Taylor's Guides to Gardening

Susan A. Roth

FRANCES TENENBAUM, Series Editor

Taylor's Guide to

Trees

Withdrawn/ABCL

**THE DEFINITIVE, EASY-TO-USE
GUIDE TO 200 OF THE GARDEN'S
MOST IMPORTANT PLANTS**

HOUGHTON MIFFLIN COMPANY

BOS

Visit our Web site: www.houghtonmifflinbooks.com.

Taylor's Guide is a registered trademark of Houghton Mifflin Company.

Library of Congress Cataloging-in-Publication Data
Roth, Susan A.
    Taylor's guide to trees : the definitive, easy-to-use guide to 200 of the garden's most
    important plants / [Susan A. Roth].
        p. cm. — (Taylor's guides to gardening)
        ISBN 0-618-06889-9
    1. Ornamental trees. I. Title: Trees. II. Title. III. Series.
    SB435 .R75 2001
    635.9'771—dc21   00-053883

Cover photograph by Dennis Frates/Positive Images
Book design by Anne Chalmers
Typefaces: Minion, News Gothic

Consultant: Nina Bassuk, Ph.D., Director of Urban Horticulture Institute,
Cornell University

Printed in Singapore

TWP 10 9 8 7 6 5 4 3 2 1

❧ Contents

INTRODUCTION

Trees Defined and Described   1
Trees in the Yard and Garden   4
Choosing and Planting a Tree   10
Right Tree, Right Place   16
Tree Care   22
Pruning Broad-leaved Trees   28
Pruning Conifers   35
Insect and Disease Problems   37

HARDINESS ZONE MAP   38

GALLERY OF TREES   41

ENCYCLOPEDIA OF TREES   189

APPENDIX

Trees that Tolerate Alkaline Soil   359
Trees with Ornamental Bark   362
Trees that Attract Songbirds, Hummingbirds, and Other Wildlife 363
Trees that Tolerate Drought   365
Trees with Outstanding Fall Color   367
Trees with Showy Flowers   370
Trees that Tolerate Road Salt and Sea Salt   373
Trees for Windbreaks and Screens   375
Trees that Tolerate Full or Partial Shade   376
Trees with Colorful Fruits   378
Street Trees   379
Urban Shade Trees   380
Trees that Tolerate Wet Soil   382

PHOTO CREDITS   385

INDEX   387

❧ Introduction

Trees create a ceiling for the landscape, holding their flowers and foliage aloft on limbs that reach toward the sky. The beauty and serenity that trees bring to our neighborhoods and gardens are without compare. Trees create an overhead structure to both block and frame views of the sky, neighbors' houses, or distant scenery. And their large size brings a sense of peace, calm, and permanence to a landscape, softening streets and sidewalks and creating a comfortable hometown feeling. A city becomes friendlier when trees grace the streets and shield the buildings and when parks and green spaces offer people refuge from urban life. A new housing development looks more established when trees are planted or left standing.

Not only are trees beautiful, but they also serve a practical purpose. A mature tree, with its thousands of leaves, acts like a super air filter, trapping dust and soot and recycling carbon dioxide into oxygen for all to breathe. A single large tree removes about 25 pounds of carbon dioxide from the air each day, and in the process of photosynthesis, it releases about 12 pounds of oxygen—enough to supply a family of four.

❦ TREES DEFINED AND DESCRIBED

Although we all know a tree when we see one, it is helpful when buying, planting, and especially when pruning a tree, to understand how it grows. A tree is a woody perennial plant that grows at least 20 feet tall and has a single freestanding main stem, or *trunk,* which may

Most flowering trees strut their stuff in springtime and none does it with quite so much drama as Kwanzan cherry (Prunus × 'Kwanzan'), whose shocking pink blossoms become the focal point of any garden scheme.

branch at an early stage into several more trunks of equal importance. The main stem is called the *leader;* as it grows, it adds height to the tree. The large main branches growing from the trunk are called *scaffold branches.* The swollen area at the scaffold base (where the branch meets the trunk) is called the *branch collar,* and the roughened area of compressed bark in the *crotch* between the trunk and the branch is called the *branch bark ridge. Secondary branches* grow from the scaffolds, and these in turn may have *twigs* growing from them. The trunk of a well-formed tree is wider at its base and narrower at its tip, indicating that the tree has a healthy *taper;* the widened area near the ground is called the *flare.*

Roots are woody underground parts that not only absorb water and nutrients from the soil but also anchor the tree in the ground, preventing it from toppling over. Most trees have a complex root system that is as large as or larger than the tree's aboveground structure. Some types of trees, especially when they are young, have a deep *taproot* that grows straight down. This taproot may die off as the tree matures. All trees have 5 to 10 main roots, called *lateral roots,* which grow from the base of the trunk and radiate outward to support the tree. Lateral roots are usually 2 to 3 feet beneath the soil surface. From these grow many smaller roots, called *transport roots,* which are about ½ to 1 inch in circumference and are closer to the soil surface, about 4 to 12 inches down. From these grow numerous tiny *feeder roots,* which are only about 1 to 2 inches long and a fraction of an inch around and reside within 1 inch of the surface. Feeder roots do most of the work of absorbing water and nutrients; they are not woody and die back every year.

Leaves contain the green pigment *chlorophyll,* which converts the energy from sunlight into sugars that feed the tree. If the leaves persist on the tree for several years, the tree is *evergreen.* If the leaves drop off in autumn and regrow months later, the tree is *deciduous.* Leaves grow from *buds,* which contain tiny, unexpanded, dormant leaves and are arranged along the twigs. A shoot gets longer by growing from its *terminal bud* and forms branches from *lateral buds* at the leaf axils on the shoots. When a leaf drops from the tree, a *leaf scar* marks where it grew. Twigs also show *terminal bud scale scars,* which indicate where the previous years' growth started and ended; the distance between sets of terminal bud scale scars indicates how much a tree has grown each year.

The spread of the tree's branches and leaves is called the *canopy,* and the outer perimeter of the canopy is the *drip line.* The tree's root system extends at least as far underground as the drip line, and usually much farther.

Types of Trees

Trees may be divided into two main botanical groups—broad-leaved and coniferous. A *broad-leaved tree* is characterized by flattened leaves that show a network of veins. The leaves may be deciduous, such as on a maple or crab apple, or evergreen, such as on a holly or southern magnolia. All broad-leaved trees reproduce by forming flowers that contain pollen-bearing stamens and ovule-bearing pistils, which when fertilized develop into fruits that contain seeds. The flowers may be colorful with showy petals or tiny and inconspicuous.

The leaves of a *coniferous tree,* or *conifer,* are sharp like a needle, as on pines, or flattened and scalelike, as on arborvitaes. Conifers bear male and female flowers in separate structures called *cones.* Female cones have ovaries on their scales, which develop into seeds after they are pollinated by the windblown pollen shed by male cones. The female cones then mature into woody cones that drop to the ground in autumn. A few species have modified cones that look like berries. Most conifers are evergreen, but a few, such as larches and bald cypress, drop their leaves during winter dormancy.

❦ TREES IN THE YARD AND GARDEN

The tallest deciduous trees can grow 80 to 100 feet tall and live for 50 to 300 or more years in yards and gardens. They may grow even taller and live even longer in their native forest habitats. These *shade trees* are valued in home landscapes because their wide branches and leafy canopies cast cooling shade during the hot summer but allow the sun to shine through bare branches in winter. Besides casting shade, tall deciduous trees beautify the landscape with their green foliage. Most tall trees do not have showy flowers, but their leaves often turn brilliant shades of red, orange, or yellow before falling to the ground in fall. Many medium-size trees (about 35 feet tall) and small trees (20 to 30 feet tall) have attractive flowers in spring or early summer and are valued as *flowering ornamentals.* Many of these trees also produce showy berries or fruits and eye-catching fall color. Some offer colorful mottled or shiny bark that adds interest during the winter. In the wild, these *understory trees* are often found growing at the edges of forests that consist of tall *canopy trees* (a garden's shade trees) and conifers.

Conifers have foliage in various shades of green, blue-green, gray-green, and gold-green and thus bring color and beauty to a landscape

A mature shade tree, such as this black walnut (Juglans nigra), *casts a light cooling shade with its high branches and creates a leafy ceiling that brings a cozy feeling to a backyard.*

throughout the year. But their color is especially appreciated in winter, when most other plants are bare. Because evergreen trees keep their leaves throughout the year, they cast shade year-round. Too many evergreens growing close to a house or yard can block light, especially in winter, and create a gloomy atmosphere. But if sited correctly, at a distance from the house or yard, they can be used as a *windbreak* to block cold winter winds and drifting snow. They also can create year-round privacy and may be used as a living *screen* when planted at the edge of a property.

Proper Positioning

Trees are the largest and most permanent plants in your yard, so you need to position them carefully. Planting the wrong tree in the wrong place can be an expensive mistake if the tree needs to be removed once it begins to reach its mature size. It's very difficult to imagine how large a young tree will become in just a few years. Healthy trees grow 1 to 2 feet in height and width each year when they are young; some grow 3 or more feet a year.

Before you start digging a hole for a new tree, find out the mature height and width of the tree. Mark where you intend to place the trunk and pace off half its mature width on the ground. (A rule of thumb is to place the tree's trunk at least 20 feet from a house.) You also might use a rope or garden hose to mark the tree's potential drip line. Consider whether the branches will hit the house or any outbuildings, rub against the roof, interfere with utility lines, or crowd other trees. You'll quickly get an idea of how much space the tree needs.

Blocking Sun and Wind

The angle of the sun changes throughout the year. It sinks lower on the horizon and casts longer shadows in winter, and it rises higher and casts shorter shadows in summer (in the Northern Hemisphere). The shadow cast by a tree also changes during the year. The farther a tree is from a house, the taller it must be to effectively shade the house. A rule of thumb is to plant a tree to the east, west, or south of where you want shade to be cast, at a distance equal to three-quarters of its mature height. In summer, when the sun is high, the hottest sun comes from the west in the afternoon, so a 40-foot tree planted about 30 feet from the house on the west side has a cooling effect during the hottest time of the year, significantly lowering air-conditioning bills. A similar tree planted on the east side of the house blocks the morning sun and provides further summer cooling. If these are deciduous trees, they will allow the sun to warm the house in winter, lowering heating bills. Thus in most climates, the tallest deciduous trees are best planted on the west and east sides of the house. A

Conifers, such as these pines and spruces, work to block wind and snowdrifts without blocking sunlight when planted on the northeast side of the property.

tree planted on the south side of a house casts shade on the house during winter, so avoid planting evergreen trees in that location.

A row of trees works best as a windbreak when planted on the side of the house or property where the prevailing winds originate. These winds usually come from the northwest in winter and the southwest in summer, but the direction varies with each situation. How much the wind is blocked depends on the height and density of the windbreak. A windbreak generally cuts wind speed in half over a distance two to three times the windbreak's height. A dense windbreak actually slows wind more, but for a shorter distance, than a more open windbreak because a solid impediment causes a downdraft to form on the leeward side of the windbreak. A row of 30-foot-tall evergreens planted 40 to 50 feet from the northwest side of a house will block cold winter winds but not desirable winter sun. If hot, drying summer winds are your problem, plant deciduous or evergreen trees as a windbreak on the southeast side of your property. Trees used as windbreaks are most effective if they branch all the way to the ground and are spaced at a distance about one-half their mature width. If the trees thin out at the bottom, you can plant shrubs in front of the gaps.

Creating Visual Effects

Where you position trees affects your home's appearance. In general, trees planted in front of a house look best if they are placed toward the sides of the structure, not in the middle, so that they frame the front entrance rather than block it. In back of the house, locate trees where they will shade a patio, frame or block a view, or direct your eye to a particular scene.

Depending on the size of your house, which direction it faces, and the effect you wish to create, you might plant large trees to create shady privacy or small flowering trees for ornamentation. A big two-story house demands large trees to keep the landscape in scale and bring the house visually down to earth. If large trees would block desirable sun, group smaller trees together to create a visual mass that balances the large house. Or plant large trees farther to the sides to modify the sun as needed. A small house can be made to look like a quaint cottage if it is surrounded by large trees. But if you want to make the house look bigger, use small trees.

Purple-leaved plum (Prunus 'Thundercloud') has a graceful vase shape that accommodates tall perennials beneath its boughs, and its lovely purple leaves create a wall of color throughout the growing season.

You can plant trees close together—with their trunks spaced at a distance of about two-thirds the tree's mature width—in groups of three or more to create a grove. This naturalistic effect works best on large properties. If tall, mature trees already exist on your property, you can plant lower-growing understory trees near them to create a layered, gardenlike appearance.

Using Complementary Shapes

Trees come in many shapes and sizes, and you should consider these characteristics when you select a tree for a particular purpose in your landscape design. Each species or cultivar has a genetic predisposition to grow into a certain form, and it is best to select a tree whose ultimate shape and size suit the site.

Vase-shaped trees have high arching branches that flare upward and outward, making them useful for shading a street or driveway where you need clearance or a view beneath the branches. *Rounded* trees often have branches low to the ground and are well suited for informal lawns. *Oval* trees have a uniform upright shape that can be used to create a formal appearance, such as along a driveway to form an allée. *Weeping* trees have cascading branches that drip to the ground; use these trees on a hillside or in an open setting as specimens where their lovely shape can be appreciated. *Columnar* trees are narrow and upright, looking rather like exclamation marks in the landscape. They can be jarring when sited alone in

A weeping tree, such as this weeping Higan cherry (Prunus subhirtella var. pendula), is at its best where its graceful flowering branches are reflected on the mirrorlike surface of a pond or where they can echo the shape of a slope or hilly terrain.

an open landscape. But when a columnar tree is used as an accent in a mixed border, it becomes a nice focal point. Columnar trees can be planted close together in a row to make a screen in a space that is too small for wider trees. *Pyramidal* trees are wide at the base and become narrower near the top, rather like a triangle. Pyramidal trees, especially conifers, often have a single straight trunk and low branches that sweep the ground, so they usually take up a lot of space. As with weeping trees, pyramidal trees can stand alone as specimens or be used where other plantings won't interfere with their branches. Some other trees have wide-spreading horizontal branches, which makes for a nice counterpoint to their upright main trunks. Like pyramidal conifers, these trees need to be placed where there is sufficient space for their branches to grow.

With age, many pyramidal or rounded trees broaden at the top and take on an irregular flat-topped shape. This gives them a very interesting craggy appearance that adds character to the garden.

CHOOSING AND PLANTING A TREE

The best time to plant a tree is in spring or autumn, when the weather is mild and rain is plentiful. Nurseries also have large selections of trees to choose from at this time of year. You'll find trees either balled-and-burlapped (B&B) or grown in containers. Each type has its advantages and disadvantages.

Whether you start with a B&B tree or a container-grown tree, be sure to choose one with a good branching structure—the branches should be evenly spaced up and down a single trunk, not lopsided or crowded to-gether. If you are purchasing a multitrunked or clumped tree, be sure the trunks originate from the ground and are well separated. Two or more trunks, or leaders, squeezed together will only grow more crowded and are likely to crack and split apart. The trunk should be straight, with an unbranched leader, and free of bark damage. If the trunk is wrapped, un-wrap it to make sure the bark is intact.

Choosing a B&B Tree

Most trees are grown in a nursery field for about 4 years and then dug up. The root ball is traditionally wrapped in natural burlap so that it will de-compose in the soil. During digging, a tree loses as much as 90 percent of its roots. The tree doesn't start growing again in height until roots regen-erate. Regardless of a tree's size, its roots grow about 1½ feet a year. A large B&B tree loses a higher percentage of its roots than a small one when they are dug. Because both regrow roots at about the same rate, a small tree will recover faster and grow more during the first few years after transplanting. Thus a small tree may be a better choice than a larger, more expensive one.

Check a B&B tree before buying it to make sure it was properly dug and is in good condition. If possible, ask nursery personnel to unwrap some of the root ball. Make sure the trunk flare is visible at the top of the ball, which should be flat. Feel the soil to be sure the roots are at the top of the ball—loose soil should not be mounded up over the solid ball of field soil and over the trunk flare. The trunk should be solid and not rock back and forth in the ball. If any of these conditions is not met, the tree was dug too shallowly and has lost more roots than necessary. Avoid these trees. Also avoid trees with root balls that show many torn or crushed roots rather than cleanly cut ones.

Choosing a Container-Grown Tree

Container-grown trees do not suffer as much transplant shock as B&B trees, but they are subject to other problems. If the tree was left in the container too long, its roots may be circling around and around the perimeter of the container or girdling the trunk. Even after transplanting, these roots continue to grow in a circle, rather than outward, and can strangle the trunk or not anchor the tree properly. Check to make sure the trunk is centered in the container. Check the top of the soil in the container to be sure that you can see the trunk flare and that no large roots are bulging up near the trunk or twisting and turning around the container. If possible, ask nursery personnel to remove the tree from the container so that you can inspect the root ball. The outside of a healthy root ball should reveal a network of roots. One or two large circling roots are OK, because they can easily be cut away, but avoid trees with a mass of circling, tangled roots.

Proper Planting

A well-shaped tree with a healthy root ball needs to be planted properly to give it a good start and ensure its future health. Sometimes a tree seems to be doing fine for the first few years after planting, then begins to decline. When this happens, a circling root system or improper planting is usually the cause. The latest tree-planting methods, which are based on research findings, differ quite a bit from the methods in common practice not too many years ago, so it pays to follow the procedures outlined here.

Proper positioning in a correctly dug planting hole is essential to a tree's long-term health. Dig a wide hole only as deep as the depth of the rootball. Refill the hole with native soil.

Dig a planting hole that is as deep as the root ball and no deeper—you can measure the depth with a shovel handle and compare it with the root ball's height. (A tree planted in a hole that is dug deeper and refilled with soil may settle and sink too low.) Make the hole two to three times as wide as the root ball to encourage new roots to grow outward.

Pick up a container-grown tree by the container's edges, not by the trunk. Remove the tree from the container by wetting the soil and then sliding the tree out; don't yank on the trunk. If the tree is reluctant to come out of the container, cut the container's sides to free the tree. Using a sharp knife or pruning shears, cut off any large roots that bulge up next to the trunk and circle tightly around it. Also cut back any large roots that circle around the outer edges of the root ball to the point where they no longer circle. Make three 3-inch-deep cuts in the sides of the root ball, spacing them an equal distance apart. This will encourage new roots to grow outward. Position the root ball in the hole so that the top is level with or slightly higher than the surrounding soil. Lay a shovel handle across the planting hole to help you judge the position of the root ball in the hole. When the tree is planted, you should be able to see the trunk flare just above the soil surface. If you can't see the flare, you have planted the tree too deep.

Pick up a B&B tree by the root ball, not by the trunk. Place it in the hole while it is still wrapped. Once it is properly positioned (see the previous paragraph), add soil to cover the lower one-third of the root ball, then unwrap and cut away the top two-thirds of the burlap. It used to be safe to leave a B&B tree wrapped because the burlap rapidly rotted once it was in the ground. But today's burlap is often treated to prevent rotting so that it remains intact longer at the nursery, or the tree may be wrapped in synthetic burlap, which will never rot. It's best to remove any wires and ties and fold back the wrapping, being careful not to destroy the integrity of the ball. If any roots are torn or ragged, use a sharp knife to make clean cuts that will heal more quickly.

Once the tree is at the proper level and you are sure the trunk is straight, refill the hole with the same soil that you removed by digging. Don't add any soil amendments or fertilizer. Research has shown that if soil is amended with materials such as peat moss or compost, the new roots may circle around in this amended soil and fail to penetrate into the native soil. Fertilizer can actually burn new roots. As you refill the hole, gently press the soil down, but do not stamp on the soil, or you will pack it too tightly and remove necessary oxygen.

Spread a 3- to 4-inch-deep layer of organic mulch, such as aged wood chips or shredded leaves, under the newly planted tree. Place the mulch in a circle that measures about 2 feet in diameter for every 1 inch of trunk diameter. (For instance, a 4-inch-diameter tree would require an 8-foot-diameter circle of mulch.) Be sure to pull back the mulch a few inches from the trunk. The mulch will help keep the soil from drying out and also suppress weeds, which can compete with the young tree for water. (See "Using Mulches and Ground Covers" for more on mulching.) As the tree grows, increase the size of the mulched area accordingly. Keep the area mulched at least until the tree is established—about three growing seasons. Then plant grass or a ground cover if desired.

Keep the newly planted tree well watered during the first two growing seasons. Allowing the roots to dry out will slow the tree's growth. Water when the soil under the mulch feels dry.

Do not prune a newly planted tree except to fix broken branches. The tree needs as many leaves as possible to help it recover from transplant shock. Research has shown that pruning the top to compensate for lost roots, as was once the practice, actually harms the tree. Begin corrective pruning and training, if needed, 1 year after planting.

Proper Staking and Wrapping

A newly planted tree should not be routinely staked. Research shows that a tree grows much better and forms a stronger trunk and a better root system if it is not staked but is allowed to sway in the wind. Stake a newly planted tree only if it cannot stand up by itself, if it is in a particularly windy spot, or if it is in a public setting where it might be bumped or otherwise injured. Do not leave it staked for more than 1 year. More damage is done to trees by leaving them staked for too long a time than for too short a time. Evergreen trees may need to be staked for the first winter, even if they can stand by themselves, in areas where heavy snow may cause them to lean or fall over.

Trees are often staked by securing them with ropes or wires to short, ground-level stakes. That method is fine in a garden border, but in open lawns or other areas where people walk, stakes like this are difficult to see, and someone may trip over them. It's safer to use tall stakes that are easily seen.

A small, light tree may only need one stake placed on its windward side. Larger trees may need two or three stakes spaced equally around the tree. Choose 8-foot-tall pressure-treated two-by-twos, metal posts, or rebar as stakes. Drive the stakes 18 to 24 inches into the soil outside the planting hole, where they will be more stable. Secure the stakes to the trunk using flexible flat rubber straps sold for this purpose. These straps will do less damage to the trunk than cords or guy wires, even if the latter are cushioned with garden hose. (Garden hose rubbing against the trunk can harm the bark if the ties loosen.) Never tie the straps around the trunk, which will cut the bark and girdle the trunk as it grows stouter. Remove the ties after 1 year to prevent strangling the trunk.

Sometimes the trunk of a young tree at the nursery is spirally wrapped with a special paper tree wrap. This wrap was originally thought to serve two purposes: to prevent the fragile bark from being injured during shipping and while at the nursery, and to prevent sunscald (splitting and cracking of bark). Research has shown, however, that tree wrap is superfluous and can do more harm than good. If left on too long, it can strangle the expanding trunk, especially if it is held in place with twine,

Stakes should be driven into firm soil outside the planting hole. Tall stakes are easier to see and won't cause passersby to trip. Keep stakes in place for no longer than 1 year; ties should not bind the trunk or rub the bark.

Remove any burlap or special protective wrap from a newly planted tree, because it can encourage pests and disease, and if it is held in place with twine it can actually strangle the trunk as it grows. If garden hose is used to cushion ties, be sure the ties are taut enough to prevent the hose from rubbing the trunk's tender bark.

string, or wire ties. The wrap also is an excellent hiding place for insects that can damage the tree. A wrap that is coming off in some places and still intact in others results in uneven heating of the trunk, which can encourage sunscald. It's best to remove any tree wrap after planting.

❧ RIGHT TREE, RIGHT PLACE

Different tree species vary quite a bit in their ability to adapt to heat, cold, drought, poor soil, air pollution, and other stresses. When choosing a tree for your yard or garden, select one that is right for your region, site, and growing conditions and that is also right for the function you have in mind. For instance, you wouldn't choose a tree that requires full sun for a shady location or one that requires loamy soil for a sandy location. Or you wouldn't choose a tree that drops lots of fruits that could cause a slipping hazard for a location next to a walkway. There is no single "right" tree for any location, but it is best to choose a tree that is well suited to the growing conditions your site has to offer rather than one that will struggle where you put it.

Trees with Bad Reputations

Certain trees have bad reputations—sometimes well deserved and sometimes not. For instance, some trees' thirsty roots invade sewer lines, some trees' weak wood breaks apart in heavy snowstorms, or some trees' prolific seeds germinate in natural landscapes and crowd out native trees. No tree is without a potential problem or two, and each tree described in this book is right for some situations, although it might not be right for yours. Make sure you have a valid reason for choosing a "bad" tree over a "good" one if you have a choice. If a better-behaved tree will fill the bill, choose it instead. The pros and cons of each tree are mentioned in the encyclopedia entries.

Norway maple *(Acer platanoides)* is an example of a tree with a bad reputation. Although it is a beautiful, round-headed tree and commonly planted, its dense shade and greedy surface roots prevent grass and other plants from growing beneath its limbs. Its big surface roots can lift up sidewalks and patios, and its large flowers and prolific seeds drop to the ground throughout the spring and create a mess. The prolific seeds also result in prolific seedlings, which at best can cause a weed problem in gardens and at worst can invade woodlands and compete with slower-growing native species in some regions. Yet Norway maple is one of the most widely planted urban trees, because it is tough, fast growing, and attractive. In the Northeast, there are many other better-behaved trees to choose from, and Norway maple is not the best choice there. But in the Midwest and Plains, where few big shade trees can survive winter's cold and summer's heat, humidity, and regular drought, Norway maple (especially its seedless cultivars) is a good option.

Fast-growing trees often have weak wood and therefore are not durable or long-lived. They also can be hazardous. Silver maple *(Acer saccharinum)* is a prime example. When this fast-growing native is mature, it can pose a danger because strong winds and heavy snow or ice can cause large limbs to break off, crushing cars, roofs, or even people. Yet this tree adapts well to cold, harsh growing conditions and urban stresses. It is overplanted as a street tree in areas where there are better—and safer—

choices. However, if located in the right place—for instance, in a large natural setting away from buildings in the Midwest or Mountain States—silver maple will provide valuable shade where few other trees can survive. It is also an excellent native tree to use for land reclamation projects, especially in wet or damp areas, where its fast growth is a particularly valuable asset.

TREES TO AVOID

The following trees are best avoided as street or landscape trees if other choices will work just as well. In some instances, an improved cultivar may make the tree more acceptable.

Acer negundo (box elder, ash-leaved maple)	Messy, weak wooded, attracts insects
Acer platanoides (Norway maple)	Heavy shade, surface roots, invasive
Acer saccharinum (silver maple)	Weak wooded, subject to storm damage, invasive roots
Aesculus hippocastanum (horse chestnut)	Unsightly defoliating diseases in some areas, messy fruits
Albizia julibrissin (silk tree, mimosa)	Weak wooded, short-lived, invasive
Elaeagnus angustifolia (Russian olive, wild olive)	Invades natural sites in some climates
Juglans nigra (black walnut)	Husks stain concrete, toxins may inhibit garden plants
Morus alba (white mulberry)	Fruits stain concrete, birds spread seeds and cause weed problem
Populus spp. (poplars, cottonwoods)	Weak wooded, short-lived, some species messy, invasive roots
Salix spp. (willows)	Weak wooded, messy, invasive roots
Ulmus pumila (Siberian elm, Chinese elm)	Weak wooded, short-lived

Urban Trees

Cities are particularly inhospitable places for trees to grow. It's surprising that trees survive in urban sites at all, considering that most trees are designed to grow in a forest where they have deep rich soil covered with natural humus, clean cool air, and foot traffic consisting only of deer and squirrels. Cities are hot because the concrete and glass absorb and reflect heat, and the air is often polluted with soot and noxious fumes. The soil in a sidewalk tree well is infertile and compacted, excluding vital oxygen and making it difficult for roots to penetrate, and it is often contaminated with construction debris and deicing road salt. Most urban street trees are subject to a constant state of drought because of the small area they are allotted and because most of the rainwater runs off into the streets and sewers. Roots usually do not extend far under paved streets because

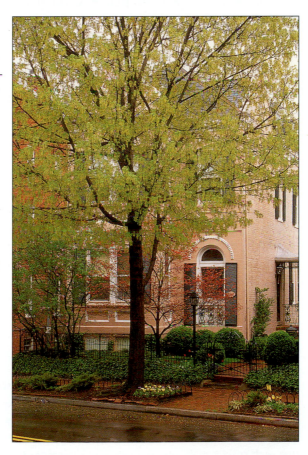

An ideal street tree, such as this sugar maple cultivar (Acer saccaharinum), *must have a shape whose branches do not interfere with traffic and whose constitution is hardy enough to withstand polluted air, heat, and compact dry soil.*

the soil there is compacted, usually dry, and often excessively hot. To all these stresses add the possibility of serious injury to tree trunks and limbs from pedestrians, vehicles, and dogs.

Trees in city parks often have better soil and more room to grow than street trees, but soil can be compacted due to heavy foot traffic, and vandalism is a constant threat. Air pollution is still a problem. But a wider array of trees grow well in city parks than on city streets.

Urban trees fare best if they are planted in wide beds or long, wide strips called parkways or tree lawns than in small wells. The soil space in a bed is large enough to absorb sufficient rainwater and will become less compacted if it is mulched or planted with a ground cover. The right species also must be selected. Trees whose leaves tolerate soot and pollution and those whose roots can survive in excessively dry, poorly aerated soil are the best choices for urban settings. Each tree must be given the best soil possible and protected from mechanical injury by a 4-foot-tall guardrail.

Trees stressed by drought, poor nutrition, and injuries are more likely to be attacked by pests. Thus a municipal tree maintenance and protection program is important to ensure city trees' health and longevity.

Street Trees

Tall trees were once favored for city and neighborhood streets because of the welcoming feeling provided by a canopy of majestic trees. Elm trees, with their tall vase shape and arching branches that allow plenty of room for traffic to pass beneath them, were once the street trees of choice. But large trees can interfere with utility lines and require skilled pruning to give them a shape compatible with those lines. In addition, storm damage to tall trees can cause branches to break, carrying electric or phone lines with them to the ground. The roots of large trees can break sidewalks and curbs. Thus many communities now plant smaller trees along streets. They require less maintenance and do not interfere with utility lines, although they cast less shade and look less impressive than tall trees.

Arborists recommend planting a mixture of tree types, rather than numerous trees of the same species, along streets to avoid the pitfalls of monoculture. As many communities learned with the American elm, if all the trees on a block or in a community are the same species, the risk of a disease or insect wiping out the entire tree population is great. When numerous types of trees are planted, if one species dies from an uncontrollable pest, the others are usually spared. Urban foresters recommend that each species make up no more than 5 percent of the tree population

Where the sidewalk abuts the curb and street, trees such as this Japanese maple (Acer palmatum) can be planted in the lawns of the homes and buildings that line the street, where they will have sufficient good soil to thrive while still beautifying the community.

in an area. Thus if one species is destroyed, 95 percent of the trees will survive.

Large trees should be spaced at most 45 feet apart along a street to create a hospitable feeling. Closer spacing (up to 25 feet apart) encourages large trees to take on a more upright shape, which requires less pruning to remove low branches that might interfere with cars and pedestrians. Small to medium-size trees should be spaced 20 to 30 feet apart. The best place to locate street trees is in a tree lawn at least 8 feet wide between the sidewalk and the street. A wide planting area allows room for each tree's trunk flare and large roots to develop without harming the sidewalk and curb. A line of trees creates a sense of security to pedestrians on the sidewalk because the trunks provide a barrier to passing traffic. Where the sidewalk abuts the road, trees can be planted in the front lawns of homes. Although different communities have different laws governing street trees, most communities allow municipal tree planting up to 20 feet inside each homeowner's property line.

❦ TREE CARE

Once established, trees are the easiest plants to take care of in the landscape. But some tender loving care will still go a long way toward ensuring each tree's long-term health.

Watering Trees

Trees have extensive root systems but also compete for water with whatever is planted around them. A rule of thumb is that most garden plants need an inch of water a week during the growing season—that means an inch of rainfall or irrigation. Plants in sandy soil may need more water, those in clayey soil less. Some drought-tolerant trees do just fine with less water. Except for very drought-tolerant trees, you should water during periods of drought. Shallow watering is bad for trees (and all other garden plants) because it encourages the growth of surface roots that dry out quickly and are more susceptible to drought damage. Turn on the sprinkler and let it run slowly under and beyond each tree's canopy so that the water can soak into the ground. Measure the amount of water you apply by putting a small container in the sprinkler's spray pattern.

In periods of severe drought, when municipalities restrict landscape watering, trees that have been watered deeply fare better than those that have been shallowly watered or continually thirsty. Trees that grow in mulched, rather than planted areas, also do better, because they are not competing with other plants for water. The mulch keeps the ground cool and slows down water loss through evaporation.

Using Mulches and Ground Covers

A tree grown where an organic mulch such as aged wood chips, shredded leaves, or compost is spread beneath the canopy grows better than one planted in bare soil, a lawn, or a border with other plants because the tree's roots are healthier. The mulch provides many benefits. The soil stays cooler and moister and is better aerated, competitive weeds are suppressed, and erosion is controlled. The mulch also protects the trunk from mechanical injury caused by a lawn mower or string trimmer. Finally, mulch looks more attractive under a dense or low-branched shade

A circle of mulch beneath the limbs of this saucer magnolia (Magnolia × soulangeana) makes mowing easier and creates a healthy soil space where the tree's roots are free of competition from grass.

tree than does a struggling lawn, which becomes thin and weedy in the heavy shade.

Spread organic mulch under the tree in a 3- to 4-inch-deep layer that extends as far under the canopy as seems visually appropriate, removing any weeds and grass first. Keep the mulch about 6 inches away from the trunk. Mulch piled up around the trunk can cause the tree to rot and encourage rodent damage, which may contribute to tree failure.

Alternatively, try planting a shade-loving ground cover, such as pachysandra or myrtle (vinca), beneath the tree. Or plant a garden of shade-loving plants such as hostas, ferns, and astilbes. Keep in mind that you'll need to supply enough water for both the tree and the plants for both to thrive. Bishop's hat *(Epimedium)* and dead nettle *(Lamium)* are two flowering ground covers that flourish in dry shade under trees.

Inorganic mulches such as rocks and pebbles are not good for most trees. The rocks heat up in the sun and work their way into the soil, destroying its water-holding capacity and nutrient content. Never put an impermeable sheet of plastic mulch under a tree to suppress weeds, because this prevents water from reaching the roots. Also avoid weed-suppressing landscape fabric, even though it does allow water and air to penetrate. The fabric must be camouflaged with wood chips, and as the mulch decays, weeds can actually sprout in it. The tree's feeder roots also may weave themselves into the fabric and thus be injured if the fabric is removed or replaced.

Fertilizing Trees

Trees growing in humus-rich soil in a woodland setting get all the nutrients they need from the soil, and most garden and landscape trees do, too. But trees growing in poor soil or mature trees that seem to be ailing often benefit from nitrogen fertilizer applied at the start of the growing season. If young trees put on 9 to 12 inches of twig growth a year, they need no fertilizer. A mature tree should add 6 to 8 inches of growth a year. If growth is less, the tree's vigor can be improved with proper fertilization. Where soil is infertile and sandy or alkaline, micronutrients such as magnesium, manganese, and iron might be needed to correct a specific nutrient deficiency, often manifested by chlorotic (abnormally yellow) leaves. This is a common problem in areas of the Midwest and plains where the soil is alkaline. A soil or leaf test is the best way to tell what your soil needs.

A tree growing in a fertilized lawn needs no more fertilizer than that applied to the lawn, because the tree's feeder roots coexist in the same top

Many popular street trees, such as this pin oak (Quercus palustris), *need acid soil, and their leaves turn yellow (chlorotic) when grown in the alkaline soil of the Midwest. In these areas it's best to choose trees that adapt to the soil conditions.*

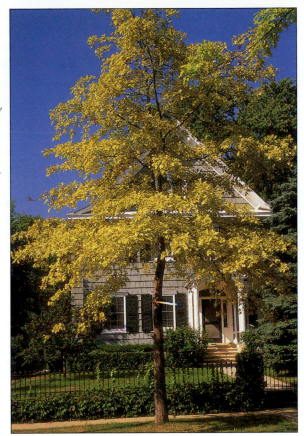

6 to 8 inches of soil as the grass roots and absorb the nutrients applied to the lawn. If the lawn is overfertilized, this may be detrimental to the tree. Be especially cautious about applying a weed killer or "weed and feed" product to the lawn, as it may harm the tree. Read the product's label and follow the instructions carefully.

Fertilize trees not growing in a lawn by broadcasting a controlled-release high-nitrogen fertilizer (which will not leach from the soil) in early spring, when tree roots are actively growing. (Water-soluble fertilizers will quickly leach from the soil.) The tree's feeder roots occupy the outer two-thirds of the tree's canopy and often well beyond, depending on the species, so that's where you should apply the fertilizer. Do not apply fertilizer within 1 foot of the trunk, as it may cause damage. How much fertilizer to apply depends on the concentration of nitrogen in the fertilizer and the size of the tree's canopy. Apply 2 pounds of actual nitrogen for each 1,000 square feet of tree canopy. The amount of fertilizer you apply to equal 2 pounds of nitrogen depends upon the nitrogen source and concentration in the product you choose; follow label directions.

Deep-root feeding is sometimes used to fertilize an ailing tree growing in a ground cover or lawn without also fertilizing the ground cover or grass, which might be harmed by the extra fertilizer. Using a high-pressure hydraulic device, an arborist can inject liquid fertilizer below the plant or grass roots, at a depth of 4 to 12 inches, at 2- to 3-foot intervals beneath the tree canopy. Another way to deep-feed a tree is to drill 1-foot-deep holes, spaced 1½ to 2 feet apart, under the canopy and, using a funnel, fill the holes half full with granular fertilizer, then top them off with soil. To avoid injuring the root collar, the holes should be at least 3 feet from the trunk. Water the tree after deep-root feeding.

Avoiding Mechanical Injury

One of the greatest threats to a tree's health is a lawn mower or string trimmer. When a mower bumps up against a tree, it can damage the trunk. The thinner the bark, the more damage there will be. String trimmers can actually cut into or strip the bark off trees, especially young ones. Car doors being opened into trees are another source of injuries. Bruises and cuts are open invitations to insects and diseases to enter the tree and hasten its decline.

The best way to avoid such injuries is to plant trees in mulched beds or garden borders where they are not surrounded by grass. However, this is not always possible or desirable. In such cases, create a small grass-free ring around each tree. Pull up the grass within 6 inches of the trunk and fill the ring with a 1-inch-deep layer of mulch, but do not pile the mulch against the trunk. The mower's wheels can ride along this ring without bumping the trunk, and there will be no need to use the trimmer to cut tall grass that the mower misses.

Avoiding Construction Damage

Mature trees add value to any property, so it makes sense to protect them during construction. But often builders and developers don't know how to protect trees or don't care enough to do it right. Trees injured during construction may not die immediately, but instead may decline over several years before they succumb.

Trees are often damaged during construction because the heavy equipment compacts the soil so much that air and water cannot penetrate. Equipment also can rip off limbs or bump into tree trunks and bruise or tear the bark. Digging and excavating can sever roots. Any change in grade—even a few inches—may result in roots being dug up and exposed or buried and suffocated. Keep in mind that 90 percent of a tree's feeder roots are within the top 6 to 12 inches of soil. Even tunneling to install utilities and sewers can sever roots and kill upper portions of a tree, depending on how close the cut is to the trunk. If one major root is severed, as much as 20 percent of the tree may die. If all the major anchoring roots are cut on one side of the tree, it may topple in a windstorm before it has time to grow new roots

Trees can be protected in several ways. First, it is vital to fence off areas beneath trees that you want to save, to prevent equipment from driving over the roots and bumping the trunks. Fence off as much of the area as possible beneath each tree's canopy, keeping in mind that a tree's roots can extend two to three times the width of the canopy. An area with a diameter measuring 1 foot for every 1 inch of trunk diameter is usually sufficient. To limit the area of soil that gets compacted, designate one area—perhaps the future driveway—as an access to the property and a place to park vehicles. Likewise, specify one area where building materials and debris are stored.

If the grade must be changed, create terraces or tree wells. To lower the grade near a large tree, leave undisturbed as much of the soil under the canopy as possible (half of the canopy spread is probably sufficient), then cut a terrace down to the desired level and build a stone or timber retaining wall, adding steps if desired, to accommodate the change in grade. The wall can actually be a landscape asset, while also saving much of the tree's root system. A tree well is just the opposite of a terrace. Build a stone wall around the tree at least halfway between the trunk and the edge of the canopy, or drip line. Then bring in soil only to the top of the tree well on its outside perimeter, leaving the well itself empty. Existing roots won't be smothered, and new ones will seek the appropriate level.

When tunneling or trenching to install utility or sewer lines, stay as far away from trees as possible. Better yet, tunnel deep enough under each trunk to avoid the roots.

If you are clearing a wooded lot, saving individual trees can be problematic, but it's worth trying. A tree's shape, structure, and root system are partly determined by where it grows. In a wooded community, trees grow taller and more upright than if they were out in the open; each tree is protected from wind and sun by neighboring trees. When suddenly standing alone and exposed, a tree will not have the same strength as it had among other trees. The trunk may be susceptible to sunscald, and the limbs will break more readily in wind or winter storms. Although it might seem desirable to save the largest, most majestic trees on a lot, smaller trees may be more adaptable. An arborist can help you select the best trees to save. Aim for a diversity of healthy, desirable species and trees of different sizes and ages.

Make sure your builder or contractor—and any subcontractors he or she hires—understand how much you value your trees and what you want done to protect them. Have these instructions written into the contract. Visit the building site daily if possible, and take before, during, and after photographs to document construction procedures and any violations of the contract.

❧ PRUNING BROAD-LEAVED TREES

Trees are pruned for several reasons: to develop a strong branching structure, to repair storm or disease damage, or to change their size or density.

PRUNING TOOLS

LOPPERS

BYPASS PRUNING SHEARS

PRUNING SAW

FOLDING PRUNING SAW

Keep in mind that any pruning cut directs the way a tree grows and that a cut cannot be undone. Pruning is for keeps, so proceed with caution.

Also remember that a pruning cut is actually an open wound that is an invitation to insects and diseases. A *callus* consisting of cambium tissue will eventually cover the injured site, but this is a slow process. Depending on the size, a cut can take several years to heal completely. Smooth, round pruning cuts, rather than oval ones, that are properly placed heal best.

Mature trees are best pruned by an arborist. Arborists understand the way trees grow and how they should be pruned. They also have the proper tools and equipment to climb and prune trees safely. Hire only a certified arborist, licensed by the International Society of Arboriculture (ISA), the American Society of Consulting Arborists (ASCA), or a similar organization, to prune your large trees.

Correct Pruning Cuts

Whenever removing any branch, cut it close enough to the trunk so that it does not leave a stub, but not so close that the trunk tissue is injured and the wound cannot heal. Use a sharp pruning saw (not a wood saw) that cuts on both the push and pull movements. Make sure that the weight of the falling branch won't tear the bark all the way down the trunk.

A heavy branch should be cut in three steps.

1. Cut about halfway through the limb on the underside, about a foot or so from the trunk. This cut will sever the bark so that it will not tear along the trunk.
2. Saw through the top of the branch at a point a few inches farther out along the limb than the undercut until it breaks from its own weight. Hold the branch if it is light, or let it fall safely to the ground if it is heavy.
3. Cut off the remaining stub by sawing at the outer edge of the trunk's branch collar without cutting into the branch-bark ridge. This cut should leave a round—not oval—wound if it is made at the correct angle.

Pruning and Training Young Trees

It's best not to prune anything other than broken branches during the first year after a tree is planted. Thereafter, you may begin corrective pruning to fix misplaced branches and to develop a set of strong perma-

When removing a limb from a tree, cut along the branch collar—where trunk tissue and branch tissue meet—and not into the trunk, so that the wound heals quickly. A cut that makes a round, not oval, wound indicates that the cut was made at the correct angle.

nent branches. Make these cuts while the tree is young, because wounds will be smaller and heal faster than if you wait to prune an older, larger tree.

Check the center of the tree to see if it has one main leader, or central trunk. If the trunk forks into several leaders, cut back any competing leaders by one-half or remove them entirely. Cut the competing leaders back to a lateral twig or bud; do not leave a stub. Do not cut the tip of the remaining leader; doing so will cause it to branch and form more leaders. Even if the tree's natural form is to have multiple leaders, these usually develop with age, so the tree will grow stronger if it is first trained into a single leader.

If the tree is still small, its branches may not be permanent. The lowest permanent scaffold branches on a broad-leaved tree are usually high

TRAINING A YOUNG TREE

FIRST-YEAR PRUNING
Plant tree in spring or fall, and do not prune until late winter or very early spring of the following year. Keep pruning to a minimum to encourage vigorous growth.

Prune out rubbing or crossing branches.

Remove vertical branches that may form a double trunk.

Widen narrow crotch angles with wooden braces or stakes and string.

Remove branches that may compete with the central leader.

Rub or pinch off small branches that will compete with the main scaffold branches.

SECOND-YEAR PRUNING
Watch for wayward growth that may cause structural problems. To minimize stress on the tree, correct problems as early as possible.

THIRD- AND FOURTH-YEAR PRUNING
In winter or very early spring, continue removing lateral branches growing at awkward angles, as well as rubbing and crossing branches. If it's necessary to remove the lowest branches, wait until at least the fourth year. Remove them over several years; retaining these branches has been shown to help increase the girth of the trunk.

enough so that people or vehicles can pass beneath them. You may earmark permanent branches on a small tree, but do not remove all the branches under them. Leave them in place so that they can nourish the tree and shade the trunk. When the young tree is taller, select several main scaffold branches, which arise directly from the trunk. These branches should be vertically spaced 1½ to 2 feet apart and radiate around the trunk so that they are evenly distributed and do not grow directly above each other. Choose branches that emerge from the trunk at an angle greater than 45 degrees; they are stronger than branches with a shallower angle. (Columnar or fastigiate forms of trees naturally branch at a tight angle.) Remove excess or undesirable branches, cutting them just outside the branch collar as described previously.

As the tree begins to mature, branches are usually appropriately spaced naturally and take on the tree's characteristic shape. You may need to do some corrective pruning, but this is usually not required.

Maintaining Mature Trees

As a tree grows and matures, it may need some routine maintenance.

- Cut off any sprouts or suckers that emerge from the base of the tree, unless it is meant to be a multitrunked specimen.
- Remove branches that emerge at a 45-degree or tighter angle— those creating a V shape—because as they grow larger, the trunk and branches will press against each other and have "included" bark, which makes for a weak attachment susceptible to breakage.
- Prune off any branches that grow across and touch each other. As they grow larger, the rubbing will injure the bark.
- If the main leader forks near the top into two or more leaders, select the tallest and straightest stem. Remove the others, except on trees that normally form multiple leaders.
- Thin very dense trees by selectively removing branches equally throughout the crown to reduce resistance to wind and prevent storm damage. Cut branches where they fork; do not head them back to a stub.

Crown Thinning, Reduction, and Drop Crotching

Sometimes a mature tree is so dense that nothing can grow beneath it or it resists wind so much that it can be damaged or blown over during a

PRUNING MATURE TREES

Mature trees that were not trained at an early age may have a variety of problems, such as those shown here, that can be corrected by an arborist. Specimens that were pruned and trained early generally need only occasional attention.

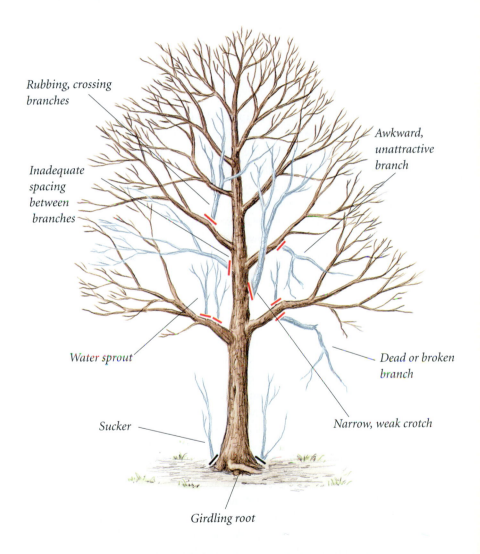

Rubbing, crossing branches

Awkward, unattractive branch

Inadequate spacing between branches

Water sprout

Dead or broken branch

Sucker

Narrow, weak crotch

Girdling root

storm. When this is the case, the tree's crown may be thinned to reduce the density of the canopy.

To thin a tree, cut back small branches (less than 1 inch in diameter) throughout the tree. Each of these branches must be cut back to where it forks with a larger branch so that no stub is left behind. This kind of pruning does not stimulate growth and creates a more open-branched tree.

If the tree has grown too tall—for instance, if it is growing into utility lines—the crown can be reduced by thinning out more major branches from the center. Again, each of these must be cut where it meets a larger branch so that the cut does not leave a stub and thus stimulate more branching.

The overall height can be lowered without destroying the tree's natural shape by using a method called *drop crotching*. This means that a large branch is removed all the way down to a crotch, or fork, where it meets another major branch. The terminal leader is usually removed, but the pruning cuts are made so that a new leader—the tallest upright branch—becomes the main leader.

It is much better to prune a tree by using these methods than to simply limb it up—cut off the lower branches—because doing so causes the tree to lose its natural shape, and it ends up looking like a lollipop. The worst thing that you can do to a tree is to top it.

Topping Trees

Pruning trees severely by cutting back all the branches to stubs is called *topping* or *heading*. This is a fashionable, but misguided, practice in some parts of the country when a property owner thinks that a tree is too tall or prone to storm damage. Topping disfigures and injures the tree and actually encourages fast, weak growth that is even more susceptible to storm damage. A tree can add 20 feet of new growth in response to topping, and then, ironically, it requires pruning again.

Topping can remove up to half of a tree's leaves, which it needs to manufacture food. This will severely weaken the tree. The wounds left by these indiscriminate cuts do not heal properly and provide easy access for insects and diseases. The many new shoots that are stimulated are weakly attached and do not develop like normal branches that grow from a socket of strong wood, so they break easily during storms.

If a tree's size or density must be controlled, prune it by thinning, reducing the crown, or drop crotching. Do not top it.

❧ PRUNING CONIFERS

Conifers usually need very little pruning when young to train them to
have strong branches. Mostly, you need to prune only to fix injuries.

Fixing a Broken Leader

Most conifers have a single main trunk and leader, and it's very important that this leader not be removed. If the leader on a young tree is broken or dies due to insect damage, you'll need to train a side branch into a
new leader to counteract the tendency for the injured tip to branch out in
a bushy growth of multiple leaders that will ruin the tree's classic pyramidal shape.

You can train a new leader by choosing one of the side shoots growing up around the dead leader and cutting off all the other competing
side branches arising from the same level. To encourage your new leader
to grow as straight as possible, wrap insulated wire around the top of the
trunk and the side shoot, then bend the shoot into an upright position.
Remove the wire in a year and rewrap it if necessary.

Repairing Damaged Limbs

If a conifer limb is broken in a storm or dies, it should be cut back to a live
crotch, or fork with a side branch, or removed at the trunk. To remove a
dead or broken limb, saw it in the same manner as described for broad-
leaved trees. The branch collar on most conifers is usually more prominent and swollen than on broad-leaved trees and so is more easily seen.
Be sure to cut just to the outside of the branch collar, not into it or too far
from it, to promote rapid healing of the wound.

Shearing a Screen or Hedge

You can encourage density and control the size of a coniferous screen or
hedge by shearing the new growth in spring or summer. Most conifers,
such as pines and spruces, produce new growth in a single flush in spring.
This new growth consists of flexible stems called *candles* and tiny expanding needles. If you cut through the candles before they expand, you
can control the plant's size. Some conifers, such as yews, do not form candles but grow in several flushes from spring through summer, so they can
be sheared anytime in spring or early summer. Keep in mind when cutting back and pruning a conifer that most species will not resprout if they
are cut back to old wood that does not contain any leaves.

Downsizing a Conifer

A conifer that has grown too tall for its site may be made smaller by thinning the branches in spring about the time new growth begins. Cut back all the branches where they fork with a side branch, in the same manner described for broad-leaved trees. Be sure to keep the tree's pyramidal shape by leaving the lower branches longer than the higher ones, and never cut off the top of the leader. After pruning, the tree should retain its natural layered look, and the pruning cuts will be barely noticeable. If you want to cut greens for holiday decorations, you can use the same method. Never head back a branch to a stub, however, because the resulting new growth will be full and bushy and destroy the tree's shape.

Most conifers, such as this Black Hills Spruce (Picea glauca *var.* densata), *have a very symmetrical shape, with their lower branches sweeping the ground. Do not prune off the lower branches or the tree will look deformed.*

Removing Lower Branches

Most conifers have branches that extend all the way to the ground, and they look best if they are very dense and symmetrical. If, as a tree matures, this skirt of branches becomes too large for the landscape, you may be tempted to prune off the lower limbs. Resist that temptation, because pruning in this way will make a very symmetrical, dense tree such as a spruce look ungainly or even comical, although it will not harm the tree. Trees such as pines, which have more open or irregular shapes, look fine if the lower limbs are pruned off. In fact, limbs often die naturally due to shading, and these should be removed.

🌱 INSECT AND DISEASE PROBLEMS

Pests can harm landscape trees, disfiguring or killing them. Nevertheless, it is not a good practice to routinely spray trees with an insecticide or fungicide as a preventative measure. Doing this can actually harm beneficial insects that keep pests under control, as well as pollute the environment and cost a lot of money. Save pesticide applications for serious problems. Most well-cared-for trees can withstand some pest damage without undue harm.

The worst pests and diseases are often ones that have been inadvertently imported from other continents and unwittingly released to prey on native trees. This is the case with the Japanese beetle, gypsy moth, Dutch elm disease, and the woolly adelgid, to name just a few. The plants have no natural resistance to these problems, and there are no natural enemies to control them.

If you see evidence of insects or disease—such as marred or chewed leaves, wilting branches, premature leaf drop, or brown or off-color foliage—and suspect a serious problem, consult a certified arborist. A capable professional will be able to diagnose the problem and know the best way to treat it.

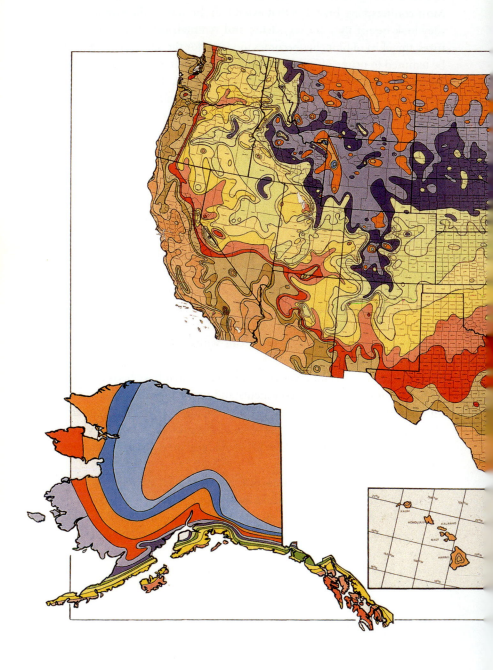

HARDINESS
ZONE MAP

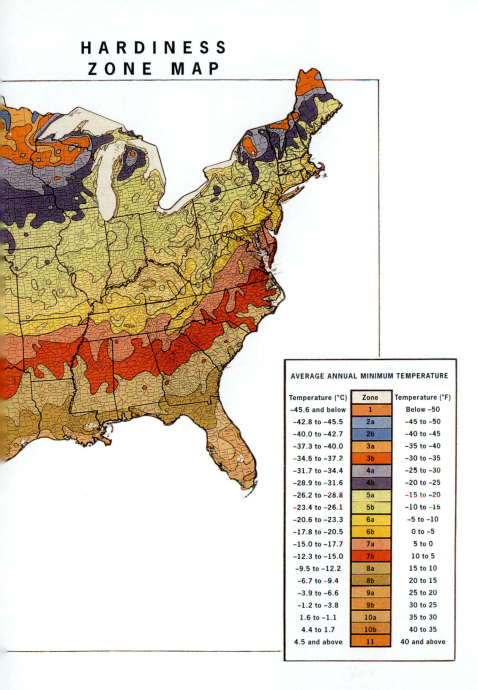

AVERAGE ANNUAL MINIMUM TEMPERATURE

Temperature (°C)	Zone	Temperature (°F)
–45.6 and below	1	Below –50
–42.8 to –45.5	2a	–45 to –50
–40.0 to –42.7	2b	–40 to –45
–37.3 to –40.0	3a	–35 to –40
–34.5 to –37.2	3b	–30 to –35
–31.7 to –34.4	4a	–25 to –30
–28.9 to –31.6	4b	–20 to –25
–26.2 to –28.8	5a	–15 to –20
–23.4 to –26.1	5b	–10 to –15
–20.6 to –23.3	6a	–5 to –10
–17.8 to –20.5	6b	0 to –5
–15.0 to –17.7	7a	5 to 0
–12.3 to –15.0	7b	10 to 5
–9.5 to –12.2	8a	15 to 10
–6.7 to –9.4	8b	20 to 15
–3.9 to –6.6	9a	25 to 20
–1.2 to –3.8	9b	30 to 25
1.6 to –1.1	10a	35 to 30
4.4 to 1.7	10b	40 to 35
4.5 and above	11	40 and above

Gallery of Trees

Acer buergerianum (A. trifidum)
Trident Maple
Slow growing to 20 to 35 feet. Multitrunked and rounded.

Glossy dark green leaves with three points.

Full sun. Sandy to clay, acid to alkaline soil. Tolerates heat and drought.

Showy dark red and orange fall color. Colorful patchwork bark.

Zones 5b to 8a

P. 192

Acer campestre
Hedge Maple
Slow growing to 35 feet. Rounded.

Matte green three- to five-lobed leaves with hairy undersides. Variable yellow fall color. Corky branches.

Full sun. Tolerates poor sandy soil, heat, and drought.

Zones 4b to 7b

P. 192

Acer capillipes
Snakebark Maple

Moderate growth rate to 30 to 35 feet. Rounded.

Three-lobed leaves reddish in spring, mature to dark green, turn red in fall. Twigs red, trunk dark green-and-white striped.

Part to light shade. Well-drained, moist, humus-rich soil. Tolerates some heat.

Zones 5a to 7a

P. 196

Acer griseum
Paperbark Maple

Slow growing to 20 to 40 feet. Upright to oval.

Jagged-edged oval leaves, dark green in summer, turn glowing shades of red and orange in fall. Very ornamental gleaming cinnamon brown bark peels in curls.

Full sun to part shade. Well-drained, humus-rich, acid to neutral moist soil.

Zones 5a to 7b

P. 193

Acer japonicum var. *acontifolium* ('Filicifolium')

Fernleaf Japanese Maple

Slow growing to 15 to 30 feet. Vase shaped to rounded, often multitrunked.

Deeply lobed rounded leaves with jagged edges. Small red flowers in spring. Brilliant red, scarlet, or gold fall color.

Full sun to light shade. Moist, humus-rich, near-neutral soil.

Zones 6a to 9a

P. 203

Acer negundo

Box Elder, Ash-Leaved Maple

Fast-growing to 30 to 50 feet. Open-branched and rounded.

Compound bright green leaves. Gray-brown deeply ridged bark.

Pendulous yellow-green flowers in spring. Brown seedpods.

Full sun to light shade. Tolerates most soils and wet or dry sites and flooding. Best used where other trees can't survive.

Zones 2a to 8a

P. 195

Acer palmatum
Japanese Maple

Slow growing to 15 to 30 feet. Vase shaped to rounded.

Deeply cut star-shaped leaves, green in summer, turn brilliant yellow to red in fall. Smooth gray bark. Red or green twigs.

Full sun to part shade. Humus-rich, moist, well-drained soil.

Zones 5b to 8a

P. 202

Acer platanoides 'Crimson King'
Crimson King Norway Maple

Moderate growth rate to 30 to 40 feet. Rounded.

Dark blood red five-lobed leaves all summer, bright red in fall. Numerous seedpods.

Full sun. Tolerates any soil, even poorly drained and compacted. Tolerates urban sites.

Zones 4a to 7b

P. 196

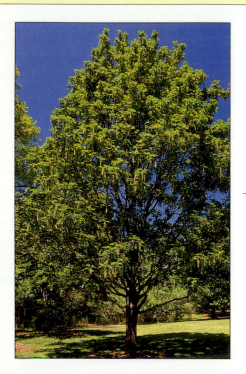

Acer pseudoplatanus
Sycamore Maple

Fast growing to 40 to 60 feet. Arching to rounded.

Large five-lobed dark green leaves. Pendulous bright green flower clusters and numerous samaras. Yellow fall color. Flaking orange-brown bark.

Full to part sun. Tolerates most soils and urban conditions.

Zones 5a to 7b

P. 198

Acer rubrum
Red Maple, Swamp Maple

Fast growing to 60 to 80 feet. Pyramidal to rounded.

Dark green lobed leaves with pale undersides turn variable shades of yellow and red in fall. Misty red flowers in spring; numerous samaras. Silvery gray bark.

Full sun to part shade. Adapts to most soils, wet to dry. Tolerates air pollution.

Zones 4b to 9a

P. 198

Acer saccharum
Sugar Maple, Hard Maple, Rock Maple

Slow to moderate growth rate to 80 feet. Oval to rounded.

Star-shaped green leaves turn flaming shades of yellow, gold, orange, and red in fall. Light yellow flowers in spring followed by tan samaras. Rough gray bark.

Full sun to part shade. Fertile, well-drained, neutral to acid moist soil.

Zones 3b to 7b

P. 201

Acer saccharum 'Bonfire'
'Bonfire' Sugar Maple

Fast-growing cultivar with consistent scarlet to red fall color.

P. 201

▲*Acer shirasawanum* 'Aureum'
(*A. japonicum* var.
microphyllum 'Aureum')

Golden Full-moon Maple

Slow growing to 20 to 30 feet. Vase shaped.

Beautiful rounded chartreuse leaves cut into shallow toothed lobes. Red flowers and samaras. Gold fall color.

Part to light shade. Moist, humus-rich soil.

Zones 5a to 7a

P. 203

▼*Acer tataricum*

Tatarian Maple

Slow to moderate growth rate to 15 to 20 feet. Multitrunked and rounded.

Oval unlobed toothed leaves dark green with lighter undersides. Red to scarlet fall color. Showy pink to red fruits in summer and fall.

Full sun to light shade. Well-drained, fertile soil best. Tolerates alkaline soil and urban conditions.

Zones 2b to 7a

P. 194

Aesculus × carnea 'Briotii'
Briotii Red Horse Chestnut

Moderate growth rate to 30 to 40 feet.
Rounded.

Large shiny green leaves divided into fingers.
Very showy tall spires of rosy red flowers in
late spring. Spiny green fruits in fall contain
brown nuts.

Full sun. Moist, well-drained, acid to alkaline
soil. Tolerates some drought.

Zones 5a to 7b

P. 205

Aesculus × carnea 'Briotii'
Briotii Red Horse Chestnut

Spectacular clusters of rose pink flowers bloom
at the branch tips in late spring.

P. 205

Aesculus flava (A. octandra)
Yellow Buckeye

Moderate growth rate to 60 to 80 feet. Upright to oval.

Glossy green five-fingered leaves. Spectacular gold, yellow, or orange early-fall color. Spires of creamy yellow flowers in mid-spring. Smooth-husked fruits in fall contain nuts. Trunk bark brown and gray broken into large plates.

Full sun to light shade. Humus-rich, moist, slightly deep acid soil.

Zones 3a to 8b

P. 205

Aesculus glabra
Ohio Buckeye

Moderate growth rate to 30 feet. Rounded.

Bright green five-fingered leaves open in very early spring. Bright gold, yellow, or orange early fall color. Spires of yellow-green flowers in midspring. Prickly fruits in fall contain nuts. Furrowed corky bark.

Full sun to light shade. Humus-rich, moist, slightly acid soil.

Zones 3a to 8b

P. 205

Aesculus hippocastanum 'Baumanii'

Baumanii Horse Chestnut

Moderate growth rate to 50 to 75 feet. Upright to oval.

Tall spires of long-lasting double white flowers in late spring and early summer. Produces no fruits. Bold-textured leaves divided into seven fingers. Yellowish fall color.

Full sun. Humus-rich, moist soil.

Zones 4a to 8b

P. 206

Aesculus pavia

Red Buckeye

Moderate growth rate to 25 feet. Multitrunked and rounded.

Glossy green leaves open early. Spires of slender red to coral pink flowers in mid- to late spring. Smooth-husked fruits contain nuts.

Full sun to light shade. Humus-rich, moist soil.

Zones 6a to 9a

P. 206

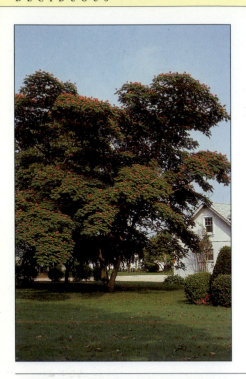

Albizia julibrissin
Silk Tree, Mimosa

Fast growing to 30 feet. Wide spreading and flat topped.

Green leaves divided into lacy leaflets. Pink powderpuff flowers in mid- to late summer. Foliage remains green through fall. Brown seedpods hang onto tree in winter.

Full sun. Well-drained acid to alkaline soil. Tolerates drought, urban and seashore conditions.

Zones 6a to 9a

P. 206

Albizia julibrissin
Silk Tree, Mimosa

Puffy deep to pale pink flowers cover the tree in midsummer, creating tropical feeling.

P. 206

Alnus glutinosa
Black alder, European Alder

Fast growing often multitrunked to 40 to 50
    feet. Oval to pyramidal.

Yellowish catkins decorate bare branches in late
    winter. Glossy green oval leaves.

Glossy dark brown bark.

Full sun to part shade. Tolerates infertile, sandy
    or gravelly soil and wet sites. Urban tolerant.

Zones 3b to 7b

P. 207

Amelanchier × grandiflora
Apple Serviceberry

Moderate growth rate to 25 to 40 feet. Rounded
    to oval shape.

Showy white flowers. Downy purple-tinged
    new leaves mature to green, turn orange and
    red in fall. Large fruits eaten by birds.

Full sun to part shade. Humus-rich, well-
    drained fertile soil.

Zones 3b to 8a

P. 209

Amelanchier laevis
Allegheny Serviceberry

Moderate growth rate to 25 to 30 feet. Multi-trunked and upright

Fluffy white flowers in early spring. New leaves glossy reddish green, mature to dark green, turn glorious shades of red and gold in early fall. Smooth gray bark on young trunks, scaly with age. Early summer fruits eaten by birds.

Full sun to part shade. Humus-rich, well-drained fertile soil.

Zones 4b to 8a

P. 208

Aralia elata 'Variegata'
Japanese Angelica Tree, Devil's Walking Stick

Fast growing to 40 feet. Multitrunked and horizontally spreading.

Bold compound leaves with creamy-white edges. Thorny leaves and branches. Huge creamy white flower clusters in late summer. Blue-black fruits eaten by birds.

Full sun to part shade. Tolerates sandy to clay soil, drought, and urban sites.

Zones 4a to 9a

P. 210

Asimina triloba
Pawpaw

Fast growing to 25 to 30 feet. Pyramidal and often suckering.

Three-parted maroon flowers in spring. Huge drooping green leaves turn glowing yellow in fall. Long green edible fall fruits.

Full sun to shade. Moist rich soil. Tolerates wet site.

Zones 5b to 8a

P. 211

Betula ermanii
Erman Birch

Fast growing to 70 feet. Open and wide spreading.

Very showy creamy white to pink peeling bark. Orange-brown twigs. Triangular heart-shaped green leaves with prominent veins turn yellow in fall.

Full sun. Moist, humus-rich soil.

Zones 5b to 7b

P. 215

Betula nigra
River Birch

Fast growing to 40 to 50 feet. Oval to pyramidal, often multitrunked.

Triangular green leaves. Beautiful yellow fall color.

Highly ornamental exfoliating bark with creamy white and pinkish tan patches.

Full to part sun. Moist, humus-rich, acid soil. Tolerates clay and wet feet, heat and drought.

Zones 4a to 9a

P. 212

Betula papyrifera
Paper Birch, Canoe Birch

Moderate to fast growing to 50 to 70 feet. Often multitrunked, pyramidal to irregular.

Creamy white papery bark peels off in shreds on trees taller than 15 feet. Oval to triangular dark green leaves turn bright yellow in fall.

Full to part sun. Moist, humus-rich soil.

Zones 2b to 5a

P. 213

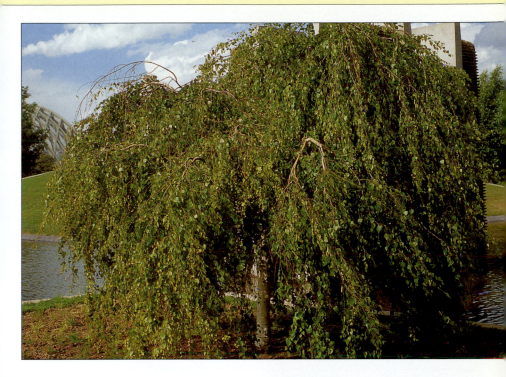

Betula pendula 'Youngii'
Weeping European Birch

Moderate growth rate. Weeping top on grafted
trunk to 15 feet.

Pendulous black-barked branches on grafted
white-barked trunk. Glossy green oval to
triangular leaves. Yellow fall color.

Full to part sun. Deep, humus-rich, moist acid
soil.

Zones 4a to 7b

P. 214

Betula utilis ssp. *jacquemontii* (*B. jacquemontii*)
White-barked Himalayan Birch

Fast growing to 60 feet. Oval shape.

Oval toothed leaves turn rich golden yellow in
fall. Stunning chalk white peeling bark.

Full sun. Moist, humus-rich soil. Tolerates
slight alkalinity.

Zones 5a to 8a

P. 214

Carpinus betulus 'Fastigiata'
Fastigate European Hornbeam

Slow to moderate growth rate to 40 to 60 feet. Symmetrical oval.

Toothed dark green oval leaves with prominent veins. Smooth gray bark. Yellow to reddish brown fall color.

Full sun to light shade. Deep, humus-rich, moist well-drained soil best. Tolerates most soils and urban sites.

Zones 5a to 7a

P. 215

Carpinus caroliniana
American Hornbeam, Blue Beech, Musclewood

Slow growing to 20 to 30 feet. Rounded to flat topped, often multitrunked.

Attractive foliage and excellent fall color. Leafy nutlets are attractive in summer and fall.

Smooth slate gray bark and muscular-looking trunks.

Part to full shade. Moist, well-drained, humus-rich soil. Tolerates wetness and flooding.

Zones 3a to 9a

P. 216

Carpinus caroliniana
American Hornbeam, Blue Beech, Musclewood

Pointed oblong toothed leaves open pale green, mature blue-green, turn red and orange in fall.

Zones 3a to 9a

P. 216

Carya ovata
Shagbark Hickory

Moderate growth rate to 60 to 80 feet. Oval shape.

Long compound leaves rich green in summer, turn golden brown in fall. Thick gray bark peels off in ragged vertical strips. Edible nuts in fall.

Full sun to part shade. Humus-rich well-drained soil. Tolerates most soils and drought.

Zones 4b to 8b

P. 217

Castanea mollissima
Chinese Chestnut

Slow to moderate growth rate to 35 to 40 feet. Rounded.

Coarse-textured glossy green leaves with downy undersides. Showy malodorous yellowish catkins in midsummer. Coppery yellow fall color. Spiny-husked edible nuts in fall.

Full sun. Well-drained slightly acid to slightly alkaline soil. Tolerates heat and drought.

Zones 5a to 8b

P. 218

Castanea mollissima
Chinese Chestnut

Edible nuts with sweet meat ripen in fall and are enclosed in spiny husks.

P. 218

Catalpa bignonioides
Southern Catalpa, Indian Bean

Fast growing to 30 to 40 feet. Rounded.

Large heart-shaped leaves. Eye-catching spires of white flowers in early summer. Dark brown slender seedpods hang on bare branches in winter.

Full sun to part shade. Rich moist soil best; tolerates most soils, heat, drought, and urban sites.

Zones 5a to 9a

P. 220

Catalpa bignonioides
Southern Catalpa, Indian Bean

Showy tall spires of purple- and yellow-speckled white flowers decorate the branch tips in early summer.

P. 220

Celtis occidentalis
Common Hackberry

Moderate to fast growing to 40 to 50 feet. Pyramidal to broadly arching.

Oval, pointed, toothed green leaves turn dull yellow in fall. Deeply furrowed corky bark. Small purple fruits attract birds in fall.

Full sun to part shade. Best in rich moist soil, but tolerates extreme sites, heat, cold, wind, and seashore conditions.

Zones 3b to 8b

P. 220

Cercidiphyllum japonicum
Katsura Tree

Fast growing to 40 to 50 feet. Multitrunked and pyramidal becoming broad and flat topped.

Small heart-shaped blue-green leaves turn glowing orange, gold, and apricot in fall. Misty red flowers before the leaves in spring. Shaggy gray-brown bark.

Full sun to part shade. Rich, moist, well-drained acid to alkaline soil.

Zones 4b to 8b

P. 221

Cercis canadensis
Eastern Redbud

Moderate growth rate to 20 to 30 feet. Rounded
to flat topped, multitrunked.

Two-lipped bright pink or white flowers before
the leaves in spring. Large matte green
heart-shaped leaves emerge reddish, change
to yellow in fall. Very dark gray bark.

Full sun to light shade. Moist, well-drained acid
to alkaline soil.

Zones 5b to 9a

P. 222

Cercis canadensis
'Forest Pansy'
Forest Pansy Redbud

New heart-shaped leaves emerge brilliant reddish-purple, mature to dark purplish green,
change to red in fall.

Zones 6a to 9a

P. 222

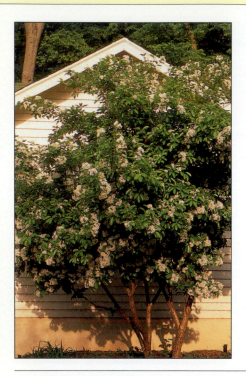

Chionanthus retusus
Chinese Fringe Tree

Slow growing to 20 feet. Multitrunked and
spreading to rounded.

Clusters of pure white fringelike flowers bloom
early summer. Oval leaves glossy green on
top, pale on undersides. Attractive yellow
fall color. Peeling bark a patchwork of green,
brown, and gray. Showy purple fruits on female trees.

Full sun with some afternoon shade. Rich,
moist, acid soil best, tolerates occasional wet
conditions.

Zones 4a to 9b

P. 223

Chionanthus virginicus
Fringe Tree, Old Man's Beard

Slow growing to 15 to 20 feet. Multitrunked and
rounded.

Showy clusters of fragrant creamy white blossoms in late spring. Dark waxy green leaves
turn yellow in late fall. Smooth gray bark.
Showy blue fall berries attract birds.

Full sun to light shade. Rich, moist, acid soil
best, tolerates wet or dry conditions.

Zones 4a to 9b

P. 223

Chionanthus virginicus
Fringe Tree, Old Man's Beard

Large clusters of honey-scented creamy white
  flowers cover the tree in a billowy mass in
  late spring as the new leaves emerge.

P. 223

Cladrastis kentukea (C. lutea)
Yellowwood

Slow growing to 30 to 35 feet. Open and
  rounded.

Long chains of fragrant white flowers in early
  summer. Bright green compound leaves
  turn soft yellow in fall. Smooth silvery gray
  bark.

Full sun. Deep, fertile, well-drained acid to alkaline soil.

Zones 4b to 8a

P. 224

Cornus alternifolia 'Argentea'
Variegated Pagoda Dogwood

Slow growth rate to 15 feet. Wide spreading with horizontal branches.

Lacy white flowers in flattened clusters in late spring. Glossy creamy white and green leaves turn white and purple-red in fall. Blue-black berries on red stalks. Glossy purple twigs, gray trunks.

Part shade. Humus-rich, well-drained, moist soil.

Zones 4a to 7a

P. 225

Cornus florida
Flowering Dogwood

Moderate growth rate to 20 to 30 feet. Wide spreading with horizontal branches.

Very showy white, pink, or rose-red flowers in early to midspring. Dark green leaves turn scarlet or wine red in fall. Red fruits attract birds. Checkered gray bark.

Full sun to part shade. Humus-rich, moist soil.

Zones 5b to 8b

P. 226

Cornus florida
Flowering Dogwood

White-bracted blossoms bloom along the layered branches in spring and remain showy for two weeks or more if weather is cool.

P. 226

Cornus kousa 'Summer Stars'
Summer Stars Kousa Dogwood

Slow growing to 20 to 30 feet. Vase shaped to horizontally spreading.

Star-shaped white flowers with pointed bracts bloom in early summer, remain showy for a month. Pointed oval leaves shiny dark green in summer, turn glossy dark red in fall. Mottled brown, gray, and creamy white bark. Large showy pink to red fall fruits attract birds.

Full sun. Fertile, well-drained, moist acid loam. Tolerates some drought.

Zones 5a to 8b

P. 228

Cornus mas
Cornelian Cherry, Cherry Dogwood

Moderate growth rate to 20 to 25 feet. Rounded and multitrunked.

Yellow flowers in late winter and early spring. Satiny green pointed oval leaves turn purplish in fall. Dark red cherrylike fruits attract birds in summer. Exfoliating gray and tan bark on older trunks.

Full sun to light shade. Humus-rich, moist acid or alkaline soil. Tolerates clay.

Zones 6a to 8

P. 228

Cornus mas
Cornelian Cherry, Cherry Dogwood

Numerous misty mustard yellow flowers bloom all over leafless branches for several weeks in late winter and early spring.

P. 228

Cornus × rutgersensis (C. florida × C. kousa) 'Aurora'

Stellar Dogwood, Hybrid Dogwood

Moderate to fast growth rate to 20 to 25 feet. Upright.

Profuse rounded white blossoms with overlapping bracts in midspring. Glossy dark green leaves turn red in autumn.

Full sun. Humus-rich, moist, well-drained soil.

Zones 6a to 8a

P. 229

Corylus colurna

Turkish Filbert, Turkish Hazel

Moderate growth to 50 feet. Round to oval.

Yellowish tan catkins dangle from leafless branches in late winter. Heart-shaped shallowly lobed glossy leaves have little fall color. Bark exfoliates into brown and white patterns. Edible nuts in fringed husks in fall.

Full sun. Well-drained acid to alkaline soil. Tolerates wind, heat, drought.

Zones 5a to 8b

P. 230

Cotinus coggygria
Smoke Tree, Smoke Bush

Moderate growth rate to 15 to 20 feet. Rounded to open and multitrunked.

Rounded leaves on long stems open pinkish bronze; mature to blue-green; turn yellow, red, and purple in fall. Showy pink flower plumes in early summer ripen into even showier summer seed heads.

Full sun to light shade. Moist, well-drained, sandy to clay soil. Tolerates alkalinity and drought.

Zones 4a to 7b

P. 231

Cotinus obovatus
American Smoke Tree, Smoke Bush

Moderate growth rate to 20 to 30 feet. Rounded and multitrunked.

Oblong leaves on long stems open pinkish bronze, mature to blue-green, turn a vivid mix of colors in fall. Pinkish gray flower plumes in late spring and early summer ripen into even showier summer seed heads. Scaly gray-brown bark.

Full sun to light shade. Moist, well-drained, sandy to clay soil. Tolerates alkalinity and drought.

Zones 4b to 8b

P. 231

Crataegus laevigata
English Hawthorn

Moderate growth rate to 15 to 20 feet. Multi-trunked and rounded.

Zigzag thorny branches decorated with clusters of white, pink, or red flower clusters in mid-spring. Glossy green shallowly-lobed toothed leaves. No fall color change. Numerous deep red berries in fall.

Full sun. Well-drained light to clay soil; tolerates cold and drought.

Zones 5a to 7b

P. 233

Crataegus laevigata
English Hawthorn

Rounded clusters of tiny pink, white, or red flowers with pink or purple anthers blanket the branches in midspring, creating a spectacular show.

P. 233

Crataegus phaenopyrum (C. cordata)
Washington Hawthorn

Moderate growth rate to 20 to 35 feet. Rounded to oval.

Clusters of white flowers bloom in early summer set off against glossy leaves. Shallowly lobed toothed leaves open reddish, turn dark green and then orange, red and scarlet in fall. Glossy red fruits remain showy through winter on leafless branches with long thorns.

Full sun. Any well-drained soil.

Zones 4b to 8b

P. 233

Crataegus viridis 'Winter King'
Winter King Green Hawthorn

Moderate growth rate to 30 feet. Vase shaped to flat topped.

Lacy white flowers in late spring. Glossy scalloped-edged wedge-shaped leaves. Scarlet and purple fall color. Persistent large bright red fruits remain showy all winter. Small thorns on silver-gray branches. Flaky trunk bark with orange patches.

Full sun. Tolerates dry to wet soil, wind, and urban sites.

Zones 5a to 9a

P. 234

Crataegus viridis 'Winter King'

Winter King Green Hawthorn

Extremely showy, the large bright red berries hang from the leafless branches all winter set off against the beautiful gray bark.

P. 234

Davidia involucrata

Dove Tree, Handkerchief Tree

Moderate growth rate to 30 to 50 feet. Open pyramidal shape.

Unique white flowers in late spring and early summer. Heart-shaped toothed green leaves with red stems. Smooth gray bark on branches, scaly orange bark on trunks. Green pearlike fruits in fall.

Light to part shade. Humus-rich, moist, acid, well-drained soil.

Zones 6b to 8b

P. 235

Davidia involucrata
Dove Tree, Handkerchief Tree

The unusual inflorescences consist of small yellow flowers surrounded by two large dangling white bracts that suggest the wings of a dove or a fluttering handkerchief.

P. 235

Diospyros virginiana
Common Persimmon

Slow to moderate growth rate to 60 to 80 feet. Pyramidal.

Bold-textured dark green leaves turn yellow, gold, and red in fall. Very fragrant small creamy bell-like flowers on male and female trees in early summer. Tasty green fruits ripen to orange and drop from female trees in fall. Attractive rugged bark.

Full sun to part shade. Moist rich soil best, tolerates poor soil, flooding, drought, heat, and wind.

Zones 5b to 9a

P. 235

Diospyros virginiana
Common Persimmon

The distinctive bark is deeply fissured and
  cracked into a checkerboard pattern.

P. 235

Elaeagnus angustifolia
Russian Olive, Wild Olive

Fast growing to 20 feet. Rounded and multitrunked.

Lance-shaped willowy leaves gray-green on tops
  and silver on undersides. Thorny silvery
  twigs and branches. Very fragrant creamy
  yellow flowers in late spring. Silver-scaled
  yellow berries in late summer and fall.
  Shaggy bark.

Full sun. Light to sandy well-drained soil. Tolerates drought, alkalinity, and urban and
  seashore sites.

Zones 3a to 7b

P. 236

Elaeagnus angustifolia
Russian Olive, Wild Olive

The creamy bell-shaped blossoms give off a
very strong sweet fragrance and are nestled
among the silvery new leaves in late spring.

P. 236

Eucommia ulmoides
Hardy Rubber Tree

Moderate growth rate to 40 to 60 feet. Vase
shape.

Attractive glossy green leaves with no fall color
change. Inconspicuous flowers and fruits.
Strong wood. Rough gray-brown bark.

Full sun. Adapts to any well-drained soil, acid to
alkaline, heavy to light. Tolerates heat,
drought, and urban sites.

Zones 5b to 8b

P. 237

Eucommia ulmoides
Hardy Rubber Tree

The dark green oval leaves have toothed margins and exude a white latexlike substance when broken, accounting for the name hardy rubber tree.

P. 237

Fagus sylvatica
European Beech

Slow growing to 50 to 60 feet. Rounded.

Arrow-shaped leaves with undulating edges, glossy dark green in summer, turn golden brown in fall. Massive trunks and branches covered with silvery gray smooth bark.

Full sun to part shade. Moist, well-drained acid soil. Somewhat drought tolerant.

Zones 5a to 8b

P. 238

Fagus sylvatica 'Tricolor' ('Roseo-marginata')

Tricolor European Beech

Slow growing to 30 feet. Pyramidal.

Arrow-shaped leaves emerge bright rosy red, mature to purple with pink and creamy variegations on the margins. Reddish purple fall color. Trunks and branches covered with silvery gray smooth bark.

Full sun to part shade. Moist, well-drained acid soil.

Zones 5a to 8b

P. 239

Franklinia alatamaha (*Gordonia alatamaha*)

Franklinia, Franklin Tree

Slow growing to 20 to 30 feet. Multitrunked open oval.

Narrow glossy green leaves turn stunning gold and wine red in fall. White camellialike flowers in late summer and fall. Slender trunks with dark gray bark and white striations.

Full sun to part shade. Humus-rich, well-drained acid soil.

Zones 6b to 7b

P. 239

Franklinia alatamaha (Gordonia alatamaha)

Franklinia, Franklin Tree

The lovely yellow-centered white flowers begin
to bloom in late summer set against green
leaves, but continue to open well into fall
when foliage changes to fiery colors.

P. 239

Fraxinus americana

White Ash

Fast growing to 50 to 80 feet. Pyramidal to oval.

Dark blue-green compound leaves with white
undersides. Vivid yellow, orange, and maroon early-fall color. Winged seeds ripen
from green to tan. Ash gray to gray-brown
furrowed bark broken into diamond-shaped
ridges.

Full sun. Deep, moist soil. Tolerates brief flooding and some drought.

Zones 4a to 9a

P. 240

Fraxinus pennsylvanica
Green Ash, Red Ash

Fast growing to 50 to 60 feet. Pyramidal to upright and spreading.

Shiny yellow-green compound leaves turn bright yellow in early fall. Single-seeded green fruits. Ash-gray bark furrowed into diamond-shaped ridges.

Full sun. Most soil types; tolerates infertile and alkaline soils, brief flooding and drought.

Zones 2a to 9a

P. 241

Ginkgo biloba
Ginkgo, Maidenhair Tree

Slow to moderate growth rate to 80 feet. Pyramidal to broad spreading.

Unique fan-shaped bright green leaves turn golden yellow in fall. Massive branching when old. Pale gray rough bark. Edible fruits on female trees become malodorous after dropping.

Full sun to part shade. Deep, well-drained acid to alkaline soil. Tolerates heat and urban sites.

Zones 4b to 8b

P. 242

Ginkgo biloba
Ginkgo, Maidenhair Tree

The beautiful fan-shaped leaves resemble the foliage of maidenhair ferns and take on glowing yellow color in autumn.

P. 242

Gleditsia triacanthos var. *inermis*
Thornless Honey Locust

Fast growing to 35 to 70 feet. Broad spreading.

Lacy compound leaves cast a light shade, turn yellow in fall. Inconspicuous flowers give off an intense sweet perfume in spring. Long brown seedpods in fall and winter . Thornless branches.

Full sun. Rich, moist, acid to alkaline soil best, tolerates wet to dry conditions and poor soil.

Zones 4b to 9a

P. 243

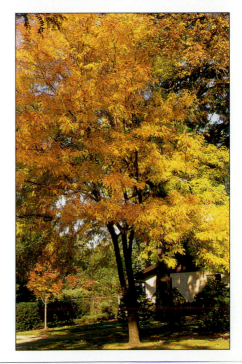

Gleditsia triacanthos var. *inermis* 'Sunburst'

Sunburst Thornless Honey Locust

Fast growing to 30 to 35 feet. Broad pyramid to irregular.

Lacy compound leaves emerge bright yellow, mature to yellow-green, turn bright yellow in fall. Inconspicuous flowers give off an intense sweet perfume in spring. Long brown seedpods in fall and winter. Thornless branches.

Full to part sun. Rich, moist, acid to alkaline soil best, tolerates wet to dry conditions and poor soil.

Zones 4b to 9a

P. 243

Gymnocladus dioica

Kentucky Coffee Tree

Slow to moderate growth rate to 50 to 70 feet. Craggy oval shape.

Compound leaves composed of long pointed leaflets. Leaves emerge pinkish green in late spring, mature to blue-green, turn pale yellow in fall. Showy greenish white fragrant flowers in spring. Reddish brown seedpods on female trees hang on all winter and into spring. Deeply furrowed and ridged bark.

Full sun. Humus-rich, moist, acid to alkaline soil. Tolerates drought and urban sites.

Zones 3b to 8a

P. 244

Gymnocladus dioica
Kentucky Coffee Tree

The reddish brown seedpods, which contain poisonous seeds, remain on the silvery branches all winter and may not drop off until after the new leaves unfold in late spring.

P. 244

Halesia carolina
(H. tetraptera)
Carolina Silverbell

Moderate growth rate to 20 to 30 feet. Rounded.

Showy bell-shaped white blossoms mid- to late spring. Oval leaves yellow-green with pointed tips. Nice yellow fall color. Winged seedpods ripen from green to brown. Gray bark with white furrows.

Full sun to part shade. Moist, well-drained, humus-rich soil,

Zones 5a to 9a

P. 245

Halesia carolina (H. tetraptera)

Carolina Silverbell

Bell-shaped white blossoms dangle from the undersides of the branches in mid- to late spring as the new leaves are emerging.

P. 245

Juglans nigra

Black Walnut

Moderate to fast growing to 75 feet. Rounded to spreading.

Dark green feathery compound leaves. Yellowish early-fall color. Inconspicuous catkins in early summer. Brown thickly furrowed trunk bark. Large edible nuts in green husks drop in fall.

Full sun. Deep, rich, moist soil best, tolerates drier sites.

Zones 4b to 9a

P. 246

Koelreuteria paniculata
Goldenrain Tree

Moderate to fast growth rate to 30 to 40 feet. Rounded.

Large compound jagged leaves with a tropical texture. Large clusters of yellow flowers in mid- to late summer. Orange, gold, or yellow fall color. Interesting papery fruits that resemble Japanese lanterns ripen from green to pinkish tan in fall.

Full sun. Any well-drained acid to alkaline soil. Tolerates drought and urban sites.

Zones 5a to 9a

P. 247

Koelreuteria paniculata
Goldenrain Tree

Starlike yellow flowers bloom in large clusters at the branch tips in mid- or late summer, an unusual time and color for a flowering tree.

P. 247

Laburnum × *watereri*
Golden Chain Tree, Waterer Laburnum
Eye-catching yellow flowers dangle in long
chains from the branches, creating an unusual sight in spring

P. 248

Laburnum × *watereri* 'Vossii'
Golden Chain Tree, Waterer Laburnum
Moderate growth rate to 15 feet. Upright oval
shape.

Extremely showy long clusters of golden yellow
blossoms in late spring and early summer.
Bright green dainty three-parted leaves. No
fall color. Smooth olive green bark on
trunks and branches.

Full to part shade. Humus-rich, well-drained,
moist soil. Tolerates alkaline soil.

Zones 6a to 7b

P. 248

Lagerstroemia indica
Crape Myrtle

Fast growing to 15 to 25 feet. Multitrunked and rounded to vase shaped.

Gorgeous pink, lavender, white, or purple yellow-marked flowers in huge clusters bloom at the branch tips in summer and fall. Shiny oval leaves in whorls of three emerge reddish, mature to dark green, change to fiery shades in fall. Very showy colorful mottled bark.

Full sun to part shade. Well-drained, moist, acid loam or clay. Tolerates heat and drought.

Zones 7b to 9a

P. 248

Lagerstroemia indica × faureii 'Natchez'
Natchez Hybrid Crape Myrtle

Fast growing to 15 to 25 feet. Multitrunked and broadly rounded.

Gorgeous white yellow-marked flowers in huge clusters bloom at the branch tips in summer and fall. Shiny oval leaves in whorls of three emerge reddish, mature to dark green, change to orange-red in fall. Alluring mottled cinnamon brown bark.

Full sun to part shade. Well-drained, moist, acid loam or clay. Tolerates heat and drought.

Zones 7b to 9a

P. 250

Liquidambar styraciflua
Sweetgum, Gum Tree

Moderate to fast growth rate to 65 to 70 feet. Pyramidal becoming rounded.

Beautiful glossy green leaves turn a mixture of fiery shades late fall. Spiny tan seed heads drop in late winter or early spring. Deeply furrowed trunk bark, silvery twigs with corky ridges.

Full sun to part shade. Humus-rich, moist, acid to slightly alkaline soil. Tolerates drought and poor drainage.

Zones 5b to 9a

P. 250

Liquidambar styraciflua
Sweetgum, Gum Tree

The star-shaped glossy green leaves have five to seven lobes. Fall color is a stunning mixture of yellow, orange, red, and purple.

P. 250

Liriodendron tulipifera
Tulip Tree, Yellow Poplar

Fast growing to 70 to 90 feet. Pyramidal becoming wide spreading.

Shallow-lobed bright green blocky leaves turn vibrant yellow in late fall. Tulip-shaped flowers bloom at the branch tips in early summer. Gray-brown furrowed trunk bark.

Full sun to part shade. Deep, humus-rich, moist soil. Tolerates drought.

Zones 5a to 9a

P. 251

Liriodendron tulipifera
Tulip Tree, Yellow Poplar

The beautiful yellow-green orange-marked flowers bloom high up on the branches so are easy to overlook.

P. 251

Maackia amurensis
Amur Maackia

Slow growing to 20 to 35 feet. Rounded to spreading.

Compound gray-green to dark olive green leaves drop with little color change in fall. Creamy white blue-marked flowers bloom in tall spires at the branch tips in summer. Shiny amber bark peels off in curls. Flat small seedpods develop in fall.

Full sun. Moist loam best. Tolerates well-drained light to heavy, acid to alkaline soil. Very drought tolerant.

Zones 3a to 7b

P. 252

Maackia chinensis
Chinese Maackia

The beautifully textured compound leaves unfold covered with downy silvery hairs that shimmer in the sun.

P. 252

Magnolia acuminata
Cucumber Tree

Moderate to fast growing to 80 feet. Pyramidal becoming wide spreading.

Bold, heart-shaped leaves with wavy edges and pointed tips turn yellow in late fall. Greenish yellow to yellow flowers in late spring and early summer. Green cucumberlike fruits split open to reveal red seeds in fall. Smooth gray bark becomes rough with age.

Full sun to part shade. Deep, moist, acid loam.

Zones 4a to 8b

P. 253

Magnolia × liliflora
Kosar Hybrid Magnolia

Fast growing to 12 to 15 feet. Multistemmed and rounded to upright.

Gorgeous lily-shaped pale pink, purple, wine red, or two-toned flowers bloom after danger of frost. Dark green leaves drop with little color change in fall. Smooth gray bark.

Full sun to light shade. Deep, acid, moist loam.

Zones 5b to 9a

P. 254

Magnolia × *liliflora* 'Ann'

Ann Kosar Hybrid Magnolia

Beautiful purplish pink lily-shaped flowers
bloom at the branch tips in midspring and
give off a sweet cinnamon scent.

P. 254

Magnolia × *loebneri* 'Ballerina'

Ballerina Loebner Magnolia

Moderate growth rate to 20 to 30 feet. Multistemmed and rounded.

Profuse fragrant double white flowers with
strap-shaped petals in early spring. Medium
green leaves do not change color in fall.
Reddish kobby seedpods split open to reveal
orange-red seeds. Smooth silvery gray bark.

Full sun to light shade. Deep, acid, moist,
humus-rich soil.

Zones 4b to 9a

P. 254

Magnolia × soulangeana
Saucer Magnolia

Moderate growth rate to 20 to 30 feet.
Rounded.

Saucer-shaped flowers with nine satiny pink,
white, or wine red petals bloom at the
branch tips before the foliage in early
spring. Oblong, smooth, bold-textured
green leaves turn golden brown in fall.
Smooth gray bark. Attractive furry buds.

Full sun to light shade. Deep, acid, moist,
humus-rich soil.

Zones 5a to 9a

P. 255

Magnolia × soulangeana
Saucer Magnolia

Flowers are often bicolored, wine red on the
outside of the petals and pink or white on
the interior. Blooming commences before
the leaves unfold but new leaves may expand before the petals drop.

P. 255

Magnolia stellata (M. tomentosa) 'Rosea'
Pink Star Magnolia

Moderate growth rate to 15 to 20 feet. Rounded and multistemmed.

Fragrant flowers made up of straplike petals bloom in very early spring on bare branches. Leaves with a finer texture than most magnolias. Silvery gray smooth bark. Attractive furry buds.

Full sun to light shade. Deep, acid, moist, humus-rich soil.

Zones 5a to 8b

P. 255

Magnolia stellata (M. tomentosa) 'Rosea'
Pink Star Magnolia

The profusion of pale pink flowers is a sight to behold in late winter and early spring, but sometimes frost ruins the show.

P. 255

Malus 'Adams'
Adams Crab Apple

Moderate growth rate to 20 to 25 feet. Rounded.

Red buds open to a profusion of purple-pink blossoms in early to midspring. Foliage dusky purple in spring matures to dark purplish green and changes to reddish purple in fall. Persistent glossy orange-red fruits.

Zones 3a to 7a

P. 257

Malus × *floribunda* 'Harvest Gold'
Japanese Flowering Crab Apple

Fast growing to 20 feet. Upright.

Cardinal red buds open to a profusion of fragrant pink blossoms that fade to white in midspring.

Large yellow fall fruits on red stems last well into winter. Dark green oval leaves with little fall foliage color.

Full sun. Well-drained, acid loam or clay soil.

Zones 4b to 8a

P. 258

Malus × floribunda 'Red Jewel'

Moderate growth rate to 15 feet. Upright and spreading.

Dawn pink buds open to numerous white flowers. Large red fruits turn cider gold in winter and persist well. Glossy leaves are green in summer and turn yellow in fall.

Full sun. Well-drained acid loam or clay soil.

Zones 4b to 8a

P. 258

Malus × floribunda 'Sugar Tyme'

Fast growing to 20 feet. Upright to oval.

Pale pink buds open to fragrant white flowers. Large very showy red fruits and golden yellow fall color.

Full sun. Well-drained acid loam or clay soil.

Zones 4b to 8a

P. 258

▲*Malus hupehensis*
Tea Crab Apple

Moderate growth rate to 20 to 25 feet. Vase shaped.

Deep pink buds open to fragrant blush pink flowers that fade to pure white in early to midspring. Oval pointed green leaves with toothed edges. Showy yellow fruits change to red.

Full sun. Moist, well-drained, acid to alkaline loam.

Zones 4b to 8b

P. 259

▼*Malus* × *hupehensis* 'Strawberry Parfait'
Strawberry Parfait Crab Apple

Large glossy fruits are yellow with a red blush or orange-red.

P. 259

Malus sargentii
Sargent Crab Apple
Slow-growing to 10 feet. Wide spreading.

Pale pink buds open to very fragrant large white flowers. Dark green slightly lobed leaves. Bright red small fruits in fall paired with yellow fall foliage. Fruits remain showy well into winter.

Full sun. Well-drained acid loam or clay soil.

Zones 4b to 8b

P. 259

Malus sargentii
Sargent Crab Apple
Flowers are so numerous the tree is transformed into a white cloud when it blooms.

P. 259

Malus × zumi 'Calocarpa'

Zumi Crab Apple, Redbud Crab Apple

Moderate growth rate to 15 feet. Rounded to horizontally spreading.

Abundant pink buds open into large white flowers in late spring. Dark green lobed oval leaves turn golden orange in fall. Large glossy red fruits hang from long stems in autumn and put on a show well into winter.

Full sun. Well-drained acid loam or clay soil.

Zones 4b to 8b

P. 260

Morus alba

White Mulberry

Fast growing to 30 to 50 feet. Rounded.

Inconspicuous spring flowers ripen to black-berry-like fruits in summer. Fruits may be messy but attract birds. Glossy dark green lobed to unlobed leaves turn attractive yellow in fall. Orange-brown bark.

Part to full sun. Tolerates any soil, heat, drought, and seashore.

Zones 5a to 9a

P. 261

Nyssa sylvatica

Black Gum, Sour Gum, Pepperidge, Tupelo

Slow to moderate growth rate to 30 to 50 feet. Pyramidal becoming rounded to irregular.

Outstanding reliable fall color changing from yellow to orange to scarlet then deep maroon. Inconspicuous spring flowers ripen into glossy blue fruits. Silvery limbs and chunky trunk bark.

Full sun to half shade. Moist, humus-rich, acid to neutral soil. Wet to dry conditions.

Zones 5a to 9a

P. 262

Nyssa sylvatica

Black Gum, Sour Gum, Pepperidge, Tupelo

The blue berries make a magnificent sight in fall when shown off against the fall-colored leaves. Birds, however, quickly eat the ripe fruits.

P. 262

Ostrya virginiana
Ironwood, Hop Hornbeam

Slow growing to 30 to 40 feet. Pyramidal becoming rounded.

Fine-textured toothed oval leaves with a felty texture. Golden yellow fall color. Small catkins ripen into pale green capsules with papery bracts in summer. Nuts provide food for wildlife. Reddish shredding bark on trunk and older branches.

Full sun to shade. Any well-drained soil. Tolerates urban conditions except for road salt.

Zones 3a to 9a.

P. 263

Ostrya virginiana
Ironwood, Hop Hornbeam

The catkin's unopened buds decorate the trees in winter, but when opened are usually obscured by the new foliage.

P. 263

Oxydendrum arboreum
Sourwood, Sorrel Tree

Moderate growth rate to 25 to 35 feet. Pyramidal.

Lance-shaped to oblong glossy green leaves. Nodding clusters of creamy white bell-like flowers at branch tips in midsummer. Beautiful yellow, scarlet, and burgundy red fall color. Buff-colored seedpods in fall. Deeply furrowed blocky bark.

Full sun to part shade. Moist, well-drained, fertile acid soil.

Zones 5b to 9a

P. 264

Oxydendrum arboreum
Sourwood, Sorrel Tree

The pretty flowers ripen into buff-colored seedpods that look quite decorative, especially when seen against the fall foliage.

P. 264

Parrotia persica
Persian Parrotia, Persian Ironwood

Slow growing to 30 to 40 feet. Single- to multi-trunked rounded form.

Tiny dark red mophead flowers cover branches in late winter. Wedge-shaped leaves emerge glossy reddish purple, mature to dark green, turn spectacular fiery shades in fall. Mottled reddish brown bark flakes to reveal showy green, silver, and cream patches.

Full sun to light shade. Well-drained, humus-rich, slightly acid to alkaline soil. Tolerates drought and urban sites.

Zones 5b to 9a

P. 265

Paulownia tomentosa
Empress Tree, Princess Tree

Fast growing to 35 to 50 feet. Irregular pyramidal to rounded.

Huge downy green heart-shaped to shallowly lobed leaves emerge late. Very showy fragrant lavender flower clusters at the branch tips in midspring. Decorative pale green seed capsules last all winter. Smooth gray trunk bark.

Full sun to part shade. Tolerates almost any soil, acid to alkaline, wet to dry. Thrives in urban sites.

Zones 6b to 9a

P. 265

Paulownia tomentosa
Empress Tree, Princess Tree

Spires of fragrant lavender to purple yellow-
striped flowers bloom at the branch tips in
midspring before the leaves emerge.

P. 265

Phellodendron amurense
Amur Cork Tree

Moderate growth rate to 30 to 45 feet. Rounded
and open branched.

Inconspicuous green spring flowers ripen to
showy red then blue fruits on female trees.

Large compound deep green leaves turn flaming red and orange in late fall. Orange-
yellow twigs and deeply furrowed corky
gray-brown bark.

Full sun. Moist, well-drained, acid to alkaline
soil. Tolerates heat, drought, and urban
sites.

Zones 6b to 9b

P. 266

Phellodendron amurense
Amur Cork Tree
The beautiful gray-brown corky bark develops
on trunks of older trees into a distinctive
deeply ridged pattern.

P. 266

Pistacia chinensis
Chinese Pistache, Chinese Pistachio
Moderate growth rate to 25 to 35 feet. Open and
rounded.

Small deep green compound leaves turn flaming shades of red and orange in fall. Inconspicuous greenish flowers in spring ripen
into showy clusters of red fruits that change
to bright blue on female trees. Fruits eaten
by birds. Mottled gray and salmon orange
flaking bark.

Full sun. Moist, well-drained acid to alkaline
soil. Tolerates heat, drought, and urban
sites.

Zones 6b to 9b

P. 267

Platanus × hispanica (P. × acerifolia)
London Plane Tree

Moderate growth rate to 50 to 60 feet. Pyramidal becoming rounded and irregular.

Dark green maplelike lobed leaves turn yellowish brown in fall. Striking creamy white, olive green, and tan flaking bark. Large tan prickly seedballs drop in winter.

Full to part sun. Fertile, moist, acid soil. Tolerates infertile and alkaline soil, wetness and drought, and urban sites.

Zones 5b to 9a

P. 268

Platanus × hispanica (P. × acerifolia)
London Plane Tree

The rugged trunk and branches of mature trees are covered with eye-catching peeling creamy white, olive green, and gray patchwork-patterned bark.

P. 268

Poncirus trifoliata
Trifoliate Orange, Hardy Orange

Moderate growth rate to 10 to 20 feet. Oval
shape, often multitrunked.

Green-barked thorny branches and trunks.
Star-shaped fragrant white blossoms in
spring. Shiny green leaves divided into three
leaflets turn bright yellow in fall. Citruslike
golden yellow fruits adorn branches in fall
and winter.

Full sun to part shade. Moist, well-drained, acid
soil. Tolerates heat and drought.

Zones 6b to 9a

P. 269

Poncirus trifoliata
Trifoliate Orange, Hardy Orange

The showy sour-tasting golden yellow fruits are
eye-catching in fall and winter.

P. 269

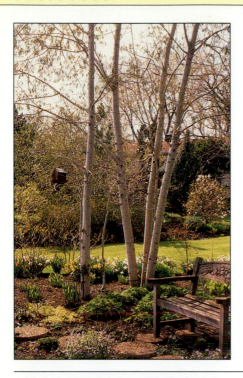

Populus alba
White Poplar

Fast growing to 40 to 70 feet. Multitrunked oval to rounded clump.

Three-lobed leaves shiny dark green on top with felty white undersides that flash in the breeze. Yellow fall color. Grayish white trunks.

Full sun. Moist soil best. Tolerates poor sandy site, salt spray, and air pollution.

Zones 4a to 9a

P. 270

Populus deltoides
Cottonwood

Fast growing to 75 to 100 feet. Pyramidal to vase shaped.

Triangular bright green leaves with blue-green undersides rattle in the wind. Yellow, gold, or brown fall color. Female trees produce masses of cottony seed heads. Deeply furrowed brown bark. Best used where other trees can't grow.

Full sun. Moist, fertile site best. Tolerates dry and alkaline soil.

Zones 3a to 9a

P. 271

Populus deltoides
Cottonwood

The rugged trunk and branches are covered with furrowed brown bark, creating a dramatic silhouette in winter, especially when lit by the setting sun.

P. 271

Populus nigra 'Italica'
Lombardy Poplar

Fast growing to 70 to 90 feet. Narrow column.

Triangular bright green leaves with light green undersides. Bright yellow fall color. Gray-green bark on young trunks, turning black on old trunks.

Full sun. Best in moist site. Tolerates wetness and drought. Best used as temporary tree.

Zones 3a to 9a

P. 272

Populus tremuloides
Quaking Aspen

Fast growing to 40 to 50 feet. Pyramidal to rounded, often multitrunked.

Bright white to gray-green bark. Small wedge-shaped green leaves with silver undersides flash in the breeze. Glorious yellow fall foliage.

Moist loamy soil best. Tolerates rocky soil, sandy and alkaline sites. Performs best in the West above 7,000 feet elevation.

Zones 2b to 6b

P. 271

Prunus cerasifera
'Thundercloud'
Purple-Leaved Plum, Cherry Plum

Moderate growth rate to 15 to 30 feet. Vase shaped to oval.

Fragrant dark pink flowers in early spring when rich purple leaves begin to unfold. Deep purple foliage all summer. Reddish-purple fall color. Small purple plumlike fruits.

Full sun. Moist, acid, well-drained loam best. Tolerates slightly alkaline soil.

Zones 4b to 9a

P. 273

Prunus maackii
Amur Chokecherry, Goldbark Cherry

Moderate growth rate to 30 feet. Single or multitrunked and rounded.

White flowers in spring ripen to small black
fruits eaten by birds. Green toothed leaves
turn yellow in fall. Outstanding gleaming
honey gold bark on trunk and branches.

Full to part sun. Moist, humus-rich, well-
drained soil.

Zones 3b to 7a

P. 273

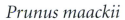

Prunus maackii
Amur Chokecherry, Goldbark Cherry

The pretty dangling clusters of white spring
flowers ripen into bird-attracting black
fruits in summer.

P. 273

Prunus × 'Okame'
Okame Cherry

Moderate growth rate to 20 to 30 feet. Vase shaped.

Very early long-lasting bright pink flowers in profuse clusters. Fine-textured sharp-toothed green leaves turn bright yellow and orange in fall.

Full sun. Well-drained moist soil. Heat tolerant.

Zones 6b to 9a

P. 274

Prunus × 'Okame'
Okame Cherry

Dark pink buds with red calyxes open to pink flowers with jagged petals. Flowers remain showy for as long as three weeks, beginning in very early spring.

Rounded to vase shaped.

P. 274

Prunus sargentii
Sargent Cherry

Moderate growth rate to 30 to 50 feet.

Delicate pink to white flowers bloom before the leaves in early spring. Large toothed leaves open reddish, mature to dark green, change to orange-red and yellow in fall. Small black fruits. Polished chestnut brown bark.

Full sun. Well-drained acid to neutral soil. Tolerates clay and drought.

Zones 4b to 9a

P. 275

Prunus serotina
Black Cherry, Wild Black Cherry

Moderate growth rate to 80 to 100 feet. Oval shape.

Drooping clusters of creamy white flowers in late spring. Leathery oval leaves turn orange in fall. Clusters of small red to black cherries provide food for birds. Rough peeling bark on trunks and branches, very shiny bark on young branches and twigs.

Full sun. Moist, neutral to acid soil best. Tolerates sandy and gravelly sites.

Zones 3b to 9a.

P. 274

Prunus serrulata 'Shirofugen'

Shirofugen Oriental Cherry, Japanese Flowering Cherry

Moderate growth rate to 25 to 30 feet. Wide-spreading and flat topped.

Large clusters of double blush pink blossoms fade to pure white then age to deep pink over three weeks. New growth bronze, matures to deep green, changes to scarlet in fall. Shiny reddish brown bark.

Full sun. Well-drained, moist, acid to neutral soil.

Zones 6b to 8b

P. 275

Prunus subhirtella
var. *pendula* (P. pendula)

Higan Cherry, Weeping Cherry

Moderate growth rate to 20 to 40 feet. Rounded weeping shape.

Single or double pink or white blossoms on cascading branches in early spring. Deeply toothed dark green leaves. Little fall color change. Wonderful winter silhouette.

Full sun. Moist, well-drained soil. Tolerates clay.

Zones 5b to 8b

P. 276

Prunus × yedoensis
Yoshino Cherry, Potomac Cherry

Moderate growth rate 40 to 50 feet. Broadly
  rounded.

Profuse single pale pink to white flowers in
  early spring on leafless branches. Dark green
  glossy toothed leaves turn yellowish before
  falling. Tiny black fruits in summer.

Full sun. Moist, well-drained soil.

Zones 6b to 8b

P. 277

Pyrus calleryana
Callery Pear, Flowering Pear

Fast growing to 30 to 50 feet. Oval to rounded.

Blanketed with fluffy white flowers in early
  spring. Leaves emerge bronze, mature to
  glossy dark green, turn spectacular shades of
  red, purple, orange, and gold in fall. Green
  to russet small fruits attract birds in summer.

Full sun to part shade. Well-drained light to
  heavy, acid to alkaline soil. Tolerates
  drought and urban sites.

Zones 4b or 5a to 9a

P. 278

Pyrus salicifolia 'Pendula'
Weeping Willowleaf Pear

Moderate growth rate to 25 feet. Rounded to irregular with weeping branches.

Narrow silvery leaves create a light-reflecting
show from spring through fall. Small white
flowers obscured by leaves. Sparse green
fruits. Attractive winter silhouette.

Full sun. Well-drained soil. Tolerates drought,
light or stony soil.

Zones 5b to 8a

P. 279

Quercus acutissima
Sawtooth Oak

Moderate growth rate to 35 to 45 feet. Pyramidal becoming rounded.

Unlobed oblong leaves with bristly edges open
light golden green, mature to dark green,
turn bright yellow to gold in late fall. Numerous brown acorns with shaggy caps feed
wildlife.

Full sun. Rich, moist, well-drained acid to neutral soil. Tolerates drought, poor drainage,
and salt spray.

Zones 5a to 9a

P. 282

Quercus alba
White Oak

Slow to moderate growth rate to 80 to 100 feet.
Rugged trunk and horizontal branches with
shaggy bark. Round-lobed leaves emerge
pinkish, mature to deep matte blue-green,
turn excellent crimson to purple in fall.

Full sun. Deep, moist, well-drained acid to neutral soil. Tolerates occasionally wet sites.

Zones 4b to 9a

P. 284

Quercus coccinea
Scarlet Oak

Moderate growth rate to 75 feet. Pyramidal to
rounded.

Deeply cut bristly leaves emerge bright red, mature to glossy dark green, and turn maroon to
brilliant scarlet in fall. Small reddish brown
acorns mostly covered by bowlike cup.

Full sun. Moist, acid, sandy soil. Tolerates slight
alkalinity, clay and dry sandy sites.

Zones 5a to 9a

P. 280

Quercus coccinea
Scarlet Oak

The most reliable of the oaks for fall color, scarlet oak's leaves turn brilliant scarlet to maroon-red in autumn.

P. 280

Quercus imbricaria
Shingle Oak

Slow to moderate growth rate to 50 to 60 feet. Pyramidal becoming open and rounded and wide spreading.

Pale yellow-green catkins in early spring. Dark green unlobed leathery green leaves turn yellow or tan in fall. Round acorns with thin bowl-shaped caps.

Deep, moist, humus-rich, acid to slightly alkaline soil. Tolerates dry soil and urban sites.

Zones 5a to 9a

P. 285

Quercus palustris
Pin Oak

Fast growing to 60 to 70 feet. Pyramidal with horizontal branching. Yellow-green catkins in spring. Deeply cut sharp-pointed leaves deep green in summer, turn yellow to coppery red in autumn. Round light brown acorns with shallow cups.

Full sun. Moist, rich, acid soil. Tolerates wet and dry sites, and air pollution.

Zones 5a to 8b

P. 281

Quercus phellos
Willow Oak

Moderate growth rate to 50 to 90 feet. Pyramidal becoming rounded.

Slender long unlobed fine-textured leaves, shiny dark green in summer, turn red to yellow in fall or remain green until early winter. Copious quantities of small acorns feed wildlife.

Full sun. Well-drained, moist, acid soil. Tolerates intermittent poor drainage.

Zones 6b to 9a

P. 285

▲*Quercus phellos*

Willow Oak

The slender unlobed smooth-edged leaves resemble those of a willow more than those of
an oak and offer a beautiful fine-textured
effect.

P. 285

▼*Quercus robur*

English Oak

Slow to moderate growth rate to 50 to 100 feet.
Broad and rounded.

Short massive trunk and wide branches. Dark
matte green leaves with rounded lobes do
not change color in fall. Shiny dark brown
narrow acorns. Rough-textured bark.

Full sun. Well-drained average to clay soil. Tolerates slight alkalinity, drought, and urban
sites.

Zones 5b to 9a

P. 285

Quercus robur
English Oak

The rugged, deeply furrowed gray-black trunk bark hosts an attractive colony of jade green lichen.

P. 285

Quercus rubra (Q. borealis)
Northern Red Oak

Fast growing to 60 to 70 feet. Upright to rounded with horizontal branching.

Shallowly lobed sharp-pointed leaves unfold pinkish red, mature to dark green with gray-green undersides, turn russet-red to bright red in fall. Dark brown acorns. Deeply furrowed bark on mature trunks.

Full to part sun. Well-drained light acid to neutral soil. Tolerates drought and urban sites.

Zones 3b to 9a

P. 282

Rhus glabra
Smooth Sumac
Fast growing to 15 feet. Multitrunked upright.

Bold-textured compound green leaves turn scarlet in autumn. Showy clusters of creamy white flowers in summer ripen on female plants into bright red fruits in fall and winter. Leaves and stout stems are hairless.

Full sun. Fertile, moist, acid soil best. Tolerates poor soil and drought.

Zones 3a to 9a

P. 287

Rhus typhina 'Laciniata'
Cut-leaved Staghorn Sumac
Fast growing to 15 to 30 feet. Multitrunked.

Bold, deeply cut velvety green leaves. Brilliant red fall color. Greenish summer flower clusters ripen on female plants into showy fuzzy red fruits in winter. Stout fuzzy stems.

Full sun. Fertile, moist, acid soil best. Tolerates poor soil and drought.

Zones 3b to 8a.

P. 286

Robinia pseudoacacia
Black Locust

Fast growing to 75 feet. Upright to spreading and irregular.

Fine-textured blue-green compound leaves. Clusters of fragrant creamy white flowers in early summer. Variable yellow fall color. Thorny branches.

Full sun. Fertile, moist soil best, tolerates infertile site, drought, and urban conditions.

Zones 4b to 9a

P. 287

Robinia pseudoacacia 'Frisia'
Golden Black Locust

Fast growing to 30 to 50 feet. Upright to rounded and irregular.

Fine-textured chartreuse compound leaves. Clusters of fragrant creamy white flowers in early summer. Yellow fall color. Thorny branches.

Full sun where cool; morning sun and afternoon shade in hot climate. Fertile, moist soil best; tolerates infertile site, drought, and urban conditions.

Zones 4b to 9a

P. 288

Salix alba 'Tristis' (*S. × specularis* 'Chrysocoma')

Niobe Willow, Golden Weeping Willow

Fast growing to 50 to 70 feet. Rounded weeping shape.

Narrow leaves with silvery undersides. Massive trunk and limbs with slender weeping gold-barked twigs. Golden fall leaves.

Full sun. Moist to wet soil.

Zones 3a to 9a

P. 289

Salix matsudana 'Torulosa'

Corkscrew Willow

Fast growing to 20 to 30 feet. Rounded to irregular shape with corkscrew branches.

Slender, curled olive green leaves on twisted and curled branches.

Full to part sun. Moist, acid to alkaline soil.

Zones 5a to 9a

P. 289

▲*Sophora japonica*
Japanese Pagoda Tree

Moderate growth rate to 50 to 75 feet. Rounded to spreading.

Fine-textured bright green compound leaves turn yellow in fall. Large airy clusters of creamy flowers in summer. Showy seedpods in fall and winter. Rugged bark.

Full sun. Well-drained, fertile, acid to alkaline soil. Tolerates drought and urban sites.

Zones 5b to 8b

P. 290

▼*Sorbus alnifolia*
Alder Whitebeam, Korean Mountain Ash

Fast growing to 40 to 50 feet. Pyramidal to rounded.

Lacy white flowers in late spring. Pointed leaves turn glorious shades in fall. Shiny rose-red berries showy in fall and winter. Attractive silver-gray bark.

Full sun to light shade. Well-drained, moist, acid to alkaline soil.

Zones 3a to 7a

P. 291

Sorbus aucuparia
European Mountain Ash

Fast growing to 35 feet. Oval shape.

Dark green ferny compound leaves. Showy clusters of white flowers in late spring. Large clusters of orange or red berries in late summer and fall.

Full sun. Moist, acid to alkaline soil.

Zones 2b to 6b

P. 292

Stewartia pseudocamellia
Japanese Stewartia, Korean Stewartia

Slow growing to 30 feet. Oval to vase shaped.

Dark green oval leaves turn brilliant orange to red in fall. Showy white flowers in midsummer. Flaky colorful trunk bark.

Morning sun and afternoon shade. Moist, fertile, acid soil.

Zones 5b to 8b

P. 293

▲*Stewartia pseudocamellia*

Japanese Stewartia, Korean Stewartia

White flowers with yellow centers and ruffled petals bloom for 2 to 3 weeks in midsummer.

P. 293

▼*Styrax americanus*

Fragrant Snowbell

Moderate growth rate to 10 feet. Multistemmed and rounded.

Bell-shaped white flowers with narrow petals in early summer. Gray-green fruits in fall and winter.

Full sun to light shade. Rich, well-drained, moist, acid soil.

Zones 6b to 9a

P. 294

Styrax japonicum
Japanese Snowbell

Moderate growth rate to 20 to 30 feet. Rounded to spreading.

Bell-shaped white flowers in late spring and early summer. Gray-green fruits in fall and winter. Yellow to rusty red fall color. Gray bark with orange-brown fissures.

Full sun to light shade. Rich, well-drained, moist, acid soil.

Zones 6a to 8b

P. 294

Styrax obassia
Fragrant Snowbell

Moderate growth rate to 30 feet. Rounded.

Large bell-shaped fragrant white flowers in early summer. Large fuzzy leaves with silvery undersides.

Full sun. Rich, well-drained, moist soil.

Zones 6b to 8b

P. 295

Syringa pekinensis
Peking Lilac

Moderate growth rate to 15 to 20 feet. Multi-trunked and vase shaped to rounded.

Small clusters of creamy flowers in summer. Shiny cinnamon brown bark.

Full sun. Fertile, moist soil.

Zones 3b to 7b

P. 296

Syringa reticulata
(S. amurensis var. japonica)
Japanese Tree Lilac

Moderate growth rate to 20 to 30 feet. Upright to rounded.

Large clusters of creamy white flowers in summer. Heart-shaped leaves with gray undersides.

Shiny dark brown bark.

Full sun. Well-drained acid to alkaline loam or clay. Tolerates drought.

Zones 3a to 7b

P. 295

Tilia americana 'Redmond'
Redmond American Linden
Fast growing to 70 feet. Pyramidal.

Coarse-textured glossy green leaves, bright yellow fall color. Small clusters of fragrant yellow-green flowers in summer.

Full sun to light shade. Deep, rich, moist, acid to alkaline soil. Tolerates drought.

Zones 3a to 8a

P. 297

Tilia americana 'Redmond'
Redmond American Linden
Glossier than those of the species, the large heart-shaped leaves also turn brighter yellow in autumn.

P. 297

Tilia cordata
Littleleaf Linden

Moderate growth rate to 60 to 70 feet. Rounded
   to oval.

Small heart-shaped leaves. Creamy yellow
   flower clusters in midsummer. Green pea-
   shaped fruits in fall attached to spoon-
   shaped bracts. Yellowish fall color. Rough
   bark.

Full to part sun. Fertile, moist, well-drained
   acid to alkaline soil.

Zones 3b to 8a

P. 297

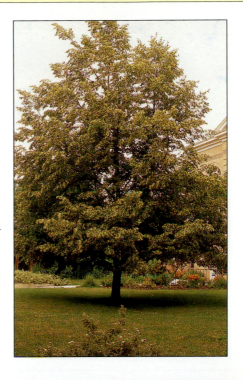

Tilia cordata
Littleleaf Linden

Numerous clusters of creamy yellow fragrant
   flowers create a two-tone effect with the
   bright green heart-shaped leaves in midsummer.

P. 297

Tilia tomentosa
Silver Linden

Moderate growth rate to 70 feet. Pyramidal to rounded.

Large glossy green leaves with woolly silvery gray undersides. Fragrant but inconspicuous flowers attached to pale green spoon-shaped bracts in early summer.

Full sun to part shade. Moist, well-drained acid to alkaline soil best.

Zones 5a to 8a

P. 298

Ulmus americana
American Elm

Fast growing to 60 feet. Vase shaped.

Reddish new growth matures to dark green. Bright yellow fall color. Reddish flowers in early spring mature to winged seeds that attract birds.

Full sun. Humus-rich moist to wet soil. Tolerates drought.

Zones 2b to 9a

P. 299

▲ *Ulmus glabra* 'Camperdownii'

Fast growing to 20 to 25 feet. Umbrella shaped.

Large lobed leaves. Reddish flowers in early spring followed by attractive pale yellow fruits.

Yellow fall color.

Full sun. Well-drained acid to alkaline soil.

Zones 4a to 7b

P. 301

▼ *Ulmus parvifolia*

Lacebark Elm, Chinese Elm

Moderate growth rate to 50 feet. Rounded to vase shaped.

Dark glossy green leaves turn yellow to reddish purple in autumn. Inconspicuous flowers; papery seedpods last into winter. Ornamental bark.

Full sun to part shade. Fertile, moist, well-drained soil. Tolerates drought and urban sites.

Zones 5b to 9a

P. 301

Ulmus parvifolia
Lacebark Elm, Chinese Elm
Bark is a fine-textured orange, gray, tan, and
   green patchwork.
P. 301

Ulmus pumila
Siberian Elm, Chinese Elm
Fast growing to 50 to 70 feet. Oval to vase
   shaped.

Oval, toothed green leaves. Inconspicuous
   green flowers and messy green seedpods.

Full sun. Sandy to clay, acid to alkaline soil. Tolerates cold, drought, and urban sites.

Zones 2b to 9a

P. 302

Zelkova serrata 'Green Vase'
Green Vase Japanese Zelkova

Fast growing to 65 to 70 feet. Vase shaped.

Narrow pointed leaves open pale green, mature to dark green, change to orange or rust-red in fall. Bark a colorful mottled orange-and-gray patchwork.

Full sun. Humus-rich, moist, well-drained soil best. Tolerates urban sites, drought, and alkaline soil.

Zones 6a to 9a

P. 303

Zelkova serrata 'Village Green'
Village Green Japanese Zelkova

Moderate growth rate to 50 to 60 feet. Rounded vase shape.

Narrow pointed leaves open pale green, mature to dark green, change to orange or reddish purple in fall. Bark a colorful mottled orange and gray patchwork.

Full sun. Humus-rich, moist, well-drained soil best. Tolerates urban sites, drought and alkaline soil.

Zones 5b to 9a

P. 303

Ilex aquifolium
English Holly

Moderate growth rate to 30 to 50 feet. Pyramidal.

Glossy dark green leaves with spiny margins. Glossy red, orange, or yellow berries from fall through winter.

Full sun to light shade. Well-drained, moist, acid soil. Tolerates urban sites.

Zones 7a to 9a

P. 304

Ilex aquifolium
English Holly

Clusters of brightly colored berries form at the bases of the leaves and look colorful through winter.

P. 304

Ilex opaca
American Holly

Moderate growth rate to 25 to 50 feet. Pyramidal.

Spiny-margined matte dull leaves. Orange-red or yellow berries are showy from fall through winter.

Full sun to light shade. Moist, well-drained acid soil. Tolerates light sandy soil, urban and seashore conditions.

Zones 6a to 9a

P. 305

Ilex opaca 'Canary'
Canary American Holly

Clusters of light yellow berries ripen near the stem tips.

P. 305

Ilex pedunculosa
Long-stalk Holly

Moderate growth rate to 20 to 30 feet. Pyramidal.

Glossy, pointed oval spineless leaves with wavy margins. Clusters of small red berries form on long dangling stalks near the branch tips and are showy from fall through winter.

Full sun to part shade. Well-drained, moist, acid soil. Tolerates clay, heat, and wind.

Zones 5b to 9a

P. 306

Laurus nobilis
Bay Laurel

Moderate growth rate to 20 to 50 feet. Multi-trunked and conical.

Long narrow, pointed leathery green leaves with wavy edges. Aromatic when crushed or broken. Inconspicuous flowers ripen into shiny black berries.

Full sun to part shade. Fertile, well-drained, moist soil. Tolerates heat, drought, sandy soil.

Zones 7b to 8a

P. 306

Magnolia grandiflora
Southern Magnolia, Bull Bay

Moderate growth rate to 60 to 80 feet.

Oblong leathery leaves with fuzzy gray or rusty undersides. Huge fragrant white flowers in summer. Interesting seedpods in fall.

Full sun to part shade. Humus-rich, moist, acid soil.

Zones 6b or 7a to 9b.

P. 307

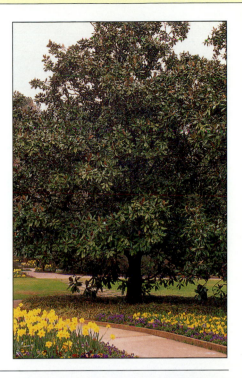

Magnolia grandiflora 'Edith Bogue'
Southern Magnolia, Bull Bay

Slow growing to 30 feet. Pyramidal.

Narrow, leathery leaves with tan undersides. Fragrant white flowers in summer. Interesting seedpods in fall. Compact and cold hardy.

Full sun to part shade. Humus-rich, moist, acid soil.

Zones 6b or 7a to 9b

P. 307

Magnolia virginiana
Sweet Bay Magnolia

Moderate growth rate to 20 to 50 feet. Often multistemmed, rounded to oval.

Silvery green new leaves mature to glossy dark green with white undersides. Fragrant white flowers in summer. Small green cucumber-like fruits reveal red seeds in fall.

Half to full shade. Moist, acid soil. Tolerates wet to swampy sites.

Zones 5b to 9a

P. 308

Prunus lusitanica
Cherry Laurel

Fast growing to 15 to 20 feet. Multistemmed and rounded to oval.

Glossy lance-shaped leaves with reddish stems. Pendulous clusters of white flowers in early summer. Red fruits ripen to purple in autumn.

Full sun to part shade. Moist, well-drained soil. Tolerates some drought.

Zones 7a to 9a

P. 309

Prunus lusitanica
Cherry Laurel

Numerous clusters of cherrylike red fruits, which ripen to purple, adorn the tree in late summer and fall, and provide food for birds and other wildlife.

P. 309

Quercus agrifolia
Coast Live Oak

Moderate growth rate to 50 feet. Rounded and wide spreading.

Dense, hollylike glossy green leaves. Smooth dark gray bark.

Full sun to part shade. Well-drained neutral to alkaline soil. Tolerates sandy dry soil.

Zones 7b to 9a

P. 311

Quercus virginiana
Live Oak

Moderate growth rate to 80 to 120 feet. Massive and wide spreading.

Smooth, leathery, unlobed green leaves with gray-green undersides. Yellowish brown catkins in spring. Fissured bark. Black acorns in late summer attract wildlife.

Full sun to part shade. Well-drained acid to alkaline soil. Tolerates sandy dry soil.

Zones 7b to 9b

P. 311

Trachycarpus fortunei
Hardy Windmill Palm

Moderate growth rate to 30 feet. Upright.

Circular bright green leaves cut into fingerlike segments.

Clusters of yellow spring flowers ripen into blue fruits in autumn. Rough bark.

Full sun to light shade.

Moist, well-drained soil. Tolerates seashore conditions.

Zones 8b to 9a

P. 312

Abies balsamea
Balsam Fir

Moderate growth rate to 50 to 70 feet. Narrow pyramid.

Blunt, shiny dark blue-green needles in two ranks with piney fragrance. Violet purple young cones.

Full sun to light shade. Humus-rich, moist to damp acid soil.

Zones 2a to 5a

P. 313

Abies concolor
White Fir

Moderate growth rate to 35 to 50 feet. Conical.

Gray-green to silver-blue round-tipped curved needles. Purplish immature cones ripen to brown.

Full sun to part shade. Moist, well-drained average to sandy soil, acid to slightly alkaline.

Zones 4a to 8a

P. 314

▲*Abies concolor* 'Candicans'

Candicans White Fir

Moderate growth rate to 40 feet. Narrow pyramid.

Narrow silvery blue needles.

Full sun to part shade. Moist, well-drained average to sandy soil, acid to slightly alkaline.

Zones 4a to 8a

P. 314

▼*Abies firma*

Momi Fir

Slow growing to 50 feet. Broad-spreading pyramid.

Glossy dark green needles lighter on the undersides.

Full to part sun. Tolerates heavy soil and heat.

Zones 6b to 8b

P. 313

Abies koreana
Korean Fir

Slow growing to 30 feet. Pyramidal.

Rich green needles with silver bands arranged in V-shaped ranks. Showy cones are red and chartreuse when young, turn blue-purple when mature.

Full to part sun. Moist, humus-rich, acid soil. Tolerates some heat.

Zones 5a to 7a

P. 315

Abies lasiocarpa
Rocky Mountain Fir, Alpine Fir

Slow growing to 15 feet. Narrow pyramid.

Narrow pale blue-green two-ranked needles. Creamy white bark.

Full sun. Well-drained moist soil. Tolerates dry heat and light soil.

Zones 4b to 7b

P. 315

Abies nordmanniana
Nordmann Fir

Moderate growth rate to 60 feet. Pyramidal.

Glossy blackish green forward-pointing needles, two white bands on undersides. Showy cones greenish black with protruding bracts. Very dark bark broken into plates.

Full to part sun. Moist, neutral to acid soil. Tolerates some adversity.

Zones 4b to 7b

P. 315

Calocedrus decurrens
(Libocedrus decurrens)
Incense Cedar

Fast growing to 30 to 50 feet. Columnar.

Beautiful shiny green scalelike foliage. Furrowed, shredding cinnamon brown bark. Inconspicuous cones.

Full sun to light shade. Moist, deep, well-drained soil. Tolerates clay and slight alkalinity, also heat, humidity, drought, and urban sites.

Zones 6a to 8b

P. 316

▲ *Calocedrus decurrens* *(Libocedrus decurrens)*

Incense Cedar

Fanlike sprays of glossy emerald green scalelike foliage emit a spicy aroma when crushed.

P. 316

▼ *Cedrus atlantica* 'Glauca'

Blue Atlas Cedar

Slow growing to 60 to 120 feet. Pyramidal and horizontally spreading.

Tufts of silver-blue needles. Blocky blue-green female cones mature to brown.

Full sun to part shade. Moist, humus-rich, well-drained sandy to clay soil, acid to slightly alkaline. Very drought and heat tolerant.

Zones 6a to 9a

P. 317

Cedrus atlantica 'Glauca'
Blue Atlas Cedar

Short silver-blue needles form dense tufts
spaced along tops of branches.

P. 317

Cedrus deodara
Deodar Cedar

Moderate growth rate to 50 to 80 feet. Pyramidal.

Slightly pendulous, graceful branches. Soft,
feathery blue-green needles. Large jade
green cones mature to reddish brown.

Full sun. Well-drained soil. Tolerates alkalinity,
drought, wind, and heat.

Zones 7a to 9a

P. 318

Cedrus deodara 'Aurea'
Deodar Cedar
Feathery new needles are light yellow-green and
mature to blue-green by midsummer.

P. 318

Cedrus libani
Cedar of Lebanon
Moderate growth rate to 50 to 60 feet. Pyramidal to irregular.

Stiff sharp needles in dense tufts. New growth
emerald green, maturing to dark green. Purple cones mature to brown.

Full sun. Well-drained fertile soil. Tolerates dry
infertile sites and alkalinity.

Zones 5a or 6a to 8b

P. 318

▲*Cedrus libani* 'Pendula'

Cedar of Lebanon

Horizontal branches of this weeping form can be trained as an espalier.

P. 318

▼*Cephalotaxus harringtonia*

Japanese Plum Yew

Fast growing to 25 feet. Pyramidal.

Long very glossy dark green pointed needles in two ranks. Reddish brown peeling bark. Fluffy yellow flowers in spring followed by large olive-brown fruits in fall.

Part to full shade. Moist, well-drained sandy to clay soil.

Zones 6a to 9b

P. 319

▲ *Cephalotaxus harringtonia*
Japanese Plum Yew

The lustrous bold-textured needles somewhat resemble yew foliage, but the olivelike fruits are quite distinctive.

P. 319

▼ *Chamaecyparis lawsoniana* 'Glauca'
Blue Lawson False Cypress

Moderate growth rate to 60 feet. Pyramidal to conical.

Blue-green scalelike leaves in flattened sprays. Small brown cones with umbrella-like scales. Red-barked butressed trunk and short side branches.

Full sun. Well-drained, moist loam.

Zones 5b to 8a

P. 320

Chamaecyparis lawsoniana 'Lanei'

Lane Lawson False Cypress

Slow growing to 15 feet. Compact conical to pyramidal.

Golden-green scalelike leaves in flattened sprays. Small brown cones with umbrella-like scales. Red-barked buttressed trunk.

Full sun. Well-drained, moist loam.

Zones 5b to 8a

P. 320

Chamaecyparis nootkatensis 'Lutea'

Golden Nootka False Cypress

Moderate growth rate to 40 feet. Conical to pyramidal with weeping branches.

New growth gold maturing to green. Sharp scales form flattened sprays. Gray- to red-brown stringy bark. Small brown cones.

Full sun to part shade. Moist, sandy to loamy acid soil. Tolerates heat and humidity.

Zones 5b to 7b

P. 321

Chamaecyparis nootkatensis 'Pendula'

Weeping Nootka False Cypress

Moderate growth rate to 40 feet. Conical to pyramidal with weeping branches.

Dark green sharp-pointed scales form flattened sprays. Gray-brown to red-brown stringy bark. Small brown cones.

Full sun to part shade. Moist, sandy to loamy acid soil. Tolerates heat and humidity.

Zones 5b to 7b

P. 321

Chamaecyparis obtusa 'Crispii'

Crispii Hinoki False Cypress

Slow growing to 35 feet. Loose pyramid.

Flattened sprays of glossy dark green scalelike leaves with white crosses on their undersides. Golden tips on new growth. Reddish brown peeling trunk bark.

Full sun to part shade. Moist, well-drained neutral to acid sandy or loamy soil.

Zones 5a to 8a

P. 321

Chamaecyparis obtusa 'Gracilis Aurea'

Golden Hinoki False Cypress

Slow growing to 25 feet. Pyramidal.

Fan-shaped sprays of golden green new growth and dark green older growth. Glossy scalelike leaves have white crosses on their undersides. Reddish brown peeling trunk bark.

Full sun to part shade. Moist well-drained neutral to acid sandy or loamy soil.

Zones 5a to 8a

P. 322

Chamaecyparis pisifera

Sawara False Cypress, Retinospora

Moderate growth rate to 25 to 60 feet. Conical to pyramidal.

Dark green scalelike needles with white markings on undersides in flattened sprays arranged in cordlike branches, plumelike clusters, or billowy masses. Reddish brown bark.

Full sun. Well-drained neutral to acid soil.

Zones 5a to 8a

P. 322

Cryptomeria japonica
Japanese Cedar, Cryptomeria

Moderate growth rate to 50 feet or more. Pyramidal to conical.

Beautifully textured bright green to blue-green
awl-shaped needles in plumelike clusters.
Needles may turn bronze in winter. Small
dark brown cones. Shredding reddish
brown bark.

Full sun to light shade. Deep, fertile, moist, acid
soil.

Zones 6b to 9a

P. 324

Cryptomeria japonica 'Lobbii'
Lobbii Japanese Cedar, Cryptomeria

Compact with moderate growth rate to 30 feet.
Pyramidal to conical.

Beautifully textured bright green awl-shaped
needles in dense clusters. Retains good winter color. Small dark brown cones. Shredding reddish brown bark.

Full sun to light shade. Deep, fertile, moist, acid
soil.

Zones 6b to 9a

P. 325

Cunninghamia lanceolata
China Fir

Moderate growth rate to 60 feet. Broad pyramid with rounded top.

Glossy blue-green pointed needles with two white lines on their undersides arranged in two ranks. Prickly cones. Retains old brown needles and small branchlets. Reddish brown peeling trunk.

Full sun to light shade. Tolerates urban conditions if soil is moist.

Zones 6b to 9a

P. 325

Cunninghamia lanceolata 'Glauca'
China Fir

Pointed needles are especially blue-gray and glossy and arranged in two ranks.

P. 325

× *Cupressocyparis leylandii*
Leyland Cypress

Fast growing to 65 feet. Columnar to narrowly
pyramidal.

Soft bright green needles in ropelike bunches
form flattened fans.

Full sun to part shade. Fertile, moist site, acid to
alkaline. Tolerates heat and seashore conditions.

Zones 7a to 9a

P. 326

Cupressus arizonica
var. *glabra* 'Blue Ice'
Arizona Cypress

Fast growing to 35 feet. Dense pyramid.

Gray-green to blue-green white-flecked scales
create braided-looking branches. Shiny red-
brown bark. Small brown cones.

Full sun. Well-drained acid to alkaline, heavy to
light soil. Tolerates drought, wind, and heat.

Zones 7a to 9b

P. 327

Cupressus macrocarpa
Monterey Cypress

Slow-growing to 40 feet. Flat topped and irregular.

Dark green scales with pointed tips are closely pressed against the stems to form irregular sprays. Aromatic when crushed. Reddish brown ridged bark.

Full sun. Well-drained sandy to loamy soil. Tolerates wind and seashore conditions.

Zones 8a to 9a

P. 327

Juniperus scopularum
'Blue Heaven'
Blue Heaven Rocky Mountain Juniper, Western Red Cedar

Moderate growth rate to 20 feet. Narrow pyramid.

Bright blue-gray scalelike needles with good winter color. Disease-resistant form. Reddish brown shredding bark.

Full sun. Well-drained average to sandy, acid to alkaline soil. Tolerates heat and drought.

Zones 3b to 6b

P. 329

Juniperus scopularum 'Wichita Blue'

Wichita Blue Rocky Mountain Juniper, Western Red Cedar

Moderate growth rate to 20 feet. Narrow pyramid.

Brilliant blue scalelike needles with good winter color. Reddish brown shredding bark.

Full sun. Well-drained average to sandy, acid to alkaline soil. Tolerates heat and drought.

Zones 3b to 6b

P. 329

Juniperus virginiana

Eastern Red Cedar

Moderate growth rate to 50 feet. Columnar to pyramidal.

Dark green needles may turn brownish in winter. Waxy blue fruits. Shredding reddish brown bark.

Full sun. Well-drained soil, acid to alkaline, heavy to light. Tolerates urban and seashore conditions.

Zones 3b to 9a

P. 329

Larix decidua
European Larch

Moderate growth rate to 75 feet. Conical to pyramidal.

Bright green needles in spring, mature to dark green, turn to ocher yellow and drop off in fall. Bare winter branches. Violet spring cones mature to brown with overlapping scales. Deeply fissured bark.

Full sun. Moist, rich, acid soil.

Zones 2a to 6b

P. 330

Larix kaempferi
Japanese Larch

Moderate growth rate to 70 to 90 feet. Open pyramid.

Bright green spring needles with white bands on undersides arranged in tufts on short reddish brown spurs. Deep blue-green summer color changes to golden orange in fall before dropping. Bare winter branches. Small brown cones with rolled-back scales.

Full sun. Well-drained moist acid soil.

Zones 4a to 6b

P. 331

Larix larcinia
American Larch, Tamarack

Moderate growth rate to 40 to 80 feet. Open narrow pyramid.

Bright lime green new growth matures to blue-green. Clear golden yellow fall color. Needles in tufts. Very small brown cones.

Full sun. Moist, well-drained, humus-rich, acid soil. Tolerates wet sites.

Zones 2a to 6

P. 331

Metasequoia glyptostroboides
Dawn Redwood

Fast growing to 80 to 120 feet. Conical.

Small flattened soft needles in opposite pairs.

New growth bright green, matures to dark green, turns red-brown to orange in fall. Leafless in winter. Clusters of small brown cones. Attractive bark and trunks.

Full sun. Moist, slightly acid soil, well drained to wet.

Zones 5a to 8b

P. 332

Metasequoia glyptostroboides
Dawn Redwood
Reddish brown to bright orange shredding bark
covers the buttressed trunks.

P. 332

Picea abies 'Cranstonii'
Cranston Norway Spruce
Fast growing to 90 feet. Pyramidal with long
weeping branches.

Dark green blunt-tipped stiff needles. Reddish
purple young cones mature to cigar-shaped
cylinders. Reddish brown bark.

Full sun. Well-drained moist, acid soil. Tolerates
well-drained clay.

Zones 3a to 7b

P. 334

Picea glauca var. *albertina* 'Conica'
Dwarf Alberta Spruce
Very slow growing to 20 feet. Conical.

Tiny feathery green sharp-pointed needles. Small brown cones all winter. Rough gray-brown bark.

Full sun to part shade. Moist, humus-rich soil.

Zones 2a to 8a

P. 334

Picea omorika
Serbian Spruce
Slow-growing to 60 feet. Narrow pyramid with weeping branches.

Dense, sharp-pointed dark blue-green needles with gray-white undersides. Cylindrical blue-purple cones ripen to cinnamon brown.

Full sun to part shade. Deep, fertile, well-drained, moist, acid to alkaline soil.

Zones 4b to 8a

P. 335

Picea orientalis

Oriental Spruce

Moderate growth rate to 60 feet. Broad cone.

Fine textured glossy green needles four-sided with blunt tips pressed tightly against the stems. Reddish-purple spring cones mature to dark brown.

Full to half sun. Well-drained soil, acid to slightly alkaline.

Zones 4b to 8a

P. 335

Picea orientalis 'Aureo-spicata'

Gold-tipped Oriental Spruce

Moderate growth rate to 60 feet. Broad cone.

Fine-textured glossy needles create densely needled twigs. Ivory-yellow new growth stands out against the older dark green needles.

Full sun. Well-drained soil, acid to slightly alkaline.

Zones 4b to 8a

P. 336

Picea pungens var. *glauca*
Colorado Blue Spruce

Moderate growth rate to 60 feet. Pyramidal.

Sharp-pointed blue-gray to steel blue needles encircle stems. Stiff horizontal branches. Green cones mature to light brown.

Full sun. Fertile, well-drained, moist soil best; tolerates poor soil and drought.

Zones 3a to 7b

P. 336

Pinus aristata
Bristlecone Pine

Very slow growing to 15 to 20 feet. Irregular and flat topped.

Dark green needles with white resin dots in bushy bundles of five densely arranged to create bottlebrush effect. Brown cones with sharp bristles.

Full sun. Any well-drained acid to alkaline soil. Tolerates drought and rocky soil.

Zones 3b to 7a or 9a

P. 337

Pinus aristata
Bristlecone Pine

Cones and stems are distinctive. Needles live for 10 or more years, creating a dense bottle-brush effect along the sparsely branched stems. Cones feature bristles at the tip of each scale.

P. 337

Pinus bungeana
Lacebark Pine

Slow growing to 30 to 50 feet. Multiple trunks and flat topped shape.

Glossy dark green sharp-pointed needles in bundles of three. Light brown cones with triangular spines. Colorful bark mottled green, pink, cream, and tan.

Full sun. Any well-drained acid or alkaline soil.

Zones 5a to 9a

P. 338

Pinus densiflora 'Oculus-draconis'

Dragon's-Eye Pine

Slow growing and multitrunked to 30 to 40 feet. Pyramidal to flat topped.

Long green needles variegated with bright yellow bands arranged in bundles of two. Bright reddish orange bark. Small yellowish cones are showy all winter.

Full sun. Well-drained slightly acid soil. Tolerates seashore conditions.

Zones 5b to 7b

P. 339

Pinus flexilis 'Glauca'

Blue Limber Pine

Moderate growth to 45 feet. Loose pyramid.

Slender, slightly twisted silver-blue needles arranged in bundles of five create fluffy texture. Large light brown pendulous cones.

Full sun to part shade. Moist, well-drained soil; tolerates rocky sites, drought, and salt.

Zones 3b to 7b

P. 339

Pinus koraiensis 'Glauca'
Blue Korean Pine

Fast growing to 25 feet. Compact pyramid.
Densely needled horizontal to upright
    branches. Long stiff needles in blue-green
    bundles of five. Smooth gray-brown trunks.
Full sun to part shade. Most garden soils.
Zones 4 to 7b or 8b

P. 340

Pinus koraiensis 'Glauca'
Blue Korean Pine

The long blue-green needles have white stripes,
    which creates a blue-gray effect when seen
    from a distance.

P. 340

Pinus parviflora 'Glauca'
Japanese White Pine

Slow-growing to 30 feet. Conical to flat topped.

Slightly twisted short narrow silvery blue-green needles with white bands arranged in bundles of five. Numerous reddish brown oval cones. Scaly dark gray bark.

Full sun. Well-drained moist, acid soil. Tolerates seashore conditions.

Zones 5b to 9a

P. 340

Pinus ponderosa
Ponderosa Pine, Western Yellow Pine

Moderate growth rate to 60 to 100 feet. Narrow pyramid to irregular.

Long green sharply pointed needles in bundles of three. Resinous reddish brown oblong cones. Deeply fissured brown to reddish-brown bark, broken into plates on old trees.

Full sun. Well-drained moist loam. Tolerates alkalinity, drought, and salt.

Zones 3b to 8a

P. 341

Pinus resinosa
Red Pine, Norway Pine

Moderate growth rate to 50 feet. Oval to pyramidal.

Dense tufts of yellow-green needles. Brittle needles snap when bent. Reddish brown bark in diamond-shaped plates. Light brown cones.

Full sun. Well-drained acid soil. Tolerates sandy to rocky soil and drought.

Zones 2a to 6b

P. 341

Pinus strobus
Eastern White Pine

Fast-growing to 50 to 80 feet. Pyramidal to spreading.

Fine-textured long slender green to blue-green needles with white stripes in bundles of five. Needles soft to the touch. Deeply furrowed brown-gray bark. Long pendulous brown cones.

Full to part sun. Well-drained moist, acid soil. Drought tolerant.

Zones 3a to 9a

P. 341

Pinus strobus var. *glauca*
Eastern White Pine

This variety has blue-green needles with white bands giving an overall silvery blue effect.

P. 341

Pinus sylvestris 'Fastigiata'
Scotch Pine, Scots Pine

Slow growing to 25 feet. Narrow column.

Blue-green short stiff twisted needles in bundles of two. Needles often turn yellow-green in winter. Showy orange-brown bark. Gray-brown cones.

Full sun. Well-drained acid to slightly alkaline soil. Tolerates infertile, dry soil and road salt.

Zones 3a to 8b

P. 343

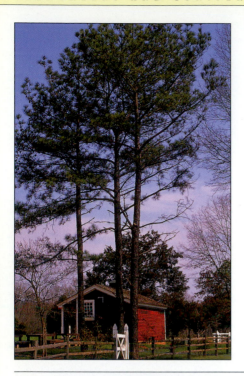

Pinus taeda
Loblolly Pine

Fast growing to 45 to 60 feet. Pyramidal to rounded.

Long dark yellow-green needles in bundles of three. Narrow cones with sharp spines. Deeply furrowed and ridged gray bark.

Full sun to part shade. Moist, acid loam to clay. Tolerates wet and dry sites.

Zones 7b to 9a

P. 343

Pinus thunbergii (P. thunbergiana)
Japanese Black Pine

Fast growing to 35 to 60 feet. Open branched and irregular.

Shiny short dark green needles in bundles of two. Dark gray trunk bark broken into large plates. Silvery buds. Shiny light brown cones.

Full sun.

Fertile, moist soil best; tolerates sandy soil, drought, heat, and salt spray.

Zones 6a to 9a

P. 343

Pinus thunbergii 'Thunderhead' *(P. thunbergiana)*

Thunderhead Japanese Black Pine

This cultivar has very large silvery buds and a more upright shape.

P. 344

Pinus virginiana

Slow to moderate growth to 15 to 40 feet. Pyramidal to flat topped and irregular.

Stout green twisted needles in pairs. Spiny red-brown pendulous cones. Orange-brown bark.

Full sun. Tolerates poor soil, drought, seashore conditions.

Zones 5a to 7b; 8b in West.

P. 344

Pinus virginiana 'Watt's Gold'
Watt's Gold Virginia Pine

Slow growing to 15 to 25 feet. Pyramidal to flat topped.

Stout needles in bundles of two, slightly twisted, light green in summer, bright gold in winter. Spiny reddish brown cones. Orange-brown bark.

Full sun. Clay loam, acid to alkaline. Tolerates drought and seashore conditions.

Zones 5b to 9a

P. 345

Pinus wallichiana
(P. griffithii)
Himalayan Pine, Bhutan Pine

Moderate growth rate to 30 to 50 feet. Broadly pyramidal.

Sharp-pointed long gray-green needles with white stripes arranged in bundles of five. Needles softly cascading. Long light brown pendulous cones.

Full sun. Well-drained, moist, fertile, acid, sandy loam.

Zones 5b to 8b

P. 345

▲*Podocarpus macrophyllus* 'Mackii'

Dwarf Yew Pine,
Dwarf Yew Podocarpus

Slow growing to 10 feet. Upright to oval.

Lance-shaped glossy dark green leathery needles. Compact growth. Pea-sized blue fruits on red stalks in fall. Reddish brown bark.

Full sun to light shade. Moist, well-drained, fertile, well-drained sandy loam or clay.

Zones 8a to 9a

P. 346

▼*Podocarpus macrophyllus* 'Mackii'

Dwarf Yew Pine,
Dwarf Yew Podocarpus

Showy blue fruits on red stalks decorate the branches in autumn.

P. 346

Pseudolarix amabilis (P. kaempferi)

Golden Larch

Slow growing to 50 feet. Open-branched broad pyramid.

Very narrow flattened needles are light green in spring, soft green in summer, and russet-gold in fall. Leafless in winter. Showy yellow-green cones ripen to reddish brown in fall.

Full to part sun. Well-drained moist, acid to neutral sandy loam.

Zones 6a to 8a

P. 347

Pseudolarix amabilis (P. kaempferi)

Golden Larch

Needles are arranged in rosettes on short spurs on older wood, but are spirally arranged around the stems on young growth. Fall color is dramatic russet-gold.

P. 347

Pseudotsuga menziesii ssp. *glauca*
Rocky Mountain Douglas Fir

Moderate growth rate to 50 to 80 feet. Narrow pyramid.

Fine-textured blue-green to blue-gray needles arranged spirally in two ranks around the stems. Rose-red cones ripen to cinnamon brown with forked bracts protruding from the scales. Reddish bark with deep fissures.

Full sun. Well-drained deep, moist, acid to neutral soil. Tolerates slight alkalinity.

Zones 3b to 6b

P. 347

Pseudotsuga menziesii ssp. *menziesii*
Douglas Fir

Moderate growth rate to 50 to 80 feet. Narrow pyramid.

Fine-textured green needles arranged spirally in two ranks around the stems. Rose-red cones ripen to cinnamon brown with forked bracts protruding from the scales. Reddish bark with deep fissures.

Full sun. Well-drained deep, moist, acid to neutral soil.

Zones 6a to 8b

P. 347

Sciadopitys verticillata
Japanese Umbrella Pine

Very slow growing to 25 to 30 feet. Conical to pyramidal.

Dark green glossy flattened long needles arranged in spirals. Egg-shaped green cones ripen to dark reddish brown.

Full sun to part shade. Fertile, moist, well-drained acid soil.

Zones 6a to 8a

P. 348

Sciadopitys verticillata
Japanese Umbrella Pine

Needles are long and dark glossy green with a waxy texture. Arranged in dense spirals around the twigs, they create a distinctive billowy effect.

P. 348

Sequoia sempervirens

Redwood, Coast Redwood, California Redwood

Moderate growth rate to 60 to 80 feet in gardens, 300 feet in the wild. Slender pyramid.

Dark green flattened needles with white bands on the undersides, arranged in two opposite ranks. Small reddish brown cones. Ruggedly furrowed reddish brown bark.

Full sun. Rich, moist, acid soil.

Zones 7a to 9a

P. 349

Sequoiadendron giganteum (Sequoia gigantea)

Giant Sequoia, Big Tree, Giant Redwood, Sierra Redwood

Moderate growth rate to 60 to 100 feet in gardens, 250 to 300 feet in the wild. Narrow pyramid.

Blue-green awl-shaped pointed scales are pressed against the stems, creating cordlike branches. Small reddish brown cones. Massive trunk with red-brown fibrous bark.

Full sun. Fertile, moist, well-drained acid to slightly alkaline soil.

Zones 6b to 9a

P. 350

Sequoiadendron giganteum (Sequoia gigantea)

Giant Sequoia, Big Tree, Giant Redwood, Sierra Redwood

The massive trunks are covered with attractive reddish brown shredding bark, which is resistant to fire.

P. 350

Taxodium distichum

Bald Cypress, Swamp Cypress

Fast growing to 60 feet. Columnar.

Small pointed flattened green needles arranged in two alternate ranks on green twiglets. Foliage bright green in spring, gray-green in summer, golden rust-brown in fall. Bare branches in winter. Buttressed trunk with shredding brown bark and odd knobby knees near base in wet site.

Full to part sun. Wet to swampy site but tolerates deep, moist, acid, sandy loam.

Zones 4b to 9a

P. 351

Taxodium distichum var. *imbricarium (T. ascendens)* 'Prairie Sentinel'

Prairie Sentinel Pond Cypress

Fast growing to 60 feet. Narrow column.

Small pointed green needles pressed to the green twiglets create a threadlike effect. Foliage bright green in spring, gray-green in summer, golden rust-brown in fall.

Full to part sun. Wet to swampy site but tolerates deep, moist, acid, sandy loam.

Zones 6a to 9a

P. 351

Taxus baccata 'Fastigiata Aurea'

Golden English Yew

Slow growing to 20 feet. Narrow column.

Golden new growth matures to green.

Full to part shade. Well-drained moist, acid to alkaline soil.

Zones 6b to 7b or 8a

P. 352

Taxus baccata 'Standishii'
Standishii English Yew

Moderate growth rate to 25 to 30 feet. Compact
column.

Flat waxy needles sickle shaped with bluntly
pointed ends. Spirally arranged around upright shoots, two-ranked on spreading
shots. Golden new growth matures to dark
green. Red berrylike fruit in fall. Reddish
brown trunk.

Full to part shade. Well-drained moist, acid to
alkaline soil.

Zones 6b to 7b or 8a

P. 352

Taxus cuspidata 'Capitata'
Capitata Japanese Yew

Slow growth rate to 25 to 40 feet. Multitrunked
and pyramidal.

Pointed flattened glossy needles arranged in
two irregular ranks. Bright green new
growth matures to dark green with yellow-
green undersides.

Full to part shade. Well-drained moist, acid to
alkaline soil.

Zones 4b to 7a

P. 353

Taxus cuspidata 'Capitata'
Capitata Japanese Yew

Flattened dark green needles are arranged in two irregular ranks around the twigs and have two olive green bands on their undersides. Red fruits ripen in fall.

P. 353

Thuja occidentalis
Arborvitae, Eastern White Cedar, White Cedar

Fast growing to 30 to 40 feet. Columnar.

Glossy green scalelike leaves in flat horizontal fans. Dark grayish brown peeling bark. Small cones ripen from yellow-green to brownish yellow.

Full sun to light shade. Fertile to moist acid to alkaline soil. Tolerates wet and clay sites. Tolerates drought if soil is cool.

Zones 3a to 7b

P. 353

Thuja occidentalis

Arborvitae, Eastern White Cedar, White Cedar

Glossy green scalelike leaves are pressed closely to the twigs, forming horizontal fans. Scales do not have white markings like other species and may turn bronze in winter if exposed to full sun.

P. 353

Thuja orientalis (Platycladus orientalis) 'Aurea Nana'

Dwarf Golden Oriental Arborvitae

Slow-growing dwarf. Columnar to 5 to 7 feet.

Golden scalelike leaves without white markings are pressed closely to the stems, forming flattened vertical sprays. Small cones ripen from purple-blue to brown.

Full sun. Moist, well-drained soil. Tolerates heat and humidity.

Zones 6b to 8b

P. 354

Thuja plicata
Western Red Cedar, Giant Arborvitae

Fast growing to 50 to 60 feet in the garden; to 120 feet in the wild. Narrow pyramid.

Horizontal narrow sprays of glossy green scale-like leaves with white markings. Small cones ripen from green to brown.

Full sun to part shade. Moist, fertile, acid to alkaline soil. Tolerates wet sites.

Zones 4b to 7b

P. 355

Thujopsis dolbrata
Hiba Arborvitae

Slow growing to 30 to 50 feet. Dense pyramid.

Shiny dark green scalelike leaves with white stripes on the undersurfaces, forming flattened sprays.

Full sun to light shade. Moist, humus-rich, acid soil.

Zones 6b to 9a

P. 356

Tsuga canadensis
Canada Hemlock , Eastern Hemlock

Fast growing to 75 feet or more. Pyramidal with slightly pendulous branches.

Very small flat dark green blunt needles with white-striped undersides arranged in two opposite rows on yellowish brown hairy twigs. Deeply furrowed brown bark. Tiny green cones ripen to brown.

Full sun to light shade. Moist, well-drained, acid, humus-rich soil.

Zones 3a to 8a

P. 357

Tsuga caroliniana
Carolina Hemlock

Fast growing to 50 feet. Open pyramid.

Small dark green blunt needles spirally arranged around reddish brown hairy twigs. Small green cones ripen to brown.

Full sun to light shade. Moist, well-drained, acid, humus-rich soil. Somewhat tolerant of heat.

Zones 5b to 7b

P. 358

Tsuga diversifolia
Northern Japanese Hemlock

Moderate growth rate to 25 to 30 feet. Broadly pyramidal.

Very small, dark green, white-banded, flat, blunt needles arranged radially around the stems. Small green cones mature to brown.

Light to full shade. Moist, well-drained, humus-rich, acid soil. Somewhat tolerant of clay, drought and urban conditions.

Zones 5b to 7b

P. 358

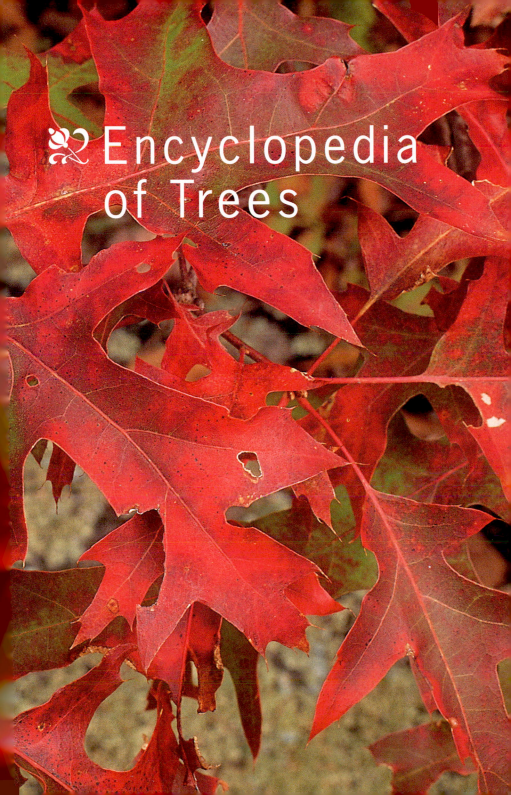

Encyclopedia of Trees

❧ Encyclopedia of Trees

❧ DECIDUOUS

❧ *Acer*

AY-ser. Maple family, Aceraceae.

This important genus, which includes some of our most beloved and best-known deciduous landscape trees, contains approximately 124 species. Most hail from North America, Asia, and Europe, with a few from Central America and northern Africa. Leaves are opposite and may be simple, lobed, or compound, with three to seven leaflets. Flowers are arranged in clusters and are not usually showy. Fruits, called samaras, consist of two winged seeds joined together.

Landscape maples can be grouped for convenience into three main groups: small maples, tall shade-tree maples, and Japanese maples. Each group has its own cultural needs and landscape uses. Many of the small garden maples adapt to poor, dry soil and thrive in urban areas. Most shade-tree maples need full sun and moist, rich, acid soil and may develop scorched leaves under drought or hot wind, although some tolerate adverse conditions. Japanese maples prefer humus-rich soil and full sun to partial shade, and they need protection from harsh wind and hot sun.

The small maples make excellent choices as street trees near or under power lines and as ornamentals for small-space gardens, especially where growing conditions are tough. Use tall maples as shade trees to cool the house, yard, or street, keeping in mind that their competitive roots can affect nearby plants. Japanese maples display gorgeous lobed or dissected foliage and ornamental bark; use them as focal points in a garden. Most maples have unrivaled displays of red, scarlet, or gold foliage in fall.

SMALL MAPLES

A. buergerianum (A. trifidum)   P. 42

a. BURR-jar-ee-AY-num. Trident Maple. This attractive, rounded, multi-trunked tree grows about 20 to 35 feet tall and 25 feet wide and is quite heat tolerant. Leaves are very glossy dark green with blue-green undersides and measure about 4 inches long. Their three pointed lobes sketch the outline of a tulip. Leaves change color in late fall, turning an excellent dark red and orange. Trunk bark is gray and peels attractively on older trees to reveal a patchwork of orange, gray, and brown underbark. Yellowish green flowers bloom in spring with the new leaves. The red-tinged green samaras ripen to brown by summer's end. Trident maple makes an excellent medium-size street or garden tree where growing conditions are demanding. Use as a specimen in a border or as a patio tree. Or mass as a privacy screen or windbreak. From China and Japan.

HOW TO GROW. Neutral to acid soil. Tolerates urban conditions and sandy, clayey, or chalky soil. Very tolerant of heat, poor soil, and drought. Train to a single trunk. Pest-free. Zones 5b–8a.

CULTIVARS AND SIMILAR SPECIES. 'Streetwise' is a fast-growing selection with reddish purple new growth maturing to dark green and burgundy in fall; grows more upright, with a single trunk; Zones 6–9. *A. glabrum* (Rocky Mountain maple) is a beautiful 20-foot-tall native with 1- to 3-inch, lobed or trifoliate, red-veined leaves; red twigs; smooth bark; and clear yellow fall color; useful in the North and Mountain States in gravelly or damp areas, on slopes, or in shade; Zones 3–7.

A. campestre   P. 42

a. kam-PES-tree. Hedge Maple. Hedge maples are low-branched, round-headed trees that reach 35 feet tall and wide. They are often planted about 10 feet apart to make a dense screen or windbreak. Leaves are dull green on top and hairy on the undersides. They measure 2 to 4 inches long and have three to five rounded lobes. Fall color is often lackluster but may be a pleasing yellow in late fall. Bark on branches is corky and attractive in winter. Use as a specimen tree in a small garden, as a patio tree in a difficult site, as a street tree under power lines, or as a hedge. From Europe and Asia Minor.

HOW TO GROW. Full sun and almost any soil. This tough tree tolerates heat; poor, sandy, alkaline soil; and urban conditions. Zones 4b–8b.

CULTIVARS AND SIMILAR SPECIES. 'Queen Elizabeth' ('Evelyn') is a fast-growing, upright or oval selection with uniform growth and excellent gold fall color. 'St. Gregory' is upright or oval and uniform, with deep green, very durable foliage and smooth bark. 'Nanum' ('Compactum') is slow growing and dense, reaching 6 feet tall. *A. miyabei* (miyabe maple) is a similar-looking tree from Japan with larger leaves and scaly trunk bark; Zones 4b–7b.

A. griseum

P. 43

a. GRIS-ee-um. Paperbark Maple. This slow-growing, upright or oval tree eventually reaches 20 to 40 feet tall and 15 to 25 feet wide. The shiny, cinnamon brown bark peels off in large papery curls, even on young trees, and glistens with a metallic sheen. The bark makes an outstanding contribution to the garden throughout the year, especially in winter, and is complemented in other seasons by the compound leaves, which are formed of three 3- to 6-inch-long, jagged-edged leaflets. These are dark green in summer and change in very late autumn to glowing shades of deep reddish orange. Locate this lovely tree in a mixed border or use it as a patio or courtyard tree, where it can be seen throughout the year. From central China.

HOW TO GROW. Full sun to partial shade and well-drained, humus-rich soil with a pH of 5 to 7. Needs plentiful moisture. Prune when dormant to remove lower limbs and reveal attractive bark. Usually pest-free. Zones 5a–7b.

CULTIVARS AND SIMILAR SPECIES. *A. triflorum* (three-flowered maple) has colorful peeling bark, three-part compound leaves, and dazzling yellow and scarlet fall color; grow in full sun to full shade; Zones 4b–8a. *A. maximowiczianum* (*A. nikoense*) (Nikko maple) is similar but with smooth-edged, three-part compound leaves and smooth, gray to gray-brown bark. Hybrids of the two trees are 'Gingerbread', a fast-growing, heat-tolerant tree with flaky cinnamon-colored bark and glowing red and orange fall color, and 'Cinnamon Flakes', similar but with red very late fall color; both Zones 5a–8a.

A. tataricum ssp. *ginnala* (*A. ginnala*)

a. jin-NAL-la. Amur Maple. This very pretty multitrunked tree has branches low to the ground and forms a 15- to 20-foot-tall specimen with a dense, rounded head. The 1½- to 3-inch-long, dark green leaves have light green or gray-green undersides and are divided into three narrow lobes with toothed edges. Leaf shape varies, with some trees exhibiting very feathery leaves. Trunk bark is smooth and gray with darker stripes; young twigs are deep reddish purple. Flowers are yellowish and surprisingly fragrant. Pinkish red samaras ripen in summer and look so showy that from a distance the tree appears to be in bloom right up to fall, when the foliage changes to deep red or bright scarlet. This is a tough, durable tree for cold climates. Use as a garden or patio tree, a hedge, or a screen. From Asia.

HOW TO GROW. Full sun to partial or light shade; fall color is showiest in full sun. Best in well-drained, fertile soil. Tolerates poor alkaline soil, road salt, and urban conditions. Withstands heavy pruning; plant as a hedge or windbreak by spacing trees 10 feet apart and shearing yearly in winter. May be pruned to a single trunk. Numerous seeds may cause a weed seedling problem. To use as a specimen, remove lower branches. Susceptible to verticillium wilt. Best in cold climates in the Northeast, Midwest, and Mountain States. Zones 2b–7a.

CULTIVARS AND SIMILAR SPECIES. The species is variable, so named cultivars are best. 'Beethoven' is columnar, with a central leader, brilliant red samaras, and superior fall color. 'Compactum' ('Bailey Compact') is bushlike, growing to 10 to 12 feet tall, and makes an excellent hedge; red fall color. 'Embers' features brighter red samaras and scarlet fall color. 'Flame' has brilliant red fall color. 'Mozart' is pyramidal with a central trunk; brilliant red samaras and fall color. 'Red Rhapsody' has brilliant red fall color. 'Red Wing' displays very showy red samaras. *A. tataricum* (Tatarian maple), **P. 48**, is very similar to Amur maple, but its leaves are oval and unlobed.

TALL SHADE-TREE MAPLES

A. × freemanii

a. × free-MAN-ee-i. Freeman Maple. This hybrid of red maple and silver maple was developed at the National Arboretum. Specimens grow into oval trees about 50 feet tall with beautiful, often deeply cut, leaves. Selected cultivars offer the best of both of the hybrid's parents: a strong branch structure, excellent fall color, and tolerance to adverse growing conditions. Use Freeman maple as a shade, lawn, or street tree (away from power lines) or to create a woodland effect, especially in the Upper Midwest and Plains, where shade tree choices are few.

HOW TO GROW. Full sun and acid to slightly alkaline soil. Prune if necessary to develop strong branching. Disease and insect problems similar to red maple. Zones 4–7.

CULTIVARS. *Note:* Sometimes nurseries mistakenly sell these cultivars as *A. rubrum.* 'Autumn Blaze' is upright or oval, with glowing red fall color and strong branches; drought tolerant and nearly seedless. 'Autumn Fantasy' is broadly oval, with large leaves and ruby red fall color. 'Armstrong Two' is an improved version of 'Armstrong', with a tall columnar shape and dependable yellow-orange fall color. 'Celebration' is seedless (less messy) and has a compact oval shape, very strong branches, and golden yellow to red early-fall color. 'Scarlet Sentinel' is seedless and has a narrow oval or columnar shape, large leaves, and unreliable yellow-orange to scarlet fall color.

A. negundo   P. 44

a. neh-GOON-doh. Box Elder, Ash-Leaved Maple. One of those trees that is best appreciated in harsh sites where few other trees flourish, this broad, rounded, open-branched native grows 30 to 50 feet tall and spreads even wider, with ragged good looks at maturity. Box elder is among the few maples with compound leaves, which are divided into three or five 2- to 4-inch-long, pointed leaflets that resemble ash tree leaves. Usually bright green on top with slightly hairy, light green undersides, the leaves also may be attractively variegated. Stems of young branches are green to reddish brown and waxy. Trunk bark is gray-brown and deeply ridged and furrowed. Yellow-green male and female flowers develop in pendulous clusters on separate trees in early spring before the leaves. Dry brown samaras hang on to female trees well into winter and may look messy. An unremarkable yellow-green fall color develops early. This picturesque tree is native to streambanks and edges of lakes and swamps throughout most of North America. Unfortunately, it is weak wooded and subject to storm damage, making it short-lived, although improved cultivars do not have this problem. Despite its drawbacks, this native is valuable for streambank stabilization or as a shelterbelt tree in the Midwest and Plains, where more desirable trees do not survive the extreme cold and drought. Variegated forms make pretty accents in large garden borders. From North America.

HOW TO GROW. Full sun to light shade; variegated forms need partial or light shade in the South. Very tolerant of soil type; flourishes in wet or dry sites and in alkaline soil; withstands flooding. Prune when dormant to develop strong branch angles and to thin the crown; prune when mature to reduce wind resistance. Needs regular pruning to remove storm-damaged wood. Box elder bugs are annoying pests that feed on box elder seeds on female trees and can invade houses in autumn; plant male trees or locate female trees away from buildings and outdoor living areas. Female trees also are messy; choose seedless male types to reduce cleanup. Anthracnose can be a problem during rainy years. Zones 2a–8a.

CULTIVARS AND SIMILAR SPECIES. 'Baron' is a male form of the species and seedless. 'Flamingo' is a female with pink new growth that matures to green-and-white variegation; grows to 20 feet tall. 'Kelly's Gold' produces gold leaves in spring, chartreuse in summer. 'Variegatum' is a female with irregular white-edged leaves. 'Violaceum' has attractive purplish twigs, purplish male flowers, and no seeds. 'Sensation' has a stronger, more uniform shape; grows to 30 feet tall and has brilliant red fall color. *A. cissifolium* (ivy-leaved maple) is a drought-tolerant trifoliate maple from Japan; grows to 20 to 30 feet tall; has a spreading mushroom shape, gnarled branches, and glossy dark green leaves that turn brilliant red and yellow in fall; uncommon but should be grown more; Zones 5b–8a.

A. pensylvanicum

a. pen-sill-VAHN-eh-kum. Striped Maple, Moosewood. Naturally growing as an understory tree in tall forests, this flat-topped or rounded maple grows 20 to 30 feet tall and wide and is valued for its interesting bark. Young trunks and branches have smooth, dark pea green bark with prominent bright white stripes, while twigs are red or reddish brown. Bark on the lower trunks of old trees becomes rough and brown, but branches higher up retain the green-and-white-striped character. Leaves are 5 to 7 inches long and three lobed, in the shape of a tulip cutout. Bright light green during the growing season, leaves change to an excellent yellow in autumn. Best used in an informal or naturalistic landscape and located where the bark is visible in winter. From eastern North America.

HOW TO GROW. Partial or light shade and humus-rich, moist, well-drained soil. Performs poorly in heat and drought. Bark is thin; protect from mechanical injury. Prune as needed to reveal bark. Verticillium wilt, aphids, and scale sometimes are troublesome. Zones 3b–7a.

CULTIVARS AND SIMILAR SPECIES. 'Erthrocladum' has scarlet twigs with white stripes and a green trunk with white stripes. *A. capillipes* (snakebark maple), P. 43, has red young twigs, green-and-white-striped trunk bark, and scarlet fall foliage; Zones 5–7. *A. tegmentosum* 'White Tigress' is an Asian species with smooth, rich green to purple-green bark with white stripes; Zones 5a–7a. *A. davidii* (David maple) is another Asian species with very showy striped bark; performs well in the South; Zones 7a–9a.

A. platanoides   P. 45

a. plat-an-NOY-deez. Norway Maple. Widely planted—many say over-planted—in North America, this European maple is a beautiful, dense, round-headed tree that grows to 50 or more feet tall and wide. In spring showy clusters of airy yellow-green flowers cover the tree before the leaves appear. In summer bright green samaras develop and then turn tan before dropping. The lustrous dark green leaves have five pointed lobes and measure 4 to 7 inches across. They become brilliant golden yellow in late fall in the North but drop with little color change in the South. Despite its beauty, the tree has many drawbacks: its roots are very shallow and feed greedily, robbing garden plants of moisture and nutrients; the shade it casts is so dense that lawn and garden plants struggle in it; and so many seeds develop (on the species) that tree seedlings create a cleanup and weed nuisance. In some areas, Norway maple has invaded natural areas and may be crowding out native trees. In these areas, choose another tree or plant a seedless form of Norway maple. Despite these drawbacks, Norway maple is an indispensable shade or street tree (away from power lines) in the extremely cold, windy, drought-ridden regions of the Plains, Midwest, and Mountain States, where few other tall shade trees will grow. Other trees make better choices elsewhere. From Europe.

HOW TO GROW. Full sun and sandy to heavy, acid to alkaline soil. Tolerates poorly drained, compacted soil and road salt. Best with moderate to plentiful moisture. Tolerates air pollution and urban conditions. Plant a ground cover suited to dry shade, or mulch with wood chips beneath the tree instead of trying to grow grass. Prune mature trees in midsummer or when dormant to reduce wind resistance. Verticillium wilt and aphids can be serious. Leaf scorch is a problem with the species but not with selected cultivars. Zones 4a–7b.

CULTIVARS AND SIMILAR SPECIES. Many improved cultivars are available and should be used rather than unnamed choices. *Columnar:* 'Cleveland' has upswept branches; grows 50 feet tall and half as wide. 'Columnare' is very narrow, with dense, erect branches; grows to 35 feet tall and 15 feet wide. *Gold leaves:* 'Princeton Gold' is a uniform oval with bright yellow leaves on new growth; similar to 'Sunburst' honey locust. *Purplish red summer leaves:* 'Crimson King' is rounded and dense, with dark, blood red foliage all summer. 'Crimson Century' is columnar, growing to 25 feet tall and 15 feet wide, with blood red foliage all summer. 'Deborah' is oval and has red new growth that turns green in summer. 'Fairview' is a narrower version of 'Deborah'. 'Royal Red' is identical to 'Crimson King' but perhaps more cold hardy. *Variegated leaves:* 'Drummondii' has light green leaves with wide white edges; protect from wind. *Cut leaves:* 'Oregon Pride' is a rounded tree with deeply cut, lacy leaves. *Especially heat, cold, and drought resistant:* 'Alberta Park' resists frost cracking. 'Emerald Luster' has a strong, rounded crown and glossy, cupped leaves. 'Medallion' has red and gold fall color and is seedless. 'Summershade' is one of the best—very tall with lustrous green, insect-resistant leaves. 'Emerald Queen' is fast growing, very tall, and drought tolerant. *A. truncatum* (Shantung maple, purpleblow maple) grows to 25 feet tall; similar to Norway maple but with purplish new growth and orange late-fall color; very heat and drought tolerant; makes an excellent tall maple for the Southwest and Plains. *Stress-tolerant hybrids of the two:* 'Norwegian Sunset' is a compact, upright oval with purplish new growth and yellow-orange to red fall color. 'Pacific Sunset' grows upright or rounded and is of medium height; purplish new growth and excellent bright red to orange-yellow early-fall color; infertile seeds; excellent in the Midwest. *A. mono* (painted maple) is related to these two trees but in form resembles a large Japanese maple, with bright light green leaves that may turn orange-yellow in fall; grows to 50 feet tall; Zones 4–7a.

A. pseudoplatanus   P. 46

a. sue-doe-PLAT-tan-us. Sycamore Maple. This broadly arching, handsome tree grows 40 to 60 feet tall and has attractive flaking or peeling orange-brown bark. It grows well in difficult sites that challenge other maples, but it may self-seed and become invasive in Zone 6b and warmer. The bold, rounded leaves are about 6 inches across and cut into five lobes, closely resembling sycamore leaves. They are dark green on top and gray-green on the undersides, turning an unremarkable yellow in autumn. Flowers form in large, bright green, pendulous clusters, blooming after the new leaves emerge. Use as a sturdy lawn, park, or street tree or as a seaside tree, as it tolerates salt spray. From Europe.

HOW TO GROW. Full to partial sun. Tolerates a wide range of soil, from clay to sand, acid to alkaline, but grows best in a humus-rich site with even moisture. Tolerates road salt. Numerous seeds may require cleanup in early summer and create a weed seedling problem in beds. Excellent in the maritime climates of the East and West Coasts, but performs poorly in the South; best in Zones 5a–7b.

CULTIVARS. 'Atropurpureum' has green leaves with deep purple undersides. *A. pseudoplatanus* var. *erythrocarpum* has bright red samaras.

A. rubrum   P. 46

a. ROO-brum. Red Maple, Swamp Maple. Pyramidal when young and becoming rounded with age, red maple grows rapidly to 60 to 80 feet tall and 45 feet wide and is one of the most popular landscape maples. In the wild, it usually inhabits wet areas and partly shaded woodlands, but it also can be found in fallow fields and on dry hilltops. In early spring, small, bright red flowers cover the silvery branches before the leaves appear. They are followed by red samaras in early summer. The 2- to 4-inch-wide, dark green leaves are gray-green on their undersides and change to a variable combination of red and yellow in early fall. Autumn color varies from tree to tree; some trees color more consistently and better than others. Red maple makes a good shade or street tree (away from power lines), although surface roots may interfere with a garden or lawn beneath the tree. From eastern North America—Canada to the Gulf Coast.

HOW TO GROW. Full sun is best, but tolerates partial sun. Adapts to a wide range of soils, from wet to dry, clayey to rocky; grows best in fertile, acid soil with plentiful moisture. Tolerates air pollution but not salt. Fallen seeds can be messy and pose a weed seedling problem; consider seedless forms. Prune when dormant; train young trees to develop evenly spaced scaffold branches. Protect thin bark from mechanical injury. Borers and leafhoppers are not serious problems. Leaf scorch disfigures leaves during hot, windy summers in unprotected sites. Chlorosis from manganese deficiency develops in alkaline soil. Verticillium wilt and trunk decay are sometimes serious. Zones 4/5–9a, depending on the selection.

CULTIVARS. Choose cultivars adapted to your region for best performance and fall color. *Northeast:* 'Autumn Flame' is a rounded, dense, seedless tree with small leaves and long-lasting, bright red early-fall color. 'Embers' is pyramidal with brilliant red fall color. 'New World' resists potato leafhoppers, has orange-red fall color, and grows into an upright, spreading or weeping shape; Zones 4–8. 'Red Sunset' is broadly oval, with wonderful, long-lasting, orange-red fall color and scorch-resistant leaves; tolerates flooding. 'Karpick' is seedless and has a narrow oval shape, red twigs, and gold and red fall color. *South: A. rubrum* var. *drummondii* is of southern origin, so it colors well in the South and tolerates salty soil. 'October Glory' is rounded, with very late crimson fall color. 'Legacy' has an oval outline and strong branches; turns red to yellow-orange in fall. Also use 'Red Sunset'. 'Steeple' has a dense oval or columnar shape, with yellow to orange fall color. *Midwest:* 'Brandywine' is resistant to potato leafhoppers; wine red fall color; Zones 4–8. 'Doric' forms a narrow column, with very late red to orange fall color. 'Northfire' is broadly oval, with fiery scarlet fall color. 'Scanlon' grows densely upright, with orange fall color. Also use 'Red Sunset' and 'New World'. *Upper Midwest:* 'Autumn Spire' is columnar or oval and seedless, with excellent red fall color. 'Firedance' is oval and seedless, with brilliant red fall color. 'Northwood' is oval or round, with orange-red fall color; seedless and intolerant of flooding. 'Red Rocket' is very narrow, with fiery red fall color; Zones 3–8. 'Rubyfrost' has strong branches, is drought and cold tolerant, and has bright red fall color. Also use 'North Fire'.

A. saccharinum

a. sak-ah-RYE-num. Silver Maple. Native to moist streambanks, lake edges, and floodplains, silver maple is a beautiful oval tree with slightly pendulous branches that grows 60 to 80 feet tall. Older trees can be unsightly and even hazardous due to weak wood and consequent storm damage. The 3- to 5-inch-wide leaves are star shaped and cut into five jagged-edged lobes. The tree's name comes from the silvery undersides of the light green leaves, which sparkle as they wave in the breeze. Fall color is light yellow. The greenish yellow or red flowers open in late winter or very early spring, creating a pretty effect. Trunk bark is smooth when young, but rough and flaky on older trees. Because branches are easily broken during wind-, rain-, and snowstorms, the tree poses a hazard if planted close to a street or house. Old trees have surface roots that can tear up sidewalks and lawns, and the large seeds and abundant seedlings create a cleanup problem. This fast-growing maple is one of the best shade trees for poor-soil areas, but it should not be planted where stronger trees will grow. It is best planted in natural sites near wetlands, on reclamation projects, or as a landscape tree in the northern Plains and Mountain States, where few other shade trees flourish. Only improved cultivars should be chosen for landscape situations. From eastern North America.

HOW TO GROW. Full sun. Best in deep, fertile, acid soil with plentiful moisture, but performs well in slightly alkaline, wet or dry soil; withstands flooding. Heat and drought tolerant. Begin pruning when young to develop a single leader and strong branches. Older trees should be cabled. Anthracnose may occur during rainy summers. Verticillium wilt and scale can be serious problems. Chlorosis occurs in alkaline soil due to manganese deficiency. Zones 3a–9b.

CULTIVARS. 'Blair' has shorter limbs that are less prone to breakage. 'Silver Queen' has deeply cut leaves with silvery undersides, has stronger upright branching, and is nearly seedless. 'Skinneri' is probably the best form, with lacy leaves and strong horizontal branches. 'Northline' is slow growing and strong, good in the Midwest and Plains. For improved hybrids, see A. rubrum.

A. saccharum

P. 47

a. SAK-kar-um. Sugar Maple, Hard Maple, Rock Maple. The sugar maple is one of North America's finest trees, its foliage painting the landscape with fiery hues in September and October. It grows into a magnificent, long-lived, 80-foot-tall specimen with a strong, symmetrical, oval silhouette, and its sap is the source of maple syrup. Medium green leaves are broad (to 6 inches across) and star shaped. In autumn they turn scarlet, orange-red, orange, or yellow, depending on sun exposure. Trunk bark is rough and gray. Light yellow flowers bloom before the leaves appear and are followed by tan samaras. Sugar maple makes a stunning shade or background tree with a beautiful winter silhouette, but it casts deep shade and has surface roots that make growing grass around it difficult. From eastern North America—Canada south to Georgia and west to Texas.

HOW TO GROW. Full sun to partial shade and fertile, moist, well-drained, neutral to slightly acid soil. Performs poorly in urban conditions with road salt and dry, compacted soil. Some cultivars tolerate heat and drought better than others. Prune when dormant or in midsummer to maintain a single leader and develop strong branch angles. Usually pest- and disease-free, although verticillium wilt, leafhoppers, and aphids can be serious problems. Zones 3b–7b.

CULTIVARS. For best performance, choose a cultivar adapted to your region. *North and Northeast:* 'Bonfire' is broader than most, fast growing, and heat resistant, with red fall color; likes acid or slightly alkaline soil; resists leafhoppers. 'Majesty' forms a narrow oval, with red and orange early-fall color. 'Goldspire' is very narrow and city tolerant; resists leaf scorch; bright yellow late-fall color. 'Green Mountain' features thick, dark green leaves that do not scald in heat and drought; fall color is golden in alkaline soil and red in acid soil. 'Newton Sentry' forms an extremely narrow column, with several leaders and gold fall color. *South:* 'Legacy' forms a dense oval with thick, scald-resistant, dark green leaves and red, pink, and orange fall color. *Midwest:* 'Caddo', a selection from Oklahoma, tolerates drought and alkaline soil; features yellow, orange, and red fall color. 'Commemoration' is vigorous and turns golden yellow-orange in early fall. 'Steeple' grows into a dense column or oval. 'Sweet Shadow' has lacy leaves and yellow fall color. *A. saccharum* ssp. *nigrum* (black maple) is endemic to the Midwest; more heat tolerant than the species, with more shallowly lobed, droopy leaves, but just as beautiful. Also use 'Green Mountain', 'Goldspire', 'Legacy', 'Majesty', and 'Newton Sentry'. *Mountain States:* 'Legacy' and 'Green Mountain'. *Southwest: A. saccharum* var. *grandidentatum,* a naturally occurring form with good fall color, is heat and drought tolerant. 'Highland Park' is a tight pyramid with tatter-proof foliage and very showy, orange-red fall color. 'Rocky Mountain Glow' has an oval shape, with smaller leaves and coral red fall color. Also use 'Caddo'.

JAPANESE MAPLES

A. japonicum   P. 44

a. jah-PON-eh-kum. Full-Moon Maple. This lovely, small, rounded or vase-shaped, multitrunked maple grows 15 to 30 feet tall and makes a stunning garden addition. Its attention-grabbing, rounded, 4-inch-wide leaves have 7 to 11 lobes with jagged edges. Small red flowers in bold, nodding clusters make a pretty show in early spring before the new leaves unfold. Fall color is brilliant scarlet, red, or gold. This is a perfect shade tree for a patio or small garden, or use it in a mixed border. From Japan.

HOW TO GROW. Full sun to partial or light shade and evenly moist, rich soil that has a near neutral pH. Mulch soil to retain moisture. Zones 6a–9a.

CULTIVARS AND SIMILAR SPECIES. *A. japonicum* var. *aconitifolium* ('Filicifolium') (fernleaf Japanese maple) has large, rounded leaves that are deeply cut to the base into ferny lobes with jagged edges; deep green in summer and ruby red and orange in early fall; very cold hardy. 'Vitifolium' leaves are not as deeply divided and appear coarser. *A. circinatum* (vine maple) is native to the Pacific Northwest, tolerates dry shade, and resembles full-moon maple; 'Sunglow' has sunny yellow leaves with a coral tinge that turn yellow and crimson in fall. *A. pseudosieboldianum* (Korean maple) is a small, beautiful tree with glossy, green, 9- to 11-lobed leaves; gorgeous fall color and white young twigs; Zones 5b–7b.

A. palmatum   P. 45

a. pal-MAY-tum. Japanese Maple. A small, slow-growing, elegant tree with gorgeous foliage, Japanese maple commands attention wherever it grows. Trees are usually upright or vase shaped with layered branching. They reach 15 to 30 feet tall and have smooth gray trunks and waxy reddish or pea green twigs. The small, 1½- to 3-inch-wide, star-shaped leaves are cut past their midpoints into five to seven toothed lobes, like the fingers of a glove. Red flowers bloom with the new leaves and are followed by red-tinged samaras. Gardeners are enticed by hundreds of cultivars with more finely cut leaves or distinctive colors. Leaves may be pale green, gold, deep red, dark burgundy, or multicolored. Spring growth is often reddish or brighter colored than summer foliage, which dulls some. In autumn green-leaved types turn gold or yellow, purple- and red-leaved types turn red or scarlet, and gold-leaved forms turn orange or yellow. These small trees are especially lovely in mixed borders and small gardens. Use weeping cut-leaved forms to cascade down a slope or waterfall. Purple-leaved forms contrast beautifully with blue-needled conifers. From China, Korea, and Japan.

HOW TO GROW. Full sun to partial shade. For best color, give red-leaved types plenty of sun but protect from hot afternoon rays in exposed sites. Needs humus-rich, moist, well-drained soil; mulch to retain soil moisture. Prune deadwood from the interior; thin to expose trunk and branching pattern. Verticillium wilt can be a serious problem, suddenly killing the tree. Zones 5b–8a.

CULTIVARS. A number of cultivars are widely available. Specialty catalogs offer rarer types for collectors. 'Atropurpureum' is the name used for any form with reddish purple leaves. 'Bloodgood' is the most popular red-leaved form; its deeply incised leaves retain their dark crimson color all summer and turn clear red in fall. 'Burgundy Lace' is a spreading tree that grows to 20 feet tall and has dark purple-red leaves whose lobes are cut all the way to the base. 'Asahi Zuru' has red new growth that changes to green, with pink, red, and white variegations. 'Sango-Kaku' (coral-bark maple) has striking coral red twigs and pale green leaves that turn yellow in fall; Zones 6b–9a . 'Aoyagi' (green-bark maple) has pea green young branches, bright green leaves, and yellow fall color. 'Butterfly' has white, pink, and green variegated leaves and is bushy to 10 feet tall. 'Shishi-gashira' has dark green, curled leaves that turn brilliant orange in fall. 'Trompenburg' has dark purple leaves that turn scarlet in fall. 'Ukigumo' has orange-red leaves that turn yellow in fall. 'Viridis' has light green leaves, green branches, and yellow fall color. *A. palmatum* var. *dissectum* (threadleaf maple, laceleaf maple) is a gorgeous, low-spreading or weeping shrub that grows wider than it is tall, with lacy, deeply dissected leaves; may have several twisted trunks that grow to 20 feet with great age. 'Crimson Queen' has deep burgundy, dissected leaves that turn red in fall. 'Ornatum' has bronze leaves that turn scarlet in fall. 'Seiryu' grows upright to 20 feet, with lacy green leaves and orange-gold fall color.

A. shirasawanum (A. japonicum var. *microphyllum)*   P. 48

a. sheer-ah-SAW-ay-num. Shirasawa Maple. Very similar to *A. japonicum*, this elegant small tree is vase shaped with layered branches and grows 20 to 30 feet tall. It features rounded, 2- to 5-inch-wide, red-stemmed leaves that are cut into 9 to 11, or even 13, sharply toothed, shallow lobes. A cultivar with yellow-green leaves is particularly beautiful and widely grown. In fall Shirasawa maple's foliage turns clear red, yellow, or orange. In spring pink and creamy yellow flowers bloom as the new leaves unfold, creating a lovely sight. The samaras are quite attractive, too, as they are held upright, an identifying trait. Trunks feature smooth gray-brown bark. Use as a specimen in a shade garden. From Japan.

HOW TO GROW. Partial to light shade and evenly moist, humus-rich soil. Zones 5–7.

CULTIVARS. 'Aureum' (golden full-moon maple) is more widely grown than the species because it features beautiful chartreuse leaves that turn gold in autumn. Needs light shade to prevent leaf scorch.

❦ Aesculus

ESS-kew-lus. Buckeye or horse chestnut family, Hippocastanaceae.

This genus contains about 15 deciduous trees and shrubs from southeastern Europe, North America, and eastern Asia. Species from North America are usually called buckeyes; those from other continents are called horse chestnuts. Leaves are opposite, rounded, and boldly cut into five to seven palmate lobes. Tubular flowers bloom in tall spikes. Most species leaf out very early in spring or late winter, their frost-tolerant new growth providing welcome greenery well before other trees. Although outstandingly beautiful when in bloom in late spring and early summer, most members of this family are messy throughout the growing season, dropping flowers, leaf and twig litter, and nuts. As a group, they are prone to leaf diseases, but some are more resistant than others. All parts of these trees, especially their beautiful nuts, are poisonous to people if eaten, but the nuts provide food for wildlife.

Most buckeyes and horse chestnuts are not fussy as to growing conditions, but good air circulation and even soil moisture discourage leaf diseases. Drought increases unsightly leaf scorch. Use as shade trees or small ornamentals in open or naturalistic areas, with a ground cover planted beneath to absorb the litter and reduce cleanup. Avoid sites near sidewalks, driveways, or patios, and do not plant near playgrounds, where the nuts might tempt children to taste them.

A. × carnea   P. 49

a. × CAR-knee-uh. Red Horse Chestnut. Growing into a dense, rounded, 30- to 40-foot-tall tree, this hybrid of horse chestnut and red buckeye is very showy and disease resistant. Eye-catching 6- to 8-inch-tall spires of rose pink flowers rise up from the branches in late spring. The glossy, dark green leaves are big and bold, divided like fingers into five to seven leaflets. In autumn spine-covered, green fruits drop from the tree and reveal lustrous, chestnut brown nuts. Leaves turn yellow-brown in early fall.

HOW TO GROW. Full sun and evenly moist, well-drained, acid to alkaline soil. Tolerates drought better than common horse chestnut *(A. hippocastanum)*. Prune in late winter if needed. Suffers somewhat from leaf scorch and mildew during dry spells and leaf blotch and anthracnose during wet spells, but less so than common horse chestnut. Prune low-hanging branches if needed. Zones 5a–7b.

CULTIVARS. 'Briotii' has 10-inch-tall, deep rosy red flowers and matures as a smaller tree. 'Fort McNair' has dark pink flowers with yellow throats and resists leaf scorch and leaf blotch. 'O'Neil Red' produces larger (10- to 12-inch-tall), brighter red flowers. 'Plantierensis' has intense rose pink flowers with yellow throats and does not set fruit, so it is less messy.

A. glabra

P. 50

a. GLAY-brah. Ohio Buckeye. Ohio buckeye is a round-headed native tree with ascending branches that grows to 30 feet tall and inhabits moist areas. Its bright green, 6-inch-wide, five-fingered leaves appear in early spring before most other plants start growing and change color earlier than most trees in fall, turning bright to golden yellow or orange. The slender, 6-inch-tall, greenish yellow flower clusters bloom in midspring. Prickly fruits are typical of the family. This adaptable tree has a rugged character with furrowed, corky, gray bark. Makes an outstanding shade tree for extreme cold areas of the Midwest and Mountain States. Adapts well to naturalistic sites and moist areas. From midwestern North America.

HOW TO GROW. Full sun to light shade and humus-rich, slightly acid soil. Likes plentiful moisture. Plant small specimens, as this taprooted tree may be difficult to transplant. Leaf blotch and powdery mildew can be serious problems during drought, although this species tolerates the heat·better than other horse chestnuts. Zones 3a–8b.

CULTIVARS AND SIMILAR SPECIES. 'Homestead' has spectacular, long-lasting, orange-red fall color. *A. flava (A. octandra)* (yellow buckeye, **P. 50**, is very similar but grows to 80 feet tall and is an elegant tree; glossy, green, disease-resistant leaves and spectacular red-orange fall color; 6-inch-tall spires of creamy yellow flowers; fruits with smooth husks; Zones 3–8.

A. hippocastanum
P. 51

a. hip-oh-kas-TA-num. Horse Chestnut. This upright or oval tree grows 50 to 75 feet tall and has down-swept branches crowned with spectacular 12-inch-tall candles of creamy, red-blotched flowers in late spring and early summer. The coarse-textured leaves may be 10 inches across and are divided into seven fingerlike leaflets. Fall color is yellowish. Spine-covered, brown fruits drop to reveal glossy, reddish brown nuts. From Europe.

HOW TO GROW. Full sun and humus-rich, moist soil, with plenty of air circulation to reduce leaf scorch and anthracnose. Zones 4a–8b.

CULTIVARS. 'Baumanii' has long-lasting double flowers that do not produce nuts, so it is less messy.

A. pavia
P. 51

a. paw-VEE-uh. Red Buckeye. This multitrunked, round-headed native is a lovely sight when in bloom in spring. It grows to 25 feet tall, with neat, bold-textured, glossy, green leaves that sprout very early. In mid- to late spring, 4- to 8-inch-tall spires of slender flowers, which vary from coral pink to bright red, adorn the branches. These tubular blooms attract hummingbirds. Fruit husks are smooth, not spiny, and contain orange-brown nuts. Use red buckeye in a woodland or naturalistic garden or as a small ornamental in a yard. Or mass it as a screen. From midwestern and southeastern North America.

HOW TO GROW. Full sun to light shade and humus-rich soil; blooms best in full sun and moist, heavily mulched soil. Does not tolerate drought well; may defoliate. Leaves are usually disease-free. Zones 6a–9a.

CULTIVARS AND SIMILAR SPECIES. *A. pavia flavescens* has yellow flowers. *A. splendens* (flame buckeye, Louisiana buckeye) has scarlet flowers and leaves with fuzzy undersides.

❧ *Albizia*

al-BIZZ-ee-uh. Pea family, Fabaceae.

This large genus contains about 150 deciduous trees and shrubs, most native to tropical and subtropical areas of Africa, Asia, and Australia. Leaves are alternate and cut into lacy leaflets. Flowers have long stamens and are arranged in fluffy heads. Only one species is commonly grown in North American gardens.

A. julibrissin
P. 52

a. jew-lee-BRIS-in. Silk Tree, Mimosa. This cold-hardy species grows rapidly into a wide-spreading, flat-topped, 30-foot-tall specimen with horizontal branches, lacy leaves, and a tropical air. Leaves, which don't emerge until late spring, are 12 to 18 inches long and dissected into tiny leaflets, which fold up at night or when touched. Leaves do not change color in autumn but remain bright green until frost. Powder puff–like flowers cover the tree in mid- to late summer, their color varying from pale to intense pink. Dark brown, 6-inch-long seedpods develop after the flowers. They remain on the tree all winter and may be unsightly. Silk tree has smooth, light brown bark and is often multitrunked. Use as a short-lived lawn or patio tree or near the seashore to cast light shade. Or arrange in a border for an exotic look. This tree is especially valued for its late-season flowers. From the Mideast, Japan, China, and India.

HOW TO GROW. Full sun and well-drained, acid or alkaline soil. Tolerates road salt, drought, and urban and seashore conditions. Numerous seedlings can be a weed problem in Zone 7a and warmer. Weak wooded and subject to storm damage. Remove deadwood and shorten wide-spreading branches in spring. Highly susceptible to mimosa webworm, which can defoliate trees, and mimosa wilt, which can kill trees suddenly; grow resistant cultivars. Zones 6a–9a.

CULTIVARS. 'Rosea' has very deep pink flowers. *Wilt resistant cultivars for Zones 7b–9a:* 'Charlotte' with light pink flowers and 'Tyron' with deep pink ones.

Alnus

ALL-nus. Birch family, Betulaceae.

Native to North America and Europe, this genus of deciduous trees and shrubs contains 60 species. Leaves are alternate and simple in outline, with coarse teeth along their edges. Flowers are conspicuous male catkins and inconspicuous female catkins that bloom from stalked buds in late winter before the leaves emerge. Female catkins ripen to small, woody cones. Trees in this genus are one of the few not in the pea family that are able to fix nitrogen from the soil and thus grow readily in poor-soil areas.

A. glutinosa   P. 53

a. glue-TIN-oh-suh. Black Alder, European Alder. This fast-growing tree, which has an irregular oval or pyramidal shape, grows 40 to 50 feet tall and 25 to 40 feet wide. Like its birch relatives, it can bend under the weight of snow without snapping. Leaves are 4 inches long, glossy, dark green, and oval, with toothed undulate margins. They remain green until frost. Young twigs and unfolding leaves are gummy, accounting for the species name. Four-inch-long, yellowish male catkins liven up the tree in late winter before the leaves unfold. Seedpods add a bit of winter interest. Trunk bark is glossy and dark brown, not black. This tree, which has naturalized in the United States, thrives in inhospitable wet sites or in areas that are periodically flooded. Use it as an urban specimen or as a woodland, streambank, or wetland tree; excellent in land reclamation projects. From Europe, northern Africa, and western Asia.

HOW TO GROW. Full sun to partial shade. Adapts to most soils, even sandy or gravelly sites. Best in moist to wet sites, but tolerates occasional dryness. Grows in infertile soil, since it can fix nitrogen. Usually pest-free, but leaf miners and tent caterpillars can be pests. Zones 3b–7b.

CULTIVARS AND SIMILAR SPECIES. 'Aurea' has leaves that emerge yellow and mature to light green. 'Pyramidalis' grows into a handsome, narrow pyramid. 'Imperialis' has finely cut leaves. *A. incana* (gray alder) is similar, with light gray bark and downy, not gummy, shoots; tolerates dry sites in Zones 2b–6b.

ꕥ *Amelanchier*

am-eel-lang-KEE-urh. Rose family, Rosaceae.

The shrubs and trees of this genus number about 25, most hailing from North America, others from Europe and Asia; all hybridize freely. Leaves are simple and oval or rounded, with toothed or smooth edges. Narrow-petaled, white flowers bloom in early spring and are arranged in showy clusters like elongated apple or pear blossoms. Edible blueberry-like fruits ripen from red to dark purple in early summer. Several species are grown in North America and are valued for their early bloom; lovely fall color; and graceful, smooth-barked trunks. Use them in informal gardens and naturalistic landscapes to attract wildlife or as street trees under power lines in cool climates. Because the many native species hybridize so freely, nomenclature is often confused.

A. laevis   P. 54

a. LAY-viss. Allegheny Serviceberry. This multitrunked native has an upright shape, reaching 25 to 30 feet tall, or even 40 feet tall in a rich, moist site. Large, fluffy, white flowers decorate the tree with a lacy mantle for 1 week in early spring. As the flowers mature, new leaves open, emerging glossy and reddish green but maturing to bright green. These round, 1- to 1½-inch-long leaves sport fine-toothed edges and turn a multitude of glorious colors, including yellow, orange, red, and purple-red, in early fall. The fruits are savored by birds and cooks. Smooth, dark gray or pinkish gray bark, which becomes scaly on old trees, cloaks the trunks, making for a pretty sight in winter. This delicate-looking tree is lovely naturalized in a woodland or used in a mixed border. Eastern North America.

HOW TO GROW. Full sun to partial shade and humus-rich, moist, well-drained, fertile soil with a pH of 5 to 7.5. Likes average to wet conditions. Does not tolerate heat or drought. Plant at least two trees to ensure fruit set. Prune when young to develop a single trunk or several strong trunks. Sometimes bothered by scale and mites in warm climates, but not by leaf spot; fire blight can be a serious problem. Zones 4b–8a.

CULTIVARS AND SIMILAR SPECIES. 'Snowcloud' has large flower clusters and scarlet fall color. 'R. J. Hilton' has pink-flushed white flowers, extra-sweet fruits, and red fall foliage with orange-yellow veins. *A. arborea* (shadblow, downy serviceberry, service tree, Juneberry) is hard to distinguish from *A. laevis,* but its flowers are somewhat smaller; its new leaves emerge downy and silver gray; it may grow taller, to 40 to 50 feet, and form suckers; Zones 3b–8a. 'White Pillar' has a columnar shape, with large flower clusters and scarlet fall foliage. *A. arborea* is sometimes confused with and labeled as *A. canadensis,* which is shrubbier, growing to 10 feet, and more stoloniferous. *A. alnifolia* (saskatoon), from western North America, is a beautiful suckering shrub that grows 12 to 15 feet tall, has downy leaves, and is the best species for edible fruit; Zones 2b–7b.

A. × grandiflora   P. 53

a. × gran-dih-FLOR-ah. Apple Serviceberry. This naturally occurring hybrid of *A. arborea* and *A. laevis* combines the best qualities of the two species: very large flowers; somewhat downy, purple-tinged new leaves; large fruits; exceptional fall color; and a tall, nonsuckering, single- or multi-trunked form. Trees have an irregular oval shape and reach 25 to 40 feet tall. Leaves mature to dark green, toothed, 3-inch-long ovals that turn orange and red in fall. This hybrid and its lovely cultivars are the showiest of the genus, making them great as street trees or as ornamentals for manicured gardens and landscapes. From North America.

HOW TO GROW. Culture is similar to that for *A. laevis.* Zones 3b–8a.

CULTIVARS. 'Autumn Brilliance' has strong, storm-resistant branches and brilliant orange-red color. 'Ballerina' has slightly pendulous flowers and large, juicy berries. 'Brilliance' forms a single trunk and has bright scarlet fall color. 'Cumulus' offers a dense cloud of white flowers and yellow-orange fall color. 'Princess Diana' has brilliant red, long-lasting fall color. 'Robin Hill' blooms very early, with pink buds that open to white flowers; gleaming yellow and red fall color and a narrow shape. 'Strata' has horizontally spreading, layered branches.

✻ *Aralia*

ah-RAY-eeh. Aralia family, Araliaceae.

This genus contains about 35 herbaceous or woody species indigenous to temperate areas of North America, Asia, and Australia. Plants have pithy stems; thorny branches; large terminal flower clusters; and alternate, pinnately compound leaves. Their bold good looks make them unusual garden specimens.

A. elata   P. 54

a. eeh-LAH-tah. Japanese Angelica Tree, Devil's Walking Stick. This exotic-looking, multitrunked tree can grow to 40 feet tall and 20 feet wide, its horizontal branches and layered foliage creating a dramatic spreading shape. Big, bold, compound leaves are triangular in outline and grow up to 3 feet long. Divided into small, pointed leaflets, they create a dramatic texture. Thorns arm the leaf undersides and branches. Flowers bloom in 18-inch-wide, creamy white clusters that are held conspicuously above the foliage in late summer or early fall and ripen to blue-black fruits that are relished by birds. Use this unusual-looking tree as an eye-catching specimen in a garden, where it will create a tropical look in a northern climate. From Asia.

HOW TO GROW. Full to partial sun and average soil. Tolerates sandy or clayey soil, drought, and urban conditions. Remove suckers to keep as a multitrunked clump. Pest-free. Because of the thorns, plant trees away from areas frequented by children. Zones 4a–9a.

CULTIVARS AND SIMILAR SPECIES. 'Aureovariegata' features green leaves with pale gold, irregular margins. 'Variegata' has gray-green leaves with white edges. *A. spinosa* (devil's walking stick) is native to eastern North America; quite similar to the Asian species, though spinier and rarely cultivated; Zones 5a–9a.

❦ *Asimina*

ass-eh-MIN-ah. Custard apple family, Annonaceae.

Closely related to the magnolias, this genus contains eight species native to North America. Only one of these is commonly grown in gardens, and it is valued for its foliage and edible fruits. Leaves are large, simple, and alternate. Flowers have three to six petals.

A. triloba   P. 55

a. tri-LOH-bah. Pawpaw. This low-branched native forms a stiff, pyramidal head and grows to 25 to 30 feet tall, sometimes suckering and forming a thicket. The foot-long, oblong leaves droop from the branches like floppy dog's ears, making a bold statement matched by few other trees. They turn a glowing yellow in autumn. Trunk bark is dark gray; twigs are reddish brown. Three-petaled, deep maroon flowers, measuring 3 inches across and resembling trillium blossoms, bloom with the new leaves. Six-inch-long, green berries ripen to dark brown in fall and taste like bananas or vanilla custard. The few seeds contained in the fruits are not edible. Grow pawpaw in a small orchard or naturalistic garden. Or use as a screen or thicket, but avoid planting near a walkway, driveway, or patio, because fallen fruits may be messy. From eastern and central North America.

HOW TO GROW. Full sun to shade; needs partial shade in hot areas. Likes moist, rich soil; tolerates wet sites. Prune suckers to maintain as a single-trunked specimen. Very difficult to transplant; best established from small container-grown plants. Zones 5b–8a.

CULTIVARS. For best fruit production, plant two clones. 'Overleese' has very large, 1-pound fruits. 'Rebecca's Gold' is very productive, with sweet aromatic fruits. 'Sunflower' has late-ripening large fruits. 'Wells' has the largest fruits of all.

❦ *Betula*

BET-yew-la. Birch family, Betulaceae.

This genus contains about 60 trees and shrubs native to northern North America, Europe, and Asia. Many have white or colorful peeling bark, making them very popular landscape subjects, although they are all relatively short-lived. Leaves are alternate, pointed, bright green ovals with toothed margins. Flowers are dangling, conspicuous male catkins and upright, inconspicuous female catkins. As a group, birches are highly susceptible to leaf miners and borers and may suffer from drought and heat. North American species are best grown in northern climates and suffer when grown in the South. Asian species are more tolerant and adapt better to poor soil, heat, and drought; these should be the choices for warmer regions. Since the bark is so ornamental, be sure to locate birches where they can be admired from indoors during winter. Naturalize birches in showy groves in a naturalistic landscape or use one as a focal point in a more formal garden. Trees that are fertilized in spring and kept well watered resist pests better than neglected or stressed trees. Do not prune birches in spring, because the bronze birch borer, the trees' most serious pest, is active then and can enter through the wounds.

B. nigra P. 56

b. Ni-grah. River Birch. In its native habitat—streambanks and marshy areas—river birch grows into a pyramidal or oval tree with slightly pendulous branches and a single trunk; it reaches 40 to 70 feet tall. In cultivation, it is often grown as a multitrunked clump. The beautiful, exfoliating trunk bark is not white, as on so many birches, but bright reddish brown, varying widely on seed-grown trees. Twigs have glossy, dark brown bark. Cultivars are even showier and tend to have apricot or creamy bark. Leaves are dark green triangles with toothed edges that turn an alluring bright yellow in autumn. Use this tree in a difficult wet area or natural site, or plant it for winter interest in a garden border. River birch also is very effective planted in groves. From eastern and midwestern North America.

HOW TO GROW. Full to partial sun. Best in moist, humus-rich, acid (pH of 6.5 or lower) soil, but adapts to clayey soil and wet or periodically flooded sites. Tolerates drought and heat once established. Does not tolerate compacted urban soil. Prune off lower limbs to expose the showy bark. Prune when young to train as a single trunk or clump. Late-summer pruning is best; sap bleeds in spring. Immune to bronze birch borers and troubled less by other pests than most birches. Leaf spot may occur in rainy years. Chlorosis due to iron deficiency occurs in alkaline soil. Deer may strip bark. Best birch for the South and Midwest. Zones 4a–9a.

CULTIVARS AND SIMILAR SPECIES. 'Heritage' is a fast-growing (to 50 feet tall) and extremely popular disease-resistant selection; very showy, creamy white and pinkish tan bark and excellent fall color. 'Fox Valley' is a dense, compact dwarf, growing only to 10 feet tall. *B. albosinensis* (Chinese paper birch) has matte orange-red, orange-brown, and beige-pink peeling bark with white patches; Zones 5b–8a. *B. alleghaniensis* (yellow birch) is native to eastern North America; polished bronze, peeling bark and glorious gold fall color; Zones 4a–7b. *B. lenta* (sweet birch, cherry birch) is native to eastern North America; glistening, almost black bark and the best golden yellow fall color of any birch; resists bronze birch borers; Zones 4a–7b.

B. papyrifera P. 56

b. pap-ee-RIFF-ur-ah. Paper Birch, Canoe Birch. Named for its creamy white bark, which peels off in papery shreds, this native tree is pyramidal when young but becomes irregular or oval when mature; it reaches 50 to 70 feet tall. Until young trees are about 15 feet tall, the bark is brown; thereafter it becomes white with horizontal black markings. Leaves are dark green, oval or triangular, and about 4 inches long, with coarse-toothed margins. Fall color is an excellent yellow. Often grown in clumps but more stunning as a single specimen, because the trunk is very stout and white. Native Americans used the bark to make canoes. From northern North America.

HOW TO GROW. Full sun in the North and light afternoon shade in the South. Needs even moisture and deep, humus-rich, acid soil. Mulch to keep soil moist, especially in warm areas. Performs poorly in compacted soil, heat, drought, and urban conditions. Less susceptible to insects than *B. pendula*, but heat- or water-stressed trees may attract borers and leaf miners. Larvae of the beautiful luna moth feed on the leaves. Best in Zones 2b–5a; grow in cool-summer mountain or coastal areas in Zones 5b–7a; a better choice than *B. pendula* in the Midwest.

CULTIVARS AND SIMILAR SPECIES. New cultivars that are highly resistant to bronze birch borers and are tolerant of high soil pH include the following: 'Renaissance Compact', which grows into a tight 40-foot-tall oval with shaggy white bark; 'Renaissance Oasis', which is a dense tree with peeling white bark; and 'Renaissance Upright', which is a distinctly narrow form with slightly exfoliating white bark. *B. populifolia* (gray birch) is native to northeastern forests and forms lovely clumps of grayish white, black-marked, slender trunks that grow to 30 feet tall; long, pointed, triangular leaves; resists borers, but leaf miners can be a serious problem; useful in wet or dry areas of Zones 4a–6b.

B. pendula (B. alba) P. 57

b. PEN-doo-lah. European Birch. Despite its botanical name, this is not a weeping tree, although the slender black branches turn downward at their tips in a pendulous manner, giving the oval tree a graceful outline. Often grown in clumps, this popular species reaches 40 to 50 feet tall and has enchanting chalk white bark, even on young trees. The lower part of the trunk turns rough and black as trees mature. The 2-inch, glossy, green leaves are oval or triangular, have toothed margins, and turn yellow in autumn. Unless grown in the North and given plenty of moisture, European birch is short-lived and highly susceptible to insects. From northern Europe.

HOW TO GROW. Full to partial sun, but protect from hot afternoon sun. Needs plentiful moisture and deep, humus-rich, acid soil. Mulch to keep soil cool and moist. Very susceptible to bronze birch borers and leaf miners, especially in warm areas. Plant 'Whitespire' as a substitute in warmer areas. Best in Zones 3b–5b.

CULTIVARS. *Weeping forms:* 'Youngii' is a weeping, moplike, grafted form that grows to 15 feet tall. 'Tristis' is a weeping form with a central leader. *Cut-leaved forms:* 'Gracilis' has very deeply cut leaves; weeping, without a central leader, to 20 feet tall. 'Crispa' has deeply cut leaves; weeping form with a central leader. *Purple leaves:* 'Purple Rain' has young purple leaves that mature to bronze-green; orange to copper fall color. 'Crimson Frost' is a hybrid with the following species and has cinnamon-tinged, exfoliating, white bark and purple leaves all summer. *Insect resistant: B. platyphylla* var. *japonica* 'Whitespire Sr.' (Whitespire Senior Asian birch) is a desirable drought-resistant cultivar that is highly resistant to bronze birch borers and moderately resistant to leaf miners; pyramidal shape and smooth, chalk white bark that does not develop until tree reaches 15 feet tall; Zones 4a–7b. 'Dakota Pinnacle' is an excellent, columnar tree for the northern Plains; cold hardy in Zone 3.

B. utilis ssp. *jacquemontii (B. jacquemontii)* P. 57

b. YEW-til-iss jack-uh-MONT-tee-ee. White-Barked Himalayan Birch. This fast-growing Asian birch is relatively new to North American gardens. It's a white-barked subspecies of the coppery brown–barked species and is known for having the whitest bark of any birch, making it a dramatic year-round statement in the garden. Its 2½-inch-long, oval leaves are sharply toothed and turn a rich golden yellow in fall. Trees are fast growing, single trunked, and oval in outline, often with low branches. They can reach 60 feet tall. From China and Nepal.

HOW TO GROW. Full sun and rich, moist soil. Tolerates slightly alkaline conditions. Some resistance to bronze birch borer and leaf miners. Zones 5a–8a.

CULTIVARS AND SIMILAR SPECIES. Several named clones exist, such as 'Ghost', 'Silver Shadow', and 'Yunnan'—all probably identical to the subspecies. *B. utilis* (red-barked Himalayan birch) has pale pink to red-brown bark that peels in narrow strips. *B. maximowicziana* (monarch birch) is an Asian species with yellow-white peeling bark; it is less susceptible to borers and more drought tolerant. *B. ermanii* (erman birch), P. 55, from Siberia, has creamy white to pinkish peeling bark with many horizontal markings; rounded green leaves with prominent veins; Zones 5a–7b.

❦ *Carpinus*

kar-PYE-nus. Birch family, Betulaceae.

This genus includes 30 species of woodland trees and shrubs from Asia, Europe, and North America. Leaves are alternate, simple, and toothed, with prominent veins. Inconspicuous male and female flowers bloom in separate catkins. Fruits are clustered, dry, brown nutlets nestled in pretty bracts; they provide food for birds. Several species tolerate adverse growing conditions.

C. betulus   P. 58

c. BET-yew-lus. European Hornbeam. This beautiful, symmetrical tree grows 40 to 60 feet tall and wide and forms a stately pyramid, with numerous slender branches radiating from the central trunk when young; it becomes a bit irregular and rounded when old. The tree's silhouette is quite becoming in winter. Leaves are 2 to 3 inches long and have sharp teeth. Their dark green surfaces are beautifully textured with prominent veins. Trunk bark is very smooth and gray and attractively marked with longitudinal ridges. In fall leaves turn a pleasing yellow and then reddish brown, often remaining on young trees through the winter. European hornbeam is an excellent easy-care, medium-size shade tree for formal landscapes. It also can be easily pruned as a screen or hedge. From Europe and Asia Minor.

HOW TO GROW. Full sun is best, but tolerates light shade. Excels in deep, rich, moist soil, but tolerates almost any well-drained soil, acid to alkaline. Usually pest-free and tolerant of urban conditions. May exhibit some leaf scorch during drought. Prune when young to prevent split-prone low double leaders. Withstands heavy pruning as a hedge. Zones 5a–7a.

CULTIVARS. The species is rarely grown. 'Columnaris' grows into a dense spire. 'Fastigiata', the most common form, grows into a very symmetrical oval shape. 'Frans Fontaine' is the narrowest form, reaching 35 feet tall and 15 feet wide. 'Heterophylla' has deeply lobed leaves. 'Pendula' is a dwarf, umbrella-shaped tree that grows to 10 feet tall. 'Purpurea' has reddish purple new foliage that turns green in summer, then orange in autumn.

C. caroliniana   P. 58

c. kar-roh-lin-ee-AY-nuh. American Hornbeam, Blue Beech, Musclewood. This handsome native matures into a rounded or flat-topped, 20- to 30-foot-tall tree with a single trunk or multiple trunks. The 2- to 3-inch-long leaves are oblong with sharp points, tiny marginal teeth, and prominent veins. Their pale green color in spring matures to dark blue-green and then becomes red and orange in autumn. From summer to fall, 2½-inch-long clusters of leafy nutlets add a decorative touch. Trunk bark is smooth and slate gray, an excellent winter feature. Use American hornbeam as an understory tree in a woodland or along a stream, as a shade tree for a small yard, or as a patio tree in a lightly shaded site. Can be pruned as a hedge or screen. The wood is very strong, which makes the tree great for climbing. From eastern North America.

HOW TO GROW. Best in partial shade, but tolerates heavy shade. Likes moist, well-drained, humus-rich, acid to neutral soil. Adapts to a wet site and occasional flooding. Does poorly in compacted soil. To avoid storm damage, train when young to several strong trunks. Remove low-hanging branches. Usually pest-free. Zones 3a–9a.

CULTIVARS AND SIMILAR SPECIES. 'Fastigiata' is narrower than the species. C. japonicus (Japanese hornbeam) is an uncommon tree with large leaves, dull red fall color, and a graceful, spreading vase shape; grows to 25 feet tall and 20 feet wide; Zones 5b–8b.

❦ Carya

KARE-ee-ah. Hickory family, Juglandaceae.

Closely related to the walnuts, the 17 species that make up this family of tall trees hail from North and Central America and Asia. Leaves are large and pinnately compound, creating a bold texture. Flowers are long, slender male catkins and smaller female catkins, which develop in spring with the leaves. Trunk bark is often rough and attractive, giving the trees a lot of character. Some species produce edible nuts prized by people and wildlife. Unlike walnuts, the husks surrounding hickory nuts split open when they ripen. These trees have deep taproots and are difficult to transplant but are worth saving or establishing in their natural habit, because they provide valuable food for wildlife.

C. ovata P. 59

c. oh-VAH-tah. Shagbark Hickory. Growing into a towering, 60- to 80-foot-tall, oval tree with low, down-swept branches, this native is named for its thick gray bark, which peels off in vertical strips, giving the trunk an appealing, shaggy texture. Leaves are a foot long and composed of five tapered, 8-inch-long, rich green leaflets, which turn a glorious golden brown in autumn. The delicious, oval nuts are thin shelled and drop from the tree when ripe. Wood from shagbark hickory is used to impart a smoky flavor to barbecue. Use as a nut-producing tree in an unmown area such as a pasture (nuts can be dangerously shot from the blades of a lawn mower), or plant in a naturalistic landscape or woodland where falling nuts won't be a hazard. From eastern North America.

HOW TO GROW. Full sun to partial shade. Best in humus-rich, well-drained soil, but tolerates a range of soils. Drought tolerant. Prune in late winter to develop a strong branch structure. Water during drought to avoid hickory bark beetle infestations. Zones 4b–8b.

CULTIVARS AND SIMILAR SPECIES. 'Wilcox' and 'Pixely' perform well in the Midwest, 'Porter' in the East, 'Harold' in the North, and 'Grangier' in the South. *C. cordiformis* (bitternut hickory) is another fast-growing native; it grows 50 to 75 feet tall and has bitter nuts and bright yellow leaf buds and fall color; Zones 5–8. *C. illinoinensis* (pecan), another native, grows into an oval, single-trunked, 70- to 100-foot-tall tree with upright branches; its massive trunk is covered with furrowed gray bark; its edible nuts can be hazardous when they fall, and their husks stain everything they touch; weak, brittle limbs can break suddenly; prone to many diseases and insects; Zones 6a–9b. *C. laciniosa* (shellbark hickory) is similar to *C. ovata* but has less shaggy bark; hardy to Zone 5b.

❦ *Castanea*

kass-TAY-nee-ah. Beech family, Fagaceae.

Twelve species native to North America, Europe, and Asia make up this genus of nut-bearing trees. Leaves are alternate, simple, and toothed.

Nuts are 1 to 2½ inches around and enclosed in husks covered with vicious spines. Flowers are born in showy, cylindrical catkins. Unlike most nut trees, chestnuts bear nuts at a young age, about 12 years. American chestnut *(C. dentata)* was once the most majestic tree of the eastern American forest, with trunks growing to 120 feet tall and 10 feet in diameter. At the time of the first European settlers, perhaps as many as 25 percent of the trees in the Appalachian forest were American chestnuts. The tree was not only beautiful but also of great economic importance, providing strong lumber and nutritious food for people, farm animals, and wildlife. Unfortunately, a fungus brought into the country from Asia in 1904 virtually wiped out all the mature chestnut trees by the 1930s. This fungus attacks only mature trees that have developed a rough bark; trees whose trunks are blighted and killed can resprout from their roots. Using genes from highly resistant Chinese chestnuts, researchers are close to developing disease-resistant American chestnuts. They hope to establish these trees in the forests and thus gradually return this grand species to its native habitat. Meanwhile, American chestnut can be grown outside its native range (west of the Mississippi) with little fear of blight. And easterners can grow young trees for many years as tall shrubs, cutting back blighted trunks and allowing suckers to grow from the roots. This way, nuts can still be harvested, and the chestnut's gene pool is kept alive.

C. mollissima   P. 60

c. mol-LISS-eh-mah. Chinese Chestnut. This dense, rounded tree grows 35 to 40 feet tall and 40 to 50 feet wide, branching close to the ground. Its shape bears little resemblance to the native chestnut, but it does make a good climbing tree for children. The coarse-textured, green leaves are glossy on top and downy on their undersides. Measuring 4 to 8 inches long, they are lance shaped or oblong with toothed margins. Fall color is a coppery yellow. The tree blooms in early summer, covering itself with decorative, upright, yellowish clusters of 5-inch catkins, whose odor may be objectionable and permeate the entire yard. Soft, spiny fruits ripen in early fall and drop to the ground, splitting open to reveal two or three shiny nuts that are not quite as sweet as those of American chestnut. Use the tree for nut-producing shade away from groomed areas, where low branches and falling nuts would be a hazard. From China and Korea.

HOW TO GROW. Full sun and well-drained, slightly alkaline to slightly acid soil. Heat and drought tolerant. Train when young to grow as a single- or multitrunked tree. Moderately resistant to chestnut blight. Zones 5a–8b.

CULTIVARS AND SIMILAR SPECIES. Plant two cultivars for best nut production: 'Dunstad' and 'Douglass' are hybrids with American chestnut and have excellent blight resistance, a straight trunk to 5 feet, and delicious nuts. *C. sativa* (Spanish chestnut) is almost identical to American chestnut and is commonly grown in the West; Zones 6b–8b.

❦ Catalpa

kah-TALL-paw. Bignonia family, Bignoniaceae.

The 11 species belonging to this genus from North America and Asia are cold-hardy trees and shrubs with a decided tropical appearance. The opposite or whorled leaves are large and without teeth, usually unlobed or shallowly lobed. Flowers are two lipped with ruffled petals and are arranged in clusters; they ripen into long, beanlike seedpods. Catalpas are valued in the landscape for their showy foliage and flowers, which rise above the leaves in early summer after most trees have finished blooming.

C. speciosa

c. spee-see-OH-sah. Northern Catalpa, Western Catalpa. Growing into an irregular, rounded tree with a stout trunk and big branches, northern catalpa can grow 40 to 50 feet tall. Its rugged good looks are highlighted by big, shallowly lobed, heart-shaped leaves, which can reach 12 inches long and are arranged opposite each other. They are glossy on top and densely hairy on their undersides. In autumn they usually turn bright yellow. In early summer 2½-inch, bell-shaped, white flowers with abundant yellow stripes and purple speckles on their throats bloom dramatically above the leaves in 8-inch clusters. The seedpods, which remain on the tree well into winter, are dark brown and slender. They grow to 2 feet long and contain beanlike seeds. Use this tree as a dramatic specimen to contrast with fine-textured plants. From southeastern North America.

HOW TO GROW. Full sun to partial shade. Best in rich, moist soil, but tolerates almost any soil, wet or dry, acid or alkaline, and salt spray. Prune in winter; train when young to develop a central leader; shorten branches on mature trees to reduce storm damage, as limbs are brittle and may break. This species continually drops small twigs, flowers, and pods; plant a ground cover to absorb the mess. Verticillium wilt, leaf spot, mildew, and catalpa worms may cause problems. Withstands hot, dry climates and urban conditions; good in the Midwest, Plains, and Mountain States. Zones 4a–9a.

CULTIVARS AND SIMILAR SPECIES. *C. bignonioides* (southern catalpa, Indian bean), P. 61, is a smaller tree, growing 30 to 40 feet tall and not quite as showy; produces 10-inch-tall spires of numerous 2-inch, purple-and-yellow-speckled, white flowers 2 weeks later than *C. speciosa;* leaves are heart shaped, grow to 8 inches long, and are whorled and less hairy, with a pungent odor; a southeastern native for Zones 5a–9a. 'Aurea' has striking chartreuse leaves. 'Bungei' ('Nana') (umbrella catalpa) is a nonflowering dwarf, growing to 14 feet tall, that forms a tight globular head. *C.* × *rubescens* 'Purpurea' has purplish new growth maturing to dark green and purple-black leaf stems and twigs.

✿ *Celtis*

SELL-tiss. Elm family, Ulmaceae.

Seventy species of deciduous and evergreen trees and shrubs make up this genus, which inhabits North and South America. Leaves are alternate, pointed ovals and are usually toothed. Female flowers bloom singly or in pairs at the leaf bases, while male flowers are clustered at the base of the twigs; neither is showy. Fruits are one-seeded sweet berries. Several *Celtis* species make useful and beautiful shade trees for tough sites.

C. occidentalis   P. 62

c. ox-ah-den-TAY-liss. Common Hackberry. Pyramidal when young, becoming broad-topped and arching with age, this fast-growing elm relative grows 40 to 50 feet tall and wide. It makes a good substitute for American elm because of its similar mature shape and disease resistance. Leaves are 4 inches long, medium green, oval, and pointed, with tiny teeth along their edges. They turn dull yellow in autumn. Trunk bark is interesting, deeply furrowed, and corky. Green flowers in spring are inconspicuous but ripen into pea-sized, purple berries that attract birds and wildlife in fall; these berries may temporarily stain walks and patios. This is a superb, deep-rooted shade tree for almost any location, but it excels in difficult sites where most other trees struggle. From northern and central North America.

HOW TO GROW. Full sun to partial shade. Best in rich, moist soil, but adapts to extremes from wet to dry, acid to alkaline, and clay to sand. Tolerates heat and cold, wind and salt spray. Prune in winter to develop strong branch angles that resist ice damage. Immune to Dutch elm disease; gall insects may disfigure leaves but are not lethal. Good in the Plains, Midwest, and Mountain States. Zones 3b–8b.

CULTIVARS AND SIMILAR SPECIES. 'Prairie Pride' has thick, wind-resistant leaves; fewer fruits; and a uniform, oval crown. *C. laevigata* (sugar hackberry) has a rounded vase shape with pendulous branches; grows to 40 feet tall, making it an excellent street tree; leaves are toothless or with a few teeth; bark is smooth and gray, sometimes with many warty projections; good in the South but not in the alkaline soils of the West; Zones 6a–9a. 'All Seasons' has a uniform shape and small leaves with bright yellow fall color. 'Magnifica' is a fast-growing, insect-resistant hybrid with large leaves. *C. sinensis* (Japanese hackberry) is similar to *C. occidentalis;* good in the West; Zones 7b–9a.

❦ Cercidiphyllum

sir-sih-dih-FILE-um. Cercidiphyllum family, Cercidiphyllaceae.

This genus contains only one species, a gorgeous tree native to the woodlands of China and Japan.

C. japonicum   P. 62

c. jah-PON-eh-kum. Katsura Tree. Pyramidal when young, but maturing into a broad-spreading, flat-topped, 40- to 50-foot-tall specimen, katsura tree is an elegant addition to the home landscape. Its delicate-looking, heart-shaped, 3-inch-long leaves emerge reddish purple in spring, mature to bluish green, and change to combinations of glowing orange, gold, and apricot in autumn. Fallen leaves give off the scent of cotton candy, most noticeable on sunny days. Tiny, red, male and female flowers bloom on separate trees before the leaves unfold in spring. Female trees can be as showy as redbud when in bloom and are broader in outline than male trees, which are more narrowly upright. This fast-growing tree is usually multitrunked, with attractive, shaggy, gray-brown bark. Surface roots may interfere with a lawn or garden beneath the tree; plant in a ground cover or heavily mulched area as a lawn or patio specimen. From Asia.

HOW TO GROW. Full sun except in Zones 8 and 9, where partial shade is best. Likes rich, moist, well-drained, acid or alkaline soil; fall color is best in an acid site. Does not tolerate drought when young; best with plentiful moisture. May be trained to a single trunk, but looks best as a multitrunked specimen. Thin and shorten the branches to reduce the possibility of storm damage. Zones 4b–8b.

CULTIVARS. 'Pendula' is a graceful weeping tree that grows to 25 feet tall. *C. japonicum* var. *magnificum* 'Pendulum' is a dramatic weeping tree that grows to 50 feet tall with irregular growth and larger leaves.

❦ *Cercis*

SEER-sus. Pea family, Fabaceae.

Six species of small trees or shrubs from North America, Asia, and the Mediterranean make up this genus. Heart-shaped leaves, two-lipped flowers blooming in clusters on both old and new wood, and slender seedpods characterize the group. Several species are prized as small, early-blooming landscape trees.

C. canadensis   P. 63

c. kan-ah-DEN-sis. Eastern Redbud. This rounded or flat-topped tree forms multiple low-branching trunks that mature to 20 to 30 feet tall. In early spring, the leafless gray branches are covered with tight clusters of 1-inch-long, bright purplish pink, pink, or occasionally white blossoms. New leaves emerge reddish purple and quickly mature into 5- to 7-inch-wide, matte green hearts that change to yellow in fall. The bark on the trunk and branches is beautiful—smooth and very dark gray. Flattened, 5-inch-long, brown seedpods decorate the tree in fall and winter. Growing naturally along woodland edges, this pretty little tree adapts well to garden borders and naturalistic landscapes. Plant alone or in groups with a dark background of evergreens to show off the blossoms. From central and eastern North America.

HOW TO GROW. Full sun to light shade. Best in moist, well-drained, deep soil; performs poorly in wet sites. Tolerates acid or alkaline soil. Protect trunk from mechanical injury. Verticillium wilt, canker, leaf spot, leafhoppers, and caterpillars can cause trees to be short-lived. Best in hot-summer areas. Zones 5b–9a.

CULTIVARS AND SIMILAR SPECIES. 'Forest Pansy' has enchanting, glossy, reddish purple leaves in spring that change to dark green in summer if nights are hot, then red and orange in fall. 'Silver Cloud' features white-variegated leaves and flowers more sparsely; grows to 12 feet tall. *C. canadensis* var. *alba* has white flowers and light green leaves. *C. canadensis* var. *texensis (C. reniformis)* is a midwestern variety that grows to 20 feet tall, with smaller, very glossy leaves; the best choice for the Southwest; Zones 6–9. 'Oklahoma' has deep magenta flowers. 'Texas White' has white flowers. *C. chinensis* (Chinese redbud) produces dense clusters of deep pink flowers on a shrubby, 12-foot-tall plant; immune to canker; Zones 6–9. 'Avondale' has profuse flowers; performs well in the Pacific Northwest. *C. occidentalis* (Western redbud) grows to 12 feet tall and tolerates alkaline soil; a better choice than *C. canadensis* for the Pacific Northwest.

❦ *Chionanthus*

kye-oh-NAN-thus. Olive family, Oleaceae.

This genus of shrubby trees includes 10, mostly tropical, Asian species; one comes from North America. Two are popular garden plants. The genus is characterized by four-petaled male and female flowers in terminal panicles, usually on separate plants. It has single-seeded fruits and alternate, simple leaves.

C. retusus   P. 64

c. rey-TUSS-us. Chinese Fringe Tree. Growing into a multistemmed, rounded or vase-shaped, 20-foot-tall specimen, Chinese fringe tree is less commonly grown than the native species but is even more beautiful. Clusters of pure white, fringelike flowers turn the tree into a snowball in early summer—a week later than the native species, because the flowers develop on new wood rather than on the previous year's growth. The tidy, oval leaves are 2 to 4 inches long, glossy on top, and densely hairy on their undersides. They may or may not develop yellow late-fall color. Female trees have purple fruits. Trunk bark is attractive, peeling away to reveal gray, brown, and green patches and eventually becoming furrowed. Use this eye-catching tree for a surprising burst of early-summer color in a border or as a screen. From Asia.

HOW TO GROW. Blooms best in full sun, but protect from direct afternoon sun in hot climates. Likes moist, humus-rich, acid soil; tolerates occasionally wet sites. Usually pest-free. Zones 6a–9a.

CULTIVARS. No named cultivars exist, although the tree is variable. Those with rounded, shiny leaves are more shrubby than those with large, dull green leaves, which are more treelike.

C. virginicus   P. 64, 65

c. ver-JIN-ee-kus. Fringe Tree, Old Man's Beard. This rounded, multistemmed, 15- to 20-foot-tall tree blooms and leafs out so late in spring that one begins to wonder whether it is dead just before it suddenly bursts into glorious bloom. The honey-scented, creamy white blossoms are made up of four strap-shaped petals and bloom in dense, 6-inch-long clusters that turn the tree into a billowy cloud for 2 weeks, masking the unfolding leaves. The waxy, dark green, oval leaves are 4 to 8 inches long and have pale undersides and smooth edges. Attractive yellow fall color develops late. Trunk bark is smooth gray, and limbs and twigs have a coarse texture when leafless in winter. Male trees are a bit showier in bloom than female ones, but in fall female trees develop showy blue berries that attract birds. Use as a slow-growing border or patio tree. From southeastern and central North America.

HOW TO GROW. Blooms best in full sun, but grows well in light shade. Likes rich, moist, acid soil; tolerates dry or wet conditions and air pollution. Train to a single trunk or several trunks; prune off low branches to make the plant more treelike. Female trees need a male nearby for best berry set, but nurseries do not label trees as to sex. Scale is sometimes a problem. Zones 4a–9b.

CULTIVARS. 'Floyd' is a rare cultivar with very showy male flowers and a dense, upright shape.

❦ Cladrastis

klad-RAS-tis. Pea family, Fabaceae.

A member of the vast pea family, this genus contains only five species native to Asia and North America. Flowers are two lipped and grow in clusters, leaves are pinnately compound, and fruits are flattened seedpods. The native species is almost extinct in the wild, due partly to overlogging, and is gaining popularity as a landscape tree.

C. kentukea (C. lutea)   P. 65

c. ken-TUCK-ee-ay. Yellowwood. This round-headed, open-branched native grows 30 to 50 feet tall and may spread even wider. Fragrant, white, 1-inch flowers in 8- to 14-inch-long, wisteria-like clusters decorate the tree in early summer. Foot-long leaves are bright light green and divided pinnately into 7 to 11 leaflets. Fall color is a pleasing soft yellow or apricot. Four-inch-long seedpods ripen in autumn. Trunk bark is smooth and silvery gray, resembling that of a beech tree. When cut, the wood reveals a yellow heart. Tall enough to cast shade and beautiful in flower and foliage, this tree belongs in more landscapes as a lawn or garden specimen. Yellowwood is slow growing and may not bloom until it is 10 or more years old. It often blooms well only in alternate years. From southeastern North America.

HOW TO GROW. Full sun and deep, fertile, well-drained, acid to alkaline soil. Drought tolerant once established, but protect from wind to avoid storm damage. Trees may develop weak branch angles; prune when young to create a strong shape and cable older trees if necessary. Prune in summer to avoid sap bleeding. Usually pest-free, but verticillium wilt and leafhoppers are occasional problems. Zones 4b–8a.

CULTIVARS. 'Rosea' ('Perkin's Pink') has enchanting, pale rose pink flowers. 'Sweetshade' grows vigorously, has larger flowers and better yellow fall color, and resists leafhoppers.

❦ *Cornus*

KOR-nus. Dogwood family, Cornaceae.

Containing many remarkable landscape trees and shrubs, this large genus encompasses 45 species from Asia and North America. Flowers are dense umbels, often surrounded by showy petal-like bracts, and develop into fleshy berries. Leaves are pointed, smooth-edged ovals with distinctive curving veins and are usually arranged opposite each other. Unfortunately, the magnificent native flowering dogwood is being decimated by anthracnose, a fungal twig blight, and should be planted in areas where the disease is prevalent only by attentive gardeners who can take measures to ward off the disease. Although no other tree can replace its beauty and bloom time, disease-resistant hybrids and other dogwood species should be considered for low-maintenance landscapes in the Northeast and Mid-Atlantic States. Infected trees should be removed and burned to prevent spread to healthy neighbors.

C. alternifolia   P. 66

c. all-ter-nih-FOL-lee-ah. Pagoda Dogwood. Growing 20 feet tall and 35 to 40 feet wide, with wide-spreading horizontal branches, this native has a beautiful layered appearance, like the tiers of a Japanese pagoda. Lacy white flowers bloom in flattened, 2½-inch-wide clusters above the leaves in late spring and are quite pretty, though not as showy as those of other dogwoods. Unlike most dogwoods, it has alternate leaves; these 4-inch-long, glossy, dark green ovals turn reddish purple in autumn. The blue-black berries have red stalks and are relished by wildlife. Twigs are glossy purple, and trunk bark is gray, adding to the eye-catching winter silhouette. Use pagoda dogwood as a focal point in a border or shade garden to emphasize its attractive horizontal branching pattern. From eastern North America.

HOW TO GROW. Partial shade and humus-rich, moist, well-drained soil. Mulch to keep soil cool and moist. Somewhat susceptible to twig blight. Zones 4a–7a.

CULTIVARS AND SIMILAR SPECIES. 'Argentea' has gorgeous creamy-white-and-green leaves that stand out against a dark background. *C. controversa* (giant dogwood) is from Asia and looks similar, with 4-inch flower clusters and alternate leaves, but grows 35 to 50 feet tall and is disease-free; Zones 6a–8a. 'June Cloud' has flower clusters that exceed 6 inches across. 'Variegata', with silver-edged leaves, grows 10 to 12 feet tall. *C. racemosa* (gray dogwood) is a stoloniferous native tree that grows to 12 feet tall; lacy, pyramidal, 2-inch flower clusters; deep purple fall color, white fruits, and attractive gray and red bark; tolerates most soil conditions and sun or shade. 'Cayahoga' is pyramidal, grows to 15 feet tall, and makes a good street tree under power lines. 'Ottawa' is columnar and grows to 12 feet tall.

C. florida P. 66, 67

c. FLOR-ih-dah. Flowering Dogwood. A tree for all seasons, with a beautiful silhouette of undulating horizontal branches, flowering dogwood is a spreading, single-trunked tree that reaches 20 feet tall in the North and 30 feet tall in the South. This beautiful species is one of the showiest spring-blooming trees, producing numerous 2-inch-wide blossoms made up of four notched white, or sometimes pink, bracts that surround a central cluster of small yellow flowers. The bracts open gradually and are held above the leaves, creating a lacy, layered pattern that lasts for 3 or more weeks if the weather remains cool. Leaves are 5 to 6 inches long and dark green, turning attractive shades of scarlet or wine red in early autumn. Pointed, ½-inch, red berries ripen in late summer and may last into fall if birds don't eat them. Trunk bark is checkered and gray, rather like alligator hide. Plant as a specimen in a border or lawn or use in a woodland garden in areas where disease is not prevalent. From eastern North America.

HOW TO GROW. Full sun to partial or light shade, but provide afternoon shade in hot climates. Best in humus-rich, moist, well-drained, acid soil; mulch soil to keep roots cool and moist. Borers are a serious problem on drought-stressed or injured trees; protect trunk from mechanical injury, because wounds allow borers to enter. Reduce anthracnose infections by planting flowering dogwood in a location with good air circulation and sun so that foliage dries quickly, by irrigating without wetting leaves, and by removing water sprouts and low branches that pick up the fungus from the soil. Control anthracnose infections with well-timed fungicide applications and low-phosphorus, high-calcium fertilizer. Prune when dormant or in summer. Pink and red forms are less heat resistant and cold hardy. Zones 5b–8b.

CULTIVARS AND SIMILAR SPECIES. *White flowers:* 'Cherokee Princess' is strongly horizontal, with 6-inch-wide, white blossoms. 'Gold Nugget' has beautiful, gold-margined, green leaves. 'Cherokee Daybreak' has sparkling, creamy white–margined, green leaves and grows upright. 'Cloud Nine' flowers profusely, has great red fall color, and blooms when young. 'Plena' ('Welch Bay Beauty') has showy double flowers made up of seven curled bracts. 'Snow Princess' has very large, abundant flowers and glossy leaves. 'Spring Grove' is a floriferous, wide-spreading tree with 4-inch-wide flowers; resists anthracnose. 'Sterling Silver' has white-and-green-variegated leaves. *Pink to reddish pink flowers: C. florida* var. *rubra* varies from pale to deep pink. 'Cherokee Chief' produces deep reddish pink flowers and red new growth. 'Cherokee Sunset' has multicolored rose-, yellow-, and-green-variegated leaves and deep pink flowers. 'Robert's Pink' has pink flowers and performs well in the Deep South. 'Red Beauty' is a compact tree with bright reddish pink bracts. 'Rubra' blooms pale to medium pink. 'Stokes' Pink' has clear pink flowers and red and purple fall color; excellent in the South. *Other species: C. nuttallii* (mountain dogwood) is native to the West Coast, grows to 60 feet tall, has rounded white flowers with six to eight bracts, and is susceptible to anthracnose; Zones 7 and 8.

C. kousa P. 67

c. KOO-sah. Kousa Dogwood, Japanese Dogwood, Korean Dogwood, Chinese Dogwood. Upright or vase shaped when young, this elegant Asian dogwood eventually spreads horizontally, growing 20 to 30 feet tall and wide. It begins blooming in late spring or early summer, a month after flowering dogwood. Its showy bracts open greenish white and mature to pure white, sometimes aging to rose, and last for a month or two, depending on the cultivar. The four petal-like bracts surrounding the yellow flowers are pointed, not notched, and they rise above the branches on 2-inch-tall stems. Leaves are 4 inches long and glossy green, with long points and curved veins. In late summer, 1½-inch pink fruits, which ripen to glossy red, dangle from the branches on 4-inch-long stems. These eye-catching fruits stand out gloriously against the green leaves but are soon eaten by birds. Fall color is glossy dark red. As the tree ages, the trunk bark develops into an attractive mixture of brown, gray, and creamy white patches. From Japan, Korea, and China.

HOW TO GROW. Full sun and fertile, well-drained, acid loam and plentiful moisture. Somewhat drought tolerant when established. Tolerates the heat of the Midwest better than *C. florida*. Plant two trees for best fruit development. Remove lower branches to show off the bark, pruning when dormant. Somewhat susceptible to borers, but immune to anthracnose. Zones 5a–8b.

CULTIVARS. Choose named cultivars for best vigor. 'Elizabeth Lustgarten' is a weeping tree that grows to 10 or more feet tall. 'Heart Throb' has profuse, reddish pink flowers. 'Gold Star' has leaves with a butter yellow central blotch. 'Rosabella' ('Satomi') has deep rose pink, long-lasting bracts. 'Snowboy' has green leaves with creamy white edges. 'Summer Stars' has showy white bracts for 6 or more weeks. *C. kousa* var. *chinensis* (Chinese dogwood) has large flowers and is very free flowering; the bracts turn pink as they mature and remain attractive for most of the summer. 'Milky Way' is the same as the previous variety but is variable. 'Milky Way Select' is more uniform, with a vase shape. 'National' is vase shaped and sports large flowers and fruits. 'Samaritan' has green leaves with creamy white edges and is vigorous. 'Galilean' has leaves twice as large as the variety and larger flowers; vase shaped or rounded.

C. mas P. 68

c. mass. Cornelian Cherry, Cherry Dogwood. This late-winter bloomer is a round-headed, low-branched, multitrunked tree that matures to 20 to 25 feet tall. Because it blooms on leafless branches when most plants are still dormant, it is a beautiful and welcome sight. Unlike other popular dogwoods, the flowers don't have showy bracts; instead they are dense, 1-inch clusters of tiny, mustard yellow flowers that turn the tree into a yellow mist for about 3 weeks. Leaves are satiny green and 2 to 4 inches long. They may be purplish in fall or have no appreciable fall color. Dark red, glossy, 1- to ½-inch berries dangle along the branches in midsummer. Tasting like tart cherries, they are prized in Turkey and Ukraine for juice, sorbet, and preserves, but in North America they are eaten primarily by birds. Trunks of older trees develop an attractive, exfoliating, gray-and-tan bark. The wood is strong; in fact, the Trojan horse may have been made from this wood. Use this lovely tree to brighten the winter landscape in a border where it can be seen from indoors or as you travel to and from the house. Most attractive with an evergreen background or where backlit by the sun. From eastern Europe and western Asia.

HOW TO GROW. Full sun to light shade and humus-rich, moist soil. Tolerates acid or alkaline soil and clay. Prune to remove suckers and create a more treelike form. Usually pest-free. Good in the Midwest. Zones 5a–8a.

CULTIVARS AND SIMILAR SPECIES. 'Aurea' has golden leaves. 'Elegantissima' has yellow-margined, pink-flushed, green leaves. 'Flava' has yellow fruits. 'Golden Glory' is pyramidal, growing to 15 feet tall, with abundant flowers. 'Jelico' has oval red fruits. 'Pioneer' has 1½-inch-long, tasty fruits. 'Redstone' is vigorous, with very dependable fruit production. *C. officinalis* (Japanese cornelian cherry) looks very similar but blooms a week earlier; its less-tasty berries ripen in early fall, and its trunk bark is more colorful, with orange patches; Zones 6a–8.

C. × rutgersensis (C. florida × C. kousa) P. 69

c. × rut-gurrs-EN-sis. Stellar Dogwood, Hybrid Dogwood. First introduced in 1990 by Dr. Elwin R. Orton Jr. of Rutgers University, hybrids between *C. florida* and *C. kousa* are stunning trees that grow vigorously to 20 to 25 feet tall. Tree shape varies from upright to spreading to rounded, depending on the cultivar. Flower shape also varies, with the 2-inch bracts being either narrow and starlike or rounded and overlapping. All cultivars bloom so prolifically that the blossoms almost completely obscure the leaves. The bloom period begins in midspring, about 2 weeks after *C. florida* and 2 weeks before *C. kousa*, and lasts for about 3 weeks. The large, glossy, dark green leaves are 2 to 5 inches long and turn red in autumn. These trees grow more vigorously than *C. kousa* and are highly resistant to both borers and anthracnose.

HOW TO GROW. Full sun and humus-rich, moist, well-drained soil. 'Constellation', 'Ruth Ellen', and 'Stardust' may suffer from powdery mildew (others are immune); keep the soil moist and the leaves dry. Zones 6a–8a.

CULTIVARS. 'Aurora' has large, overlapping, pure white, round bracts with a slight notch and forms a full, bushy, upright tree. 'Celestial' has oval, pointed, white bracts that touch but do not overlap and forms a rounded tree. 'Constellation' has delicate, long, nonoverlapping bracts with starry points and forms a narrow tree. 'Ruth Ellen' blooms a bit earlier than the other cultivars; has horizontal branches and a mounding shape; and has pure white, starlike, pointed bracts. 'Galaxy' has rounded, slightly overlapping, white bracts with a slight point that open first as greenish cups; grows upright. 'Stardust' is dwarf, growing only to 15 feet tall, with the horizontal form of *C. florida;* it has rounded, notched, separate bracts and is highly anthracnose resistant. 'Stellar Pink' has broad, pale pink, overlapping, notched bracts and a rounded shape.

❦ *Corylus*

KOR-eh-lus. Birch family, Betulaceae.

This genus of 10 to 15 shrubs and trees encompasses mostly woodland plants from the north temperate zone. They have rounded or oval toothed leaves, showy male catkins in late winter, inconspicuous female flowers, and edible nuts. Only one tree is commonly grown as an ornamental, although several shrubby ones are used in orchards for nut production. The common names hazel and filbert are interchangeable, both of English origin.

C. colurna P. 69

c. koh-LUR-nah. Turkish Filbert, Turkish Hazel. Densely pyramidal when young and eventually maturing into a rounded or oval shape with low-hanging branches, this good-looking tree, which reaches 50 or more feet tall, should be used more often in North American landscapes. Yellowish tan male catkins dangle from the branches in late winter before the leaves unfold. The rounded or heart-shaped leaves are 3 to 6 inches long, rather coarse, glossy, and dark green, with a double row of fine teeth at their margins. Fall color is usually undistinguished. Brown bark exfoliates into an attractive, rough-textured, brown-and-white pattern. Small nuts enclosed in bristly husks ripen in fall and may be messy but are eaten by wildlife. Plant as an easy-care formal lawn, urban, street, or seashore tree. From southeastern Europe and southwestern Asia.

HOW TO GROW. Full sun and any well-drained, acid to alkaline soil. Drought, heat, and wind tolerant once established. Performs well near the seashore, resisting wind and salt spray. Remove lower branches if desired. Eastern filbert blight can be a problem in some areas; otherwise pest-free. Zones 5a–8b.

SIMILAR SPECIES. *C. avellana* (European hazelnut) is a shrubby plant that grows to 20 feet tall; can be pruned into a small tree; has edible nuts.

❦ *Cotinus*

koh-TYE-nus. Cashew family, Anacardiaceae.

This genus contains only two species, both of which are handsome garden plants admired for their foliage and flowers. *C. coggygria* is often cut
to the ground every year (coppiced) to force vigorous new growth. *C.
obovatus* also may be treated this way.

C. obovatus   P. 70

c. ob-oh-VAH-tuss. American Smoke Tree, Smoke Bush. A multitrunked,
small tree reaching 20 to 30 feet tall, this native forms a round-headed
specimen with distinctive 5- to 10-inch-long, oblong leaves that are attached to long petioles. The attractive leaves open pinkish bronze, mature
to blue-green, and change to unrivaled combinations of yellow, red, reddish orange, and purple in fall. In late spring and early summer, the tree is
transformed into a smoky cloud when the flowers bloom at the branch
tips. The flowers themselves are yellowish and tiny but are grouped into
multibranched, 6-inch-long heads that are decorated with plumelike,
pinkish gray hairs. Even after the flowers fade or ripen into black seeds,
the hairs grow longer and get showier. It's these long-lasting hairs that
create the smoky show, which is a bit better on male trees and can last for
4 to 6 weeks. The bark is scaly, gray-brown, and attractive in winter. Use
this unusual native for a dramatic effect in a lawn, border, or natural area.
From south-central North America.

HOW TO GROW. Full sun to light shade and moist, well-drained,
sandy to clayey soil. Performs well in alkaline soil and is very drought tolerant. Susceptible to damage during ice storms. Trees will resprout from
stumps cut to the ground. Pest-free. Zones 4b–8b.

CULTIVARS AND SIMILAR SPECIES. *C. coggygria* (smoke tree, smoke
bush), **P. 70,** is a shrub or multitrunked small tree growing 15 to 20 feet
tall; showier, pink, 4- to 10-inch-long clusters of male and female flowers
on the same plant and rounder leaves; hardy in Zones 4a–7b, although it
dies to the ground and resprouts in Zone 4. 'Flame' is a 25-foot-tall hybrid
of the two species with showy pink flowers and scarlet to orange fall
color. 'Grace' is a 20-foot-tall upright hybrid with bronzy pink summer
foliage and deep, iridescent, orange and red fall color. *C. coggygria* var.
purpureus has blue-green leaves and pale pinkish purple flowers. 'Pink
Champagne' has green leaves and showy, light pink flowers. 'Royal Purple' is the darkest hued, with deep black-purple leaves all summer, red fall
color, and burgundy flowers that age to dusty wine-pink. 'Velvet Cloak'

has deep red-violet foliage all summer and red fall color. 'Notcutt's Variety' is similar to 'Royal Purple', but the leaves are slightly redder and not as black; flowers are rose pink.

❦ *Crataegus*

kruh-TEE-gus. Rose family, Rosaceae.

This large genus contains 200 trees and shrubs from woodlands and scrubby areas of the north temperate zones. They usually have thorny branches, simple or lobed alternate leaves, small five-petaled flowers borne in dense clusters, and small applelike berries. Most hawthorns make excellent ornamentals for year-round beauty, especially in the North. Like most rose family members, however, they suffer from many insect and disease problems, including fire blight and cedar-apple rust, a leaf and fruit fungus whose alternate host is the native eastern red cedar (*Juniperus virginiana*). This leaf disease may defoliate susceptible trees in midsummer. Hawthorns and cedars should not be planted near each other. Despite these drawbacks, hawthorns are valued landscape trees because they bloom in late spring after most other trees, and they are especially cold hardy.

C. crus-galli

c. krus-GAL-ee. Cockspur Hawthorn. A spreading tree with dramatic horizontal branches, this small, dense hawthorn grows 15 to 25 feet tall and 20 to 30 feet wide and provides year-round landscape interest. Lacy white flowers with pink anthers bloom in 2- to 3-inch-wide clusters that cloak the tree in late spring along with the young foliage and may have an unpleasant odor at close range. The glossy, wedge-shaped leaves emerge light green, mature to dark green, and turn wine red or scarlet in autumn. The ½-inch, showy berries ripen to dark red in fall and decorate the leafless branches well into winter. Rather lethal-looking, curved, 2-inch or longer thorns arm the branches, although thornless forms are available and preferred for many landscape situations. This tough tree excels in cold, harsh climates, making it an excellent choice for an impenetrable screen or garden border, where it can be grouped to have a strong horizontal impact. Its low-branched shape precludes growing grass or anything but a shade-loving ground cover underneath. From eastern and central North America.

HOW TO GROW. Full sun and any well-drained soil. Withstands urban conditions and air pollution. Fruits are moderately susceptible to rust, but leaves are only slightly affected. Zones 3b–6b.

CULTIVARS AND SIMILAR SPECIES. *C. crus-galli* var. *inermis* is thornless and very resistant to rust. 'Crusader' is denser, growing to 15 feet tall. 'Vaughn' is a hybrid with *C. phaenopyrum;* it has horizontal branches, disease-resistant leaves, and masses of long-lasting orange-red fruits. *C. × lavellei* (Lavalle hawthorn) is an upright hybrid with some-what larger flowers, scarlet-orange fruits that last through the winter, fewer spines, and rust-resistant foliage; Zones 4b–7a.

C. laevigata

P. 71

c. lee-vi-GAH-tah. English Hawthorn. The most commonly planted of all the hawthorns because it blooms so profusely, English hawthorn is a small, rounded, multitrunked tree that grows 15 to 20 feet tall and wide. Flowers bloom in clusters of 5 to 15 blossoms in midspring with the emerging leaves and may be white or shades of pink or red, with pink or purple an-thers. The glossy, 2-inch leaves have a pretty shape—three to five shallow lobes with toothed edges—and don't change color in fall. The dense zigzagging branches are covered with 1-inch-long thorns. Numerous deep red, ½-inch berries ripen in fall but are not long lasting. The showiest hawthorn in bloom, English hawthorn makes a grand statement in a spring and fall border, but it is plagued by disease. From Europe.

HOW TO GROW. Full sun and well-drained soil. Tolerates cold, drought, and clayey soil. Prone to insect and disease problems and sensi-tive to road salt. Provide good air circulation to reduce leaf diseases. Train to a single trunk and prune off lower branches if desired. Zones 5a–7b.

CULTIVARS AND SIMILAR SPECIES. 'Crimson Cloud' ('Superba') has disease-resistant foliage, very large crimson flowers with white cen-ters, and glossy berries. 'Paul's Scarlet' is widely planted and has large, double, rose-crimson flowers and thornless branches; very susceptible to leaf spot. 'Plena' has large, double, white flowers that age to pink; resistant to leaf spot. *C. × mordenensis* is a cold-hardy, thornless hybrid with dou-ble white flowers and sparse scarlet fruits; hardy to Zone 3b. 'Snowbird' is an upright or oval form. 'Toba' has a rounded shape, and the flowers age from white to pink.

C. phaenopyrum (C. cordata)

P. 72

c. core-DAH-tah Washington Hawthorn. Growing into a 20- to 35-foot-tall, rounded or pyramidal specimen, this is the largest and latest-flowering of the hawthorns. Clusters of white flowers with yellowish pink anthers bloom in early summer. New leaves open with a reddish cast, mature to dark green, and turn orange, scarlet, or purple in fall. Individual leaves are 1 to 2 inches long and shallowly cut into three to seven lobes with sharp teeth, like a maple's. The glossy, bright red berries last through the winter, adding interest. Trunk and branches sport very sharp, 3-inch-long thorns. Leaves and fruits of Washington hawthorn are less susceptible to disease than those of other hawthorns. This is the best hawthorn for the South. From eastern North America.

HOW TO GROW. Full sun and any well-drained soil. Does not tolerate road salt. Prune to a single trunk if desired. Rust-resistant leaves. Zones 4b–8b.

CULTIVARS. 'Washington Lustre' has fewer thorns, shinier leaves, and more profuse flowers and fruits than the species. 'Princeton Sentry' grows into an upright tree with very showy fruits and few thorns.

C. viridis   P. 72, 73

c. VEER-ih-dis. Green Hawthorn. This native is a tree for all seasons. Vase shaped when young, it matures into a flat-topped, horizontally spreading specimen that grows to 30 feet tall and wide. A profusion of lacy white flowers with yellow anthers bloom in 2-inch-wide clusters in late spring. The wedge-shaped leaves are 1½ to 3½ inches long. They have a fine texture, a glossy sheen, and scalloped edges, and, unlike those of most hawthorns, they are generally disease-free. Fall color is often scarlet or purple. Small, very persistent, scarlet berries ripen in fall and last most of the winter, making an outstanding color statement against the gray bark of the branches. Thorns are about 1 inch long. Mature trees have rough, flaky trunk bark with orange patches. Use as a small garden tree or in groves where it can be seen in winter. Showiest with an evergreen background.

HOW TO GROW. Full sun and almost any soil, well drained to wet. Tolerates drought, wind, and urban conditions. Thin branches and remove water sprouts when dormant. Provide good air circulation. Usually free of fire blight, leaf spot, and insects, although fruits can become diseased. Good in the Midwest. Zones 5a–9a.

CULTIVARS. 'Winter King' is an award-winning cultivar noted for its profusion of very large, long-lasting, red berries and its strong vase shape.

Davidia

dah-VID-ee-ah. Tupelo family, Nyssaceae.

This genus contains only one species, a lovely tree that is prized as an unusual specimen.

D. involucrata P. 73, 74

d. in-voh-lew-KRAH-tah. Dove Tree, Handkerchief Tree. Growing into an open pyramidal shape, this unique tree reaches 30 to 50 feet tall and is draped with eye-catching flowers in late spring or early summer. Small, round, yellow flowers are clustered together and have two pure white, papery bracts—one 6 to 8 inches long and the other shorter—suggesting the wings of a dove or a fluttering handkerchief. Unfortunately, this smooth, gray-barked tree may bloom well only in alternate years. The 3- to 7-inch-long leaves are matte green and heart shaped, with toothed margins, red stalks, and downy undersides. Fall color is variable, ranging from pastels to fiery shades of red and yellow. Green pearlike fruits, about 1½ inches long, dangle on 3-inch-long stems in summer and fall. Use this tree as a focal point in a lawn, to shade a patio, or in a border or woodland garden. From China.

HOW TO GROW. Partial or light shade and acid, humus-rich, moist, well-drained soil. To reduce storm damage, prune to develop a strong central leader. Zones 6b–8b.

CULTIVARS. *D. involucrata* var. *vilmoriniana* differs from the species in having almost hairless leaves and is more cold hardy, to Zone 6a.

Diospyros

dye-OSS-phir-us. Ebony family, Ebenaceae.

This genus from North America and Asia is known for its edible fall fruits and very strong, beautiful wood. Small blueberry-like flowers and fleshy berries characterize the genus. Native to forests of eastern and central North America, common persimmon is a beloved native that should be preserved in the wild and grown more in landscapes. It is a tough survivor that adapts to urban stress.

D. virginiana P. 74, 75

d. ver-jin-ee-AY-nah Common Persimmon. Forming a symmetrical pyramid when young and becoming craggier with age, common persimmon reaches 60 to 80 feet tall in good, moist soil and is more shrubby where soil is poor. Female flowers are very fragrant, ¾-inch, creamy bells and are borne singly. Male flowers are smaller and bloom in clusters of three, usually on separate trees. Female trees produce 1½-inch, green berries that ripen to orange after frost and cling to the bare limbs after the leaves drop. The fruits eventually fall to the ground, causing a litter problem if not immediately gathered to make persimmon pudding or preserves (two midwestern specialties). They also provide valuable food for wildlife. The bold-textured, dark green leaves are 3- to 5-inch-long, pointed ovals. Fall color varies from glorious to subdued shades of yellow, gold, and red. This deep-rooted tree is easily recognized by its distinctive trunk bark, which is deeply fissured and cracked into a checkerboard pattern. Use common persimmon in reclamation projects, native landscapes, and urban sites where the fruit litter will not be a problem. From eastern and central North America.

HOW TO GROW. Full sun to partial shade. Most vigorous and attractive in rich, moist soil, but tolerates poor soil, flooding, drought, heat, and wind. May be difficult to transplant; choose small balled-and-burlapped or container-grown trees. Leaf spot is troublesome in the South. Zones 5b–9a.

CULTIVARS AND SIMILAR SPECIES. 'Early Golden' has large, sweet fruits. 'Meader' is self-fertile, with early-ripening fruits. 'Male' produces no fruits and will pollinate female trees; use as an urban street tree. *D. kaki* (Oriental persimmon) grows to 30 feet tall and has huge, tasty, orange fruits that ripen in fall after the leaves drop; Zones 7b–9a.

❦ *Elaeagnus*

ee-lee-AG-nuss. Oleaster family, Elaeagnaceae.

Forty-five species make up this genus of evergreen and deciduous trees and shrubs that are closely related to the true olive. Members have tubular, four-petaled flowers; single-seeded, berrylike fruits; and stems and leaves that are often covered with silvery scales and thorns. Several shrubs and one tree are common garden plants valued for their fast growth and silvery foliage. From Europe, Asia, and North America.

E. angustifolia   P. 75, 76

e. an-gus-tih-FOL-ee-ah. Russian Olive, Wild Olive. This small, multitrunked tree can fix its own nitrogen from the soil, which means it flourishes in poor-soil sites. It forms a round, dense crown about 20 feet tall and wide, and its willowy leaves create a beautiful, light-reflecting sight. The 3-inch-long, lance-shaped leaves are gray-green on top and silver gray on the undersides and are borne on thorny, silvery twigs and branches. Small, tubular, creamy yellow flowers hide under the leaves but give off a very sweet fragrance that is hard to miss. The flowers are followed in late summer and fall by silvery scaled, yellow berries that attract birds. Trunk bark is shaggy and dark gray to black. Use this tree as a focal point in a border or mixed planting, or plant it as a screen. Russian olive can become a pest, spreading to wild areas in the western states, so confine it to urban areas away from natural sites.

HOW TO GROW. Full sun and light to sandy, well-drained soil. Tolerates drought, alkaline soil, road salt, and urban and seashore conditions; performs poorly in heat and humidity. Prune when young to create a well-shaped tree. Shorten brittle branches to reduce storm damage. Can be pruned into a dense screen or hedge. Verticillium wilt can be serious if soil is not well drained. Leaf spot, scale, and aphids also are problems. Zones 3a–7b.

CULTIVARS. 'Quicksilver' has extra-silvery foliage. 'King Red' has large burgundy fruits.

❦ *Eucommia*

yew-COH-mee-uh. Eucommia family, Eucommiaceae.

This genus has only one species, which is an effective, but not well-known, shade tree that thrives in tough urban sites.

E. ulmoides   P. 76, 77

e. ul-MOY-deez. Hardy Rubber Tree. This tall, wide-spreading tree grows slowly to 40 to 60 feet tall and ultimately has ascending branches and a vase shape similar to that of American elm. Its glossy, dark green leaves are also elmlike—3- to 5-inch ovals with toothed margins. When broken, the leaves and bark exude a white latex sap, hence the common name. Flowers and fruits are inconspicuous, and fall color is unremarkable, but the tree has a wonderful form and strong, storm-resistant wood, making it an excellent candidate for shading streets, parking lots, and other public areas. From southwestern China.

HOW TO GROW. Full sun and almost any well-drained soil, from sandy to heavy, acid to alkaline. Tolerates heat, drought, and urban con-

ditions, but is very sensitive to poorly drained soil. Pest-free and needs no
regular pruning. Zones 5b–8b.

CULTIVARS. None.

❦ *Fagus*

FAY-gus. Beech family, Fagaceae.

Ten tree species from the north temperate regions belong to this genus.
All have smooth gray bark, very pointed leaf buds, pointed oval leaves
with smooth or toothed edges, and triangular edible nuts borne in spiny
husks, which provide food for wildlife. Flowers are not showy. European
beech is one of the most stately shade trees. Old, magnificent specimens
often adorn estates, parks, and campuses.

F. sylvatica   P. 77, 78

f. gran-dih-FOH-lee-ah. European Beech. As a lawn or landscape specimen,
this long-lived, majestic tree grows slowly to 50 to 60 feet tall and 35 to 45
feet wide, forming a beautiful rounded pyramid that is quite striking if
the lower limbs are left to sweep to the ground. The leaves are arrow
shaped, with smooth, undulating edges. They unfold in spring a lovely
silvery green, mature in summer to glossy dark green, and turn a warm
golden brown in autumn. Leaves sometimes remain on the tree through
the winter, turning alluring shades of buff or apricot. Mature trees have
massive trunks and branches cloaked in smooth, silver gray bark, making
a dramatic silhouette in winter. Use this big tree in a lawn where it has
plenty of room to mature. It has shallow roots and casts so much shade
that grass will not grow underneath it, but mulch or bare ground is fine,
especially if lower limbs are present. From central Europe.

HOW TO GROW. Full sun to partial shade and moist, well-drained,
acid soil. Somewhat drought tolerant. Train to a single leader to prevent
breakage from multiple leaders. Leave lower branches on to create a
rounded form or prune them to show off the trunk. Prune when dormant. Leaf spot, mildew, canker, scale, and beech bark disease can be
problems. Zones 5a–8b.

CULTIVARS AND SIMILAR SPECIES. *F. sylvatica purpurea* are seed-
grown, purple-leaved forms with variable color. 'Asplenifolia' (fernleaf
beech) has delicately cut leaves. 'Dawyck' ('Fastigiata') is columnar, growing to 60 feet tall and 30 feet wide. 'Dawyck Purple' is columnar, with purple leaves. 'Dawyck Gold' features golden leaves and a narrow columnar

shape. 'Pendula' is a glorious weeping tree that grows to 60 feet tall. 'Riversii' (purple or copper beech) has dark purple leaves all summer. 'Purpurea Pendula' is a purple-leaved weeping form without a central leader; it reaches only 10 feet tall unless grafted high. 'Tricolor' ('Roseo-marginata') has bright rosy red new growth that matures to purple with pink and creamy white variegations; reaches 30 feet tall. 'Rohanii' resembles 'Riversii', but with ferny leaves. *F. grandifolia* (American beech) is a similar native tree with blue-green toothed leaves, lighter gray bark, and light yellow to golden bronze fall color; it deserves wider use in landscapes, especially in the South, but is not drought tolerant; Zones 4a–9a.

Franklinia

frank-LYN-ee-ah. Tea family, Theaceae.

Only one species belongs to this genus, which is related to *Stewartia*. It is a native America tree last seen in the wild in 1803. John Bartram, a botanist from Philadelphia, collected the tree in 1765 in Georgia and named it after Benjamin Franklin. All known specimens are believed to be descendants of the tree he collected.

F. alatamaha (Gordonia alatamaha) **P. 78, 79**

f. al-ah-tah-MAH-ha Franklinia, Franklin Tree. This graceful, multitrunked tree forms an open pyramid or oval and grows 20 to 30 feet tall and half as wide. The narrow, 6-inch-long leaves are glossy green all summer and turn a rich wine red and gold in autumn. Unusual among trees, franklinia blooms in late summer and fall. Its 3-inch-wide, white, camellia-like flowers open from pearl-like buds when the foliage is still green, and new flowers continue to open even after the leaves have taken on their glorious fall colors. This stunning combination of flowers and fall colors has no equal. The slender trunks and branches have a sinewy shape and are covered with dark gray bark marked with white striations. Use this eye-catching tree in a border or woodland or to cast light shade on a patio, where its silhouette and fall flowers can be readily admired.

HOW TO GROW. Flowers best in full sun, but performs well in light shade. Needs humus-rich, well-drained, acid soil and plentiful moisture, especially in a sunny site. May be finicky if soil conditions are not right. Can suffer from drought or from root rot in a poorly drained site. Needs no pruning and is usually pest-free. Zones 6b–7b.

CULTIVARS. None.

❦ *Fraxinus*

FRAX-in-us. Olive family, Oleaceae.

Sixty-five species of woodland trees from North America, Europe, and Asia make up this genus. Leaves are opposite and pinnately compound. Flowers are usually not showy and are borne in clusters in spring or summer. Fruits are single-seeded, winged structures and can be messy. Several species are planted as handsome, fast-growing shade trees. Seedless forms are preferred for most landscape situations.

F. americana P. 79

f. am-AIR-ih-kan-ah. White Ash. Pyramidal or oval when young, this fast-growing but strong-wooded tree becomes rounded with age, maturing to 50 to 80 feet tall and wide. Leaves emerge in late spring and are made up of five to nine dark blue-green, sparsely toothed, oval leaflets with white undersides. Fall color develops early and is vivid, including combinations of yellow, orange, and maroon, with the brighter colors usually occurring toward the tree's interior. Flowers are inconspicuous. Female trees produce clusters of 1-inch-long, winged seeds that ripen from green to tan and make a mess when they drop. Seedless cultivars are available. This tree has a more attractive fall color than green ash, but it is not as adaptable to poor soil and is more vulnerable to ash yellows disease. Trunk bark is ash gray with diamond-shaped furrows. Use seedless forms as lawn, park, or street trees where there's plenty of growing room. From eastern and central North America.

HOW TO GROW. Full sun and deep, moist soil. Tolerates brief flooding and slight drought. Leaf rust, leaf spot, borers, and fall webworms may be troublesome. Dieback (ash yellows) may be serious. Anthracnose disfigures leaves in wet years. Frost cracking can be a problem in exposed sites in cold-winter areas. Prune when young for a strong shape to prevent storm damage. Zones 4a–9a.

CULTIVARS AND SIMILAR SPECIES. 'Autumn Applause' is a seedless, compact tree with smaller leaves that turn deep red or mahogany in fall. 'Autumn Blaze' is more drought tolerant; good in the northern Plains. 'Autumn Purple' is seedless and exhibits deep purple fall color. 'Champaign County' is seedless and dense, with bronze fall color; good in the South. 'Chicago Regal' is a symmetrical oval, with excellent fall color. 'Greenspire' is narrow and upright. 'Rosehill' is a seedless, disease-resistant, broad-spreading tree with fiery bronze-red fall color; good in the South. 'Royal Purple' ('Elk Grove') has purple fall color and is hardy in

Zone 3b. 'Skyline' is a seedless, rounded tree with orange-red fall color. 'Sparticus' has longer-lasting, deep burgundy fall color and a sturdy, uniform pyramidal shape. 'Windy City' is seedless and resists frost cracking. *F. quadrangulata* (blue ash) is a similar native tree with corky twigs; it tolerates drought and alkaline soil; excellent in the northern Plains.

F. pennsylvanica   P. 80

f. pen-sil-VAHN-eh-kah Green Ash, Red Ash. This fast-growing shade tree is narrowly pyramidal with ascending branches when young, but it matures to an upright, spreading, 50- to 60-foot-tall-and-wide tree. The handsome, shiny, dark yellowish green leaves are made up of five to nine pointed, narrow leaflets with jagged edges. In early fall, the foliage turns very bright yellow. Flowers develop into clusters of single-seeded green fruits, which cause a litter and weed seedling problem. Nonseeding male cultivars are available. Green ash has an overall coarse texture, with strong, bold branching and ash gray, furrowed bark. Use the species for reclamation projects and seedless cultivars as shade trees for houses, parks, or streets in areas where cold, poor soil, drought, or flooding preclude the use of other large trees. From eastern and central North America.

HOW TO GROW. Full sun and almost any soil. Tolerates infertile or alkaline soil, drought, intermittent flooding, and salt. Excellent in the Plains and Midwest. Prune in winter to train to a single leader and develop a strong branch structure. Remove lower limbs as the tree matures. Zones 2a–9a.

CULTIVARS AND SIMILAR SPECIES. *These are all seedless.* 'Emerald' has long-lasting, golden yellow fall color and adapts to hot, dry climates. 'Foothills' is especially cold hardy. 'Lednaw' is columnar, growing to 30 feet tall. 'Marshall's Seedless' is identical to the species, except that it usually lacks seeds. The most widely planted form, 'Newport', is an excellent oval tree with a strong central trunk. 'Patmore' has a uniform oval shape with a strong central leader; shiny, dark green leaves; disease resistant. 'Prairie Spire' forms a narrow pyramid. 'Summit' is pyramidal, with golden yellow fall color. 'Urbanite' is pyramidal and especially tolerant of urban settings; thick, shiny, injury-resistant young bark tolerates sunscald; Zones 5b–9a. *F. excelsior* (European ash) has 9 to 11 leaflets and yellow-green late-fall color; popular in the Pacific Northwest; Zones 5a–8a. 'Aureafolia' has yellow summer foliage. 'Hessii' is a vigorous-growing form with undivided leaves. *F. veluntina* (velvet ash) may be a smaller form of green ash that is native to the Southwest; adapts well to alkaline soil, drought, and poor drainage; Zones 7a–10b.

❦ Ginkgo

GINK-goe. Ginkgo family, Ginkgoaceae.

This species is the only member of its genus and family and is sometimes called a living fossil, because its ancestors inhabited the Earth during the Paleozoic era, 225 million to 280 million years ago. Now thought to be extinct in the wild, the tree, valued by Buddhist monks, was preserved in temple gardens in China and thus carried through the eons as a garden plant. Today it is a popular lawn and urban tree.

G. biloba   P. 80

g. bye-LOH-bah. Ginkgo, Maidenhair Tree. Varying from pyramidal to broad and spreading when grown from seed, ginkgo matures to 80 or more feet tall and 30 to 80 feet wide, with an open, airy framework that casts only light shade despite its size. It is rather sparse and gaunt when young but grows into magnificent maturity, with massive branches and trunks. Branches of this long-lived tree are strongly horizontal, with short spurs that hold eye-catching, bright green, fan-shaped, 2- to 4-inch-wide leaves that resemble leaflets of maidenhair fern. Fall color is a brilliant clear yellow; it develops in late fall and is not long lasting. Trunk bark is pale gray and rough. Male and female flowers are borne on separate trees, but trees may not flower until they are 10 to 20 years old. Female trees, if pollinated, develop flesh-covered edible nuts that drop in fall and create a mess. The fruits quickly become malodorous if left to decay. Plant male cultivars in lawns and parks where they have plenty of space to mature. Narrower forms make useful urban street trees. From China.

HOW TO GROW. Full sun to partial shade and deep, well-drained, acid or alkaline soil. Tolerates road salt, air pollution, drought, and heat, but does not tolerate poorly drained sites. Prune in late winter to a single trunk with strong scaffold branches. Pest-free. Zones 4b–8b.

CULTIVARS. *These are all nonfruiting.* 'Autumn Gold' is broadly conical with excellent golden fall color. 'Lakeview' has a narrow, pyramidal shape. 'Magyar' is pyramidal with upright branching. 'Princeton Sentry' is columnar, growing to 15 feet wide. 'Mayfield' is very narrow. 'Saratoga' forms a broad, dense cone with weeping branches; grows to 20 feet tall; common in the Pacific Northwest. 'Shangri-la' is a fast-growing, compact pyramid. 'The President' is upright. 'Woodstock' has a strong central leader and a uniform, oval shape.

❦ *Gleditsia*

gleh-DIT-see-ah. Pea family, Fabaceae.

Hailing from Asia, North and South America, and Africa, the 14 trees in this genus are thorny and have feathery, pinnately compound leaves and beanlike seedpods. The genus contains only one garden tree, a North American native, which is popular because of the dappled shade it casts.

G. triacanthos var. *inermis*   P. 81

g. tri-ah-KAN-thoss in-ERR-miss. Thornless Honey Locust. Broadly spreading with horizontal branches, this elegant, fast-growing tree reaches 35 to 70 feet tall and wide. Foliage is delicate and lacy, consisting of compound leaves divided into twenty to thirty ½- to 1-inch-long, lance-shaped, bright green leaflets. Leaves are divided twice on young, vigorous trees; once on mature trees. Fall color is a pleasing yellow. Leaflets are so small when they drop in fall that they require little cleanup. By contrast, the 12-inch-long, twisted, dark brown seedpods are a nuisance when they drop in early winter. Clusters of inconspicuous greenish flowers bloom in spring and have a sweet, intense fragrance. Vicious, branched, 3- to 6-inch-long thorns arm the trunk and branches of the species, but this variety and most cultivars are thornless and seedless. Honey locust is a valued landscape tree because it casts light shade and does not have competitive roots, so lawn and garden plants thrive under it. Use it to shade a patio or garden, as a street tree, or in groups to create light shade. From southeastern and south-central North America.

HOW TO GROW. Full sun. Adapts to almost any soil, wet or dry, but does best in rich, moist soil with a pH of 6 to 8. Tolerates drought and road salt. Insects and diseases can be serious problems. Webworms, spider mites, and borers are common, as are leaf spot, mildew, and rust. Performs poorly in the heat and humidity of the Southeast. Zones 4b–9a.

CULTIVARS. These are all thornless and mostly seedless. 'Christie' is fast growing and rounded, with horizontal branches. 'Continental' is narrow, with large leaves. 'Halka' is very vigorous and fast growing, with horizontal branches. 'Imperial' is compact and rounded or spreading, with dainty leaves. 'Moraine' has dark green leaves, is vase shaped, and has excellent resistance to webworms. 'Shademaster' has dark green leaves, a vase shape with slightly pendulous branches, and a straight trunk. 'Ruby Lace' has ruby red new growth that turns bronze-green in summer; susceptible to webworms. 'Skyline' has dark green leaves, a broad pyramidal shape with a straight trunk, and golden fall color. 'Spectrum' has bright gold leaves in spring and summer and a rounded form with strong branches. 'Summer Lace' is tall and has light green new growth maturing to dark green. 'Sunburst' has bright yellow new growth at the branch tips all summer and yellow-green older leaves; has a broad, pyramidal, irregular shape; susceptible to webworms. 'True Shade' is rounded, with upright branches, and has golden fall color.

🍂 *Gymnocladus*

gym-know-CLAY-duss. Pea family, Fabaceae.

Closely related to *Gleditsia,* this genus of trees with compound leaves contains several species from eastern Asia and one from North America. Only the native species is grown here as an ornamental.

G. dioica   P. 82, 83

g. dye-OH-eh-kah. Kentucky Coffee Tree. A tough tree for difficult, drought-prone sites, Kentucky coffee tree possesses a craggy oval form, silvery twigs, and ascending branches. It reaches 50 to 70 feet tall and 40 to 50 feet wide. Leaves are doubly compound, measuring up to 3 feet long and 2 feet wide, and consist of a hundred or more 2- to 4-inch-long, pointed leaflets. The pinkish purple leaflets unfold in late spring after most other trees have leafed out, mature to dark blue-green in summer, and turn pastel yellow in autumn. Showy, 12-inch-long panicles of fluffy, greenish white, fragrant flowers bloom on female trees in spring. Male trees have smaller flowers. Six-inch-long, wide, reddish brown seedpods containing large seeds develop on female trees and hang on through the winter. The seeds are poisonous when raw, but European colonists roasted them and used them like coffee. Trunk bark is dark brown and deeply furrowed, with curled ridges. Use this bold, picturesque tree for shade on large properties where its messy habits will not be a problem and its lovely silhouette can be viewed against the sky. Excellent in a pasture or meadow. From southeastern and midwestern North America.

HOW TO GROW. Full sun and humus-rich, moist soil. Tolerates drought and occasional wetness. Adapts to urban conditions and a soil pH of 6 to 8. Train to a strong branch structure when young. Prune in summer to avoid bleeding sap. Pest-free. Zones 3b–8a.

CULTIVARS. 'Espresso' is vase shaped and seedless. 'Prairie Titan' is pyramidal, vigorous, and seedless.

🌱 *Halesia*

HAIL-zee-ah. Styrax family, Styracaceae.

This genus contains five trees and shrubs from North America and China. All have white, bell-shaped flowers in spring; dry, silvery, winged seed capsules; and alternate, toothed leaves.

H. carolina (H. tetraptera) P. 83, 84

h. kare-oh-lyn-ee-AY-nah. Carolina Silverbell. This charming spring bloomer has a broad, rounded shape with low, horizontal or ascending branches and several trunks. It reaches 20 to 30 feet tall and 35 feet wide. Bell-shaped, 1-inch-long, snow-white blossoms dangle in delicate clusters from the undersides of the tree's branches for 2 weeks in mid- to late spring. The dark yellow-green, oval leaves have pointed tips and measure 4 inches long. Fall color develops early and is a pleasing yellow. Two-inch-long fruits have four wings and are subtle but pretty in fall, ripening from green to tan. Trunk bark has white furrows and gray-brown plates. Use this graceful tree at the edge of a woodland, as an understory tree in a shade garden, or in a patio or border. Beautiful when planted on a hillside and viewed from below. From southeastern North America.

HOW TO GROW. Full sun to partial shade and humus-rich, well-drained, acid soil and plentiful moisture, especially in the sun. Sensitive to drought; benefits from an organic mulch. Prune immediately after flowering, removing lower limbs and training to a single trunk when young if desired. Pest-free, but becomes chlorotic in alkaline soil. Zones 5a–9a.

CULTIVARS AND SIMILAR SPECIES. 'Rosea' is pink flowered and hard to find. *H. diptera* (two-winged silverbell) flowers 2 weeks later than *H. carolina* and has two-winged seeds. 'Magniflora' has large, showy flowers. *H. monticola* (mountain snowbell) is very similar to *H. carolina* but grows to 60 feet, has larger flowers and leaves and a strong central leader.

🌱 *Juglans*

JEW-glanz. Walnut family, Juglandaceae.

The trees of this genus are closely related to hickories. They have large, pinnately compound, alternate leaves and male and female flowers on the same tree. Some species have edible nuts and are valued for their wood. Members of this genus, especially black walnut and butternut, exude a toxic chemical called juglone from their roots which inhibits the growth of some plants. Grass grows well near walnut trees, but many garden plants, such as asparagus, tomatoes, potatoes, eggplant, blueberries, mountain laurel, red pine, apples, rhododendrons, azaleas, hydrangeas, peonies, chrysanthemums, and columbines do not. The area of toxicity usually extends within a radius of 50 to 60 feet from the trunk, but it can extend up to 80 feet. Leaves contain lower concentrations of the toxin and can be composted and used in the garden, because the toxin breaks down quickly when exposed to air and water. Bark and wood chips need to be aged for 6 months before garden use.

J. nigra
P. 84

j. NYE-grah. Black Walnut. A tall native with a wide-spreading, ruggedly picturesque outline, black walnut grows to 75 feet tall and almost as wide. Dark green leaves emerge in late spring and are divided like large feathers into pointed, 5-inch-long leaflets. They lack a terminal leaflet, are aromatic when crushed, and turn yellowish in late summer or early fall before dropping. Leaves fall apart and pose little cleanup problem, although the long central rachis (leaf stem) must be raked up. Edible nuts enclosed in green, 2-inch, round husks drop in autumn, posing a hazard and a cleanup problem if the tree is near a walkway, driveway, or lawn. The nuts are valued food for people and wildlife, but the husks are hard to remove and can stain hands and clothing. Trunk bark is brown and thickly furrowed. The beautiful, fine-grained wood is valued for furniture making. Save native trees in a natural landscape and locate young trees in a large field, pasture, park, or open lawn, where they will hold the soil and provide light shade. From eastern and central North America.

HOW TO GROW. Full sun and deep, rich, moist soil. Tolerates somewhat drier sites. Zones 4b–9a.

CULTIVARS AND SIMILAR SPECIES. *J. cinerea* (butternut) is similar, but its leaves have a terminal leaflet and it is more cold hardy; Zones 3b–7a. *J. regia* (English walnut) is a smaller tree grown commercially for its easier-to-shell nuts; Zones 7a and 7b. 'Carpathian' is hardy in Zone 6a.

❦ Koelreuteria

kohl-rue-TEAR-ee-ah. Soapberry family, Sapindaceae.

This small genus is made up of four or five species from Asia. These trees are characterized by their showy yellow blossoms, pinnately or bipinnately compound leaves, and papery seedpods. Though not pests, some species have reseeded and naturalized in some parts of the country.

K. paniculata   P. 85

k. pan-ick-yew-LAY-tah. Goldenrain Tree. This large flowering tree forms a rounded crown and reaches 30 to 40 feet tall and wide. Airy, 15-inch-long panicles of tiny, starlike, yellow blossoms bloom at the branch tips for several weeks in mid- to late summer. Clusters of 1- to 2-inch seedpods ripen from green to pinkish tan in fall, resembling Japanese lanterns. The large, compound leaves emerge with a pinkish or reddish purple tinge and become bright green in summer, changing to variable shades of orange, gold, and yellow in autumn. Made up of 7 to 17 leaflets with deeply jagged lobes, the 15-inch-long leaves have a bold, exotic texture. Goldenrain tree makes a fine shade tree for a lawn or patio or a good street tree away from power lines or near the seashore. From China, Japan, and Korea.

HOW TO GROW. Full sun and almost any well-drained soil, including alkaline soil. Tolerates drought, heat, road salt, and urban conditions. The numerous seeds can cause a weed seedling problem if the tree is sited near a garden bed; best in a lawn where seedlings can be mown. Prune when dormant to develop a strong branch structure and to remove lower limbs that may die naturally from lack of light. May be weak wooded if not properly pruned. Usually pest-free. Zones 5a–9a.

CULTIVARS AND SIMILAR SPECIES. 'Rose Lantern' blooms late and has rose pink seedpods. 'September' ('September Gold') has larger flowers and blooms later than the species, in late summer or early fall; Zones 6a–9a. *K. bipinnata* (Chinese goldenrain tree) grows larger and has more delicate-looking foliage, with 50 unlobed leaflets; flowers are not as showy and bloom in late summer; seedpods are a showy pink; Zones 7–9.

❦ *Laburnum*

lah-BURR-num. Bean family, Fabaceae.

The two small European trees that make up this genus feature clusters of yellow flowers, trifoliate leaves, and narrow seedpods. All plant parts, especially the seeds, are poisonous if eaten. A very showy hybrid of the two species is grown most frequently.

L. × watereri

P. 86

l. × WAT-err-err-eye. Golden Chain Tree, Waterer Laburnum. This small, spring-blooming tree, a showy hybrid of *L. anagyroides* and *L. alpinum*, has a stiff, upright or oval form and grows to 15 feet tall and 12 feet wide. It's a gorgeous sight for two weeks in late spring and early summer when decked out with its 12-inch-long or longer, wisteria-like chains of golden yellow flowers. Leaves are bright green and dainty, made up of three pointed, 3-inch leaflets, which close up at night. Leaves drop in fall with little color change. Bark on new shoots, trunk, and branches is smooth and olive green—a lovely addition to the winter landscape. Produces few seedpods. This tree is often short-lived, but it is worth planting in a spring border or foundation planting, where it will garner a lot of attention.

HOW TO GROW. Full sun with light afternoon shade in hot climates; best where summers are cool. Likes humus-rich, moist, well-drained soil; tolerates alkaline soil. Protect from wind and full sun in winter. Prune in summer (to avoid bleeding sap) to develop a main leader. Twig blight, aphids, and mealybugs can be troublesome. Zones 6a–7b; Zone 8 where summers are cool.

CULTIVARS AND SIMILAR SPECIES. 'Vossii' is the most widely grown cultivar because of its 2-foot-long flower clusters. *L. alpinum* (Scotch laburnum) has 10- to 16-inch-long flower clusters in early summer, shiny green leaves, and shiny seedpods. 'Pendulum' is a weeping, 10-foot-tall form with 1-foot-long flower clusters. *L. anagyroides* (common laburnum) has 6- to 12-inch-long flower clusters in late spring, matte green leaves, and hairy round seedpods.

❧ Lagerstroemia

lay-gurr-STREE-meee-ah. Loosestrife family, Lythraceae.

This genus of at least 35 trees and shrubs, mostly from tropical Asia, offers several outstanding flowering trees for southern landscapes. The species described here is an extremely popular landscape plant in the Deep South, along the Gulf Coast, and in California. Recent hybrids made at the National Arboretum have extended the hardiness range and increased the disease resistance of this remarkable tree.

L. indica

P. 87

l. IN-dih-kah. Crape Myrtle. A tree for all seasons, crape myrtle forms a multitrunked, upright or spreading specimen that reaches 15 to 25 feet tall and half as wide. Sumptuous, 6- to 20-inch-long clusters of pink, purple, lavender, or white flowers with crinkled petals and yellow markings bloom from early summer to fall, depending on the cultivar. The shiny, oval leaves are 1 to 3 inches long and arranged in whorls of three. They emerge with a reddish tinge and turn deep green in summer. Fall color is superb, including light-reflecting combinations of yellow, gold, scarlet, orange, maroon, and red. The attractive trunk bark of the species peels to reveal a gray-and-cream patchwork in trees 3 to 5 years old. Hybrids have orange-and-cinnamon-brown-mottled bark. Locate this outstanding tree in a border or foundation planting where it can be seen throughout the year. Or use it to shade a patio or as a street tree under power lines. Excellent planted in groups or allées. From China, Korea, and India.

HOW TO GROW. Full sun to partial shade; flowers best in sun. Needs moist, well-drained, loamy or clayey soil with a pH of 5 to 6.5. Tolerates heat and drought once established. Train to several strong trunks. Withstands heavy pruning and blooms on new growth. Can be cut to the ground and treated as a shrub where winter cold kills the tops, but do not head back branches to stumps, which will turn this lovely tree into an unattractive lollipop. Clip off faded blossoms to encourage repeat bloom through the summer and fall. Older types suffer from mildew, aphids, and black soot fungus; hybrids are immune to powdery mildew. Zones 7b–9a.

CULTIVARS AND SIMILAR SPECIES. 'Centennial Spirit' has dark rose-red flowers and an upright form. 'Near East' has unique peach flowers and a loose, irregular growth habit. 'Potomac' has medium pink flowers, orange fall color, and an excellent form. 'Regal Red' has dark rose-red blossoms, red-orange fall color, and a broad shape. 'Seminole' has medium pink flowers and yellow fall color, grows to 15 feet tall, and is mildew resistant. 'Twilight' has heavy clusters of purple blossoms; a vigorous grower. Hybrids of *L. indica* and *L. fauriei*, a rarely grown white-flowered species, are extremely popular, mildew-resistant plants with excellent bark and flowers; they are top hardy in Zones 7a–9a and root hardy in Zone 6. Dwarf and semidwarf types are shrubs. *Intermediate trees (12 to 20 feet tall):* 'Apalachee' is columnar, with light lavender blossoms, cinnamon brown bark, and orange fall color. 'Osage' is broadly rounded, with light pink reblooming flowers, chestnut brown bark, and red fall color. 'Sioux' has a tight vase shape, medium pink blossoms, and intense red fall color. 'Tuskegee' has dark red-pink flowers, tan-and-gray-mottled bark, orange-red fall color, and horizontal branches. *Tall trees (20 to 35 feet tall):* 'Biloxi' has an open vase shape, pale pink flowers, brown-mottled bark, and orange-red fall color. 'Miami' has dark coral pink flowers, dark chestnut brown bark, and red-orange fall color.

'Muskogee' is a spreading type with light lavender-pink flowers, gray-and-tan-mottled bark, and bright red-orange fall color. 'Natchez' has a broad shape, reblooming white flowers, cinnamon brown–mottled bark, and orange and red fall color.

❦ *Liquidambar*

lick-wid-AM-bar. Witch hazel family, Hamamelidaceae.

Four species of tall trees belong to this genus, which is characterized by aromatic, star-shaped leaves; inconspicuous flowers; and spiky, dry seed balls. Juice or gum from these trees has been used as perfume, incense, and chewing gum. The species native to North America makes an excellent shade tree renowned for its long-lasting fall foliage.

L. styraciflua   P. 88

l. stye-rah-sih-FLEW-ah. Sweet Gum, Gum Tree. Named after the aromatic gummy resin that bleeds from its wounded bark, sweet gum forms a narrow pyramid with slightly pendulous branches when young and changes to a rounded tree with a tall, straight trunk and massive branches when mature. It grows 65 to 70 feet tall and 40 to 50 feet wide. The star-shaped, glossy, dark green leaves measure 7 inches long and have five to seven pointed lobes. Fall color develops late and is a combination of yellow, scarlet, and deep purple, with the brightest hues on the tree's interior. Trunk bark is deeply furrowed; twigs are silvery and often feature corky ridges. Fruits are round, spiny, 1-inch-wide, tan seed heads that remain on the tree through the winter and drop in spring, creating a bit of a mess. Use this attractive tree to shade a house, park, or street. Reduce cleanup by planting a ground cover to absorb the fruits, or choose a fruitless form. From eastern and central North America.

HOW TO GROW. Full sun to partial shade and humus-rich, moist soil with a pH of 7.5 or lower. Tolerates drought and poorly drained soil. Needs little or no pruning to develop a strong branch structure; remove lower limbs if desired. Usually pest-free. Larvae of the luna moth feed on the leaves. Zones 5b–9a.

CULTIVARS. 'Burgundy' forms a wide column and has long-lasting, deep purplish red fall leaves, which can remain on the tree into early winter. 'Corky' is an upright, fruitless form with very corky young branches. 'Festival' has a narrow shape and apricot, peach, and red fall color; Zones 6a–9a. 'Gold Dust' ('Variegata') has bright gold-and-green-variegated leaves and pink and wine-red fall color; Zones 5a–9a. 'Palo Alto' is pyramidal, with orange-red fall color; Zones 6a–9a. 'Moraine' is pyramidal, with burgundy fall color; Zones 5b–9a. 'Rotundiloba' is narrowly pyramidal and fruitless; unusual round-lobed leaves; yellow and purple late-fall color; Zones 6b–9a. 'Worpelsdon' has rich purple, orange, and yellow fall color; noncorky twigs; and multilobed leaves.

❦ *Liriodendron*

lear-ee-oh-DEN-dron. Magnolia family, Magnoliaceae.

Two species belong to this genus, one from Asia and one from North America. The North American species is a noble tree of the eastern forests—perhaps the tallest native tree east of the Mississippi, reaching 200 feet tall in the forest. Although this is a common landscape tree, the Asian species is rare.

L. tulipifera   P. 89

l. too-lip-IF-er-ah. Tulip Tree, Yellow Poplar. This magnificent tree is pyramidal when young but becomes towering and wide spreading when mature, with a massive trunk and several large, outstretched branches high on the trunk. It grows 70 to 90 feet tall and 35 to 50 feet wide. Leaves measure 3 to 5 inches across and have an unusual blocky shape, with shallow lobes. Borne on long stems, they flutter in the wind. They are bright yellow-green in spring, dark green in summer, and vibrant yellow in late autumn. In late spring, the 2-inch, upright flowers, which are reminiscent of tulips, bloom at the branch tips. Their orange-marked, yellowish green petals attract hummingbirds. Although the flowers are quite pretty, they are not profuse enough to put on a show, and because they bloom high up in the tree, they are easy to overlook. Conelike seedpods develop in fall but are not noteworthy. Trunk bark is gray-brown and furrowed. This is a good-looking shade tree for a large property or a natural landscape. From eastern and central North America.

HOW TO GROW. Full sun to partial shade and humus-rich, deep, well-drained soil. Best with plentiful moisture, especially when young; not very drought tolerant. Train to a strong central leader; trees with multiple leaders are prone to storm damage. Aphids and associated sooty mold may be a nuisance. Zones 5a–9a.

CULTIVARS AND SIMILAR SPECIES. 'Majestic Beauty' ('Aureomarginatum') has smaller leaves with wide, bright golden green margins in spring, turning solid green by midsummer. 'Arnold' ('Fastigiatum') is narrow, with upright branches. *L. chinense* (Chinese tulip tree) has greenish flowers and 10-inch-long or longer, deeply lobed leaves with pinched "waists" and pale undersides; grows to 60 feet; Zones 6b–8b.

❦ *Maackia*

MACK-ee-ah. Pea family, Fabaceae.

This genus from eastern Asia contains about eight tree species, which are closely related to *Cladrastis*, another genus of summer-blooming trees.

M. amurensis   P. 90

m. am-ore-EN-siss. Amur Maackia. This little-known tree grows 20 to 35 feet tall and 25 to 50 feet wide, with a rounded, spreading shape. It deserves wider planting, especially as a street tree. Eight-inch-long, upright flower clusters appear at the branch tips in late summer. They consist of small, creamy white, blue-marked, pealike blossoms with a pleasant grassy fragrance. The compound, gray-green to dark olive green leaves are 8 to 12 inches long and made up of seven to eleven 1- to 3-inch-long, oval, pinnate leaflets with smooth margins. Foliage drops with little color change in fall. The shiny, bright amber bark peels off in attractive curls all year. Flat, 2- to 3-inch-long seedpods develop in autumn. Use this species as a street or urban tree in a tough site or enjoy it in your yard as an easy-care shade tree. From Manchuria, Korea, and Japan.

HOW TO GROW. Full sun and any well-drained soil, light to heavy, acid to alkaline; grows best in moist loam. Very drought tolerant. When using it as a street tree, remove lower limbs when young to allow traffic to pass beneath the tree as it ages. Large pruning cuts are slow to heal. Zones 3a–7b.

CULTIVARS AND SIMILAR SPECIES. 'Starburst' has especially showy flowers. *M. chinensis* (Chinese maackia), P. 90, is a similar, showier, smaller tree with silvery new leaves; often mislabeled and sold as *M. amurensis;* Zones 4a–7b.

❦ *Magnolia*

mag-KNOW-lee-ah. Magnolia family, Magnoliaceae.

This large, ancient genus of deciduous and evergreen trees and shrubs contains 80 to 100 species from Asia and North America. Most produce exquisite, many-petaled flowers with clusters of stamens and pistils in the center and handsome foliage. Buds are often silvery, furry, and quite attractive. Fruits are coblike seedpods with red seeds and can be eye-catching in autumn. Many species and hybrids are favorite garden trees. The Asian species usually bloom on bare branches in late winter or early spring, making them among the first trees to bloom. The North American species bloom in summer. (For the evergreen species, see page 307.) Magnolias are somewhat difficult to transplant because of their wide-spreading roots. Container-grown trees planted in spring do better than balled-and-burlapped ones. All prefer mulched, undisturbed soil.

M. acuminata P. 91

m. ah-kew-min-NAY-tah. Cucumber Tree. One of the tallest deciduous magnolias, this pyramidal tree becomes wide spreading with age and reaches 80 feet tall and 60 feet wide. The 3-inch-wide, greenish yellow flowers (brighter yellow in the cultivars) are sprinkled all over the branch tips in late spring and early summer. These flowers develop into upright green fruits that look like cucumbers and turn deep pink in autumn. They provide food for wildlife. Leaves are somewhat heart shaped, measuring up to 10 inches long and half as wide, with a pointed tip and wavy edges. They are dark yellow-green on top and light green on the undersides and may turn pale yellow in late fall. Bark is smooth and gray when young, with the lower trunk becoming ridged and brown with age. This great-looking, cold-hardy tree is an excellent shade tree for a lawn or park. From eastern North America.

HOW TO GROW. Full sun to partial shade and deep, loamy, slightly acid soil. Keep moist and mulched after transplanting. Does not tolerate drought or excessive moisture. Prune when young to develop a strong structure; pruning wounds do not heal readily. Zones 4a–8b.

CULTIVARS AND SIMILAR SPECIES. *M. acuminata* var. *subcordata* (yellow cucumber tree) is smaller and features very pretty, canary yellow flowers. 'Golden Glow' has bright yellow flowers. 'Elizabeth' is a very showy hybrid of *M. acuminata* var. *subcordata* and *M. denudata;* has 7-inch, creamy yellow flowers on bare branches in late spring; resembles a pale yellow–flowered, 15- to 20-foot-tall saucer magnolia; Zones 5b–8b. 'Butterflies' has 4- to 5-inch butter yellow flowers. 'Yellow Bird' has later, bright yellow blossoms. *M. macrophylla* (bigleaf magnolia), from the Southeast, grows 30 to 40 feet tall; huge, oblong, tropical-looking leaves up to 3 feet long; fragrant, white, dark-centered, 8- to 20-inch-wide flowers; Zones 5b–9a.

M. liliiflora (M. quinquepeta)   P. 91

m. lil-ih-FLOR-ah. Lily-Flowered Magnolia. This multistemmed magnolia
grows to 12 feet tall and wide and blooms in mid- to late spring (later
than most deciduous Asian magnolias) as the leaves are unfolding. It
bears 4-inch-wide flowers with six slender petals that are white inside and
purple outside. Leaves are oval and pointed, dark green on top and light
green on their undersides. Although this species makes a fine specimen,
it's often used in hybridizing to combine a later bloom time with other
desirable characteristics. Hybrids with *M. stellata* produce flowers late
enough in spring to avoid frost damage but still bloom on bare branches
so that the magnificent effect is unsullied. Their only drawback is that
they bloom so late that they compete with other flowering trees. The National Arboretum has developed eight shrubby, 15- to 20-foot-tall, very
late blooming hybrids between *M. liliiflora* and *M. stellata*, collectively
called the Kosar hybrids or the Little Girl Series. From China.

HOW TO GROW. See *M. × soulangeana*. Zones 6–9.

CULTIVARS. 'Nigra' has larger and later, deep purple flowers. The
most treelike Kosar hybrids are hardy to Zone 5b and include the following: 'Ann' blooms the earliest, with cinnamon-scented, reddish pink flowers. 'Betty' is similar to 'Ann' but blooms later, with 8-inch, purple flowers.
'Pinkie' is the latest bloomer, with pastel pink, 6-inch flowers. 'Ricki' has
flowers whose petals are wine red outside and lavender-pink inside.
'Susan' has reddish purple flowers with slightly twisted petals.

M. × loebneri   P. 92

m. × LOBE-nerr-eye. Loebner Magnolia. This hybrid of *M. kobus* and *M.
stellata* is a rounded, wider-than-tall tree that blooms in early spring. It
reaches 30 feet tall. Even young plants bloom profusely, producing white
or pink flowers with 12 or more strap-shaped petals on bare branches in
late winter or early spring. Leaves are mid-green, oval, and up to 6 inches
long. Site this small tree in a bed or border planted with early bulbs such
as *Chionodoxa* or *Scilla siberica*, which bloom at the same time.

HOW TO GROW. See *M. × soulangeana*. Zones 4b–9a.

CULTIVARS. 'Leonard Messel' has lovely pink flowers that open from
dark purplish pink buds and have crinkled petals. 'Merrill' is upright,
reaching 25 feet tall; 15-petaled, white flowers are flushed pink at the base.
'Spring Snow' blooms late enough to escape most unexpected frosts and
has pure white flowers with 15 to 20 wide petals. 'Ballerina' is a late-
blooming form that has very fragrant, pure white flowers with 30 petals.

M. × soulangeana

P. 93

m. × sue-lan-gee-AY-nah. Saucer Magnolia. A hybrid of *M. denudata* and *M. liliiflora* dating back to the 1800s, saucer magnolia is the most commonly planted deciduous magnolia—which does not decrease the wonder of its early-spring bloom one iota. It grows into a rounded, low-branched, 20- to 30-foot-tall-and-wide tree. Magnificent saucer-shaped, 5- to 10-inch blossoms made up of nine satiny white, pink, purple, or bicolored petals decorate the branches in profusion before the leaves emerge in early spring. The dark green, smooth-edged, 6-inch-long, oblong leaves have a bold texture. They turn golden brown in fall. Trunk and branches feature smooth gray bark, and twigs are adorned with lovely, fur-covered flower buds in winter, making this open-branched tree an attractive winter specimen. Use it in a border or lawn or to shade a patio. Combine with daffodils, which bloom at the same time.

HOW TO GROW. Full sun to partial or light shade and humus-rich, deep, acid, moist soil. Even though the tree is cold hardy, the early blossoms may be killed by a late frost in warmer areas. Plant in a colder microclimate to delay bloom and thus avoid frost damage; a southern exposure may encourage earlier bloom that could be killed by frost. Train to several trunks with low, spreading branches. Prune immediately after bloom if necessary. Usually pest-free, but may be susceptible to mildew, leaf spot, and scale. Zones 5a–9a.

CULTIVARS. 'Alba Superba' has large white flowers that are sometimes flushed pink at the base. 'Alexandrina' has large, early-blooming flowers whose petals are white inside and purple-pink outside. 'Rustica Rubra' has a treelike form; flowers are rose-red outside and white inside. 'Lennei' is an open, shrubby form with enormous, later-blooming, globular flowers that are magenta-purple outside, white inside; Zone 4b. 'Bronzzonii' is an upright form with 10-inch, white flowers.

M. stellata (M. tomentosa)

P. 94

m. steh-LAY-tah. Star Magnolia. This multistemmed, rounded tree grows 15 to 20 feet tall and features very early, starry, white flowers that cover bare branches in late winter or early spring, about a week before saucer magnolia blooms. The fragrant, 3- to 4-inch-wide flowers consist of a dozen or more straplike, white or pale pink petals surrounding a yellow center. In some areas, a late frost can ruin the flowers without harming the tree. The oblong leaves are 2 to 4 inches long and dark green, with a finer texture than those on most magnolias. They often turn yellowish in autumn. The smooth, silver gray branches are decorated with furry silver buds in winter. Use this lovely early bloomer in a border or foundation planting, sited where it can be enjoyed from inside or as you go in and out of the house. From Japan.

HOW TO GROW. See *M.* × *soulangeana*. Performs well in hot climates. Zones 5a–9a.

CULTIVARS AND SIMILAR SPECIES. 'Centennial' has 5-inch, pink-tinged, white flowers with 30 petals. 'Rosea' is pale pink. 'Royal Star' has pink buds that open to white blossoms with 30 petals; late blooming. 'Waterlily' is bushy and late flowering, with 14 or more white petals that open from pink buds. *M. kobus* (Kobus magnolia) is a similar multi-trunked tree that grows to 40 feet tall; has 4-inch flowers with nine white petals and a faint purple marking; Zones 5a–8b.

❦ *Malus*

MAHL-us. Rose family, Rosaceae.

This genus contains 35 species from Asia, Europe, and North America, including apples, which are generally orchard trees grown for their large edible fruits, and crab apples, which are primarily ornamental, although their much smaller showy fruits are edible (though not always palatable). Both apples and crab apples have clustered, five-petaled blossoms with 15 to 20 yellow stamens in the center. They usually begin blooming before the leaves unfold and are later joined by the young greenery. Blossoms often open from pink or red buds and change to paler shades after opening, creating a beautiful pink cloud lasting several weeks. The Asian crab apple species are usually preferred for ornament, because their fruits are more colorful and last into winter, providing food for birds. Crab apples are favorite spring-flowering trees in the North and Midwest, where cold winters and heavy soil prevent other spring bloomers from performing well.

Because the genus is subject to numerous serious diseases and insects, which vary from region to region and year to year, it's best to choose disease-resistant cultivars adapted to your area. Four diseases are serious. Apple scab, a fungus characterized by black sooty spots on leaves and corky spots on fruits, may defoliate trees in summer. Although it is unsightly, it is not lethal. Fire blight is a bacterium that turns twigs and branches black, eventually killing the tree. Cedar-apple rust is a fungus that creates rusty, corky spots on leaves and, if serious, can defoliate the tree. The fungus must have native cedars and junipers (*Juniperus scopulo-*

rum, J. virginiana, or *J. horizontalis)* as alternate hosts to complete its life cycle, so do not plant susceptible crab apple cultivars within a mile of junipers. Powdery mildew is a white fungus that attacks leaves, flowers, and fruits during warm, humid weather and is unsightly.

The *Malus* species hybridize easily, resulting in an enormous number of horticultural selections. Older cultivars of hybrid crab apples were selected primarily for blossom size and color, not disease resistance or fruit size and color. Fruits of these older cultivars may be more than ½ inch around and drop in fall; they are quite messy and can cause a slippery hazard on sidewalks. Better are newer cultivars that are disease resistant and offer numerous fruits measuring less than ½ inch or that remain on the branches into winter, adding color to the winter landscape. These fruits are just the right size for birds, and if they do fall, they are not messy. When selecting a crab apple, choose one based on size, shape, and fruit color rather than flower color. Be sure to avoid the inferior older cultivars; many are still sold even though much better choices are available. Some of the worst are 'Almey', 'Bechtels', 'Evelyn', 'Eleyi', 'Flame', 'Hopa', 'Red Silver', 'Radiant', 'Sparkler', and 'Vanguard'.

M. baccata   P. 95

m. bah-KAH-tah. Siberian Crab Apple. This round-headed, wide-spreading species is one of the largest crab apples, reaching 20 to 50 feet tall. In midspring the profuse pink flower buds open into very fragrant, white, five-petaled flowers. Leaves are bright green. Fruits are small, about ⅛ inch around, but are profuse and a very showy, glossy red. They persist on the bare branches through most of the winter. Use this large, very cold hardy crab apple as a lawn, border, or street tree. From northeastern Asia.

HOW TO GROW. Full sun and well-drained, acid or alkaline, loamy or clayey soil. Susceptible to scab and sometimes fire blight. Provide good air circulation, apply fungicide in spring, or choose disease-resistant cultivars. Zones 3a–7a.

CULTIVARS. 'Columnaris' has creamy white buds that open to white blossoms and large, red-blushed, yellow fruits; columnar to 30 feet. 'Jackii' blooms and fruits well annually; purplish red, ½-inch fruits; resists scab and fire blight; Zone 2. 'Walters' is one of the best gold-fruited crab apples; pink buds open to white flowers; ½-inch fruits last all winter, changing from gold to bright amber; rounded and growing to 30 feet tall; resists scab and fire blight. *Rosybloom crab apples* are hybrids with reddish purple flowers; leaves are purple in spring, very dark green in summer, and orange-red in fall; most are very susceptible to scab. 'Adams' has deep reddish pink buds and crimson flowers that fade to pink; very persistent, ½-inch, glossy, red fruits; broadly rounded and growing 20 to 25 feet tall; scab resistant. 'Indian Summer' has ruby red buds that open to light magenta flowers; very persistent, ⅝-inch, bright oxblood red fruits; rounded and growing to 18 feet tall; scab resistant. 'Prairiefire' is highly scab resistant and one of the best cultivars; grows into a rounded, 20-foot-tall tree; purple-red flowers and leaves that turn orange-red in fall; persistent, ½-inch, oxblood red fruits that turn maroon in winter. 'Weeping Candied Apple' is stiffly weeping, growing to 15 feet tall; large crimson flowers; ½-inch, oxblood red fruits last all fall and winter; green foliage with red veins and light red undersides; scab resistant.

M. floribunda P. 95

m. flor-ih-BUN-dah. Japanese Flowering Crab Apple. This species is extinct in the wild but is still commonly grown in gardens around the world. A beautiful, disease-resistant tree with horizontal branches and a dense, rounded head, it reaches 20 feet tall and 30 feet wide. Blanketed with clusters of deep reddish pink flower buds that open into 1-inch-wide, fragrant, pink flowers that fade to white, the tree is a sight to behold for 2 or more weeks in early to midspring. The 3-inch, oval leaves are dark green and sometimes slightly lobed. Yellow, ⅓-inch fruits adorn the tree in fall and turn reddish amber after a freeze, but are quickly eaten by birds and squirrels. Fall color is negligible. This tree is a parent of many hybrid crab apples, which may be rounded, spreading, vase shaped, or even columnar and usually grow 8 to 25 feet tall. The best ones feature red, pink, or white blossoms; disease-resistant green or purple foliage; and attractive red, orange, or golden yellow fruits that persist on bare winter branches and are not messy.

HOW TO GROW. Full sun. Best in well-drained, acid, loamy or clayey soil, but tolerates alkaline soil. Fruits are not messy. Seedlings create a minor weed seedling problem. Prune to a single leader with a good branch structure when young. Remove suckers and water sprouts as needed. The species is moderately resistant to scab, rust, and mildew; fire blight is rarely a problem. Susceptibility to diseases varies widely among cultivars, but all diseases are worse in the South. The species is hardy in Zones 4b–8a; some cultivars perform in Zones 3b and 8b.

CULTIVARS. These are all disease-resistant hybrids with long-lasting, nonmessy fruits. 'Amberina' has crimson buds that open to blush pink blossoms; ⅜-inch, cardinal red fruits turn oxblood red in winter; fall foliage is red and gold; upright oval, growing 10 to 12 feet tall. 'Coral Cascade' has deep coral red buds that open to blush-white flowers; ½-inch fruits are persistent and coral-orange; semiweeping to arching tree that reaches 15 feet tall. 'Harvest Gold' features cardinal red buds opening to pink flowers that fade to white; late-ripening, ½-inch fruits on red stems; grows upright to 20 feet tall; tolerates road salt; one of the showiest crab apples in winter. 'Red Jewel' has dawn pink buds opening to white flowers; ½-inch fruits are currant red in fall and amber in winter; glossy leaves may turn yellow in fall; upright and spreading, growing to 15 feet tall. 'Red Swan' is an improved 'Red Jade' with smaller, brighter crimson fruits and extremely weeping branches; rose pink buds open to white, bell-shaped blossoms; grows to 10 feet tall. 'Sugar Tyme' has pale pink buds that open to fragrant white flowers; very showy, ¾-inch, red fruits may be messy if tree is not planted in a ground cover; golden yellow fall color; grows to 18 feet tall. 'White Angel' has pale pink buds opening to pure white blossoms; heavy crops of ½- to ¾-inch, glossy, red berries; vase shaped and growing to 20 feet tall.

M. hupehensis   P. 97

m. who-puh-HEN-sis. Tea Crab Apple. This widely grown species is a graceful, vase-shaped, open-branched tree that reaches 20 to 25 or more feet tall and wide. The deep pink flower buds open to 1½-inch, blush pink blossoms that fade to white and have a lovely scent, turning the tree into a cumulus cloud in early to midspring. The deep green, 4-inch leaves are oval or elliptical and pointed, with toothed edges. They are rarely marred by disease. The showy, ½-inch fruits are yellow with a rosy blush, changing to red. This tree's shape makes it a good street tree under power lines. Or use it as a patio or border tree where people can walk under its branches. From Asia.

HOW TO GROW. Full sun and moist, well-drained, acid or alkaline loam. Highly resistant to scab, but slightly susceptible to fire blight. Prune water sprouts and crossed branches as needed. Zones 4b–8b.

CULTIVARS. 'Cardinal' is a broad form that grows to 15 feet tall; bright rose-red flowers; small, deep red fruits; red-tinged summer leaves. 'Strawberry Parfait' is a 25-foot-tall, vase-shaped hybrid; fragrant pink flowers with rosy margins; leaves emerge reddish purple and mature to dark green; ¾-inch fruits are yellow with a red blush or glossy orange-red.

M. sargentii   P. 98

m. sare-GENT-ee-i. Sargent Crab Apple. This small crab apple is a mound-like, spreading tree with a single trunk that grows to only 10 feet tall and

15 feet wide, although it is often grafted to a 6-foot trunk to make it taller. In midspring the pale pink flower buds open to very fragrant, 1-inch-wide, white flowers, turning the tree into a snowball. Numerous bright red, ⅓-inch fruits stand out in autumn against yellow leaves and hang on well into winter, making this one of the best fall performers among the crab apples. Leaves are dark green and slightly lobed. Some trees bloom and fruit well only in alternate years; others bear annually. The tree is popular because of its unique shape and tidy size. It works well in a foundation planting or border, where it will add interest. Does not hybridize readily and comes true from seed. From Japan; not known in the wild.

HOW TO GROW. Full sun and moist, well-drained, loamy soil. Suckers form on grafted plants; prune as needed. Remove any crossed branches. Resistant to scab. Zones 4b–8b.

CULTIVARS. 'Firebird' has ½-inch fruits that keep their red color exceptionally well in winter. 'Pink Princess' has rose pink flowers and purple-bronze foliage. 'Rosea' has larger, dark pink buds opening to white flowers and large fruits. 'Tina' is smaller but is usually grafted to a trunk to reach 16 feet tall. 'Jewelberry' is a 6- to 7-foot-tall hybrid that looks much like *M. sargentii* but blooms and fruits annually. 'Mary Potter' is another hybrid that looks like a larger, more horizontally branched *M. sargentii*.

M. × *zumi* 'Calocarpa'   P. 99

m. × ZOO-mee. Zumi Crab Apple, Redbud Crab Apple. This disease-resistant tree, a hybrid of *M. baccata* var. *mandschurica* and *M. sieboldii*, is a rounded, horizontally spreading form that grows to 15 feet tall and 25 feet wide and is one of the best crab apples for fall display. It has abundant, large, white flowers that open from pink buds in late spring, later than most crab apples. Leaves are 3½-inch-long, dark green ovals, often lobed, that may turn golden orange in fall. The glossy, cherry red, ½- to ¾-inch fruits, which hang from 1½-inch-long stems, persist through the winter, making this tree and its hybrids some of the best for a year-round landscape effect. Leaves are dark green, lobed, and toothed and turn bright yellow to gold in autumn. The species tends to bloom and fruit well every other year, but the cultivars do so annually. Use this eye-catching tree where it can be appreciated throughout the year, especially in fall and winter. Do not confuse it with *M.* 'Zumi', which is a less desirable tree.

HOW TO GROW. Full sun and well-drained, loamy to heavy soil. Very scab resistant, but sometimes suffers from fire blight. Zones 4a–8a.

CULTIVARS. These hybrids are like the species in flower and fruit unless noted. 'Donald Wyman' has rose pink flower buds, ½-inch cardinal red fruits, and bronze-yellow fall color; rounded to 20 feet tall; susceptible to apple scab in some areas. 'Bob White' has ½-inch, persistent, yellow fruits; rounded and dense to 20 feet tall; alternate bearer. 'Ormiston Roy' has red buds opening to white flowers and ½-inch, red-blushed, orange-yellow fruits that are amber through the winter; grows 20 to 25 feet tall. 'Professor Sprenger' has cardinal red buds opening to white flowers and unusual, brilliant orange-red, ⅝-inch fruits; rounded and upright to 35 feet tall; Zones 3–7. 'Snowdrift' has orange-red fruits; rounded to 20 feet tall. 'Volcano' has red buds opening to white flowers, orange-red fruits, and golden yellow with orange fall color; grows upright to 10 feet tall. 'Winter Gem' is an upright form. 'Winter Gold' has deep carmine buds opening to white flowers and orange-blushed, yellow fruits; broadly pyramidal to 20 feet tall. 'White Cascade' has pink buds opening to white flowers and buttercup yellow fruits that turn amber in winter; grows to 15 feet tall, with gracefully weeping branches.

❦ *Morus*

MOOR-us. Mulberry family, Moraceae.

This genus contains 7 to 12 species, all used in Asia to host silk-producing caterpillars. *M. alba* has been used in China for nearly 4,000 years for silk production. All species produce tasty fruits that resemble blackberries but are too fragile and soft to be marketable.

M. alba   P. 99

m. al-BAH. White Mulberry. This sturdy, adaptable, small shade tree forms a rounded head and grows 30 to 40 feet tall and wide. It is weak wooded and can sucker badly, so it is suitable for only the most hostile environments, where more attractive trees do not prosper. Flowers bloom in spring but usually go unnoticed, except by some allergy sufferers who react to the pollen. Leaves are quite variable and may be lobed or unlobed, but they are usually a lustrous dark green and measure 2 to 7 inches long. Fall color is often a nice yellow. Clusters of pink to purple, ½- to 1-inch, blackberry-like fruits ripen in summer. These berries are very messy, staining sidewalks and outdoor furniture, but they are so relished by birds that if you have a home orchard, you might wish to plant several mulberries to lure birds away from your cherries, apples, or blueberries. Otherwise, plant one of the fruitless forms. This unfussy, fast-growing tree has orange-brown bark and grows very well in the harsh climates of the Southwest, Midwest, and Plains, where few trees flourish. It is best limited to use as a quick-growing shade tree or screen in these regions. From China.

HOW TO GROW. Partial to full sun and any soil, wet to dry, acid to alkaline. Tolerates heat, drought, road salt, and seashore conditions. Fruit drop can be annoying, and bird-distributed seeds may cause a weed seedling problem. Susceptible to storm damage and numerous insect pests. Zones 5a–9a.

CULTIVARS. 'Chaparral' features slender, twisted branches that cascade to the ground and deeply cut leaves; grows 8 to 20 feet tall, with a beautiful silhouette; fruitless. 'Fan-San' is fruitless and has very shiny, lobed leaves. 'Kingan' is fruitless and very durable under stressful conditions. 'Mapleleaf' is fruitless and has large lobed leaves. 'Pendula' is identical to 'Chaparral' but produces fruit. 'Stribling' is fruitless and noted for its excellent yellow fall foliage.

Nyssa

NIH-sah. Tupelo family, Nyssaceae.

Most of the 5 to 10 species in this genus are native to wet sites. They are grown in gardens for their outstanding fall color and easy-care nature. The most widely grown species, *N. sylvatica*, is highly attractive to bees when in bloom and is the source of the prized tupelo honey.

N. sylvatica   P. 100

n. syl-VAH-tih-kah. Black Gum, Sour Gum, Pepperidge, Tupelo. With a strong pyramidal shape, a central leader, and horizontal to ascending branches when young, this beautiful native eventually becomes irregular or rounded and matures to 30 to 50 feet tall and 20 to 30 feet wide. Producing the most reliable and outstanding fall color of all our native trees (although color is not always dependable in the South), black gum should be grown more in home gardens. Leaves are pointed ovals, 3 to 6 inches long, and a highly polished dark green in summer. They change color over a long season, first turning yellow, then orange and scarlet, and finally deep red or maroon before falling in late autumn. Spring flowers go unnoticed except by bees, but clusters of deep blue berries on female trees look spectacular in fall when they ripen against the red leaves. Birds quickly eat the berries. Trunk bark is patterned into rough, chunky, dark gray checkers, while limbs are silvery gray. Use this medium-size tree in a lawn or border or plant it in groups in a naturalistic garden or wet site. From eastern and central North America.

HOW TO GROW. Full sun to partial shade and moist, humus-rich, acid soil. Tolerates wet and dry conditions, but not alkalinity. Plant small trees, since the taproot makes large trees difficult to transplant. Prune lower limbs in fall if desired. Remove suckers. Usually pest-free. Zones 5a–9a.

CULTIVARS. 'Miss Scarlet' has outstanding red fall color and large blue berries.

❦ *Ostrya*

oss-TRY-ah. Birch family, Betulaceae.

This genus contains 8 to 10 species from the woodlands of North and Central America, Europe, and Asia. They have simple, oval or lance-shaped leaves and male and female catkins on the same tree. Fruits with distinctive papery bracts identify these species, distinguishing them from the genus *Carpinus*, to which they are related. They are excellent performers in shady gardens.

O. virginiana   P. 101

o. ver-jin-ee-AY-nah. Ironwood, Hop Hornbeam. Forming a strong central leader and growing 30 to 40 feet tall and even wider when situated in full sun, ironwood remains pyramidal and shorter when grown in shade. Its 2- to 5-inch-long, toothed leaves are pointed, light green ovals that feel like thin felt and turn golden yellow in fall. The unopened buds of the catkins provide winter interest but are obscured by new leaves when the buds expand and bloom. In summer pale green clusters of hoplike, papery capsules hang from the undersides of the branches, adding interest, and the nuts they enclose provide food for wildlife. Like its relative hornbeam *(Carpinus caroliniana)*, ironwood has extremely hard wood. Reddish, shredding bark decorates the trunks and branches of older trees, eventually becoming very dark on the lower trunk. This fine-textured, slow-growing tree works well as an understory tree in a woodland or shaded garden. Save this native species during development. From most of North America, except the extreme Southeast.

HOW TO GROW. Very adaptable, growing in full sun to shade and almost any soil, except for wet sites. Tolerates moderate drought and all urban conditions except road salt. Somewhat difficult to transplant, so choose small container-grown trees. Pest-free except for gypsy moths, which love it. Zones 3a–9a.

SIMILAR SPECIES. *O. carpinifolia* (European hornbeam) is hardy to Zone 5b and is almost identical to the American species.

❦ *Oxydendrum*

ox-ee-DEN-drum. Heath family, Ericaceae.

Related to heaths, heathers, azaleas, rhododendrons, and other acid-loving plants, this genus contains only one species, a tree native to the woodlands and streambanks of eastern North America. It is a valuable landscape tree because of its unusual bloom time and outstanding fall color.

O. arboreum   P. 102

o. ARE-boar-ee-um. Sourwood, Sorrel Tree. A tidy, summer-blooming tree, sourwood has a pyramidal shape with low ascending branches and grows 25 to 35 or more feet tall and 15 to 20 feet wide. In midsummer this native is adorned with 10-inch-long, nodding clusters of creamy white, bell-shaped flowers. The flowers ripen to buff-colored seedpods, which are quite attractive from late summer through winter. The 4- to 8-inch-long, lance-shaped or oblong leaves are glossy dark green and turn showy shades of yellow, scarlet, and burgundy in early to midfall. Trunk bark is dark gray and deeply furrowed into blocks. This tree's shape makes it an excellent candidate for a small property, in a lawn, border, or foundation planting or grouped in a woodland setting. From eastern North America.

HOW TO GROW. Full sun to partial shade, but blooms more profusely and has better fall color when planted in sun. Likes moist, well-drained, fertile, acid soil. Somewhat drought tolerant, but keep well watered in hot climates. Sensitive to air pollution. Branches sweep low to the ground; prune if desired. Usually problem-free. Zones 5b–9a.

CULTIVARS. 'Chameleon' exhibits consistent fall color in various flaming shades.

❦ *Parrotia*

pah-ROH-tee-ah. Witch hazel family, Hamamelidaceae.

This genus has only one species, which hails from an area of the Caucasus Mountains near the Caspian Sea, where it sometimes forms dense forests with *Carpinus betulus* (European hornbeam).

P. persica
P. 103

p. per-SICK-ah. Persian Parrotia, Persian Ironwood. An attractive specimen throughout the year, Persian parrotia is a single- or multistemmed, rounded or spreading, low-branched tree that matures to 30 to 40 feet tall and wide. The flowers of this unusual tree have no petals but consist of tiny, mopheadlike clusters of dark red stamens. They cover the bare branches in late winter, well before the leaves emerge, and are splendid when viewed up close, although they may go unnoticed from a distance. The leaves are reddish purple when young, maturing to glossy, dark green, 2- to 5-inch-long wedges. Fall color is spectacular, a mixture of gold, orange, and scarlet late in the season. The dark reddish brown bark on the trunk and main branches flakes off to reveal a mottled pattern of green, silver gray, and cream, which is especially striking in winter. Use as a specimen in a border or garden where it can be seen in winter. Mulch the ground or plant a ground cover under its low branches, which will shade out grass. From Iran.

HOW TO GROW. Full sun to light shade and well-drained, humus-rich, slightly acid to alkaline soil. Tolerates drought and urban conditions once established. Does not tolerate wet sites. Most attractive if low branches are not pruned off. Protect the trunk from mechanical injury. Japanese beetles may be a problem. Performs well in the South. Zones 5b–9a.

CULTIVARS. 'Biltmore' exhibits excellent fall color. 'Pendula' forms a weeping mound. 'Vanessa' is columnar.

❦ Paulownia

paw-LOW-knee-ah. Figwort family, Scrophulariaceae.

This genus contains six species of trees from eastern Asia. All are tall specimens with showy flowers and foliage. In China and Japan, the lightweight, beautifully grained wood of *P. tomentosa* is sacred and highly prized for making furniture and jewelry boxes.

P. tomentosa
P. 103, 104

p. toe-men-TOE-sah. Empress Tree, Princess Tree. Naturalized in many places in eastern North America, this Asian tree grows rapidly into an irregular pyramidal or rounded shape, reaching 35 to 50 feet tall and wide. Leaves are 5 to 10 inches long, somewhat downy, and deep green. Varying from heart shaped to three or five lobed, they create a bold tropical texture. They drop over several weeks in fall with little change in color. Dramatic 12-inch spires of fragrant lavender or purple, yellow-striped, fox-glovelike flowers bloom at all the branch tips in midspring, before the leaves emerge, creating an unforgettable sight. Trunk bark is smooth and gray. Clusters of pale green, egg-shaped, 1- to 2-inch capsules ripen to brown in fall and last into winter as pretty ornaments. They release numerous seeds, which readily germinate in undisturbed or barren sites, sometimes causing a weed seedling problem. Use this fast-growing tree in a difficult site (it might grow 20 feet tall in 2 years), with the intention of replacing it with a longer-lived specimen. Or use it as a dense shade tree in a park or open area where its litter will not be problematic. Also valuable for reforestation and land reclamation projects. In Zones 5a–6a, empress tree dies to the ground in winter but regrows from the roots in spring, sending up 10- to 14-foot-tall stems with 30-inch-wide leaves. In warmer zones, many landscape designers deliberately create this effect by "stooling" the tree. From China and Korea.

HOW TO GROW. Full to partial sun. Tolerates most soils, from acid to slightly alkaline, although it does best in rich, moist soil. Tolerates both dry and wet conditions, as well as road salt. Train when young to a single leader. Usually pest-free. Flower buds and branch tips may winterkill in Zones 6b–7a. Cold hardy in Zones 6b–9a.

CULTIVARS. 'Lilacina' has paler flowers without spots.

🌿 Phellodendron

fell-oh-DEN-dron. Rue family, Rutaceae.

About 3 to 10 very similar species belong to this genus, which resembles *Ailanthus* (tree of heaven). The compound leaves are opposite each other and are aromatic when crushed or broken.

P. amurense

P. 104, 105

p. ah-mor-EN-see. Amur Corktree. This tough tree gets more picturesque as it matures into a wide-spreading or rounded, open-branched, 30- to 45-foot-tall-and-wide specimen. It has a stout central trunk with deeply furrowed, gray-brown, corky bark, from which radiate a few sturdy horizontal branches studded with orange-yellow twigs. The boldly attractive compound leaves are 10 inches long and consist of 9 to 13 smooth-edged, oval, 2- to 4-inch-long leaflets. They are glossy dark green with lighter undersides and turn bright yellow in fall. The greenish white spring flowers are inconspicuous. The ½-inch, round, black fruits drop in large quantities, making a mess on walkways and roads. Seedless forms are preferred as street trees or in groomed lawns and parks. From western Europe and eastern Asia.

HOW TO GROW. Full sun and moist, well-drained, acid to alkaline soil. Tolerates some drought. Performs well in urban conditions only if space is plentiful. Prune during dormancy when young to develop a single trunk with well-spaced, high branches. Fruits of female trees can cause a weed seedling problem; plant a fruitless form. Usually pest-free, but leaf scorch may develop in hot, dry situations. Zones 4b–7b.

CULTIVARS. 'Shademaster' is a fruitless form that grows 30 to 35 feet tall. 'Macho' is more upright and vase shaped, growing 25 to 30 feet tall; fruitless. *P. amurense* var. *sachalinense* has less corky bark and is hardy in Zones 3b–7b. 'His Majesty' is seedless and has an open-branched vase shape.

🌿 *Pistacia*

piss-TAY-she-ah. Cashew family, Anacardiaceae.

This genus of 10 species of trees and shrubs with compound leaves includes the commercial pistachio tree, valued for its nuts, as well as several ornamentals.

P. chinensis

P. 105

p. chi-NEN-sis. Chinese Pistache, Chinese Pistachio. Prized for its dependable fall color in the South, where few trees put on outstanding displays, Chinese pistachio grows into a rounded, 25- to 35-foot-tall-and-wide, open-branched specimen with a lacy character. The 8-inch-long, compound leaves are deep green, with 10 to 12 lance-shaped, aromatic leaflets that turn flaming red and orange in late autumn. Greenish flowers bloom before the leaves open in spring but are not remarkable. Clusters of showy red fruits, which ripen to a bright metallic blue in autumn, develop on female trees. These are not messy because they are usually eaten by birds. The attractive, flaking, mottled trunk bark is gray and salmon-orange. Although this tree may look a bit awkward when young, it grows more attractive with age and is a good choice for casting light shade on a lawn, street, or patio. From China.

HOW TO GROW. Full sun and moist, well-drained, acid to alkaline soil. Tolerates heat, drought, and urban conditions. Prune when young to develop a strong central leader. Usually pest-free. Performs well in the South and Southwest. Zones 6b–9b.

CULTIVARS. 'Keith Davey' has outstanding scarlet fall color. Other selections with improved form, fall color, and heavy fruiting may be available.

❧ *Platanus*

PLAT-ah-nus. Sycamore family, Platanaceae.

This genus contains nine species of large trees that have maplelike leaves and mottled bark. They are popular urban street trees.

P. × *acerifolia*   P. 106

p. × aye-sir-ih-FOL-ee-ah. London Plane Tree. This well-known hybrid of *P. occidentalis* and *P. orientalis* is superior to both of them, combining each one's best characteristics into a tall, attractive, disease-resistant shade tree. Pyramidal when young, the tree grows into a rounded specimen reaching 50 to 60 feet tall and 30 to 40 feet wide. Its massive trunk and sturdy, wide-spreading scaffold branches create a rugged silhouette. Leaves are 6 to 10 inches long, dark green, and lobed like those of a maple. They turn yellowish brown in fall before dropping. Bark is striking, peeling to a patchwork of creamy white and gray. Curious 1- to 2-inch-wide, tan seed balls made up of tightly packed, prickly seeds develop in fall and hang on into winter before dropping. Kids call them "itchy balls" and like to torment each other with them. London plane tree is a durable urban dweller but also looks wonderful in an open, naturalistic setting, where its ghostly bark and craggy shape can be appreciated fully.

HOW TO GROW. Full to partial sun and deep, fertile, moist, acid soil. Tolerates drought, wetness, infertile or alkaline soil, heat, and air pollution. Messy fruits need to be raked up in spring. Remove lower branches to show off trunk bark. This tree is less susceptible to anthracnose than other sycamores, but it may be disfigured during wet seasons. Mildew, borers, and lace bugs are other pests. Zones 5b–9a.

CULTIVARS AND SIMILAR SPECIES. Choose named cultivars to ensure disease resistance. 'Bloodgood' is the oldest and most common cultivar; highly resistant to anthracnose, but suffers from mildew. 'Columbia' is a pyramidal form with deeply lobed leaves from the National Arboretum; resists anthracnose (on the East, but not the West, Coast) and mildew. 'Liberty' is similar to 'Columbia', but the leaves are not as deeply lobed. 'Metroshade' is very tall and fast growing, with bronze new growth; anthracnose and mildew resistant. 'Yarwood' has large, light green leaves that resist powdery mildew and anthracnose on the West Coast. *P. occidentalis* (sycamore, American plane tree, buttonwood) is a fast-growing native that can reach 100 to 150 feet tall; bark is ghostly white and tan, and leaves are shallowly lobed; suffers from anthracnose and mildew; grows and looks best in a natural landscape with moist to wet soil; Zones 5a–9a. *P. orientalis* (Oriental plane tree) has deeply lobed leaves, is wide spreading, and grows to 25 feet tall; a useful, small street tree; resists scale; Zones 7a–9a.

❦ *Poncirus*

pon-SEAR-us. Rue family, Rutaceae.

P. trifoliata P. 107

p. try-FOE-lee-ay-tah. Trifoliate Orange, Hardy Orange. This small thorny tree, a cold-hardy relative of the orange tree, has an oval shape and grows 10 to 20 feet tall. Bark on trunk and branches is an attractive green. Star-shaped, 2-inch-wide, white flowers decorate the branches in spring and have a sweet perfume. The 3-inch-long leaves are divided into three leaflets on winged stalks. They are bright yellow-green when young, mature to glossy mid-green, and turn glowing yellow in fall. Leaves drop in autumn to reveal beautiful, bright golden orange, 2-inch, citruslike fruits. These sour-tasting fruits adorn the branches through the winter, standing out beautifully against the green branches. This tree's main attraction or detraction, depending on your point of view, is its 2-inch-long, extremely sharp, stout, green thorns, which make it very useful as a security barrier when planted on boundaries or under windows. When using the tree as an ornamental, be sure to locate it where it is visible in winter. From China and Korea.

HOW TO GROW. Full sun to partial shade and moist, well-drained, acid soil. Tolerates heat and drought. Locate where the thorns won't pose a hazard to gardeners and passersby. May be pruned into a dense screen or hedge; prune immediately after blooming. Usually problem-free, but develops chlorosis if soil pH is above 7.5. Zones 6b–9a.

CULTIVARS. 'Monstrosa' is a dwarf with twisted branches that is useful as an ornamental shrub.

❧ *Populus*

POP-yew-lus. Willow family, Salicaceae.

About 35 species of poplar and aspen trees belong to this genus, which is native throughout the northern temperate zones. These are the fastest-growing trees in temperate climates and often have ornamental white or gray bark, male and female catkins on separate trees, and leaves that flutter gracefully on long, flattened stems. They have invasive root systems and should be planted at least 30 feet from foundations, water pipes, sewer pipes, or septic systems. Their great thirst for water makes them invaluable in cleaning up sites damaged by polluted groundwater. Most poplars are weak wooded and susceptible to storm damage. Some are also susceptible to canker, so they are often short-lived. In some regions, they are grown and harvested for firewood.

P. alba

P. 108

p. AL-bah. White Poplar. Often grown as a graceful, multitrunked clump, white poplar is a round-topped, spreading tree that grows quickly to 40 to 70 feet tall and wide. Leaves are 3 to 5 inches across and three lobed, rather like a maple's. They are shiny dark green on top, with a felt of white hairs on the undersides. The slightest breeze sets the leaves in motion, flashing a silvery light. Fall color is yellow. Trunk bark is a showy, grayish white and attracts attention all year. As trunks mature, they become marked with black. Though attractive, this tree is soft wooded, short-lived, and a bit messy, continually dropping leaves during summer and fall. It is best used to create quick shade in the Midwest and West, where few shade trees thrive. From Central Europe and Asia.

HOW TO GROW. Full sun. Best in moist soil, but tolerates sandy soil, salt spray, and air pollution. Tends to form thickets if soil is moist. Prone to storm damage. Roots can clog drainpipes. Prune in summer and fall to remove lower branches and suckers. Continually drops leaves, so requires cleanup. Troubled by aphids, canker, and leaf spot, but less so than other poplars. Zones 4a–9a.

CULTIVARS AND SIMILAR SPECIES. 'Nivea' is the most common form sold (although it may not be labeled with its cultivar name); three- to five-lobed leaves with very silvery undersides. 'Pyramidalis' ('Boleana') is very narrow and does not sucker, but its leaves are less silvery; an excellent substitute for Lombardy poplar for screens and windbreaks. 'Raket' is similar to 'Pyramidalis' but has more silvery foliage. *P. angustifolia* (willowleaf poplar) is an upright native with willowlike leaves and excellent gold fall color; grow in moist soil at high elevations to 10,000 feet. *P. x canescens* 'Tower', a hybrid with *P. tremula*, grows to 45 feet tall and 10 feet wide; excellent disease resistance; makes a good substitute for Lombardy poplar. *P. tremuloides* (quaking aspen), **P. 110**, is native to the Rockies and has bright white to gray-green bark and small, wedge-shaped leaves with silver undersides that turn a beautiful yellow in fall; performs well only in the Mountain States above 7,000 feet; otherwise it is short-lived and disease prone; Zones 2b–6b. 'Pike's Bay' has lighter bark and is canker resistant.

P. deltoides   P. 108, 109

p. del-TOY-deez. Cottonwood. Pyramidal when young and becoming irregularly open and vase shaped with age, this tree has a low-branching trunk and grows 75 to 100 feet tall and 50 to 75 feet wide along watercourses in the West and Midwest. It has a rugged character and a massive silhouette, with its tall, stout trunk and big branches covered with deeply furrowed, brown bark. Leaves are triangular, 3 to 5 inches across, bright green on top, and blue-green on the undersides. They turn yellow, gold, or brown before dropping in autumn. Male trees produce a lot of pollen, which can irritate allergy sufferers. Female trees produce enormous amounts of cottony white seeds that float great distances and create quite a mess. Numerous seedlings can invade open areas and grow in seemingly hostile sites. Despite its drawbacks, cottonwood is one of the hardiest shade and shelterbelt trees for the cold climates of the North, Plains, and Mountain States, where most trees have a difficult time growing. In the home landscape, a male, cottonless form is best, used only in large-scale situations and away from drainpipes. It is also extremely valuable in stabilizing soil along watercourses and floodplains. From central and western North America.

HOW TO GROW. Full sun. Best in moist, fertile soil, but tolerates poor, dry, alkaline soil. This messy tree requires continual cleanup of twigs, leaves, and seeds; plant a ground cover to absorb the droppings. Grows very rapidly but is short-lived (by tree standards) and weak wooded; does not sucker. Susceptible to storm damage; consider cabling older trees. Zones 3a–9a.

CULTIVARS AND SIMILAR SPECIES. 'Robusta' is cottonless and has coppery new leaves; broadly oval, growing to 60 feet tall. 'Siouxland' is pyramidal, cottonless, and rust and storm resistant; grows to 75 feet tall. *P. × acuminata* (lanceleaf poplar) is a common natural hybrid with very narrow leaves, excellent fall color, and a rounded form. *P. × canadensis (P. × euramerica)* and its cultivars are superior cottonless hybrids with *P.*

nigra; they have smooth bark and triangular leaves. 'Imperial' is disease resistant and narrowly pyramidal, growing to 60 feet tall. 'No'reaster' is highly disease resistant and grows to 75 feet tall. 'Prairie Sky' is very narrow, growing to 40 feet tall and 8 feet wide, with smooth gray bark and very good resistance to canker and storm damage. 'Robusta' has coppery new growth and large ornamental leaves. The Zappetti hybrids are seven clones selected by hybridizer George Zappettini for superior disease resistance, fast growth, and strong form; they include 'Tripolo', Jacometti', 'Russo', 'Northeast 14', 'Northeast 17', and 'Northeast 224' (all males). *P. fremontii* (western poplar) is native to moist areas of the Southwest and is suitable for large-scale landscapes in that region.

P. nigra 'Italica'

P. 109

p. NYE-grah. Lombardy Poplar. This fast-growing cultivar of the wide-spreading black poplar tree reaches 70 to 90 feet tall 10 and 15 feet tall. Its numerous upright branches give it the erect appearance of a telephone pole but make it useful as a quick screen or shelterbelt. Leaves are triangular and about 4 inches long. They have light green undersides and turn bright yellow in fall. Trunk bark is gray-green on young trees, eventually becoming black on the lower trunk. Because this cultivar is susceptible to disease when mature, consider using it only as a temporary planting in a new landscape, or choose a similar but more disease-resistant cultivar or a columnar form of another tree such as a maple.

HOW TO GROW. Full sun. Best in evenly moist soil, but tolerates wetness and drought. Prune to a single leader. Protect trunks from mechanical injury. Diseases are less of a problem in the North and West, where humidity is low. Zones 3a–9a.

CULTIVARS AND SIMILAR SPECIES. 'Theves' is wider than 'Italica' and more disease resistant. *P. alba* 'Pyramidalis' and 'Raket' make good, disease-resistant columnar-shaped substitutes. *P. × canescens* 'Tower' and *P. deltoides* 'Prairie Sky' also are good substitutes.

❦ *Prunus*

PROO-nuss. Rose family, Rosaceae.

This large genus contains about 400 species of trees and shrubs, many of them ornamental cherries. *Prunus* members have five-petaled (or double), pink or white flowers, often borne in large rounded or elongated clusters; single-seeded fruits; and alternate, pointed, oval leaves. In general, flowering cherries are short-lived, about 20 years, because they are prone to numerous diseases and insect pests, including borers, scale, aphids, tent caterpillars, canker, and leaf spot. However, these trees' exceptional beauty and utility far surpass any concern over their longevity. The genus also includes apricots, peaches, plums, and almonds, as well as several broad-leaved evergreen trees and shrubs (see page 309).

P. cerasifera 'Atropurpurea'   P. 110

p. sair-ah-SIFF-er-ah. Purple-Leaved Plum, Cherry Plum. This small tree is one of the most cold-hardy purple-leaved plants available and grows into a 15- to 30-foot-tall-and-wide, rounded or vase-shaped form with gently arching branches. In early spring, fragrant, pale to dark pink, ½-inch flowers cover the limbs, blooming just as the richly colored new leaves begin to unfold. The leaves are vivid ruby red in spring and mature to greenish bronze-purple by midsummer, although some cultivars remain more vibrantly purple through the summer. Fall color is reddish purple. Small, purple, plumlike fruits ripen in midsummer, attract birds, and can be messy if they drop to the ground. This pretty little tree makes an eye-catching focal point in a border or foundation planting. From Eurasia.

HOW TO GROW. Leaf color is best in full sun. Best in moist, acid loam, but tolerates any well-drained site and slightly alkaline soil. Somewhat drought tolerant. Train to a single short leader; prune immediately after flowering. Pests are less of a problem on this species than on others. Zones 4b–9a.

CULTIVARS AND SIMILAR SPECIES. 'Thundercloud' has very deep purple foliage all summer and purple fruits; the most widely grown cultivar. 'Krater's Vesuvius' is very similar to 'Thundercloud' but has deeper red new growth, is a bit purpler in summer, and has almost no fruits; excellent in the Southwest. 'Mt. St. Helens' is rounded, has light pink flowers, and has rich purple leaves all summer and fall. 'Newport' has light pink flowers, few fruits, and dark purple foliage all summer, with reddish fall color. P. × blireana (blireana plum) is widely vase shaped and twiggy, growing 15 to 20 feet tall and wide; very early, bright pink, double, 1-inch flowers and reddish purple or greenish bronze summer foliage; leaves are duller than purple-leaved plum's, but flowers are showier; Zones 6a–9a.

P. maackii   P. 111

p. MAK-ee-eye. Amur Chokecherry, Goldbark Cherry. Grown for its gorgeous bark, Amur chokecherry is pyramidal when young and grows into a rounded, single- or multitrunked, 30-foot-tall tree. Bark is smooth or ex-foliating and has no equal—it's a glistening, metallic honey gold, with lighter horizontal bands. It attracts attention all year but is especially beautiful when the tree is leafless. Dangling, 3-inch clusters of tiny white flowers bloom in mid- to late spring but are partly obscured by the leaves. The medium green leaves, which measure 2 to 4 inches long and have tiny teeth on the margins, turn yellowish and drop in early autumn. Small black fruits ripen in summer but are eaten by birds, so they are not usu-ally messy. Use this medium-size tree to shade a patio, in a winter border, or as a street tree where it can be seen up close. It is an especially good or-namental choice for cold climates. From Manchuria and Korea.

HOW TO GROW. Full to partial sun and moist, well-drained, humus-rich soil. Prune to a single trunk or several strong trunks and remove small limbs to show off the bark. Subject to the usual cherry pests, but is relatively pest-free in the coldest zones. Zones 3b–7a.

SIMILAR SPECIES. *P. serotina* (black cherry, wild black cherry), **P. 113,** has rough, peeling, black bark on the trunk and main branches but shiny bark on young branches; 5-inch-long, drooping clusters of creamy flowers; leathery leaves turn orange in fall; ½-inch fruits ripen from green to red to black in summer and provide food for birds but stain concrete if they drop to the ground; the tallest cherry, growing 80 to 100 feet tall; Zones 3b–9a. *P. serrula* (paperbark cherry, birchbark cherry) is a pyrami-dal or rounded, 20- to 30-foot-tall tree; gleaming, dark red-brown bark with horizontal brown bands; narrow, willowlike leaves; white flowers that bloom in late spring; Zones 5b–8a.

P. × 'Okame'   P. 112

p. × oh-CALM-ee. Okame Cherry. This award-winning cultivar is a hybrid between *P. incisa* and *P. campanulata* and is the earliest- and longest-blooming of all the cherries. It grows into a gracefully spreading, 20- to 30-foot-tall vase shape. Opening from dark pink buds set into red ca-lyxes, the profuse, clear pink flowers have jagged petals and bloom before the leaves unfold; they remain showy for about 3 weeks until the leaves mature. Blooming is early, often starting in late winter when the magno-lias are still in bloom. Leaves are 1 to 2½ inches long, dark green, fine tex-tured, and sharp toothed. They turn bright yellow and orange in fall. Use as a small specimen in a garden or border or plant in groups to create a flowering grove.

HOW TO GROW. Full sun and moist, well-drained soil. Tolerates heat. Zones 6b–9a.

CULTIVARS AND SIMILAR SPECIES. 'Hally Jolivette' is a shrubby hybrid that grows 15 to 20 feet tall; profuse, semidouble, 1¼-inch, white flowers with pink centers open over 3 weeks in early spring on slender branches; Zones 5b–8b. *P. mume* (Japanese flowering apricot) has very early, single, pink flowers; double forms with dark pink, red, and white flowers also are available; Zones 7a–9a.

P. sargentii   P. 113

p. sar-JEN-tee-eye. Sargent Cherry. Perhaps the loveliest of all the cherries, Sargent cherry grows into a 30- to 50-foot-tall-and-wide, rounded or vase-shaped specimen that is a mist of pink when in bloom. Flowers are single and delicate rose pink, or sometimes white, 1 to 1½ inches across, and borne in groups of two or three. They bloom before the leaves open, enhancing their appeal. The toothed leaves are about 6 inches long and 3 inches wide, wider than most cherry leaves. They are a shiny reddish green when they open, mature to dark green, and finally turn orange-red and yellow in fall. This is one of the best cherries for reliable fall color. The black fruits are small and not messy. Bark is a very attractive polished, chestnut brown with prominent horizontal bands. Sargent cherry makes a beautiful flowering shade tree for year-round interest. Use in a lawn or garden or as a street tree where there is plenty of soil. This is the most cold hardy of the flowering cherries. From Japan and Korea.

HOW TO GROW. Full sun and well-drained, acid to neutral soil. Tolerates clayey soil and drought. Prune when young to create a short, single trunk. Japanese beetles are a serious problem, but other pests are not as troublesome as on other cherries, and the tree is longer-lived than most. Zones 4b–9a.

CULTIVARS. 'Columnaris' ('Rancho') is narrowly upright, growing to 30 feet.

P. serrulata Sato-zakura Group   P. 114

p. sair-yew-LAH-tah. Oriental Cherry, Japanese Flowering Cherry. These double- or single-flowered hybrids have few equals, as they provide dramatic spring beauty coupled with great foliage and bark. Oriental cherries are usually flat topped and wide spreading, growing 50 to 75 feet tall and wide. In midspring large clusters of 2-inch-wide flowers with 10 to 30 petals hang down from the limbs beneath the unfolding leaves, blooming in white or shades of pink. The single-flowered types are more delicate, while the double-flowered ones are more sensational. The oval or lance-shaped, 3- to 5-inch-long, glossy leaves usually emerge with a soft bronze tinge, mature to dark green, and then turn rich orange, red, or scarlet in fall. The reddish brown bark on the stout trunk and branches is shiny and marked with light horizontal bands. Use these trees in a garden where their shape can be accommodated. Vase-shaped types make good street trees if the soil is adequate. From Korea and Japan.

HOW TO GROW. Full sun and well-drained, moisture-retentive, acid to neutral soil. Susceptible to many insects and diseases, including viruses, so may be short-lived. Zones 6b–8b.

CULTIVARS. 'Amanogawa' has light pink, semidouble flowers with 5 to 15 petals and yellow-bronze new growth; columnar, reaching 20 feet tall and 5 feet wide. 'Kwanzan' has amazingly large clusters of shocking pink, double flowers with 20 to 30 petals in late spring (some gardeners find it too aggressive a color); a strong vase shape if grafted; one of the cherries planted in the Washington, D.C., tidal basin; hardy in Zone 6a or 5b. 'Royal Burgundy' is like 'Kwanzan', but with shiny red-purple leaves. 'Shiro-fugen' is perhaps the best cultivar; the large clusters of 30-petaled, blush pink blossoms fade to pure white, then become deep pink again before dropping after a 3-week bloom; new growth is bronze; flat topped and wide spreading to 25 to 30 feet tall. 'Shirotae' ('Mt. Fuji') has large clusters of pure white, fragrant flowers with 12 petals; new growth is green; grows 15 to 20 feet tall. 'Shogetsu' has 30-petaled, white flowers and green new growth; reaches 15 feet tall with a flat top. 'Tai Haku' has white, 2½-inch, five-petaled flowers opening from pale pink buds; coppery bronze new growth; a broad vase shape, growing to 35 feet tall.

P. subhirtella var. *pendula (P. pendula)*   P. 114

p. sub-her-TELL-ah pen-DEW-lah. Higan Cherry, Weeping Cherry. This graceful weeping tree grows rapidly to 20 to 40 feet tall and 15 to 30 feet wide and is most dramatic in early spring, when its leafless branches become a waterfall of single or double, pink or white, 1½-inch blossoms. The glossy, dark green leaves measure 3 inches long, are deeply toothed, and usually remain green well into fall before dropping without changing color. In some cases, however, they may change briefly to yellow. The tree's silhouette is wonderful in winter, especially when outlined against the sky or dusted with snow or ice. Locate it where it can be reflected in a pool of water, or plant it at the top of a slope to emphasize its cascading branches. From Japan.

HOW TO GROW. Full sun and moist, well-drained soil. Tolerates clayey soil. Prune when young to a single strong leader and allow branches to weep to the ground for the best effect. Mulch or plant a ground cover beneath the branches rather than attempting to grow grass. More pest tolerant than Oriental cherries if the soil is kept moist. Zones 5b–8b.

CULTIVARS AND SIMILAR SPECIES. 'Yae-shirdare-higan' ('Plena Rosea') has long-lasting, double, dark pink, 1-inch flowers. 'White Fountain' ('Snow Fountains', 'Wayside White Weeper') is a naturally weeping (not grafted) hybrid that grows 12 to 15 feet tall and has large white flowers, shiny bark, and gold fall color. *P. subhirtella* 'Autumnalis' has semi-double pink flowers that bloom in early spring and again lightly in autumn; more rounded and less weeping.

P. × yedoensis   P. 115

p. × yea-doe-EN-sis. Yoshino Cherry, Potomac Cherry. One of the cherries that made Washington, D.C., famous for its cherry blossoms, Yoshino cherry is a graceful, medium-size, broadly rounded tree that grows 40 to 50 feet tall. It's extremely showy when in bloom, as the fragrant, single, 1¼-inch-wide blossoms are so profuse before the leaves emerge that they turn the tree into a translucent cloud. Flowers open pale pink and then turn snowy white. They are borne in clusters of three to six. The dark green leaves are 2 to 4 inches long and turn yellowish before dropping. Tiny black fruits ripen in early summer. Use this dramatic tree where its spring bloom can be appreciated—in a border, garden, or lawn, or even as a street tree where there is plenty of room for root growth. From Japan.

HOW TO GROW. Full sun and moist, well-drained soil. Tolerates some drought. Zones 6b–8b.

CULTIVARS. 'Afterglow' has rich pink flowers that do not fade to white. 'Akebono' has soft pink flowers and a rounded shape; very vigorous; hardy in Zone 6a. 'Shidare Yoshino' is a dwarf weeping form with small white flowers.

❦ *Pyrus*

PYE-russ. Rose family, Rosaceae.

This genus contains about 30 species of Old World trees that produce small clusters of white flowers in spring and usually small, seedy, inconspicuous fruits, although several are orchard trees that produce edible pears. The leaves are glossy ovals with toothed or scalloped edges; branches are sometimes thorny. Several species are popular for their ornamental flowers and handsome leaves. One, *P. calleryana* 'Bradford'

(Bradford pear), has been overplanted as a street tree, and its susceptibility to storm damage has become an expensive problem for many municipalities.

P. calleryana   P. 115

p. kal-ler-ee-AY-nah. Callery Pear, Flowering Pear. Cold hardy and beautiful in bloom and in leaf, Callery pear and its many cultivars have become popular as garden and street trees because they grow into manageable oval or rounded shapes that

30 to 50 feet tall and 20 to 35 feet wide. In early spring, fluffy clusters of white, five-petaled, 1-inch flowers with dark-tipped anthers transform the tree into a snowy mass. Most cultivars have an offensive odor up close that can permeate a yard, especially when several trees are grown together. The dark green, oval leaves have a high polish and lovely scalloped edges. They open when the flowers begin to fade and are 4 to 5 inches long. Color is spectacular in late fall and often lasts for several weeks. A single tree may include red, purple, orange, and scarlet foliage. The green or russet, ¼- to ½-inch fruits ripen in summer and are so attractive to birds that the tree should not be planted in quantity near airports. Although the fruits themselves are not messy, the resulting bird droppings may be. Most cultivars tend to have a stiff oval shape, which makes them good street trees, because the limbs do not interfere with traffic. But the shape is often too formal for their use as shade trees in home landscapes. Plant at a distance from the house or outdoor sitting areas to avoid the flowers' bad smell. An excellent performer in the Midwest and North. From Asia.

HOW TO GROW. Full sun to partial shade and almost any well-drained soil, light to heavy, acid to alkaline. Best with even moisture, but tolerates drought and intermittently wet soil. Performs well in urban settings; tolerates air pollution. Large limbs of cultivars with tight branch angles may be susceptible to storm damage. Choose improved cultivars or prune when young to develop strong crotch angles. Because this pear goes dormant so late, choose early-coloring cultivars for northern zones to prevent frost damage. Susceptible to several insects and diseases, including blister mites, scab, and rust; the worst problem is fire blight in the South. Zones 3b/5b–9a, depending on the cultivar.

CULTIVARS AND SIMILAR SPECIES. 'Aristocrat' is fast growing and pyramidal when young, and rounded with strong, more horizontal branches as it ages; leaves are narrow, turning red and yellow in fall; does not flower well when young. 'Autumn Blaze' is a cold-hardy tree with strong, wide crotch angles and the widest, most informal crown of any cultivar; grows to 35 feet tall and 20 feet wide; excellent, long-lasting, cardinal red early-fall color and bad-smelling flowers; susceptible to fire blight; Zone 5a. 'Bradford' has a uniform oval shape, growing to 45 feet tall; prone to storm damage because of its crowded, narrow crotch angles; widely planted but now out of favor. 'Burgundy Snow' has profuse white flowers with burgundy centers; pyramidal, growing to 40 feet tall; Zones 4b–9a. 'Capital' is columnar, has a strong central leader, and grows to 40 feet tall and 12 feet wide; purple and bright red early-fall color. 'Chanticleer' ('Cleveland Select') is a 35-foot-tall, formal pyramid or oval with strong branches and a central leader if properly pruned; abundant, bad-smelling flowers; gold, red, and purple early-fall color; fire blight resistant; Zones 4b–9a. 'Frontier' is narrow and upright, growing to 35 feet tall and 20 feet wide, and is the most cold-hardy selection to Zone 3b. 'Redspire' is a dense, narrow pyramid, growing to 35 feet tall and 15 feet wide; strong branches, large flowers, and yellow, red, and maroon early-fall color; somewhat susceptible to fire blight. 'Metropolitan' has a wide-spreading shape, growing to 45 feet tall, with strong branch angles. 'Whitehouse' is a narrow, pyramidal oval reaching 40 feet tall and 18 feet wide; reddish purple early-fall color. 'Valiant' is short and compact, reaching 30 feet tall and 20 feet wide; crimson early-fall color; Zone 4b. *P. ussuriensis* (Ussuri pear) is a very cold hardy, fire blight–resistant Asian species; rounded and growing 40 to 50 feet tall; prolific white flowers, leathery leaves, and reddish purple fall color; excellent in cold northern areas; Zones 3b–6b. 'Mountain Frost' is vigorous and upright, reaching 30 feet tall. 'Prairie Gem' is smaller and more rounded, reaching 18 to 25 feet tall.

P. salicifolia 'Pendula'
P. 116

p. sal-eh-seh-FOL-ee-ah. Weeping Willowleaf Pear. This graceful weeping tree grows to 25 feet tall and makes a spectacular light-reflecting focal point against a dark background. Its main attraction is its narrow silvery leaves, which are 3½ inches long and covered with white fuzz. Combined with the cascading branches, these leaves create the same effect as a weeping Russian olive. The spring-blooming flowers are white and showy, but they are obscured by the leaves. The green, pear-shaped, 1½-inch fruits are sparse and also go unnoticed. Plant this specimen as a focal point at the axis of a path or near a patio where its silvery glow can stand out against a background of evergreens or a dark wall. From southwestern Asia.

HOW TO GROW. Full sun and well-drained soil. Tolerates drought and light or stony soil. Remove suckers. Susceptible to fire blight. Zones 5b–8a.

CULTIVARS AND SIMILAR SPECIES. 'Silver Frost' is the same as 'Pendula'. *P. betulaefolia* (birch-leaf pear) has an oval shape with strong, slightly pendulous branches; grows to 35 feet tall; coarse-toothed leaves are green on top and silvery on their undersides; white spring flowers are partly hidden by the leaves; resists fire blight. 'Dancer' has silvery leaves that flutter like an aspen's in the slightest breeze. 'Edgedell' is a hybrid with purple-tinged new leaves that mature to silver.

❦ *Quercus*

KWUR-kuss. Beech family, Fagaceae.

This large genus of 450 species contains both evergreen and deciduous trees and shrubs that hail mostly from the Northern Hemisphere and are particularly abundant in Mexico, which claims more than 100 native species. Most North American species are large, long-lived trees that make an impressive statement in the landscape. Flowers are usually inconspicuous male and female catkins. Fruits are highly recognizable acorns—the seeds rest in a rough, caplike cup. Leaves are alternate and usually lobed, with blunt or pointed tips, but some species have unlobed leaves. Deciduous oaks are divided into two groups: *black (red) oaks*, with bristle-tipped pointed lobes and acorns that take 2 years to mature, and *white oaks*, with rounded lobes and acorns that take 1 year to mature. (For the evergreen species, see page 310.) Many of these forest dwellers are important for lumber and wildlife, but they also are popular and useful shade trees for home and public landscapes. Until recently, most species were not widely propagated by nurseries because cuttings were difficult to root and many species have taproots. Modern growing techniques are overcoming these problems, and oaks are now more widely available.

Many diseases and insects attack oak trees, although most are not life threatening. Gypsy moths defoliate oaks during epidemic years. Red oaks are highly susceptible to oak wilt; they should not be pruned during the growing season, because beetles carrying this deadly fungus can easily enter the wounds; infected trees should be destroyed. White oaks are susceptible to mildew during wet years.

BLACK (RED) OAKS

Q. coccinea   P. 117, 118

q. kok-SIN-ee-ah. Scarlet Oak. This pyramidal or rounded tree is beloved for its scarlet fall color and grows to 75 feet tall and 40 feet wide. More reliable and more colorful than most oaks in autumn, scarlet oak turns maroon to brilliant scarlet in midfall, in a good year rivaling the best of the maples. Leaves are deeply cut into seven to nine C-shaped lobes with bristly points. They measure 3 to 6 inches long and 2½ to 4½ inches wide, emerging bright red and maturing to a glossy dark green on top with waxy, dull green undersides. The reddish brown acorns are ½ to 2 inches long and are mostly covered by a bowl-like cup. Like many native oaks, this one was difficult to find in nurseries until recently. It should be saved during development and makes an excellent lawn or street tree. From eastern and central North America.

HOW TO GROW. Full sun. Best in moist, acid, sandy soil, but tolerates slightly alkaline, clayey, or dry soil. Zones 5a–9a.

SIMILAR SPECIES. Similar to *Q. palustris* (pin oak) and *Q. rubra* (northern red oak).

Q. palustris   P. 119

q. pal-US-truss. Pin Oak. This strongly pyramidal tree grows 60 to 70 or more feet tall and 25 to 40 feet wide. It has a distinctive straight trunk and a strong horizontal branching pattern, with the lowest branches sweeping downward and creating a skirt near the base of the tree. The yellow-green catkins bloom along with the emerging foliage. The 3- to 6-inch-long, deep green leaves are deeply cut into five to seven U-shaped lobes with sharp points. In fall the leaves change to yellow or coppery red, then become paper bag brown and may remain on the tree through the winter. Pin oak produces numerous crops of round, ½-inch, light brown acorns with thin, shallow cups. This is probably the oak that is most widely planted as a lawn and street tree. However, it needs plenty of room for its low, ascending branches and therefore actually makes a poor street tree. From eastern North America.

HOW TO GROW. Full sun and moist, well-drained, rich, acid soil. Tolerates wet sites, air pollution, and drought. Acorns may be a litter problem. Easy to transplant because of its shallow, fibrous root system. Prune when young to remove competing leaders. Remove lower branches if they interfere with traffic, but other branches may droop lower as a result. Chlorosis is serious in neutral to alkaline soil, so the tree performs poorly in the Plains and Midwest. Zones 5a–8b.

CULTIVARS AND SIMILAR SPECIES. 'Crownright' has strongly horizontal branches that do not droop, but it is subject to breakage, so is no longer recommended. *Q. ellipsoidalis* (northern pin oak) is very similar to pin oak but is native to a more northerly area; Zones 3b–6a. *Q. nuttallii (Q. texana)* (Nuttall's oak) resembles pin oak but hails from the South;

a very fast grower with a pyramidal shape and red fall color, it withstands the wet soil and urban conditions of the South and Midwest; Zones 5b–9a.

Q. rubra (Q. borealis) P. 121

q. RUE-bra. Northern Red Oak. Upright with horizontal branching, northern red oak grows to 70 feet tall and wide and can rival scarlet oak for fall color. The 4- to 8-inch-long leaves are deeply cut into 7 to 11 shallow lobes with sharp points. They unfold pinkish red in spring and mature to dark green with gray-green undersides. In autumn they turn russet-red to bright red. The 1-inch acorns are dark brown with smooth ridges and gray stripes. Bark on mature trees is deeply furrowed and quite ornamental. Use this fast-growing, long-lived oak as a shade tree for a lawn or park. Makes a good street tree except under power lines. From eastern and midwestern North America.

HOW TO GROW. Full to partial sun and well-drained, light, acid to neutral soil. Tolerates drought and urban conditions. Acorns may be a litter problem. Train to develop a strong central leader with evenly spaced branches. Chlorosis can develop in alkaline soil. Zones 3b–9a.

SIMILAR SPECIES. *Q. shumardii* (shumard oak) is very similar, with red fall foliage, but is native to southeastern and south-central North America; fast growing, it performs well in its native regions in wet or dry soil; Zones 5b–9a. *Q. falcata* (southern red oak, Spanish oak) has red-or-ange to russet-orange fall color and can grow in very poor soil; Zones 6b–9a. *Q. velutina* (black oak) is native to eastern and midwestern North America; not widely available commercially, but should be saved during development; seven- to nine-lobed, stiff, shiny, green leaves turn russet in autumn; ½-inch, light brown acorns; grows in sandy to heavy soil but performs best in a rich, moist site; Zones 4b–8b.

WHITE OAKS

Q. acutissima P. 116

q. ay-quew-TIS-sih-mah. Sawtooth Oak. Pyramidal when young, sawtooth oak becomes rounded with age, growing 35 to 45 feet tall and wide, with large, low branches. The leaves of this beautiful, fine-textured shade tree resemble chestnut leaves: unlobed and oblong (7 inches long and 2¼ inches wide), with softly bristled edges. They open light golden green in spring and mature to shiny dark green. Fall color is bright yellow to gold and develops late; dry leaves often persist through the winter. Attractive, golden, 4-inch-long catkins decorate the tree in spring when the leaves open. One-inch-long, round, rich brown acorns with shaggy caps are borne profusely, providing excellent food for wildlife but posing a cleanup problem if not eaten. Bark is deeply ridged and furrowed, becoming corky with age. This heat-tolerant tree makes an exceptional shade tree in the South. From Asia.

HOW TO GROW. Full sun and rich, moist, well-drained, acid to neutral soil. Tolerates intermittent poor drainage, drought, and salt spray. Train to a single leader with evenly spaced main branches. May be defoliated by oakworms and become chlorotic in an alkaline site. Zones 5a–9a.

CULTIVARS AND SIMILAR SPECIES. 'Gobbler' has an especially reliable, heavy crop of acorns and is very cold hardy. The following North American trees are valuable natives with similar leaves. Though not widely sold, they should be preserved during site development. *Q. muehlenbergii* (yellow chestnut oak) is native to east-central and southwestern North America and is often found on limestone outcroppings; its yellow-green leaves are unlobed with round-toothed edges and have felty white undersides; the tree's shape is narrow and vaselike; grows to 50 or more feet tall; a good choice for neutral to alkaline soil; Zones 5a–8b. *Q. prinus* (chestnut oak) is native to eastern North America; it forms a dense, rounded tree that reaches 60 feet tall; its leaves measure up to 7 inches long, open pale green, mature to dark green, and turn red-orange and golden brown in autumn; acorns are large and can pose a cleanup problem; excels in dry, rocky, acid soil; Zones 5a–9a. *Q. michauxii* (swamp chestnut oak) is very similar to *Q. prinus* but is native to wet sites in southern and central North America; Zones 6b–9a.

Q. bicolor

q. BYE-cull-or. Swamp White Oak. The winter silhouette of this mighty oak is rugged and coarse, with a round, low, open canopy that grows 50 to 60 feet tall and spreads even wider. Leaves are 3 to 7 inches long, blunt lobed or wavy edged, and shiny dark green on top with velvety gray-green undersides. They form a dense foliage that turns yellow-brown to red in autumn. The bark on the branches peels like that of a birch, and the trunk bark is roughly furrowed and marked with white. Light brown acorns ripen in early fall and are about 1 inch long. Native to swampy sites, this massive oak also tolerates drought and is one of the easiest white oaks to transplant. It makes an excellent choice for parks, wetlands, and open spaces. From eastern North America.

HOW TO GROW. Full to partial sun. Best in moist, acid to neutral soil, but also grows well in wet sites. Tolerates drought. Pruning is not usually necessary to form a good shape, but lower limbs may be removed as the tree matures to reveal the bark. Suffers from chlorosis in highly alkaline soil. Trees saved during development are very sensitive to soil compaction or disturbance during construction and should be mulched heavily rather than having grass planted beneath them. Usually not bothered by pests, except for gypsy moths. Performs well in the Midwest and Mountain States. Zones 4a–8b.

CULTIVARS AND SIMILAR SPECIES. *Q. alba* (white oak), **P. 117**, is a massive, spreading, slow-growing native oak that has only recently been offered by nurseries; it has upright to horizontal branches and a picturesque, rugged, 80- to 100-foot-tall silhouette; trunk and limbs are covered with light brown or gray shaggy bark; leaves are 4 to 8 inches long with rounded lobes; they emerge pinkish, mature to a deep, matte bluegreen, and usually turn purplish or crimson before dropping in fall; one of the finest fall displays of any oak; leaves are mildew resistant; tolerates alkaline and occasionally wet soil; Zones 4b–9a. *Q. macrocarpa* (bur oak, mossycup oak) is slow growing to 60 to 80 feet tall; it has a straight trunk and low branches; leaves are blunt lobed; twigs are corky; acorns are 2 inches around and provide food for wildlife; tolerates drought and wet soil; an excellent shade tree or windbreak in acid or alkaline soil in its native midwestern Plains and Rocky Mountains; Zones 3a–9a. 'Boomer' is more upright, with spreading branches and vigorous growth.

Q. nigra

q. NYE-grah. Water Oak, Possum Oak. This upright or rounded tree is a fast-growing, rough-barked native that reaches 50 to 80 feet tall and half as wide. It is a popular street and shade tree in the South because of its shape and slender branches. Its fine-textured, dull blue-green leaves measure 2 to 4 inches long and half as wide and vary from unlobed to slightly lobed to paddle shaped. They stay green until they drop in early winter and may be semievergreen in the Deep South. Acorns are ½ inch long, are striped brown and black, have shallow caps, and require little cleanup, although they can stain concrete when they drop. Use this tall tree where there is plenty of room for it to grow. From southeastern North America.

HOW TO GROW. Needs full sun. Best in moist, well-drained soil, but tolerates wet sites and heavy, compacted soil. Prune to a strong branch structure; weak wooded compared to other oaks. Remove lower limbs as the tree matures to reveal the massive trunk. Acorns can sprout and cause a weed seedling problem. Mistletoe, aphids, scale, and borers can be problems. Zones 6b–10a.

CULTIVARS AND SIMILAR SPECIES. New cultivars may be available with columnar shapes. *Q. imbricaria* (shingle oak), **P. 118**, is pyramidal when young; becomes open and rounded, with widely spaced, horizontally spreading branches, with age; dark green, unlobed, leathery leaves turn yellow in fall; tolerates slightly alkaline soil; Zones 5a–9a.

Q. phellos P. 119, 120

q. PHIL-loos. Willow Oak. This fine-textured oak is pyramidal with weeping lower branches when young and becomes rounded with age, growing 50 to 90 feet tall and 40 feet wide. The leaves are unusual for an oak—long, slender, and unlobed, measuring about 4 inches long and 1 inch wide. These shiny, dark green leaves create a much more refined texture than that of most oaks. In the coldest zones of its range, the leaves often turn red or yellow in fall, but in the warmest zones, they remain green into winter. The tree produces copious ½-inch acorns, which are excellent food for wildlife and, because of their small size, do not pose a cleanup problem in groomed landscapes. Use this graceful tree to shade a lawn or street. It is easily transplanted and readily available. From southeastern North America.

HOW TO GROW. Full sun and moist, well-drained, acid soil. Tolerates intermittent poor drainage. The small leaves are easy to rake. Prune when young to develop an even crown and a strong central leader; remove lower ascending branches if they interfere with traffic. Chlorosis develops in alkaline soil; otherwise problem-free. Zones 6b–9a.

CULTIVARS. None.

Q. robur P. 120, 121

q. ROW-burr. English Oak. This distinguished European oak is broad and rounded, with a short massive trunk and huge low branches, making an impressive specimen 50 to 100 feet tall and wide. The dark, matte green leaves are 2 to 5 inches long, with three to seven rounded lobes. They drop in early winter without changing color. One-inch-long, shiny, dark brown acorns have a distinctive narrow shape and grow on long stalks. Trunk bark is rugged, deeply furrowed, and gray-black. The species grows quite large and is best used in parks. Smaller and narrower cultivars perform well as screens, windbreaks, and garden shade trees. From Europe and western Asia.

HOW TO GROW. Full sun and well-drained soil. Tolerates clayey or slightly alkaline soil, urban conditions, and drought. Acorns may pose a litter problem. Prune when young to maintain a central leader and evenly spaced branches. May suffer from mildew. Excellent in the Midwest and Mountain States. Zones 5b–9a.

CULTIVARS AND SIMILAR SPECIES. 'Crimson Spire' is a tight, columnar hybrid with *Q. alba,* growing to 45 feet tall and 15 feet wide; mildew-resistant leaves and rusty red fall color. 'Skymaster' has very dark green leaves and is narrowly pyramidal, with a strong central leader; grows to 50 feet tall and 15 feet wide. 'Skyrocket' ('Fastigiata') grows to 50 feet tall and 15 feet wide. 'Rosehill' is a narrow oval that reaches 40 feet tall and 20 feet wide; glossy, mildew-resistant leaves. 'Westminster Globe' is rounded and symmetrical, with a strong branch structure; grows to 45 feet tall and wide. *Q.* × *warei* 'Regal Prince' is an upright, oval hybrid with *Q. bicolor* that grows to 50 feet; dark green leaves with silvery undersides; tolerates wet or dry sites.

❦ *Rhus*

russ. Cashew family, Anacardiaceae.

This large genus includes deciduous and evergreen trees and shrubs as well as a few vines. Some of its members, including poison ivy, poison oak, and poison sumac, are notorious for causing allergic skin reactions; all species are poisonous to some degree if ingested. Leaves are usually compound and divided into three or more pinnate parts. Flowers are often inconspicuous, with male and female flowers borne on separate plants. Several species feature strikingly showy foliage and make interesting landscape plants.

R. typhina   P. 122

r. tye-FYE-nah. Staghorn Sumac. Often forming a thicket due to its suckering roots, this 15- to 30-foot-tall, multitrunked, sparsely branched tree has a strong, upright architectural form and makes a bold foliage plant. Leaves are dark green and velvety, 2 feet long, and divided into 11 to 31 pointed leaflets that measure 4 inches long and are arranged pinnately along a reddish brown midrib. Young, twiggy branches are stout and densely covered with velvety hairs, reminiscent of a buck's antlers. In early summer, greenish male and female flowers bloom at the branch tips in 8-inch clusters on separate plants. On female plants, the flowers ripen into attractive, clublike clusters of fuzzy red fruits that last well into winter until they are eaten by birds. In early autumn, the leaves turn glowing shades of light orange, crimson, and red, creating one of the finest foliage displays of any small tree. Site this suckering tree as a focal point or specimen in an uncluttered landscape where its bold tropical appearance is an asset. Or plant it in a mass in a naturalistic or informal garden where its spreading habit is welcome. It also is an excellent choice for erosion control. From eastern North America.

HOW TO GROW. Full sun. Best in fertile, moist, well-drained soil, but adapts well to poor soil and drought. May suffer from canker and dieback. Prune out old or diseased trunks to make room for new growth. May be cut to the ground every year or every other year to control growth; resulting new shoots grow to about 6 feet in one season. Difficult to eradicate and may become weedy in the wrong site or if not controlled. Zones 3b–8a.

CULTIVARS AND SIMILAR SPECIES. 'Dissecta' and 'Laciniata' (cut-leaved staghorn sumac) are fruit-bearing females with very finely cut, ferny leaves that have a bold but lacy appearance. *R. glabra* (smooth sumac), **P. 122**, is native throughout North America and is almost identical to *R. typhina*, but its stems and leaves are smooth and hairless; grows to 15 feet tall; Zones 3a–9a. 'Laciniata' is a rare cut-leaved form. *R. javanica* var. *chinensis* (Chinese sumac) has 12-inch-long leaves divided into 7 to 13 leaflets, showy white flowers in late summer, and scarlet fall color and fruits; grows to 20 feet tall; Zones 6–9. 'September Beauty' has larger, more beautiful flower clusters but no fruits.

❧ *Robinia*

row-BIN-ee-ah. Pea family, Fabaceae.

The four members of this North American genus have alternate, pinnately compound leaves and clusters of fragrant flowers. They can fix their own nitrogen from the soil, so they adapt well to poor, infertile sites.

R. pseudoacacia   P. 123

r. sue-doe-ah-CASE-ee-ah. Black Locust. Varying within its native range from a very narrow tree with an arrow-straight, 75-foot-tall trunk to an irregularly branched, spreading, 45-foot tall tree, black locust casts a dappled shade that's perfect for many garden situations. The fine-textured leaves appear in late spring and are divided into 15 rounded, 1- to 2-inch-long, blue-green leaflets, which fold up at night. Some trees have yellow fall color; others lose leaves without changing color. In late spring and early summer, 8-inch-long clusters of very fragrant, creamy white flowers hang beneath the foliage. They can ripen into flat, 6-inch-long, brown seedpods. The branches have a zigzag pattern and are slightly thorny. Trunk bark is deeply furrowed and light brown, with a lot of winter character. Although the branches are brittle, the trunk wood is very durable, and tall trunks are used for ships' masts and fence posts. Use this fast-growing tree in difficult, poor-soil sites and to create light shade in a lawn. From eastern and central North America and naturalized throughout most of the continent.

HOW TO GROW. Full sun. Best in fertile, moist soil, but adapts to poor, infertile soil. Tolerates drought and urban conditions. Fast-growing suckers can sprout at great distances from the trunk, especially in poor-soil sites, and should be cut out promptly. The tree has shallow roots and can topple during high winds if the ground is soggy. Prune in fall or winter to develop a single leader; multiple trunks are weak. Drop crotch tall trees to reduce height and prevent storm damage. Borers are sometimes a serious problem and encourage broken limbs. Zones 4b–9a.

CULTIVARS AND SIMILAR SPECIES. 'Appalachia' has a straight trunk and resists borers. 'Bressoniana' is thornless, compact, and oval; grows to 30 feet tall. 'Frisia' has lovely chartreuse leaves all season and makes an outstanding focal point against a dark background; grows 30 to 50 feet tall; provides afternoon shade in hot climates. 'Inermis' is thornless, dense, and rounded; grows to 20 feet tall and wide. 'Purple Robe' is a dense hybrid with bronze-red new growth, bronze-green mature leaves, and beautiful rose pink spring flowers; grows 30 to 50 feet tall, with variable thorniness. 'Pyramidalis' is thornless and columnar; grows to 40 feet tall and 15 feet wide. 'Umbraculifolia' is a dense, rounded, thornless, shrublike form; grows to 15 feet tall with few flowers. *R* × *ambigua* 'Idahoensis' is a hybrid with purple-pink flowers and an upright, oval shape; grows to 35 feet tall; good in places with hot, dry summers and cold winters.

Salix

SAY-lixs. Willow family, Salicaceae.

This genus contains 300 to 500 deciduous trees and shrubs, most native to wet-soil areas in the Northern Hemisphere, from the tropics to the Arctic. Leaves are usually long and narrow with a fine texture. Flowers are borne in male and female catkins on separate plants. Although 100 or so willows are native to North America, the popular landscape trees are from Europe. These picturesque garden specimens are messy and weak wooded, however, so site them with care.

S. alba 'Tristis' (*S.* × *sepulcralis* 'Chrysocoma') P. 124

s. AL-bah TRISS-tiss. Niobe Willow, Golden Weeping Willow. This popular willow forms a large, rounded canopy of long, gracefully weeping branches and grows 50 to 70 feet tall and wide. The trunk and main branches are massive and cloaked in rough brown bark. The slender weeping branches and twigs feature bright gold bark that is especially pretty in winter. Leaves are narrow and lance shaped, measure 4 inches long and ½ inch wide, and have whitish undersides. They are bright yellow-green very early in spring, mature to dark green with silver undersides in summer, and change to golden yellow in late fall. Plant Niobe willow beside a pond or stream, where its form will be reflected in the water, or use it in any informal site with moist to wet soil. Avoid groomed areas, as it is messy. From Europe, northern Africa, and western and central Asia.

HOW TO GROW. Full sun and moist to wet, average to fertile soil. Drops leaves and small branches through the summer and fall, so cleanup is a constant need. Wood is weak and subject to storm damage. Prune to develop a strong shape; brace heavy branches. Attacked by many insects and diseases, including twig blight, gall, canker, aphids, borers, and sawflies. Zones 3a–9a.

CULTIVARS AND SIMILAR SPECIES. 'Niobe' is another name for 'Tristis'. 'Prairie Cascade' is a 45-foot-tall hybrid with glossy, leathery, green leaves and gold weeping branches; Zones 3a–7b. *S. alba* (white willow) is an upright tree with greenish twigs. *S. alba* var. *vitellina* (golden willow) is round headed and nonweeping, with gold to bright yellow twigs and very narrow leaves. *S. babylonica* (weeping willow) is very similar to Niobe willow but is even more pendulous, with green twigs; Zones 7a–9a.

S. matsudana (*S. babylonica* var. *pekinensis*) P. 124

s. mat-sue-DAY-nah. Hankow Willow, Peking Willow. This large willow is a nonweeping tree with a rounded or oval shape, bright green twigs, and fine-textured branches. It matures to 40 to 50 feet tall and wide and looks very similar to *S. babylonica*, except that it does not weep. Leaves are slender, emerging pale green and maturing to olive green in summer. They drop without changing color in fall. Forms with twisted branches are the most common landscape types, and they make unique accent plants that stand out in the winter garden. From northern China.

HOW TO GROW. Partial to full sun and moist, acid to alkaline soil. Tolerates road salt and dry soil better than most willows, but does not tolerate drought. Weak wooded and messy. Train to a single leader and space branches evenly to develop a more storm-resistant structure. Protect trunk bark from injury. Zones 5a–9a.

CULTIVARS. 'Tortulosa' (corkscrew willow) has ornamental, very twisted branches and twigs and curled leaves; train to a single trunk; grows 20 to 30 feet tall. 'Scarlet Curls' has semipendulous, slightly twisted branches, red twigs, and curly leaves; grows to 30 feet tall and 15 to 20 feet tall. 'Golden Curls' is a hybrid with slightly twisted, gold stems and somewhat curled leaves; rather shrubby, growing to 30 feet tall and half as wide.

✿ *Sophora*

sow-FOR-ah. Pea family, Fabaceae.

This varied genus includes 50 to 80 species of trees, shrubs, and herbs. Leaves are pinnately compound, and seedpods are rounded or winged and tightened between the seeds. One species is an increasingly popular landscape tree.

S. japonica (Styphnolobium japonicum) P. 125

s. jah-PON-eh-kah. Japanese Pagoda Tree, Chinese Scholar Tree. Fifty to 75 feet tall and wide, with a rounded spreading crown, this graceful, fine-textured summer bloomer has become a recent favorite as an urban street tree. Leaves can reach 9 inches in length and are shiny, bright green, and divided into 7 to 17 pointed, 1-inch-long leaflets, which drop in late fall with no color change. In mid- to late summer, large, airy, pyramidal clusters of small creamy flowers adorn the tree for 2 to 3 weeks, creating a lovely lacy look, but flowering may not commence until the tree is 10 years old. As with all trees in the pea family, 4- to 8-inch-long seedpods are a showy yellow in fall, ripen to dark brown, and remain on bare branches during the winter, dropping intermittently. Trunk bark is dark gray and corrugated on mature trees. Use this tree to cast light shade on a house, patio, or lawn or to line a street away from power lines. From China and Korea.

HOW TO GROW. Full sun and fertile, moist, acid to alkaline soil. Tolerates drought, heat, air pollution, and urban conditions, but not poorly drained soil. Fall cleanup is minimal due to the small leaflets. Flowers fall in late summer; pods fall in winter and may be slippery. Train when young to develop a single tall trunk with well-spaced branches. Cable large scaffold branches of mature trees to prevent storm damage, or prune back side branches in late summer to reduce weight. Usually pest-free, but leafhoppers, mildew, and twig blight are sometimes trouble-some. Zones 5b–8b.

CULTIVARS. Seed-grown trees are variable in form and often slow growing; choose a named cultivar. 'Princeton Upright' is upright and compact, growing 40 to 50 feet tall; a good street tree. 'Regent' has an oval crown, reaches 40 to 50 feet tall, is disease resistant, and blooms well when young.

Sorbus

SORE-buss. Rose family, Rosaceae.

This large genus contains 120 species of mountain ashes from North America and Europe. Flowers are usually creamy white in flattened, el-derlike heads and ripen into clusters of small, showy, red apples. Leaves are variable, from compound to simple. Species with compound leaves are called mountain ashes; those with simple leaves are called white-beams. Most hail from cool, moist, northern climates and do not fare well when grown in hot sites or in poor, dry soil, hence their reputation for being disease ridden. When planted in a favorable climate, however, they are very showy and desirable garden trees that offer year-round beauty.

S. alnifolia   P. 125

s. al-neh-FOL-ee-ah. Alder Whitebeam, Korean Mountain Ash. This pest-resis-tant tree has an upright or pyramidal shape when young and becomes rounded with age. It grows 40 to 50 feet tall and 20 to 30 feet wide and draws attention throughout the year. In late spring, 3-inch, lacy clusters of white flowers bloom above the foliage, creating a show for a week or so. Leaves are 4-inch-long, pointed ovals with slightly toothed edges, re-sembling beech leaves. They turn glorious colors in autumn—first yel-low-green, then yellow, and finally deep coral red. When the leaves drop, the ripened clusters of pendulous, shiny, rose-red or scarlet berries are displayed to full advantage. The berries remain on the tree well into win-ter and provide food for birds. The silver gray trunk and limbs resemble those of a small beech and are very attractive in winter. Grow as a low-branched border tree so that you can appreciate the flowers and fruits at eye level. This species may bloom and fruit well only every other year. From Asia.

HOW TO GROW. Full sun is best for fall color, but tolerates light shade. Likes moist, well-drained, acid to alkaline soil. Mulch to keep roots cool and moist. Grow as a single- or multitrunked tree. Resists borers, but may suffer from scab and fire blight in hot, humid areas. Highly disease resistant in cool, dry climates. Zones 3a–7a.

CULTIVARS. 'Redbird' forms a narrow column, growing to 25 feet tall; numerous red berries and golden yellow fall color.

S. aucuparia P. 126

s. oh-kew-PAR-ee-ah. European Mountain Ash. Growing 35 feet tall and 20 feet wide, this species makes a fine, medium-size shade tree for a lawn or border, but only in cool climates, where it is most pest-free. Leaves are 9 inches long, dark green, and divided into 11 to 17 fernlike, rounded leaflets with toothed edges. Flattened, 5-inch-wide clusters of white flowers bloom in late spring and ripen by fall into orange berries that turn dark red. The berries are quite showy against the green leaves in late summer, but they blend into the fiery shades of the leaves as they change to orange and red in midfall. Berries do not remain on the tree into winter because they are eaten by birds, but the shiny, cherrylike bark adds winter interest. Grow in northern or high-elevation regions to avoid fire blight and other problems. From Europe and Asia.

HOW TO GROW. Full sun and moist, well-drained, acid to alkaline soil. Mulch to keep roots cool and moist. Prune to develop a single trunk and strong branching. Highly susceptible in the South to fire blight, scab, borers, and numerous other pests. Best grown only in the North and West in Zones 2b–6b.

CULTIVARS AND SIMILAR SPECIES. 'Black Hawk' is somewhat columnar, growing to 30 feet tall and 20 feet wide, with large orange fruits and green fall color. 'Brilliant Yellow' has large clusters of yellow berries. 'Cardinal Royal' is vigorous and tightly upright, with very dark green leaves, bright white flowers, and outstanding red fruits. 'Rossica' is a uniform oval, growing to 30 feet tall, with bright red fruits and rusty fall color. *S. americana* (American mountain ash) is very similar to European mountain ash but is bushier, growing 10 to 30 feet tall, and more disease resistant; not widely grown by nurseries. 'Belmonte' is tightly upright. *S. decora* (showy mountain ash) is native to Canada and grows 20 to 30 feet tall; free of fire blight, it has an oval shape, showy flowers, red fruits, and red fall foliage; Zones 2b–6a. *S. rufoferrugenia* 'Longwood Sunset' resembles European mountain ash but is highly disease resistant and tolerates heat and drought; it features large clusters of orange berries and stunning burgundy fall color on a rounded, 30-foot-tall tree; Zones 4a–7b. *S. × thuringiaca* 'Fastigiata' (oakleaf mountain ash) is disease resistant; it has 5-inch white flower clusters, bright red berries, and 6-inch-long, divided, leathery, green leaves; it forms a broad, 30-foot tall dome and is often mislabeled *S. × hybrida;* Zones 5a–8a.

🐦 *Stewartia*

stew-ARE-tee-ah. Tea family, Theaceae.

Related to *Camellia* and *Franklinia,* the 15 members of this genus bloom in summer and have lovely, camellia-like flowers. Several species are valued in temperate gardens for their ornamental bark, fine foliage, and unusual summer blossoms.

S. pseudocamellia   P. 126, 127

s. sue-doe-cam-EEL-ee-ah. Japanese Stewartia, Korean Stewartia. Open branched and oval or vase shaped, this pretty garden tree grows slowly to 30 feet tall and 20 feet wide. The oval, pointed leaves are 2 to 4 inches long and dark green. Bloom commences in early to midsummer. The 2- to 3-inch-wide, cup-shaped, yellow-centered, white blossoms open from prominent round buds and have slightly crinkled petals. Each lasts only 1 day, but many flowers bloom each day for 2 to 3 weeks. Fall foliage is luscious, turning many shades of orange, gold, and red, depending on sun exposure. After the dense leaves drop, the flaky bark on the trunk and branches is displayed to perfection as an orange, tan, and apricot patchwork. Place this tree in a mixed border where it can be enjoyed throughout the year. From Japan and Korea.

HOW TO GROW. Light afternoon shade and humus-rich, moist, acid soil. Easy to grow and pest-free as long as soil and light requirements are met. Train to a single trunk or several trunks and remove lower branches to expose the attractive trunk bark. Faded flowers drop and require daily cleanup. Zones 5b–8b.

CULTIVARS AND SIMILAR SPECIES. 'Ballet' has 3½-inch flowers and graceful down-turned branches. 'Korean Splendor' *(S. pseudocamellia koreana* and *S. koreana)* (Korean stewartia) is very similar to the species, but flowers are 3 inches across and open more widely. *S. monodelpha* (tall stewartia) has metallic orange bark and is blanketed with 1¼-inch, violet-centered, white flowers through the summer; grows 40 to 50 feet tall. *S. ovata* (mountain stewartia) is a southeastern native that forms a bushy, 20-foot-tall tree; 6-inch-long leaves have downy undersides; 4-inch, cup-shaped flowers bloom in mid- to late summer; Zones 5b–8a.

❦ *Styrax*

STYE-raks. Styrax family, Styracaceae.

This genus, a relative of *Halesia,* contains 100 to 130 species from tropical and temperate regions, but only a few are grown as small ornamental trees in North American gardens.

S. japonicum P. 128

s. jah-PON-eh-kum. Japanese Snowbell. Rounded to spreading, with distinctive horizontal branches, this small, multitrunked tree reaches 20 to 30 feet tall and wide and puts on a pretty show of white flowers in late spring or early summer, when most other trees are done blooming. Leaves are 3 inches long and glossy dark green, turning yellowish to rusty red in fall. Flowers are ¾-inch-long, fragrant, white bells that dangle in clusters from the outstretched branches. Seen from a distance, the blooming tree has an elegant green-and-white effect. Hard, felt-covered, gray-green berries ripen in fall and remain on the tree well into winter. Trunk bark is smooth and gray with orange-brown fissures. If possible, plant this tree on a slope or where it can be seen from below, or use it in a border or to shade a patio. Do not plant it near a walkway, because fallen pods are messy in late winter. From Asia.

HOW TO GROW. Flowers best in full sun, but light afternoon shade is preferable in hot climates. Needs humus-rich, moist, well-drained, acid soil. The tree has shallow, competitive roots, so choose underplantings that tolerate dry shade, or simply mulch the ground. Prune to a single trunk or multiple trunks and remove lower branches to encourage a tree shape. Usually trouble-free, but borers may be a problem with stressed trees. Zones 6a–8b.

CULTIVARS AND SIMILAR SPECIES. 'Carillon' is a smaller, 10-foot-tall tree with pendulous branches. 'Pink Chimes' has charming pale pink flowers. 'Sohuksan' has larger flowers and leaves. *S. americanus* (American snowbell), **P. 127**, is a round-headed, shrubby tree that reaches 10 feet tall and has narrow-petaled flowers in late spring; Zones 6b–9a.

S. obassia   P. 128

s. oh-BASS-ee-ah. Fragrant Snowbell. With the largest flower clusters of any *Styrax,* fragrant snowbell grows to 30 or more feet tall and wide and has spreading branches that form an upright or rounded crown. One-inch, bell-shaped, fragrant, white flowers bloom in 6- to 8-inch-long clusters in early summer. They hang beneath the foliage and are partially obscured, so they are best viewed from underneath. The rounded, 8-inch-long, dull green, fuzzy leaves have silvery green undersides and are quite striking because of their bold texture and color. Unfortunately, they have only a slight yellow color in fall. Use this tree in a border or lawn. From China, Japan, and Korea.

HOW TO GROW. Humus-rich, moist, well-drained soil. Performs poorly in heavy soil. Usually pest-free. Zones 6b–8b.

CULTIVARS. None.

Syringa

sigh-RING-gah. Olive family, Oleaceae.

The genus of the beloved common lilac, *Syringa* contains 20 to 30 species, mostly shrubs. A few species grow to treelike proportions and are valued in gardens for their large summer blossoms.

S. reticulata (S. amurensis var. japonica)   P. 129

s. reh-tick-yew-LAY-tah. Japanese Tree Lilac. This tree-sized lilac is an upright, round-headed, multistemmed beauty that grows 20 to 30 or more feet tall and 25 feet wide. Eye-catching, pyramidal, 12-inch-long clusters of creamy white flowers bloom at the branch tips in early summer, putting on a 2-week show. The 5-inch-long, heart-shaped leaves are dark green on top with grayish undersides and turn dull yellow in fall. The bark on the trunk and branches is shiny dark brown with prominent horizontal stripes and is quite attractive, especially in winter. This is a valuable street or garden tree in the North and Mountain States, where the choice of flowering trees is limited. It may be planted under power lines. Unlike common lilac, this tree's flowers do not have an agreeable fragrance. In fact, they smell rather unpleasant, like privet, so the tree is best planted away from windows or outdoor living areas. It is quite showy when viewed at a distance. From Japan.

HOW TO GROW. Full sun and well-drained, acid to alkaline, clayey or loamy soil with plentiful moisture. Tolerates drought once established. Tends to bloom well in alternate years unless faded flowers are removed in time to prevent seed formation. Prune to a single trunk or multiple trunks; remove lower branches to expose the bark. Resistant to mildew, borers, and scale, which plague common lilac. Zones 3a–7b.

CULTIVARS AND SIMILAR SPECIES. 'Ivory Silk' has larger, more profuse flowers, even when young; a compact, oval tree, growing 15 to 20 feet tall. 'Regent' grows vigorously. 'Summer Snow' is compact and has profuse flowers. *S. reticulata* var. *mandushurica* is very similar but is hardy to Zone 2b. *S. pekinensis* (Peking lilac), **P. 129,** is vase shaped, with 6-inch flower clusters and beautiful, shiny, cinnamon brown bark; needs a fertile site; Zones 3b–7b. 'Summer Charm' has a dense, uniform shape.

❦ *Tilia*

TILL-ee-ah. Linden family, Tiliaceae.

Members of this genus usually have bold, heart-shaped or rounded, toothed, alternate leaves; clusters of small, creamy, fragrant flowers attached to winglike, spoon-shaped, green bracts; and clusters of green, pea-shaped fruits. The flowers attract bees, which make a flavorful honey from the nectar. Several species are important landscape subjects, despite a host of disease and insect problems, including leaf blight, mildew, verticillium wilt, anthracnose, rust, borers, gypsy moth caterpillars, aphids, and Japanese beetles. Most of these problems are usually not life threatening. Aphids are the most annoying problem, because they secrete a sticky honeydew that collects on pavement, cars, or lawn furniture beneath infested trees.

T. americana   P. 130

t. ah-mer-eh-KAY-nah. Basswood, American Linden. This native grows 50 to 80 feet tall and has a decided oval shape created by a strong, straight trunk and a skirt of low, down-swept branches. The coarse-textured, toothed, heart-shaped leaves are 4 to 8 inches long and dark green, turning yellowish before dropping in autumn. In early summer, 2- to 3-inch-wide clusters of pale greenish yellow flowers hang among the leaves, giving off a pleasant spicy-sweet scent. Give this large tree plenty of growing space in a park or lawn where it will cast dense shade. It's ideal in a naturalistic setting. From eastern North America.

HOW TO GROW. Full sun to light shade and deep, rich, moist, alkaline or acid soil. Tolerates some drought when established. Train when young to develop a strong branch structure. Remove competing leaders and suckers. Aphids, with subsequent sooty mold, are the worst pests. Leaf scorch occurs in dry years, rust in wet ones. Zones 3a–8a.

CULTIVARS. 'Boulevard' is narrower than the species, growing to 60 feet tall and 30 feet wide, with a strong central leader. 'Frontyard' forms a very symmetrical, uniform pyramid with a strong central leader. 'Legend' is broad and has glossy, rust-resistant leaves. 'Redmond' is a fast-growing hybrid with large glossy leaves, bright yellow fall color, and a compact, tight, 70-foot-tall, pyramidal form. 'Lincoln' forms a compact pyramid, growing to 35 feet tall and 25 feet wide.

T. cordata P. 131

t. kore-DAH-tah. Littleleaf Linden. A favorite street tree because of its dense, symmetrical shape, littleleaf linden is pyramidal when young but matures into a rounded, 60- to 70-foot-tall, 40-foot-wide tree. Most cultivars are uniform and formal looking. Leaves are tidy, bright green, 2- to 4-inch-long hearts with lighter undersides and unremarkable yellowish fall color. Three-inch clusters of creamy yellow flowers bloom in midsummer, dangling beneath the dense leaves in such profusion that from a distance, the tree has a two-tone effect. Trunk bark is gray-brown, ridged, and roughly furrowed. Use as a street, lawn, or park tree. From Europe.

HOW TO GROW. Full to partial sun and fertile, moist, well-drained soil. Tolerates acid or alkaline soil, air pollution, and urban conditions. Train when young to develop a single leader and a strong branch structure. Thin branches, pruning when dormant, to reduce overcrowding in the dense canopy. Usually trouble-free, although aphids and Japanese beetles are common. Zones 3b–8a.

CULTIVARS AND SIMILAR SPECIES. 'Chancellor' forms a 50-by-20-foot, narrow pyramid with golden yellow fall color. 'Corinthian' forms a 45-by-15-foot pyramid with small, very shiny leaves. 'Fairhaven' has a straight trunk, uniform branches, and slightly larger leaves. 'Glenleven' is a fast-growing hybrid that forms an open pyramid, growing to 50 feet tall with a strong central leader; golden fall color; good in the Mountain States. 'Greenspire' is the best-known cultivar; has a straight trunk and well-spaced branches, forming a symmetrical, 50-foot-tall pyramid. 'Olympic' grows 40 feet tall and 30 feet wide; has a looser shape than most cultivars and looks better in informal settings. 'Rancho' has small leaves and a beautiful, narrow form. 'Shamrock' is similar to 'Greenspire' but grows faster and is a bit more open. *T.* × *euchlora* (Crimean linden) has beautiful, fine-textured, glossy foliage that turns bright yellow in fall; grows to 40 feet tall and 35 feet wide, forming a broad pyramid; Zones 5a–8a.

T. tomentosa P. 132

t. toe-men-TOE-sah. Silver Linden. Pyramidal or rounded and growing to 70 feet tall, silver linden has a formal shape that's suitable for manicured gardens. Its 5-inch-long leaves are outstanding—glossy dark green on top with silver gray, woolly undersides. They shimmer and flash in the sun and turn an attractive golden yellow in fall. Fragrant flowers bloom in early summer but are obscured by the dense leaves. Branches and young trunks are covered with smooth, silver gray bark. Older trunks become gray-brown and are ridged and furrowed. Use as a street or lawn tree. If possible, site the tree on a slope or above a wall so that you can look up at the leaves and enjoy their silvery undersides.

HOW TO GROW. Full to partial sun and moist, well-drained soil. Adapts to acid or alkaline conditions. Tolerates moderate drought and urban conditions, but sooty or dusty air will disfigure the leaves. Train when young to develop a central leader and a strong branch structure. Bothered much less than other lindens by diseases and pests, especially Japanese beetles and gypsy moths. Zones 5a–8a.

CULTIVARS. 'Green Mountain' grows rapidly to 45 feet tall and 35 feet wide and has thick leaves that tolerate heat and drought. 'Sterling Silver' grows to 45 feet tall and 35 feet wide, forming a neat, symmetrical oval, and has silvery new growth. 'Satin Shadow' forms a 50-by-40-foot uniform oval and has silvery leaves.

❦ *Ulmus*

ULL-muss. Elm family, Ulmaceae.

This large genus includes trees from Europe, Asia, and North America. Leaves are oval or oblong and pointed, with double-toothed margins and many prominent veins. Fruits are winged nutlets that ripen soon after the inconspicuous flowers bloom. One species in particular, *U. americana* (America elm), was a beloved street tree that lined boulevards across America at the beginning of the twentieth century. In the 1930s, Dutch elm disease (DED), a fungus so named because Dutch researchers identified it, was accidentally introduced into New York on a shipment of logs from France. The fungus was spread to native trees by elm bark beetles (both an American and an introduced European species), and within 30 years most of the elms in the Northeast and Midwest were wiped out. To make matters worse, a new, more virulent strain of DED has recently appeared, killing the remaining trees at an even faster clip.

All American species of elms are highly susceptible to DED. European species are highly resistant, and Asian ones are usually immune. Plant geneticists at the National Arboretum and the Morton Arboretum have been selecting and hybridizing among these species with the goal of developing a tree that looks like our cherished elm while warding off DED and other serious pests. Several hybrids with great potential are now available, and more are on the way.

Meanwhile, existing American elms and other susceptible elms can be protected from DED with good sanitation. Pruning out infected limbs can sometimes stop the disease. Dead or dying trees should be removed immediately. The beetles that spread the fungus burrow between bark and wood, so logs from infected elm trees should be either stripped of their bark, burned, chipped, or buried to prevent further transmission. Never stack this wood in piles with the bark intact. Elms should be separated by at least 500 feet to stop beetles from moving from tree to tree, and a pesticide program to control beetles should be considered. The fungus also is spread by root contact, so wide spacing can prevent transmission via this method. Infected trees may be saved with a fungicide or biological serum injections.

U. americana   P. 132

u. ah-mare-eh-KAHN-nah. American Elm, White Elm. This elegant, vase-shaped, 80-foot-tall, 60-foot-wide native has a distinctive, picturesque shape. The tall, stout trunk splits into several leaders that grow upward, eventually arching out to create the tree's unmistakable fountainlike silhouette. The leaves emerge reddish in very early spring, mature to glossy dark green, and change to bright yellow in fall. They measure 3 to 6 inches long and have toothed edges and asymmetrical bases. Flowers are small and reddish, blooming very early, well before the leaves. Winged seeds are insignificant but can cause a litter problem on sidewalks and a weed seedling problem in beds. This tree's high, spreading canopy makes it ideal for shading streets because traffic can flow easily beneath its branches. It also makes an excellent lawn tree, but it has become a rarity in many parts of the country, especially the Northeast and Midwest, due to severe infestations of DED, elm yellows, and elm leaf beetles. Plant only disease-resistant cultivars or hybrids. From eastern and midwestern North America.

HOW TO GROW. Full sun and humus-rich, moist to wet soil, but is quite drought tolerant once established. Tolerates acid or alkaline soil and urban conditions. Prune young trees when dormant, removing lower limbs to develop a main leader as high up as possible. DED and elm yellows (phloem necrosis) are the most deadly diseases, but wilt, canker, leaf spot, and mildew also can be problems. Elm leaf beetles can defoliate trees and are the worst pests. Aphids, Japanese beetles, leaf miners, and gypsy moths also can be troublesome. Zones 2b–9a.

CULTIVARS AND SIMILAR SPECIES. 'Augustine' is a columnar form with ascending branches. Though not totally immune, the following cultivars and hybrids are highly resistant to DED. 'American Liberty' has an excellent vase shape but is susceptible to elm yellows. 'Delaware' is vigorous and wide spreading, growing 70 to 80 feet tall. 'New Harmony' was developed by the National Arboretum and is vase shaped and resistant to elm yellows and leaf beetles; Zones 5a–9a. 'Princeton' grows quickly to 60 to 70 feet tall, has a uniform vase shape, and resists elm leaf beetles. 'Urban' is vase shaped and tolerates compacted soil, restricted root space, and drought. 'Valley Forge' was developed by the National Arboretum, is vase shaped, and resists elm leaf beetles and elm yellows; Zones 5a–9a. *U. davidiana* is an Asian look-alike of American elm. *U. davidiana* var. *japonica* 'Discovery' has a strong, upright vase shape; grows to 40 feet tall and 35 feet wide; very cold hardy; resists elm leaf beetles; Zones 3–6. *U. wilsoniana* 'Prospector' is a tough cultivar from the National Arboretum with the same vase shape as American elm; grows to 40 feet tall; resists DED, elm yellows, and elm leaf beetles; Zones 4–9. *U.* × *wilsoniana* 'Accolade' is a hybrid from the Morton Arboretum with a good vase shape; grows to 70 feet tall and 40 to 50 feet wide; Zones 4–7. 'Danada' is similar, with red-tinted new growth and a graceful shape.

U. carpinifolia (U. minor)

u. kar-pin-eh-FOL-ee-ah. Smooth-Leaf Elm. This cold-hardy elm features a tall, straight main trunk and graceful, ascending, narrow branches that create a 70- to 90-foot-tall, 30-foot-wide pyramid. Leaves are more rounded than those on most elms. Up to 4 inches long, they are shiny dark green and have fine-toothed edges and unequal bases, giving the tree a fine-textured cloak. This is Europe's most common elm and makes a useful street or lawn tree. The hybrids are more valuable in North America because they are highly disease resistant. From Europe, northern Africa, and western Europe.

HOW TO GROW. Full sun and well-drained, acid to alkaline soil. The species is somewhat susceptible to DED. Zones 5b–9a.

CULTIVARS. *All of these hybrids resist DED and elm yellows.* 'Frontier' is a 45-foot-tall hybrid with *U. parvifolia;* it has a narrow oval shape and doubly serrated leaves with long-lasting, burgundy fall color; resistant to elm leaf beetles. 'Homestead' is a complex hybrid from the USDA that forms an arching, narrow oval growing to 55 feet tall; yellow fall color. 'Pioneer' is a vigorous grower with a rounded canopy; grows to 50 feet tall; yellow fall color; a hybrid with *U. glabra* from the USDA.

U. glabra 'Camperdownii'   P. 133

u. GLAY-bra. Camperdown Elm. This unusual specimen tree forms an umbrella-like canopy of slender, weeping branches that can reach to the ground. It matures at 20 to 25 feet tall and 18 to 20 feet wide. Leaves are large for an elm (6 to 8 inches long), lobed at the tips, and dark green. Reddish flowers appear before the leaves and are not particularly showy. As the new leaves mature, they are joined by winged, pale yellow-green fruits that give the tree an enchanting two-tone appearance. Fall color is yellow. Use this tree as a specimen to create a focal point in the garden, especially where it can weep down a slope, near water, or over a low wall. The silhouette is most striking when leafless in winter, so locate it where it can be seen from indoors. From eastern Europe, western Asia, and northern Africa.

HOW TO GROW. Full sun and moist, acid to alkaline soil. Usually grafted, so remove any suckers that might arise from the rootstock. Susceptible to elm leaf beetles. Zones 4–7.

SIMILAR SPECIES. *U. alata* 'Lace Parasol' ('Pendula') is a weeping tree with corky, winged branches and an irregular, twisted branching pattern reminiscent of cut-leaved maple; 2-inch-long, dark green leaves with pale yellow fall color; grows to 10 feet tall and 12 feet wide; fairly resistant to DED and elm leaf beetles; adapts to sandy or clayey soil; Zones 6a–9a.

U. parvifolia   P. 133, 134

u. par-veh-FOL-ee-ah. Lacebark Elm, Chinese Elm. Rounded or slightly vase shaped and growing to 50 feet tall and wide, this pest-resistant Asian tree is beautiful but not commonly grown. Some cultivars and hybrids closely resemble American elm in shape and are being promoted as substitutes for the native tree. Leaves are glossy dark green, measure 3 inches long, have finely toothed edges with equal bases, and are borne in dense clusters. They turn yellowish to reddish purple in late autumn in northern areas and are almost evergreen in the South. Colorful orange, tan, and gray bark cloaks the trunk and branches with a fine-textured patchwork that is especially attractive in winter. Inconspicuous flowers bloom in late summer and are followed by papery, ½-inch seedpods that remain on the tree after leaf drop. Use this large tree to cast shade in tough sites. From China, Korea, and Japan.

HOW TO GROW. Full to partial sun and fertile, moist, well-drained soil. Tolerates urban conditions, alkaline soil, and drought. Train to a single leader when young. Thin crowded branches to reduce wind resistance and storm damage. Protect trunk from mechanical injury. Highly resistant to DED, elm leaf beetles, and Japanese beetles. Zones 5b–9a.

CULTIVARS. 'Allee' has a tall vase shape, growing to 50 feet tall, and yellow-orange and rust-red fall color. 'Athena' is a highly recommended, drought-tolerant, dense, rounded tree that reaches 50 feet tall; shiny, dark green leaves and unusual burgundy fall color; very colorful flaking bark; Zones 4b–9a. 'Drake' has almost evergreen leaves and grows to 35 feet tall. 'Dynasty' is a hybrid with a strong vase shape and red fall color. 'Elsmo' is fast growing, with a rounded vase shape, and resists elm yellows. 'Emerald Vase' grows to 70 feet tall and closely resembles American elm, with colorful flaking bark and yellow fall color. 'King's Choice' is similar to American elm, with furrowed bark. 'Milleken' is rounded and spreading, reaching 50 feet tall and wide, with colorful bark. 'Pathfinder' grows broadly upright to 50 feet tall and has glossy yellow-green leaves, reddish fall color, and especially colorful bark.

U. pumila   P. 134

u. poo-MILL-ah. Siberian Elm, Chinese Elm. This tough, drought-resistant, cold-hardy, fast-growing, disease-resistant tree has an upright oval or vase shape and matures to 50 to 70 feet tall and 35 to 50 feet wide. The 3-inch-long leaves are oval or lance shaped, with toothed margins and equal bases. Inconspicuous green flowers are followed by winged, ½-inch-long, green seedpods. It makes a useful tree in shelterbelts and reclamation projects in the cold, dry regions of the Plains and Mountain States. Despite its many assets, it is weak wooded and drops a lot of litter. From Korea, China, and Siberia.

HOW TO GROW. Full sun and almost any soil, sandy to clayey, acid to alkaline, wet to dry. Tolerates cold, heat, drought, and urban conditions. Highly susceptible to elm leaf beetles, but resistant to DED and elm yellows. Seeds may germinate in beds. Zones 2b–9a.

CULTIVARS. 'Cathedral' is an attractive, disease-resistant hybrid with *U. japonica* that resembles American elm; broadly vase shaped, growing 40 to 50 feet tall and 40 to 60 feet wide; Zones 4–7.

❦ *Zelkova*

zell-KOH-vah. Elm family, Ulmaceae.

Z. serrata   P. 135

z. sir-AY-tah. Japanese Zelkova. The species is rounded or broadly spread-ing and matures to 50 to 80 feet tall and wide. Some cultivars are tall and vase shaped with ascending branches, making them good replacements for American elm. The 2-inch-long, narrow, pointed leaves resemble elm leaves and are oval or oblong, with toothed margins and equal bases. They open pale green in spring, mature to dark green, and turn russet-orange or purplish red in midfall. The bark exfoliates into a mottled or-ange-and-gray patchwork. Use as a street tree or to shade a lawn, garden, or patio. From Japan and Korea.

HOW TO GROW. Full sun. Best in humus-rich, moist, well-drained soil, but adapts to poor or alkaline soil. Tolerates drought, air pollution, and urban conditions. Train when young to develop a strong central leader and evenly spaced branches. Resistant to DED and elm leaf beetles; susceptible to Japanese beetles. Protect the trunk from injury, as wounds can invite canker. Zones 6a–9a.

CULTIVARS. 'Green Vase' is very fast growing to 60 to 70 feet tall, with a graceful vase shape; orange-brown to rust-red fall color. 'Green Veil' is a narrow tree with weeping branch tips. 'Halka' is very fast growing to 50 feet tall and 30 feet wide, with a strong central leader; yellow fall color; most resembles American elm. 'Village Green' has an upright, rounded vase shape; grows 50 to 60 feet tall and wide; rust-red fall color; cold hardy to Zone 5b.

❧ BROAD-LEAVED EVERGREENS

❦ *Ilex*

EYE-lex. Holly family, Aquifoliaceae.

This large genus contains both broad-leaved evergreen and deciduous trees and shrubs from temperate, subtropical, and tropical regions of the world. The species grown in gardens are admired for their showy berries and handsome leaves, which may or may not have sharp spines. Male and female flowers are borne on separate plants. Only female plants produce berries, and only if they are pollinated by a male plant of the same species. For best pollination, male and female plants should be growing within 100 feet of each other. Only one male plant is needed to pollinate a number of female plants.

I. aquifolium P. 136

i. ahk-wif-FOL-ee-um. English Holly. This handsome tree forms a dense pyramid that can reach 30 to 50 feet tall and half as wide, with branches cloaking the single main trunk all the way to the ground. The glossy, dark green leaves are 1 to 3 inches long and ¾ to 2½ inches wide, with wavy leaf margins and a sharp spine on each wave. Leaves are spinier on young plants; mature trees may have spineless leaves. In spring clusters of tiny white flowers bloom at the bases of the leaves of the previous year's growth. On female plants, the flowers ripen into clusters of glossy, red, ¼-inch berries, which are quite long lasting, usually remaining on the tree until spring. Branches with berries are often cut for Christmas decorations. Plant English holly as a specimen where it has plenty of room to grow, or use it as a pruned or unpruned screen. Avoid placing it where its prickly nature may harm passersby. From Europe, western Asia, and northern Africa.

HOW TO GROW. Full sun to light shade; best with afternoon summer shade in the South and winter shade in the North. Likes moist, well-drained, acid soil. Mulch to keep soil cool and moist. Tolerates sandy soil, air pollution, and urban conditions. Foliage can burn in winter if wind and sun are too strong. Allow branches to remain on the tree all the way to the ground. Tolerates thinning and shearing if grown as a hedge or screen. To rejuvenate, cut to the ground and allow a new leader to form. Attacked by leaf miners, mites, and scale less often than other hollies. Grows best in the Pacific Northwest and Mid-Atlantic States. Zones 7a–9a.

CULTIVARS AND SIMILAR SPECIES. 'Argentea-marginata' ('Silveredge') is columnar to 40 feet tall; dark green leaves with silvery white margins; red berries. 'Bacciflava' ('Fructo-luteo') has golden yellow berries. *I. × altaclarensis* is a vigorous hybrid with larger leaves and larger berries. 'Camelliifolia' has dark green, spineless, 5-inch-long leaves and large, dark red berries. 'Ciliata Major' has red berries and purple, long-spined new leaves that mature to bronze-green. 'James E. Esson' has undulating, spiny, 4-inch leaves and glossy red berries. 'Nellie R. Stevens' is a hybrid that forms a 20-foot-tall pyramid; mostly spineless leaves; orange-red berries; performs well in the South; pollinate with 'Edward J. Stevens' or with a male *I. cornuta* shrub; Zones 6b–9b. 'Pyramidalis' is a slow-growing, narrow, female form that reaches 25 feet tall; abundant berries; makes a good hedge. 'Sparkler' forms a uniform pyramid; very shiny, dark green leaves; copious bright red berries. *I. × aquipernyi* is a hybrid with *I. pernyi.* 'San Jose' forms a dense, 25-foot-tall cone with deep green leaves; sets numerous red berries without a male pollinator. 'Dragon Lady' forms an 18-foot-tall, 5-foot-wide column with very dark green leaves and large red berries.

I. opaca   P. 137

i. oh-PAH-kah. American Holly. This noble evergreen grows slowly into a dense, 25- to 50-foot-tall, 10- to 20-foot-wide pyramid in its native areas. It isn't grown in gardens as much as it should be, given its handsome form and adaptable character. The spiny leaves are similar in size (2 to 5 inches long and 1½ to 2 inches wide) and outline to those of English holly, but they are usually matte green, rather than glossy, and are often lighter in color. Selected cultivars feature dark, shiny, more ornamental leaves. In summer the tiny, sweet-smelling, white flowers bloom in the leaf axils on new growth. Male and female flowers are borne on separate plants. If pollinated by a male plant, a female plant will produce orange-red berries near the stem tips. These ripen in fall and last into winter, when they are usually eaten by birds. Although female plants are valued in the landscape for their showy berries, male plants have glossier, darker green leaves and are handsome specimens. American holly is an excellent specimen in a formal setting. Or plant it in groups for an informal screen or in a row for a hedge. From eastern and southeastern North America.

HOW TO GROW. Full sun to partial or light shade. Light winter shade and wind protection is best in the North and Midwest to prevent winter burn. Best in rich, moist, well-drained, acid soil. Tolerates drought, sandy soil, and urban and seashore conditions. Prune multiple leaders as they form. Leaf miners are often a serious problem but can be controlled with properly timed pesticide applications. Mildew, midges, scale, and twig blight are occasional problems. Zones 6a–9a.

CULTIVARS. Dwarf, shrublike forms are available. Tree forms include the following: 'Brilliance' has semipendulous branches and ⅓-inch, bright red, prolific berries; cold hardy in Zone 5b. 'Cardinal' is compact and slow growing, with superior red berries. 'Canary' has light yellow berries and a rounded, slightly open form. 'Christmas Snow' has white-margined, dark green leaves and bright red berries. 'Golden Knight' is a male form that has golden yellow leaves with green veins; grows slowly to 15 feet tall; use as an accent. 'Jersey Princess' features lustrous leaves and abundant, dark red berries. 'Jersey Knight' is an attractive male form with glossy, dark green, 2-inch-long leaves; pollinates most other cultivars. 'Kentucky Knight' is a male form with glossy, 2½-inch-long, very wavy, spiny leaves. 'Princeton Gold' has golden yellow berries.

I. pedunculosa   P. 138

i. ped-unck-yew-LOW-sah. Long-Stalk Holly. The most cold-hardy evergreen holly, this handsome, small, multitrunked tree grows into a 20- to 30-foot-tall, narrow pyramid that is gracefully cloaked from top to bottom with glossy green foliage. Leaves are pointed ovals, 1 to 3 inches long and ¾ to 1¾ inches long, and have wavy margins but no spines. They may turn yellowish green in winter but are fairly resistant to windburn. The ¼-inch, red berries are borne on 1- to 1½-inch-long stems, so that they dangle in sprays from the branch tips. Use this attractive evergreen as a specimen in a border or foundation planting or plant it as a screen. From Japan and China.

HOW TO GROW. Full sun to partial shade. Protect from full winter sun in the North. Likes moist, well-drained, acid soil. Tolerates clayey soil, wind, and heat better than any other evergreen holly. Rarely bothered by pests. Best holly for the Midwest. Zones 5b–9a.

CULTIVARS. 'Vleck' is exceptionally cold hardy.

ꙮ Laurus

LAH-rus. Laurel family, Lauraceae.

Only two species of shrubs or trees belong to this Old World genus, and both hail from Asia Minor and the Mediterranean region. Prized for their aromatic, leathery leaves, which are arranged alternately on the stems, these trees make useful and beautiful additions to warm-climate gardens, where the leaves can be harvested and used to flavor food. The ancient Greeks used bay laurel leaves to make wreaths for crowning nobles and victors. The four-part male and female flowers are borne on separate plants.

L. nobilis   P. 138, 139

l. NO-bil-us. Sweet Bay, Bay Laurel. Growing into a dense, conical, 20- to 50-foot-tall, multitrunked tree in the warmest parts of its range, sweet bay dies to the ground each winter in colder areas, where it resprouts and is useful as a shrub. The long, narrow, pointed leaves measure 4 to 7 inches long and ½ to 3 inches wide, are leathery and dark green on top with light green undersides, and have noticeably wavy edges. They emit a lovely aroma when crushed and are used to flavor food. The yellowish flowers are very small and may go unnoticed when they bloom in spring, but they ripen into ½-inch, shiny, black fruits on female trees. Use sweet bay as a handsome screen or specimen tree or plant it as a formal hedge. From the Mediterranean.

HOW TO GROW. Full sun to partial shade and fertile, moist, well-drained soil. Tolerates heat, drought, and sandy soil. Protect from cold wind. May be clipped for a hedge or topiary. Top hardy in Zones 8b–10; root hardy in Zones 7b–8a.

CULTIVARS. 'Saratoga' features green leaves splotched with gold and gray-green. 'Sunspot' is a male form that grows without training into a large tree; large, round, medium green leaves and reddish shoots.

❦ *Magnolia*

mag-KNOW-lee-ah. Magnolia family, Magnoliaceae.

Containing both evergreen and deciduous species, *Magnolia* is one of the oldest genera of flowering plants. (For the deciduous species, see page 252.) The following species are summer-flowering landscape trees that are especially useful in the South.

M. grandiflora   P. 139

m. gran-dih-FLOR-ah. Southern Magnolia, Bull Bay. One of the most magnificent trees in the southern landscape, this rounded or pyramidal tree can grow 60 to 80 feet tall and 30 to 50 feet wide, although popular cultivars may be smaller. The 4- to 12-inch-long, leathery leaves are oblong and pointed, often with dense gray or rust-colored fuzz coating their undersides. During summer and early fall, large, cup-shaped, creamy white flowers dot the tree. These 6- to 12-inch-wide blossoms emit a heady lemony fragrance. Seed-grown trees may not flower for decades, so it's best to purchase named cultivars. The 2- to 5-inch-tall, beige or red seedpods develop in late summer and fall, then split open to reveal red seeds. Trunk bark is smooth gray on young trees and scaly on mature trees. Plant southern magnolia as a specimen where it has plenty of room to grow and where its dense shade will be welcomed. From southeastern North America.

HOW TO GROW. Full sun to partial shade and humus-rich, moist, acid soil. Tolerates wet sites. Allow lower limbs to sweep to the ground or prune off as desired. Older leaves and seedpods drop in autumn and winter, requiring cleanup. Limbs may break during ice storms. Zones 7a–9b; some to Zone 6b.

CULTIVARS. 'Little Gem' is a shrubby dwarf that reaches 20 feet tall. 'Majestic Beauty' is a full-size tree with 12-inch flowers and large leaves with green undersides. 'St. Mary' is a slow-growing, compact form that grows to 20 feet tall; 5-inch flowers bloom profusely even on young trees. 'Samuel Sommers' has 14-inch flowers and grows to 30 feet tall. *Cold-hardy forms for Zones 6b–9a:* 'Bracken's Brown Beauty' has 6-inch flowers and small leaves whose undersides are densely covered with rust-colored hairs; grows to 30 feet tall; may suffer winter leaf damage in Zone 6b during severe winters. 'Edith Bogue' is a compact, pyramidal form that grows to 30 feet tall; narrow leaves have light tan undersides; the most cold-hardy form. Spring Grove Series plants are cold hardy. 'Victoria' has broad, lustrous leaves with green undersides; grows to 20 feet tall.

M. virginiana   P. 140

m. ver-gin-ee-AY-nah. Sweet Bay Magnolia. This graceful, shrubby or multi-trunked tree forms an open-branched, rounded or oval specimen that can reach 50 feet tall in the South, where it is fully evergreen. In the coldest parts of its range, it is semievergreen and reaches only 20 feet tall. In spring the new leaves emerge silvery green on green twigs and mature to a shiny dark green with white-haired undersides. These 5-inch-long, oblong leaves create a shimmery effect in a breeze. The lemon-scented, 2- to 4-inch flowers have 9 to 12 creamy white petals and bloom at the branch tips for a month or so in early summer. They develop into green fruits that look like small cucumbers until they turn red in fall and split open to reveal orange-red seeds. Sweet bay magnolia makes an excellent understory tree in a woodland garden or shaded site. From southeastern North America.

HOW TO GROW. Partial to full shade and moist, acid soil. Suffers from chlorosis in alkaline soil. Tolerates wet or swampy sites. Leaves may suffer winter damage in the northerly parts of its range. Train to a single trunk if desired. Usually pest-free. Zones 5b–9a.

CULTIVARS. *M. virginiana* var. *australis* is the tall southern type. 'Henry Hicks' is the most cold-hardy form, and its leaves remain evergreen in the North. 'Willowleaf' has very narrow leaves.

❦ *Prunus*

PROO-nuss. Rose family, Rosaceae.

This large genus contains about 400 species of deciduous and evergreen trees and shrubs. (For the deciduous species, see page 272.) The following broad-leaved evergreens are common and very useful landscape plants, especially in the South.

P. caroliniana

p. kar-oh-lyn-ee-AY-nah. Carolina Cherry Laurel. Lush and dense, Carolina cherry laurel forms a rounded or oval, single- or multitrunked tree cloaked with lustrous foliage. It grows 25 to 30 feet tall and 15 to 25 feet wide. The ornamental, oval leaves emerge light yellow-green or bronze and mature to shiny dark green. They measure about 5 inches long and 2 inches wide and have pointed tips; some have a few marginal teeth. When the stems are crushed or broken, they give off a very distinct cherry aroma. Tight, 2- to 3-inch-long, showy, upright clusters of ¼-inch, five-petaled, white flowers bloom at the leaf bases in early spring and have an intensely sweet fragrance. They ripen into ½-inch, dry, black, cherrylike fruits that are usually hidden by the foliage and are often eaten by birds. Trunk bark is smooth and light gray. This fast-growing tree makes an excellent screen and can be clipped for a formal effect. From southeastern North America.

HOW TO GROW. Full sun to partial or light shade and moist, well-drained soil. Adapts to acid to slightly alkaline, sandy to clayey soils. Sensitive to poorly drained sites. Tolerates seashore and urban conditions. Leaves may turn bronze or suffer winter burn in full sun during the winter; protect from sun and cold wind. Train to a single trunk or several trunks as desired. The messy fruits can cause a weed seedling problem. Borers and whiteflies are occasional problems. Zones 7b–9a.

CULTIVARS. 'Cascade Snow' has 1½-inch-wide, pure white flowers that open from pink buds; bronze-tinted new growth. 'Bright 'N Tight' is a compact, pyramidal form that grows to 10 feet tall; makes a good hedge or screen.

P. lusitanica   P. 140, 141

p. loo-sih-TAN-eh-cah. Portuguese Cherry Laurel. This small, shrubby tree grows 15 to 20 or more feet tall and makes a handsome addition to the landscape throughout the year. The glossy, dark green, lance-shaped leaves are 2½ to 5 inches long and half as wide, with reddish stems and slightly toothed edges. The ⅓- to ½-inch, white flowers bloom in 6- to 10-inch-long, elongated, pendulous clusters in early summer. The red fruits ripen to dark purple, ⅓-inch-long, cherrylike fruits in autumn. Portuguese cherry laurel is most often used as a formal or informal screen, but it makes a beautiful specimen when allowed to grow into a tree. From southern Europe.

HOW TO GROW. Full to partial sun. Protect from full sun and wind in winter to reduce leaf scorch. Best in moist, well-drained soil. Tolerates some drought; withstands clipping. Zones 7a–9a.

CULTIVARS AND SIMILAR SPECIES. 'Variegata' has white-margined leaves. *P. laurocerasus* (English laurel, cherry laurel) is a very similar, shrubbier plant that grows to 20 feet tall and wide; shorter, lance-shaped leaves and elongated clusters of tiny white flowers.

❦ *Quercus*

KWUR-kuss. Beech family, Fagaceae.

This large genus of evergreen and deciduous trees and shrubs offers several evergreen landscape trees that are native to the East and West Coasts of North America. (For the deciduous species, see page 280.)

Q. chrysolepis P. XX

q. cry-so-LEP-iss. Canyon Live Oak. This round-headed or spreading evergreen grows 20 to 60 feet tall and 20 feet wide. The shiny, dark green leaves are 4 inches long and 2½ inches wide and unlobed, with or without spines along the margins. Their undersides are coated with a dense gold or gray felt. Trunk bark is smooth and whitish gray when young, becoming darker and scaly with age. The oblong or oval, 1- to 2-inch-long acorns have gold-felted caps. Use as a shade tree in a naturalistic or informal site. This native tree should be saved during site development. From western North America.

HOW TO GROW. Full sun and well-drained soil. Tolerates drought. Do not irrigate wild native trees saved during construction, as they are adapted to much less water. Prune deadwood only if dangerous, because pruning cuts allow fungal diseases to enter the tree. Zones 7b–9b.

SIMILAR SPECIES. *Q. emoryi* (Emory oak) is native to low elevations of the southwestern mountains; leathery, oval, 2- to 3-inch-long leaves; tolerates desert conditions and most well-drained soils.

Q. *virginiana*   P. 142

q. ver-JIN-ee-AY-nah. Live Oak. One of the white oaks, this fast-growing, long-lived tree grows slowly into an irregularly shaped specimen with a stout trunk and massive outstretched branches that sometimes sweep sinuously downward to rest on the ground. Trees grow to at least 80 feet tall and 120 feet wide. The 3-inch-long, 1-inch-wide, oval leaves are leathery and have smooth, unlobed edges. Leaves are bright olive green in spring and mature to dark green with gray-green, felt-covered undersides. Older leaves drop in spring when the new leaves emerge, making the tree essentially evergreen. Long, yellowish brown catkins bloom in spring. Clusters of 1-inch-long, black acorns ripen in late summer and provide food for wildlife. Trunk bark is dark brown to black and fissured into large blocks. Use as a lawn specimen, for shade, or to line a long driveway or a street where there is plenty of room for the tree to grow. From southeastern coastal North America.

HOW TO GROW. Full sun to partial shade and well-drained, acid to alkaline soil. Tolerates sandy soil and drought once established. Withstands seashore conditions. Train to a single trunk and a strong branch structure when young. Remove deadwood as the tree ages. Spanish moss hanging from the branches does no harm, but do not allow ivy to grow too high into the tree, as its weight may contribute to storm damage. Grows best in warm, humid coastal areas; performs poorly inland. Remove suckers that grow from the root system. Susceptible to oak wilt in Texas. Zones 7b–9b.

CULTIVARS AND SIMILAR SPECIES. 'Heritage' is fast growing and performs well in low desert areas. 'Highrise' has an upright, rather than a spreading, shape, making it a better street tree. 'Southern Shade' has excellent foliage and is fast growing, with the typical spreading shape. *Q. fusiformis* (upland live oak) is very similar and is native to central Texas; resists oak wilt but is susceptible to root rot. *Q. engelmanii* (mesa oak) is another evergreen, wide-spreading oak that is native to southern California. *Q. agrifolia* (coast live oak), P. 141, is native to the coastal ranges of western North America; it grows to 70 feet tall and at least as wide; dense, hollylike leaves.

❧ *Trachycarpus*

tray-key-CAR-pus. Palm family, Palmae.

This genus of six species contains palms from subtropical Asia whose fronds are shaped like large, round fans or the arms of a windmill. Their trunks feature characteristic black fibers, at least near the top. These species are among the most cold-tolerant palms.

T. fortunei P. 142

t. for-tune-ee-i. Hardy Windmill Palm. The tallest of the cold-hardy palms, hardy windmill palm brings a tropical look to a site that experiences moderately cold winter weather. The hairy-looking trunk, which is stouter at the top than near the ground, grows moderately fast to 30 feet tall in the warmest parts of its range, but only 8 to 10 feet tall in the coldest areas. The bright green, circular leaves measure 3 feet across and are cut into many fingerlike segments. They grow on 1½-foot-tall stalks to form a rounded head of boldly textured foliage at the top of the trunk. Hanging clusters of yellow flowers bloom in late spring and early summer and ripen into pretty blue fruits in fall, adding a decorative touch. Plant hardy windmill palm as a specimen in a border or use it to line a street or driveway. Plant it in a grove for a truly exotic look or in a protected courtyard to push the tree's hardiness limit. From China.

HOW TO GROW. Full to partial sun or light shade and moist, well-drained soil. Tolerates seashore conditions. Remove old leaves as they turn brown. Scale can be a problem. Zones 8b–9a; some selections are cold hardy to Zone 7b.

CULTIVARS. 'Charlotte', 'Greensboro', and 'Norfolk' are cold-hardy selections created from seeds collected in those cities; all tolerate winters in Zone 7b.

EVERGREENS AND CONIFERS

Abies

AY-beez. Pine family, Pinaceae.

The 50 or so fir species, members of the genus *Abies,* hail from northern or mountainous regions of North America, Europe, Asia, and northern Africa. They are tall, symmetrical conifers with dense, whorled branches and rigid, pyramidal or conical shapes. The mature female cones are squat, sturdy, and showy, standing upright along the high branches. They ripen and fall apart on the tree rather than dropping to the ground, easily distinguishing them from spruces *(Picea),* whose cones hang down and drop in one piece. Fir needles are more flattened than spruce needles and are blunt tipped and soft to the touch, unlike the spruces' sharp, pointed needles. They grow directly from twigs that either encircle the branch or curve up and away from the underside of the branch. If pulled off, they leave behind a round, white depression, another identifying feature. Firs look best with the lowest branches left to sweep to the ground. Be careful how you prune them, because they will not resprout from old, leafless wood.

Firs generally need cool, moist soil and cool temperatures, so they are unreliable performers in much of North America. They are usually pest- and disease-free, although aphids, bagworms, spider mites, and twig blight sometimes can be troublesome, and root rot is common in poorly drained soil. Most firs are grafted to rootstocks of *A. fraseri* or *A. balsamea,* which do not thrive in dry soil or hot summers, so they perform poorly in the South and Midwest. In these regions, choose a fir that is grafted to the more tolerant *A. firma.* Where adapted, firs make gorgeous specimens and screens.

A. balsamea   P. 143

a. ball-SAM-ee-ah. Balsam Fir. Growing into a dense, narrow, pointed pyramid that reaches 50 to 70 feet tall and 20 to 25 feet wide, this native is loved for its piny fragrance and is often cultivated as a Christmas tree. The 1-inch-long needles are blunt, rounded, shiny dark blue-green. They are arranged in two ranks along the side branches. Trunk bark is gray-brown. Cones are 2 to 3 inches long and violet-purple. Balsam fir thrives in cool northern climates, but it is the worst performer of any fir in the Upper South, Mid-Atlantic States, and Midwest. Despite this, it is often sold by nurseries in those areas. Use spire-shaped balsam fir as a specimen, with its lowest branches left to sweep the ground. From northeastern North America.

HOW TO GROW. Full sun to light shade and humus-rich, acid, moist to damp soil. Suffers sunscald in hot climates, especially during drought. Best in the North or at high elevations. Plant on a cool, north-facing slope in the warmest parts of its range. Susceptible to root rot in warm, humid regions. Zones 2a–5a.

SIMILAR SPECIES. *A. balsamea* var. *phanerolepis* (Canada fir) is fast growing, with heavy side branches. *A. fraseri* (Fraser balsam fir) forms a narrow pyramid to 40 feet tall and has very short, glossy, dark green needles; it comes from a more southerly mountainous climate than balsam fir and performs well at high elevations in the South and North; likes moist, well-drained, acid soil; a favorite Christmas tree; Zones 3b–7a.

A. concolor

P. 143, 144

a. KON-kuh-lor. White Fir. The most beautiful and adaptable of the firs, this dense, conical tree features horizontal branches and grows 35 to 50 feet tall and 15 to 30 feet wide. White fir makes an elegant, symmetrical specimen reminiscent of Colorado blue spruce. Needles are 1½ to 2½ inches long, soft gray-green to silvery blue-green, and curved upward with rounded tips. Trunk bark is smooth and gray, becoming scaly with age. Immature cones are purplish, turning light brown and growing to 5 inches long and 2 inches wide when mature. Use this tree, especially its most silvery cultivars, as an eye-catching specimen in an open area where its lowest branches can sweep the ground. White fir makes a good substitute for Colorado blue spruce in areas where the latter suffers from diseases and insects. From high elevations of western North America.

HOW TO GROW. Full sun to partial shade and moist, well-drained, sandy, acid to slightly alkaline loam. Performs poorly in wet or clayey sites. Tolerates more heat and drought than other firs, but does not tolerate urban conditions. Keep soil cool and moist with an organic mulch. Prune to a single leader if a competing one forms. This is the best fir for the Midwest and East Coast, but it performs best in the North and the Pacific Northwest. Zones 4a–8a.

CULTIVARS. 'Candicans' has vivid silvery blue or silvery white needles when grown in full sun and forms a narrow, upright pyramid. 'Glenmore' has large, gray-blue needles and a nice compact tree shape. 'Swift's Silver' has exceptionally silvery needles. 'Violacea' has bright silvery blue needles.

A. homolepis

a. hoh-moh-LEP-is. Nikko Fir. Unlike most firs, which are spire shaped, the heat-tolerant Nikko fir starts out pyramidal but matures into a broad-spreading tree that grows 40 to 50 or more feet tall and 30 feet wide. The attractive needles are denser than those of most firs, have notched tips, and are ½ to 1 inch long. They are dark green with two white stripes on their undersides, giving the tree an overall lighter color. Trunk bark is gray but tinged with pink and becomes scaly with age. The 3- to 4-inch-long, ornamental cones are green when young and pale brown when mature. They are borne lower on the tree than those of most firs. Use this distinctive tree for its full silhouette as a specimen or massed for a screen. From Japan.

HOW TO GROW. Full to partial sun and moist, humus-rich soil. Tolerates more heat than other firs. Zones 5a–6b.

SIMILAR SPECIES. *A. firma* (momi fir), **P. 144**, from Japan, is a wide-spreading tree that grows to 50 feet tall; glossy, two-tone needles (dark green on top and light green on the undersides); the only fir that adapts to heavy, acid soil and heat, making it the best fir for the South; Zones 6b–8b.

A. koreana   P. 145

a. kor-ee-AY-nah. Korean Fir. Korean fir has a compact, wide-spreading, pyramidal form and grows slowly to about 30 feet tall and 15 feet wide. The ½- to 1-inch-long needles are rich green with two broad silver bands on the undersides, creating a shimmery effect, and are arranged in V-shaped ranks. Trunk bark is dark gray-brown. Cones are red and chartreuse when young and bluish purple when mature. These beautiful cones are profuse even when the tree is young. From southern Korea.

HOW TO GROW. Full to partial sun and moist, humus-rich, acid soil. Mulch beneath the tree. More heat tolerant than other firs, but performs best in a cool climate. Zones 5a–7a.

CULTIVARS. 'Hortsmann's Silberlocke' is a compact tree that has a silvery effect because its needles twist to expose the silver undersides.

A. nordmanniana   P. 146

a. nor-man-knee-AY-nah. Nordmann Fir. This handsome tree grows to 60 feet tall and 25 feet wide, with tiers of down-swept branches. The beautiful, forward-pointing, glossy, black-green needles are about 1½ inches long and have two white bands on their undersides. Mature cones are 6 inches long and greenish black, with protruding bracts. Trunk bark is very dark gray-black and broken into plates. Locate Nordmann fir as a specimen in a lawn or border where it has plenty of growing room. From the Caucasus Mountains of eastern Europe.

HOW TO GROW. Zones 4b–7b.

CULTIVARS AND SIMILAR SPECIES. 'Pendula' is a rare form with weeping branches. *A. lasiocarpa* (Rocky Mountain fir, alpine fir), **P. 145**, is native to western North America; creamy white bark and short, narrow, pale blue-green, two-ranked needles; tolerates dry heat and light soil, but not clayey soil. 'Arizonica' is compact and narrow, has blue-green needles, and adapts better to the East. 'Compacta' has silvery blue needles and forms a dense, slow-growing pyramid.

❦ Calocedrus

Kal-oh-ced-druss. Cypress family, Cupressaceae.

Characterized by flat branchlets and scalelike leaves in whorls of four, this genus includes two or three species, all from North America and Asia. Only one, incense cedar, is common as a landscape plant. Widely grown on the West Coast, this adaptable tree should receive more attention in the East, South, and Southwest, where it makes an excellent substitute for two overused plants—arborvitae *(Thuja occidentalis)* and eastern cedar *(Juniperus virginiana)*. Unlike these two trees, incense cedar has a single leader and short branches that do not split in ice and snow, and its foliage retains its bright green color in winter.

C. decurrens (Libocedrus decurrens)   P. 146, 147

c. dee-KUR-wrens. Incense Cedar. This narrow, columnar tree reaches 30 to 50 feet tall and 10 feet wide. It has a single straight trunk that tapers to a point and spreads into a wide buttress at its base. Bark is cinnamon brown, deeply furrowed, and shredding, adding an ornamental touch. Emitting a spicy aroma when crushed, the glossy, emerald green foliage is made up of pointed scales and grows in fanlike sprays on short, slightly pendulous side branches that resist snow and ice damage. The distinctive but inconspicuous cones are ¾-inch-long, brown cylinders with several scales that spread open like small flowers in autumn to release the seeds. Use a single plant as a strong, upright accent. The narrow shape also works well planted in a grove or as a tall screen. Although this conifer comes from a cool area, it adapts to many climates. From the mountains of the West Coast of North America.

HOW TO GROW. Full sun to light shade; provide afternoon shade in the South. Best in deep, moist, well-drained, acid soil, but tolerates clayey and slightly alkaline soil. Tolerates heat, humidity, and urban conditions. Tolerates drought once established, but grows best with even moisture; does not tolerate wet soil. Shelter from drying wind. Water deeply when young to encourage drought-resistant roots. Needs no pruning but may be sheared for a hedge; do not remove lower limbs. Usually pest-free. Zones 6a–8b.

CULTIVARS. 'Columnaris' is narrow and spirelike; the form is usually offered under the species name.

❦ *Cedrus*

SEED-russ. Pine family, Pinaceae.

Many trees include "cedar" in their names, but *Cedrus* is the genus of the true cedars, which hail from Asia and northern Africa. These very large, long-lived, elegant trees grow rapidly when young and mature into breathtaking silhouettes, which then grow very slowly to a grand size with old age. The stiff needles are arranged singly on young shoots and in clustered whorls on older branches. Cones are large and showy. The species listed here all look quite similar. Use them in large landscapes.

C. atlantica (C. libani ssp. *atlantica)*   P. 147, 148

c. at-LAN-teh-kah. Atlas Cedar. Stiffly pyramidal and awkwardly angular when young, Atlas cedar becomes beautifully irregular and flat topped, with upward-reaching top branches and horizontally spreading to ascending lower branches. It matures to 60 feet tall and 30 to 40 feet wide, but it can reach 120 feet tall with great age. Needles are ¾ to 1 inch long, forming dense tufts on the tops of branches. Their color varies from dark green to blue-green, with the more commonly grown blue Atlas cedar exhibiting stunning silver-blue needles. Female cones are blocky, 3-inch-tall, blue-green cylinders with concave tips. They take 2 years to mature, eventually turning brown. Atlas cedar strongly resembles cedar of Lebanon but is taller and has a more open silhouette. It is best planted as a specimen in an open lawn. Although this tree is not particularly cold hardy, it is often sold in borderline areas, where it will not survive an unseasonably cold winter. From northern Africa.

HOW TO GROW. Full sun to partial shade. Best in humus-rich, moist, well-drained, acid soil, but adapts to any well-drained, sandy or clayey, or slightly alkaline soil. Very drought and heat tolerant in deep soil. Shorten long branches when trees are young to encourage resistance to snow and ice damage. Remove multiple leaders if they develop. Leave lower limbs to sweep to the ground or remove them to reveal trunk bark. Sometimes bothered by weevils, tip blight, borers, root rot, and sapsuckers. Zones 6a–9a.

CULTIVARS. 'Aurea' has golden yellow new growth and yellow-green older needles; grows slowly to 16 feet tall. 'Glauca' (blue Atlas cedar) has gorgeous, silvery blue needles. 'Glauca Pendula' has silvery blue needles and graceful, weeping branches; must be staked to create a tree form; grows to 15 feet tall and 20 feet wide. 'Glauca Fastigiata' is a dense, narrow, upright tree that reaches 40 feet tall and 10 feet wide; silvery blue needles.

C. deodara
P. 148, 149

c. dee-oh-DOOR-ah. Deodar Cedar. More graceful and dense when young than Atlas cedar, deodar cedar forms a 50- to 80-foot-tall, 30- to 40-foot-wide pyramid with slightly pendulous, tiered branches and a nodding leader, rather like a hemlock's, which distinguishes it from afar. With age, deodar cedar becomes spreading and flat topped, with the lower branches ascending toward the ground and then turning upward, creating a dramatic silhouette. The blue-green needles are the longest of any cedar's, measuring 1½ to 2 inches long, and have a soft, feathery appearance. Female cones are 3 to 4 inches long and pale jade green, maturing to reddish brown after 2 years. This elegant tree is suitable only for a large property and performs well in the South and Southwest. From the Himalaya Mountains.

HOW TO GROW. Full sun and well-drained to dry soil. Tolerates alkaline soil, drought, wind, and heat. If desired, cut back new growth halfway to control the tree's spread. Will not resprout from leafless wood. Usually problem-free, but weevils, canker, and cold can cause tip dieback. Zones 7a–9a.

CULTIVARS. 'Aurea' has yellow new needles that mature to golden green. 'Albospicata' has ivory new growth that turns creamy yellow and stands out against bright green older needles. 'Kashmir' is compact, growing to 20 feet tall; silvery blue-green needles; hardy to Zone 6b. 'Sander's Blue' is a narrow, bushy form with powder blue new growth that darkens to gray-blue. 'Shalimar' has a graceful, pendulous habit and blue-green needles; hardy in Zone 6b.

C. libani
P. 149

c. lib-AHN-eye. Cedar of Lebanon. The most cold-hardy species, cedar of Lebanon is tightly pyramidal when young, maturing into an irregular shape with outstretched horizontal branches that sweep the ground. It grows 50 to 60 or more feet tall and wide, has a massive trunk, and often has several leaders. Needles are ¾ to 1½ inches long, stiff, and sharp pointed. They are borne in dense tufts and emerge bright green, contrasting beautifully with the glossy, dark green, older needles. The 4-inch-tall, barrel-shaped cones are purplish when young, turning brown after 2 years. Use this conifer as a specimen in a large landscape; it looks fantastic planted near a reflecting pool or pond. From mountainous areas of the Middle East.

HOW TO GROW. Full sun. Best in deep, well-drained, fertile soil, but adapts well to infertile, dry, or alkaline soil. Intolerant of air pollution and humidity. Performs best in the West; may not do well in the South. No pruning is necessary. Usually pest-free. Zones 6a–8b, with one form hardy to Zone 5a.

CULTIVARS. 'Pendula' has long, weeping branches and forms a narrow, irregular shape if staked. *C. libani* ssp. *brevifolia (C. brevifolia)* (Cypress cedar) has ½-inch-long needles and small cones. *C. libani* ssp. *stenocoma* has a more stiffly pyramidal shape and shorter needles; cold hardy to Zone 5a.

❦ *Cephalotaxus*

seh-fall-oh-TAX-us. Plum yew family, Cephalotaxaceae.

This genus of small trees and shrubs from Asia contains nine species. Needles are flat, pointed, and usually arranged in two ranks, one on either side of the young branches. The undersides often have silver bands. Female plants produce small, fleshy, plumlike, green fruits. These shade-tolerant trees are not well known but make fine additions to the plant palette in many areas.

C. harringtonia   P. 150, 151

c. hair-ring-TONE-ee-ah. Japanese Plum Yew. This dark green, shade-tolerant, deer-proof conifer usually forms a 25-foot-tall pyramid, but some types are low, spreading shrubs. Needles are 1½ to 2½ inches long, glossy, very dark green, and arranged in two ranks along the tops of the stems. They are reminiscent of yew needles, but are much longer and more pointed, and densely cloak the whorled branches. Trunk bark is reddish brown and shredding. Yellowish flowers bloom along the stems in spring. The 1-inch-long, oval, olive-brown fruits ripen to purple in fall. This is a perfect tree for a shade garden or foundation planting. It also looks good planted in groups or as a screen. It tolerates heavier soil and more heat than do yews and is popular in the Southeast. From Japan and China.

HOW TO GROW. Partial to full shade and any moist, well-drained soil, from sand to clay. Winter burn can occur in sunny locations in the North. Needs no pruning, but may be sheared if desired; resprouts from leafless wood. Mites are the worst problem. Zones 6a–9b.

CULTIVARS AND SIMILAR SPECIES. Many dwarf, shrublike forms are available. Only tree forms are described here. 'Fastigiata' is upright and slow growing, reaching 17 feet tall and 6 feet wide; needles are arranged in spirals. *C. fortunei* is upright or oval, growing 10 to 20 feet tall, and has 3-inch-long needles.

❦ *Chamaecyparis*

kam-ee-SIP-ah-riss. False cypress family, Cupressaceae.

Native to North America and Asia, the six members of this genus are usually tall, columnar trees that thrive in cool, humid climates. Leaves are tiny scales (sometimes sharp needles on juvenile trees) and are arranged in opposite pairs that create fanlike sprays on the short branches. Cones are only about ⅓ inch around and not very noticeable. They are usually blue-green when young, with 6 to 12 umbrella-like scales, and ripen in 1 year to reddish brown. All these species make an excellent specimen in a border or foundation planting, or arrange them as a screen or in a grove.

C. lawsoniana   P. 151

c. law-son-ee-AY-nah. Lawson False Cypress, Port Orford Cedar. This pyramidal or conical evergreen can grow to 60 feet tall and 30 feet wide, although many of its popular cultivars are smaller. Depending on the cultivar, the scalelike leaves vary in color from deep green to gray-green to golden and have white marks on their undersides. They are arranged in flattened sprays that form vertical or horizontal planes, giving the tree a very soft, layered appearance. Trunk is buttressed and has red bark. Side branches are short and horizontal to drooping, so the tree usually resists snow damage. The widely available colorful forms make eye-catching specimens that bring year-round beauty to a garden. The species and its green cultivars are the best choices for a screen or hedge. From the Pacific Northwest.

HOW TO GROW. Full sun to partial shade; gold forms need full sun. Needs moist, well-drained loam. Does not tolerate clayey soil or drying wind. Performs poorly in the East; best in the West where it's cool and moist. May be sheared for a hedge, but do not cut back to bare wood, because new shoots will not grow. Phytopthera fungus causes root rot in heavy or poorly drained soil and in hot, humid climates. Mites are a severe problem in hot, dry sites. Zones 5b–8a.

CULTIVARS. 'Alumii' forms a narrow, 35-foot-tall cone; metallic blue new growth matures to blue-green. 'Dragon Blue' is a compact, upright form with blue-gray needles. 'Ellwoodii' has a dense columnar shape and reaches 10 to 20 feet tall; feathery, gray-green, prickly new growth turns steel blue in winter. 'Green Hedger' is a dense, conical tree with bright green foliage. 'Golden King' ('Golden Showers') is a 35-foot-tall pyramid with slightly pendulous branch tips, golden yellow outer needles, and yellow-green inner needles; often turns deep gold in winter. 'Lanei' ('Lane') is an upright, compact form that grows to 15 feet tall; gold-tipped new foliage and yellow-green older foliage. 'Oregon Blue' is fast growing, has silvery blue to blue-gray needles, and resists phytopthera. 'Pendula' has an upright stem that grows to 30 feet tall with weeping branches; glossy needles of variable color.

C. nootkatensis

P. 152, 153

c. neut-kah-TEN-sis. Nootka False Cypress, Alaska Cedar. This beautiful, conical evergreen has a graceful silhouette. The main trunk is strong and straight, with spreading main branches that swoop downward and then curve gracefully upward; side branches hang almost straight down, creating curtains of weeping foliage. Mature trees reach 40 or more feet tall and 15 to 20 feet wide. Leaves are usually dark blue-green or gray-green, sharp-pointed scales that form fine-textured, flattened sprays. Foliage has an unpleasant odor when crushed. Trunk bark is gray-brown or red-brown and stringy. Cones take 2 years to ripen, unlike those on other species. Weeping forms make a wonderful focal point in a lawn or border. Use nonweeping forms as a screen. The tree is very resistant to storm damage. From coastal Alaska and the Pacific Northwest.

HOW TO GROW. Full to partial sun or light shade; best with afternoon shade in the hottest areas. Needs plentiful moisture and sandy to humus-rich, acid soil. Tolerates heat and humidity and performs well in the Midwest. Old foliage may turn brown and remain on the tree; remove with a strong spray from a garden hose to improve appearance. Prune carefully, because it will not resprout from leafless wood. Usually pest-free, but scale and bagworms are occasional problems. Zones 5b–7b.

CULTIVARS. 'Aurea' forms a slow-growing pyramid with bright yellow new growth; may be mislabeled as 'Lutea'. 'Glauca' has thick, nodding, blue-green foliage. 'Glauca Pendula' is a slender tree with weeping, blue-green foliage. 'Green Arrow' forms a very narrow column with pendulous branches. 'Lutea' has pendulous branches and new growth suffused with gold. 'Pendula' has gracefully weeping, dark green foliage. 'Sullivan' is a dense, weeping form that tolerates heavy shade; grows to 20 feet tall. 'Strict Weeping' is extremely narrow and pendulous.

C. obtusa

P. 153

c. obb-TWO-sah. Hinoki False Cypress. This stunning evergreen forms a 50-foot-tall, 20-foot-wide pyramid, although the commonly grown garden forms are smaller, usually reaching only 25 feet tall and 10 feet wide. The scalelike needles are glossy dark green with white crosses on their undersides, an identifying feature. They form rounded, fan-shaped sprays that give the tree a beautiful texture. The bark on older trunks is reddish brown and shredding. The species makes an excellent tall screen or hedge, while the cultivars create a beautiful focal point in a shrub border or foundation planting. From Japan and Taiwan.

HOW TO GROW. Full to partial sun; afternoon shade is best in hot areas. Needs moist, well-drained, acid to neutral, sandy to loamy soil. Performs best in humid areas. Foliage may burn in winter wind and sun. Older inner foliage may turn brown without dropping; remove by hand or with a strong spray from a hose to improve appearance. Do not prune to bare wood; plants resprout only from wood that contains foliage. Mites may be a problem in hot, dry areas. Zones 5a–8a.

CULTIVARS. 'Aurea' is compact, with bright gold tips on new growth and dark green inner foliage. 'Crispii' is a broadly spreading, loose pyramid with dense, golden yellow new growth and bright green older foliage. 'Filicoides' (fernspray Hinoki cypress) is an irregular, slow-growing, 10-foot-tall, gaunt pyramid with long, pendulous clusters of green needles. 'Gracilis' ('Nana Gracilis') is a slow-growing, compact form with dark green, nodding fans of foliage; the most common form and very beautiful. 'Gracilis Aurea' has gold-tipped, nodding fans. 'Koster Sport' is a full-size tree with twisted, light green foliage and layered branches. 'Tetragona Aurea' forms a narrow, slow-growing pyramid with bright gold, tufted and twisted branches.

C. pisifera   P. 154

c. piss-SIF-err-ah. Sawara False Cypress, Retinospora. This broadly conical or pyramidal tree can grow to 60 feet tall and 20 feet wide, although its cultivars are usually smaller and more compact. The species is rarely grown in home landscapes, although its cultivars are commonly found in gardens as medium-size trees and dwarf shrubs. The dark green needles have white markings on their undersides and grow in flattened sprays, but they are quite variable and are found in three distinct shapes: *Filifera types* (threadleaf sawara cypress) feature closely pressed, scalelike needles that form slender, pendant, cordlike branches. *Plumosa types* (plume sawara cypress) have sharp, pointed, bright green needles that stand out from the stems, creating a plumed effect. *Squarrosa types* (mossy sawara cypress) have recurved, pointed, soft, scaly needles that stand away from the stems in a billowy mass. From Japan.

HOW TO GROW. Full sun and moist, well-drained, humus-rich, acid to neutral soil. Needs plentiful moisture and tolerates only short periods of drought. Performs best in humid climates. Sensitive to road salt. The plumosa and squarrosa types may hold their dead inner needles; remove to improve appearance. Allow branches to remain on the ground for best appearance. Prune carefully, because needles resprout only from older wood containing foliage. Mites are a problem in dry sites. Zones 5a–8a.

CULTIVARS. Many dwarf, shrublike forms are available. Only tree forms are described here. *Filifera types:* 'Filifera' is a slow-growing, broadly conical form with light green needles on long, whiplike branches. 'Filifera Aurea' has bright golden yellow foliage and is a bit smaller than 'Filifera'. 'Lemon Thread' has bright lemon yellow, whiplike branches. *Plumosa types:* 'Plumosa' is a full-size tree with bright green needles. 'Plumosa Aurea' is compact, with golden yellow outer needles that deepen to yellow-green. *Squarrosa types:* 'Squarrosa' forms a densely twiggy, broad cone with billowy sprays of soft, blue-green needles. 'Squarrosa Aurea' has golden foliage. 'Squarrosa Veitchii' is very similar to 'Squarrosa'.

C. thyoides

c. thigh-OIY-deez. Atlantic White Cedar, White Cypress, Swamp Cedar. This small to medium-size conifer, which grows naturally in coastal swamps, forms a 40- to 50-foot-tall, slender column that naturally loses its lower branches. It is an excellent choice for difficult wet sites where an evergreen is called for. Needles are blue-green or blue-gray, scalelike leaves with a conspicuous white gland on the back. They look very much like juniper needles. In fact, the plant closely resembles eastern red cedar *(Juniperus virginiana)*. Like juniper, this species' needles often take on a purplish brown hue in winter. When old inner needles die, they turn brown and remain on the tree for another year; remove them to improve appearance. Trunk bark peels in thin shreds and is gray-brown or reddish brown. Fruits are small, pointy, purple cones that turn brown; this helps distinguish the plant from eastern red cedar, which has bright blue-gray, berrylike fruits. This useful native does best in a naturalistic setting in a damp or wet site where other cedars would suffer, but it adapts well to most garden situations. From eastern North America.

HOW TO GROW. Full sun to light shade. Best in moist, sandy, acid soil, but tolerates almost any acid soil, sandy to clayey, dry to wet. Usually pest-free. Zones 5a–9a.

CULTIVARS. Many dwarf, shrublike forms are available. Only tree forms are described here. 'Andelyensis' forms a bright green, 10-foot-tall, narrow column that turns purplish in winter and has numerous cones. 'Ericoides' grows very slowly to 25 feet tall and has blue-gray, needlelike leaves. 'Glauca' has blue-green needles. 'Hopkinton' has attractive blue-gray needles and is open branched and fast growing.

☙ Cryptomeria

krip-toe-MARE-ee-ah. Bald cypress family, Taxodiaceae.

This is a one-species genus native to Asia, where it is an important timber tree. It is also a much-loved garden plant in Asia and North America.

C. japonica

P. 155

c. ja-PON-eh-kah. Japanese Cedar, Cryptomeria. This elegant conifer with a tall, straight trunk matures into a pyramidal or conical form that reaches 50 or more feet tall and 25 feet wide, with branches layered from its pointed top right to the ground. The ¼- to ¾-inch-long, awl-shaped, four-sided, scalelike needles are bright green or blue-green and slightly twisted. They are arranged spirally in plumelike clusters along slightly pendulous, spreading branches, which gives the tree an unusual and beautiful texture. In winter the foliage of the species turns bronze-blue or reddish, but some cultivars retain their summer color. Trunk bark is reddish brown and shredding. Cones are dark brown and 1 inch around, with 20 pointed scales. Japanese cedar is one of the best conifers to grow in the South. Use it as a specimen or plant it as a screen or in a grove. From China and Japan.

HOW TO GROW. Full sun where conditions are cool, but best in partial to light shade in hot areas. Needs fertile, moist, deep, acid soil. Does not tolerate drought. Performs best in humid areas. Protect from winter wind, especially in the coldest areas. Remove dead inner needles if they are unsightly. Will resprout only from wood that contains needles, but may be pruned for a hedge. Lower limbs may be removed to show off trunk bark. Usually pest-free, but mites, leaf blight, branch dieback, and leaf spot are sometimes disfiguring. Zones 6b–9a.

CULTIVARS. Seedlings are variable and do not always grow into attractive plants; named cultivars are best. 'Benjamin Franklin' grows densely to 40 feet tall; rich green needles and no dead inner foliage; resists fungus; tolerates wind and salt spray. 'Elegans' is very dense and compact, with longer needles and an attractive burgundy-plum color in winter.

'Lobbii' is compact, with slender twigs and long, deep green needles that are densely compacted at the branch tips and remain green in winter. 'Sekkan Sugi' is a slow-growing, dense tree; creamy to bright yellow new growth. 'Yoshino' is narrow, grows to 30 feet tall, and has bright blue-green foliage all year; no dead inner foliage; resists fungus; hardy to Zone 6a.

❦ Cunninghamia

kun-ing-HAM-ee-ah. Bald cypress family, Taxodiaceae.

The three species of this genus, which look rather like the monkey-puzzle tree, have flat needles that spread out from the stems in two ranks. Native to eastern Asia.

C. lanceolata   P. 156

c. lan-see-oh-LAY-tah. China Fir. This uncommon evergreen is a bold-textured, unique-looking plant with a strong central leader and open, irregular branches that form a broadly pyramidal crown with a rounded top. It reaches 60 feet tall and 30 feet wide. The glossy, blue-green, 2½-inch-long needles are broad and flat, with sharp points and two white lines on their undersides. They are arranged in two ranks on either side of the branches, creating a distinctive texture. The prickly, 2-inch-long cones grow in clusters and drop to the ground while still attached to large twigs. Trunk bark is reddish brown and peels in strips. Use this distinctive tree as a specimen on a large property. From China.

HOW TO GROW. Full sun or light shade and evenly moist soil. Tolerates urban conditions. Protect from wind in coldest areas. May form several trunks at ground level; best to prune to one trunk. Unlike most conifers, this one resprouts from leafless wood and even from stumps if cut to the ground. Cones and small deciduous branches require cleanup. Remove old brown needles by hand or with a strong spray from a hose. Usually pest-free. Zones 6b–9a.

CULTIVARS. The species is quite variable. 'Chason's Gift' is fast growing and densely symmetrical. 'Glauca' has dark green needles with a blue cast.

❦× Cupressocyparis

× kew-press-oh-SIGH-par-is. Cypress family, Cupressaceae.

The three hybrids called × *Cupressocyparis* are natural hybrids between species of *Chamaecyparis* and *Cupressus*. They were found growing in England and Wales at the end of the nineteenth century and are notable for their extremely fast growth, as much as 3 feet a year. The most popular form is Leyland cypress.

× C. leylandii

P. 157

× c. lay-LAND-ee-eye. Leyland Cypress. This vigorous, fast-growing, handsome tree is a hybrid between *Chamaecyparis nootkatensis* and *Cupressus macrocarpa*. It has a columnar or narrow, pyramidal shape and reaches 65 feet tall but only 15 feet wide, with dense growth all the way to the ground. It may get even taller with great age. The bright green needles are soft scales that are pressed into ropelike bunches along the stems and form flattened fans that resemble those of Nootka cypress. Because it grows so fast, this evergreen makes an especially valuable screen or hedge in sun or partial shade, but it is also a useful focal point in a border or lawn. Where pests and diseases are prevalent, use *Juniperus chinensis* 'Spartan' or *Thuja plicata* 'Hogan' instead for screens and hedges.

HOW TO GROW. Full sun to partial shade; will be less dense in full shade. Prefers fertile, moist soil. Adapts to acid or alkaline soil. Plentiful moisture is best, especially when newly planted. Tolerates heat, salt spray, and seashore conditions. Remove multiple leaders to avoid storm damage. May be sheared in early summer for a formal hedge. Bagworms and canker are serious in some areas. Phytophora root rot is troublesome in wet sites. Excellent in the South. Newly planted trees are susceptible to winterkill in Zone 6. Zones 7a–9a.

CULTIVARS. 'Castlewellan' has golden yellow new growth that turns bronze in winter; grows to 20 feet tall. 'Robinson Gold' is more golden and faster growing than 'Castlewellan'. 'Emerald Isle' has very dense, bright green, flattened sprays and reaches 25 feet tall. 'Gold Cup' has gold-tipped new growth. 'Green Spire' is dense and narrowly columnar, with bright green foliage. 'Naylor's Blue' has bright gray-blue, slightly pendulous foliage and loose branching; grows to 35 feet tall; looks more like Monterey cypress than other cultivars. 'Silver Dust' has lovely foliage with creamy variegation.

❦ Cupressus

kew-PRESS-us. Cypress family, Cupressaceae.

Thirteen to 25 species belong to this genus, which is very similar to *Chamaecyparis* but has shiny, marble-sized cones that remain on the tree and stay closed for many years. Most *Cupressus* species perform best in the mild climates of the West and Southwest and suffer from disease problems elsewhere.

C. arizonica var. *glabra*   P. 157

c. air-ree-ZON-eh-kah GLAY-brah. Arizona Cypress. A fast-growing, dense, pyramidal tree that reaches 35 feet tall and 15 to 20 feet wide, this species is cultivated only in the blue-leaved form described here. Foliage is made up of tiny, sharp-pointed, gray-green or blue-green, white-flecked scales that are pressed against the stems, creating ropelike branches. The bluest cultivars are quite beautiful and very popular. Trunk bark is shiny and reddish brown, like that of a cherry tree, and flaking. Cones are about an inch around, larger than those of *Chamaecyparis*. Arizona cypress makes an excellent, fine-textured screen, windbreak, or specimen in a sunny, dry site and can be used as a substitute for Rocky Mountain juniper in areas where disease limits its use. From southwestern North America.

HOW TO GROW. Full sun and well-drained soil. Tolerates a range of soils, from heavy to light, alkaline to acid. Very drought, wind, and heat tolerant and thrives in the South and Southwest. May be short-lived in the East unless soil is very well drained. Prune to a single leader if necessary. Tolerates heavy pruning or shearing. Mites and bagworms may be a problem. Susceptible to twig blight, but less so than junipers, and suffers from stem canker. Zones 7a–9b.

CULTIVARS AND SIMILAR SPECIES. 'Blue Ice' is a very narrow, conical tree that grows to 30 feet tall and 8 feet wide; powder blue needles and red-tinged twigs. 'Blue Pyramid' has handsome gray-blue needles and forms a compact pyramid, growing to 20 feet tall and 10 feet wide. 'Carolina Sapphire' has bright blue needles and a full shape and is very fast growing. *C. sempervirens* (Italian cypress) is a narrow, columnar tree with dark green needles; grows to 50 feet tall and 3 to 10 feet wide; popular as a dramatic, tall screen in mild, dry climates; Zones 7b–11. 'Glauca' has blue-green foliage.

C. macrocarpa   P. 158

c. mack-row-KAR-pah. Monterey Cypress. This tree has a strong pyramidal shape with a spiky top when young, but it matures into a picturesque, flat-topped specimen with horizontal branches which reaches 40 feet tall and 30 feet wide. When grown on the coast, the tree takes on a rugged, windswept look. Foliage consists of tiny, dark green, pointed scales that are closely pressed against the stems and borne in irregular sprays. Leaves are aromatic, releasing a lemony scent when crushed. Trunk bark is reddish brown and ridged. Use as a specimen or screen in the West. Use dwarf forms in borders and foundation plantings. From the West Coast of North America.

HOW TO GROW. Full sun and well-drained, sandy to loamy soil. Tolerates wind, salt spray, and seashore conditions. Withstands shearing. Canker is serious away from the coast. Performs poorly in the East, except right on the coast. Zones 8a–9a.

CULTIVARS. 'Golden Pillar' is a dwarf that forms a compact cone, growing to 15 feet tall; vertical fans of golden outer foliage and chartreuse inner foliage. 'Horizontalis Aurea' is a 20-foot-tall, narrow column with golden foliage.

🐦 *Juniperus*

joo-NIP-er-us. Cypress family, Cupressaceae.

This large and variable genus contains about 60 species from North America, Asia, and Europe, many of them important landscape trees, shrubs, and ground covers. Young plants have sharp-pointed, needlelike foliage, while mature plants usually feature scalelike foliage. Some cultivars have both juvenile and adult foliage at the same time; others keep the juvenile form throughout their lives. Fruits are technically cones but look like berries and are usually dark gray-blue.

J. scopulorum   P. 158, 159

j. skop-yew-LOH-rum. Rocky Mountain Juniper, Western Red Cedar. Forming a narrow pyramid with several 30- to 40-foot-tall trunks, this western native has cultivars that are smaller and more compact. Leaves are scalelike and green or blue-green; they keep their color in winter, unlike eastern red cedar (*J. virginiana*). Trunks are covered with reddish brown, shredding bark. This drought-tolerant evergreen is useful as a fine-textured, vertical accent or screen in Xeriscape gardens or areas with low rainfall. It performs poorly in areas, such as the Southeast, where rainfall and humidity are high. From the Rocky Mountains.

HOW TO GROW. Full sun and average to sandy, well-drained, alkaline to slightly acid soil. Adapts to moist or dry conditions and rocky soil, but fares poorly in heavy soil. Tolerates heat and drought. Do not irrigate established plants. Prevent storm damage by encircling narrow forms with twine in winter and by training them to a single leader. Does not respond well to shearing. Juniper blight and cedar-apple rust can be serious problems in humid areas. Zones 3b–6b.

CULTIVARS. 'Blue Heaven' ('Blue Haven') is a disease-resistant, bright blue, 20-foot-tall pyramid. 'Blue Trail' is a silver-blue, 18-foot-tall column. 'Medora' is a very narrow, dense, blue-green column that is especially tolerant of cold and drought. 'Moonglow' is a dense, 20-foot-tall, silver-blue pyramid. 'Skyrocket' is an extremely narrow, silver-blue column that grows to 15 feet tall and 2 feet wide; susceptible to storm damage. 'Sutherland' is a silvery green, 18-foot-tall column. 'Tolleson's Blue Weeping' has silver-blue foliage and gracefully arching, wide-spreading branches; grows to 20 feet tall and wide if central trunk is staked. 'Wichita Blue' is a brilliant blue, 20-foot-tall, 6-foot-wide pyramid; susceptible to disease. 'Welchii' forms a dense, 12-foot-tall, blue-green cone.

J. virginiana

P. 159

j. ver-jin-ee-AY-nah. Eastern Red Cedar. Forming a 50-foot-tall, 10- to 20-foot-wide pyramid or column, this adaptable native is common in the wild but is not well known in gardens. The dark green foliage has a strong cedar fragrance when crushed. It is needlelike on young plants, changing to scalelike with maturity. Foliage turns brownish green in winter, although improved cultivars have a more attractive winter color. Trunk bark is shredding and reddish brown. Female trees produce clusters of eye-catching, waxy, blue fruits, which provide food for birds and other wildlife. This underused tree makes an easy-to-grow screen or windbreak, especially in poor-soil sites in the East and Midwest. From eastern North America.

HOW TO GROW. Full sun and any well-drained soil—sandy, gravelly, or clayey; acid or alkaline. Grows best in moist sites, but tolerates drought. Do not irrigate established plants. Tolerates road salt, salt spray, and seashore and urban conditions. Leave lower limbs all the way to the ground or remove them to reveal trunk bark. Usually pest-free, but mites may be a problem in very hot, dry locations. Twig blight is a problem in wet areas. Eastern red cedar also is the alternate host for cedar-apple rust, which can disfigure the tree and seriously hurt nearby apples, crab apples, and hawthorns. Do not plant within a mile of an apple orchard. Zones 3b–9a.

CULTIVARS AND SIMILAR SPECIES. 'Burkii' has steel blue needles that turn an attractive purplish color in winter; grows 10 to 25 feet tall. 'Canaerti' is a dark green form with copious berries; pyramidal, growing to 25 feet tall. 'Emerald Sentinel' is a deep green, 20-foot-tall, 4-foot-wide column. 'Princeton Sentry' is a blue-green, very narrow, 25-foot-tall column. *J. chinensis* (Chinese juniper) is a 60-foot-tall, 20-foot-wide tree in the wild; its cultivars are common in gardens as compact trees or spreading shrubs; foliage usually includes both needlelike and scalelike green, blue-gray, or golden leaves; grows well in the East in well-drained sites; Zones 4a–9a. *Upright cultivars:* 'Blue Point' is a vivid blue-green, 12-foot-tall, 8-foot-wide column. 'Hetzii Columnaris' is a bright green, 15-foot-tall, 5-foot-wide column. 'Keteleeri' is a 30-foot-tall cone with dense, vivid light blue-green foliage.

🐾 *Larix*

LAR-icks. Pine family, Pinaceae.

Related to pines and spruces, this genus of 10 species from the cold regions of the Northern Hemisphere is unusual in that its members drop their needles in fall and stand bare limbed all winter. Needles are borne in whorls on short, spurlike shoots along the horizontal branches. These trees also have wonderful fall color. Three larch species are useful garden plants.

L. decidua   P. 160

l. deh-SID-yew-ah. European Larch. With a tall straight trunk, a slender crown, and whorls of horizontal branches, this tree grows into a distinct, dense cone, reaching 75 feet tall and 25 feet wide. The 1½-inch-long needles grow in clusters of 30 to 40 on short, brownish black shoots. They are bright light green in spring, mature to darker green in summer, and turn a glorious deep ocher before dropping in autumn. Bark exfoliates and is deeply fissured, revealing a gray-brown and reddish brown pattern. The clustered, 1- to 2-inch-long cones are violet-purple in spring and mature to woody brown. They have overlapping scales and stand straight up on the branches, looking showy all year. European larch makes a fine, strong-limbed screen or specimen for a large property in a cold climate. From Europe.

HOW TO GROW. Full sun and moist, well-drained, deep, humus-rich, acid soil. Does not tolerate alkaline or clayey soil or air pollution. Resists storm damage. Prune in summer. Pests include larch casebearers, gypsy moths, Japanese beetles, and canker. Zones 2a–6b.

CULTIVARS. 'Varied Directions' is a vigorous hybrid with irregular, arching branches; use as an unusual specimen.

L. kaempferi P. 160

l. KAM-fur-eye. Japanese Larch. Pyramidal, with slightly pendulous, horizontal branches and a straight, massive trunk, this picturesque tree grows 70 to 90 feet tall and 35 to 40 feet wide and has an open silhouette. The 1-inch-long needles grow in tufts of 40 on short, reddish brown spurs. They are brilliant green in spring; mature to deep blue-green in summer, with two white bands on their undersides; and turn glorious shades of gold and orange in fall. The scales of the 1½-inch-long cones are rolled back, creating a showy rosette. Makes an excellent specimen or screen. From Japan.

HOW TO GROW. Full sun and moist, well-drained, acid soil. Does not tolerate alkaline soil, heat, drought, or urban conditions. Twigs and cones may create a litter problem. Do not remove lower branches; allow a skirt of branches to form near the ground. Forms a new leader if it is injured. Larch casebearers, Japanese beetles, sawflies, gypsy moths, and aphids can be serious problems. Fairly resistant to canker. Zones 4a–6b.

CULTIVARS. 'Blue Rabbit' has blue needles and a narrow shape. 'Pendula' is irregularly weeping, growing to 60 feet tall.

L. larcinia P. 161

l. lar-SIN-ee-ah. American Larch, Tamarack. Growing 40 to 80 feet tall and 15 to 30 feet wide, with a slender trunk and horizontal branches with drooping branchlets, this tree forms an open pyramid that is usually narrower than that of other larches. New growth is bright lime green, matures to blue-green, and turns a very clear golden yellow in fall. The 1-inch-long needles are borne in tufts of 12 to 30. Cones are only about ½ inch around, the smallest of any conifer. They hang down from the branches but are hidden by the needles. This very cold hardy, strong-wooded tree grows naturally in boggy soil. Best as a specimen or screen on a large property and very useful in a wet site beside a stream or pond that may flood in spring. From northern North America.

HOW TO GROW. Full sun and moist, well-drained, humus-rich, acid soil. Tolerates wet or slightly alkaline soil and road salt. It is not very heat tolerant and prefers mountainous climates. Troubled by larch casebearers, gypsy moths, and sawflies. Zones 2a–6b.

SIMILAR SPECIES. *L. occidentalis* (western larch) is a slender tree with a massive trunk, grass green needles, and 2-inch cones; native to western North America.

ᵂ *Metasequoia*

met-ah-she-KWOY-ah. Bald cypress family, Taxodiaceae.

Twenty million years ago, when dinosaurs were becoming extinct, dawn redwoods grew throughout most of the Northern Hemisphere. They, too, became known only from fossil records and were thought to be extinct until the 1940s, when a forester discovered three trees growing beside a rice paddy in central China. Seeds of this deciduous conifer were eventually gathered from another grove nearby containing 1,500 trees and distributed to arboretums and eventually homes and parks around the world. This is a single-species genus.

M. glyptostroboides   P. 161

m. glip-toh-stroh-BOY-deez. Dawn Redwood. This magnificent tree forms a commanding, tall, narrow cone with a strong, tapering central leader, upright branches, and a buttressed and fluted trunk. It grows 80 to 120 feet tall and 20 to 40 feet wide. Leaves are flattened, ½-inch-long needles that are arranged in opposite pairs on the branchlets and create a soft, feathery look. Foliage emerges bright green in early spring, matures to dark green, and turns red-brown or orange in late fall before all the needles drop. (Individual leaves don't actually drop off, but fall while still attached to 3-inch-long, green-barked, deciduous branchlets.) The tree then stands leafless throughout the winter. Reddish brown or bright orange shredding bark covers the attractive trunk. Cones are brown and 1 inch around and persist throughout the winter, clustered in long, cascading bunches. Dawn redwood can be distinguished from bald cypress by its large winter buds and oppositely arranged needles; bald cypress has very small buds and alternately arranged needles. This very fast growing tree can add 3 feet of new growth each year and makes an excellent screen. Where space allows, it is beautiful planted in a grove. It also can be used as a street tree, except under power lines. From China.

HOW TO GROW. Full sun. Best in moist, well-drained, slightly acid soil, but adapts to a wet site at a pond's edge. Does not tolerate drought. Growth stops in late fall, and the tree can be injured by early frost; avoid planting in frost pockets. All lower branches should remain on the tree, which will form a new leader if it is injured. It responds to shearing during midsummer. Usually pest-free, but mites are sometimes problematic in dry soil. Zones 5a–8b.

CULTIVARS. 'National' forms an extremely narrow spire. 'Sheridan Spire' is a narrow pyramid with more compact growth.

☙ *Picea*

PYE-see-ah. Pine family, Pinaceae.

The 40 species of this genus, the spruces, hail from North America, Europe, and Asia, mostly from cool, moist regions. They look very similar to the firs *(Abies)*, featuring a pyramidal to conical shape with whorled branches and maintaining the same symmetrical shape even with great age. Needles are usually four angled and spirally arranged on the branchlets. Cones are oval or elongated and usually hang down, remaining on the tree without shattering. Several species of these very formal looking conifers are popular in gardens and large-scale landscapes, where they are most attractive if the lower branches are left to sweep to the ground. In general, spruces do not tolerate hot, dry climates; the heat and humidity of the Southeast; or air pollution. Spruces may be pruned to control their size and encourage density by cutting halfway through the new growth in spring before the needles reach their full size.

P. abies

p. AY-beez. Norway Spruce. This pyramidal tree reaches 90 feet tall and 35 feet wide and is quite stiff looking when young, although it becomes more open and graceful as it matures. The wide-spreading side branches are almost horizontal but turn downward and then upward at their tips. They are decorated with weeping twigs and branchlets that are densely cloaked with needles. The ½- to 1-inch-long needles are stiff and dark green with a blunt point. Young cones are reddish purple in spring and ripen into 6-inch-long, light brown, cigar-shaped cylinders that hang from the upper branches all winter. Norway spruce has rough, reddish brown bark and is fast growing and very long-lived; it resists cold and wind. It grows to a large size that can dwarf many home landscapes, so plant it where it has plenty of room to expand, and take into account its dark, somber appearance. Useful as a specimen, screen, or windbreak. From Europe.

HOW TO GROW. Full sun. Best in moist, well-drained, acid soil, but adapts to clayey soil if well drained. Does not tolerate wet soil or extreme drought. Large trees transplant well. Lower branches may die naturally and should be removed, but this spruce looks best with branches to the ground. Mites, aphids, and bagworms can be serious problems; borers are sometimes troublesome. Zones 3a–7b.

CULTIVARS. Many dwarf, shrublike forms are available. Only treelike forms are described here. 'Acrocona' has showy, raspberry-pink cones in spring and forms a 12-foot-tall, 4-foot-wide pyramid. 'Cranstonii', P. 162, is a sparsely branched, gaunt, full-size pyramid with long, weeping, snakelike branchlets. 'Cupressina' is a dense, broad column with tightly weeping branches, small needles, and cones; reaches 50 feet tall. 'Frohburg' is a vigorous, upright tree with strongly weeping branches and a tidy appearance. 'Inversa' has a straight main trunk with weeping branches and twigs on a small frame. 'Reflexa' spreads on the ground, with upward-reaching branch tips. 'Pendula' is a variable weeping form that may resemble 'Inversa' or 'Reflexa'.

P. glauca   P. 163

p. GLOUW-kah. White Spruce. When young, white spruce forms a broad, dense pyramid with horizontal branches. It matures into a spirelike, pyramidal or columnar tree with ascending branches and ultimately grows to 50 feet tall and 20 feet wide. The ¾-inch-long, pale blue-green needles are rigid with a barely sharp point. They have white bands on both sides, creating a less somber appearance than that of Norway spruce. The 2-inch-long cones are green in spring, ripen to pale brown in fall, and remain on the tree through the winter. Bark is rough and gray-brown. White spruce ultimately reaches a large size with branches all the way to the ground. Use it as a specimen or screen where it has plenty of room to grow. From northern North America.

HOW TO GROW. Full sun is best, but tolerates half shade. Best in moist, humus-rich soil, but tolerates some dryness and is the most heat-tolerant spruce. Adapts to coastal conditions. Mites, sawflies, and bagworms may be problems; trunk rot can be troublesome in overly wet sites. Zones 2a–8a.

CULTIVARS. 'Coerulea' has beautiful blue-green needles. 'Pendula' has light gray-green needles and forms a narrow, weeping pyramid; grows to 30 feet tall. P. glauca var. albertiana 'Conica' (dwarf Alberta spruce), P. 163, is a very popular dwarf form with tiny, feathery, light green needles; forms a slow-growing, dense cone that can reach 20 feet tall after many years; very susceptible to spider mites in hot locations. P. glauca var.

densata (Black Hills spruce), **P. 36**, is a slow- to moderate-growing form that matures as a 30-foot-tall, broad pyramid with very dense, dark green or blue-gray needles; an exceptional ornamental in the North.

P. omorika

P. 163

p. oh-MOR-ee-kah. Serbian Spruce. Though not well known, this slow-growing spruce, with its narrow pyramidal shape and weeping branches, is perhaps the most elegant of the genus and one of the toughest, too. It reaches 60 feet tall and 20 feet wide, has short side branches that curve gracefully upward at their tips, and has somewhat pendulous branchlets, creating a distinctive silhouette. The dense, sharp-pointed, 1- to 1½-inch-long needles are dark blue-green on top and gray-white on their undersides, which creates a two-tone effect. The 2-inch-long, cylindrical cones are dark blue-purple when young and turn cinnamon brown when mature. Use this narrow tree as a strong vertical accent in a mixed border. From western Europe.

HOW TO GROW. Full sun to partial shade and deep, fertile, well-drained, acid or alkaline soil with even moisture. Mulch to keep soil moist. Tolerates heat, humidity, and dry air, unlike most spruces. Allow branches to remain to the ground. Aphids, bagworms, borers, and mites can be troublesome. Zones 4b–8a.

CULTIVARS. 'Pendula' is variable but has a more pronounced weeping habit than the species. 'Pendula Bruns' has an extremely narrow weeping shape; grows to about 30 feet tall.

P. orientalis

P. 164

p. ore-ee-en-TAH-lis. Oriental Spruce. Less commonly grown than Norway or white spruce and much more beautiful, Oriental spruce forms a slow-growing, broad cone that reaches 60 feet tall and 20 to 30 feet wide. It has horizontal or slightly pendulous branches and short, stiff branchlets that are less pendulous than those of other spruces. The blunt-tipped, four-sided needles are noted for their fine texture and glossy, dark black-green color. They are only ¼ inch long and are pressed tightly against the stems, creating very densely needled twigs. Cones are reddish purple in spring and mature to 3½-inch-long, dangling, brown cones in fall. This very formal looking spruce is best used as a specimen in a lawn or border. The golden-needled forms look best against dark green evergreens. From eastern Europe and Asia Minor.

HOW TO GROW. Full sun is best, but tolerates half sun. Grows in any well-drained soil, from humus rich to rocky, acid to slightly alkaline. Protect from drying winter wind. Remove lower branches only if they die naturally. Aphids and bagworms may be troublesome; mites are less of a problem than with other spruces. This is one of the best spruces where summers are hot and humid. Zones 4b–8a.

CULTIVARS. 'Aurea' has creamy yellow needles at the branch tips all year. 'Aurea Compacta' forms a very slow growing, dense, 30-foot-tall cone and has golden new growth. 'Aureo-spicata', P. 164, has ivory-yellow new growth that turns green in summer. 'Atrovirens' has glossy, very dark green needles. 'Skylands' has brilliant creamy yellow new growth that darkens to rich gold; forms a very slender, slow-growing pyramid.

P. pungens var. *glauca* P. 165

p. PUN-jenz GLOUW-kah. Colorado Blue Spruce. This extremely dense, blue-needled tree forms a very symmetrical, 60-foot-tall, 25-foot-wide pyramid made up of tiers of stiff, horizontal branches and short, nonweeping branchlets. The sharp-pointed needles are about 1 inch long and encircle the stems. They range in color from blue-gray to steel blue to powder blue; the species itself has gray-green to dark green needles. Cones are green when young and mature to shiny, light brown, 4-inch-long cylinders. This poplar tree has a very formal shape that does not lend itself to all landscapes. Plant in a lawn as a specimen, in groups as a windbreak, or as a screen where there's plenty of growing room. Looks best against dark green (not golden) evergreens. From western North America.

HOW TO GROW. Best blue color develops in full sun. Likes fertile, moist, well-drained soil, but grows in any well-drained soil. Tolerates some drought and a dry climate. May not prosper in a hot, humid climate. Do not remove lower branches. Spruce gall, budworms, spider mites, and canker can be problems. Zones 3a–7b.

CULTIVARS. 'Bakeri' has deep blue needles and forms a 30-foot-tall pyramid. 'Bizon Blue' is a dense pyramid with brilliant blue needles. 'Fat Albert' has pale silvery blue needles and forms a dense, 15-foot-tall pyramid. 'Hoopsii' is fast growing and has beautiful silver-blue, almost white needles. 'Iseli Fastigate' forms a 15-foot-tall, 2-foot-wide column with steel blue needles. 'Iseli Foxtail' grows into a narrow, 15- to 20-foot-tall pyramid with twisted blue needles that form tufted branch tips; an oddity to use as a specimen. 'Koster' has silver-blue or powder blue needles and a variable form. 'Moerheim' is compact and narrow, with silver-blue needles.

❦ *Pinus*

PYE-nuss. Pine family, Pinaceae.

About 90 species of this genus are distributed throughout the Northern Hemisphere. Pine needles are very distinctive: they are linear, sprout from papery brown sheaths, and are grouped along the stems in bundles of two, three, or five (sometimes four). Pines with bundles of five needles are called white pines or soft pines; those with two or three needles per bundle are called black pines or hard pines. Spring growth consists of elongating stems, called candles, that reach their full length before their new needles mature. Pines can be pruned by cutting off half the length of the candles before the needles elongate. Limbs should be pruned back only to a fork in the branch because they will not resprout from leafless wood. Pines are popular landscape trees and offer gardeners a soft, informal texture as screens or specimens. In general, they are tough, drought-resistant trees, with different species thriving in different regions.

P. aristata   P. 165, 166

p. air-is-TAH-tah. Bristlecone Pine. This very slow growing, open-branched pine is an irregular, spreading or flat-topped, 15- to 20-foot-tall-and-wide tree that stays in scale with a small garden for many years. It has one or more trunks and rough bark. Needles are 1 to 2 inches long and dark green, marked with dots of white resin. They are arranged in bushy bundles of five on sparsely branched stems. Individual needles live for 10 or more years before dropping, so the branches have a dense bottlebrush appearance that distinguishes them from those of other pines. The brown cones are 3 inches long and have sharp, spiny bristles at the tip of each scale. Wild bristlecone pines are the longest-lived trees known; some gnarled, weather-beaten specimens are at least 4,000 years old. Use this picturesque tree in a border, foundation planting, or rock garden. It also thrives in poor-soil areas. From the high mountains of southwestern North America.

HOW TO GROW. Full sun and any well-drained, acid or alkaline soil. Tolerates poor, rocky conditions. Best with moderate moisture, but tolerates drought. Usually pest-free. Resin dots may resemble scale. Zones 3b–7a in the East; to Zone 9 on the West Coast.

CULTIVARS. 'Sherwood Compacta' has a compact, conical shape resembling that of Alberta spruce.

P. bungeana   P. 166

p. bun-jee-AY-nah. Lacebark Pine. This rare pine is admired for its open, flat-topped shape and for the showy bark that cloaks its multiple trunks. Lacebark pine grows very slowly but ultimately reaches 30 to 50 feet tall and wide. Bark is a patchwork of green, pink, and cream that is most colorful when the sun strikes the trunks, but it does not develop its distinctive colors until the tree is at least 10 years old. The glossy, dark green, 3-inch-long needles are sharp pointed and in bundles of three. Cones are 3-inch-long, light brown ovals with triangular spines. This pine is grown in temple gardens in China and makes a wonderful specimen in a border where it has plenty of space to grow and the bark can be admired up close. From China.

HOW TO GROW. Full sun and any well-drained, acid or alkaline soil. Brittle branches may break under snow or ice. Prune lower branches to reveal trunk bark, but do not remove multiple trunks. Usually pest-free. Zones 5a–9a.

CULTIVARS. 'Rowe Arboretum' forms a tight pyramid with glossy green needles.

P. densiflora   P. 167

p. den-sih-FLOR-ah. Japanese Red Pine, Tanyosho Pine. This sculptural, slow-growing pine features multiple trunks and layers of upturned, horizontal branches that form an irregular or flat-topped shape. It can reach 60 or more feet tall and wide, but its most popular form is half that size. Along with its striking silhouette comes a showy cloak of reddish orange bark that brightens a garden throughout the year. The 3- to 5-inch-long needles are bright light green, slightly twisted, and arranged in bundles of two in dense, upright tufts along the branches. Numerous clustered, yellowish, 2-inch-long cones adorn the branches all winter. Use the species or a smaller cultivar where it has plenty of room to grow, as a lawn specimen, in a border, or silhouetted in a distant view. From China, Japan, and Korea.

HOW TO GROW. Full sun and any well-drained, slightly acid soil, from sandy to slightly heavy, with moderate moisture. Tolerates salt spray and seashore conditions. Leave multiple trunks but remove lowest branches to show off bark. Often pruned into cloud formations in Japanese-style gardens. Branches are susceptible to snow damage. Usually pest-free. Zones 5b–7b.

CULTIVARS. 'Aurea' is a bushy, 8-foot-tall dwarf; new needles are golden in spring, mature to lime-yellow in summer, and turn more golden in fall. 'Umbraculifera' (Tanyosho pine) is a popular slow-growing cultivar that reaches 15 to 30 feet tall and wide; has vase-shaped trunks and a mushroom-shaped, flattened top. 'Heavy Bud' resembles 'Umbraculifera' but has large red buds. 'Soft Green' is similar to, but more dwarf than, 'Umbraculifera'. 'Morris Arboretum' is beautifully irregular, with a pronounced flat top. 'Oculus-Draconis' (dragon's-eye pine), P. 167, has green needles with bright yellow bands; produces a creamy effect when seen from a distance. 'Pendula' ('Prostrata') weeps if staked and grafted to a tall, straight trunk.

P. flexilis
P. 167

p. FLECK-sill-iss. Limber Pine. This stunning pine forms a loose pyramid when young and matures into a broad, flat-topped specimen that reaches 45 feet tall and 30 feet wide. Limber pine is not widely planted but ought to be used more in gardens, because it is quite beautiful and widely adapted. The slender, blue-green, 3-inch-long needles appear in bundles of five and are slightly twisted, giving the tree a dense, fluffy texture. Mature cones are 6 inches long, light brown, and pendulous. This pine may form single or multiple trunks that are covered with deeply fissured, dark gray bark. The young branches are so flexible that they can be bent in half without breaking. Use as a tall, soft-textured screen or specimen. From the Rocky Mountains.

HOW TO GROW. Full sun to partial shade and moist, well-drained soil. Tolerates rocky soil and some drought or salt. Do not remove lower limbs. More resistant to winter burn from sun and wind in cold regions than other five-needled pines; performs better in the West and Midwest. Usually pest-free, but white pine blister rust can occur. Zones 3b–7b.

CULTIVARS. 'Extra Blue' forms a strong pyramid with very blue needles. 'Glauca' has bluish needles. 'Glauca Thume' features very blue needles on a compact, upright plant; good for a screen. 'Millcreek' has very blue needles and a full pyramidal shape. 'Temple' is upright and open branched; grows to 30 feet tall; short, silvery blue-green needles. 'Vanderwolf's Pyramid' is a fast-growing, narrow, pyramidal tree that reaches 25 feet tall and has long, silvery blue-green needles.

P. koraiensis
P. 168

p. kor-ay-eye-EN-sis. Korean Pine. Loosely pyramidal, growing to 40 feet tall and 15 to 20 feet wide, this little-known pine is a beautiful, lush tree with long, densely needled, horizontal or upright branches. Korean pine resembles the much more common eastern white pine, but it has longer needles and a more layered shape when young. The thick, stiff needles are arranged in bundles of five. They are 3½ to 4½ inches long and glossy dark green with white stripes, giving the tree an overall blue-green or gray-green hue. Blue-needled forms are the most striking. Dense, reddish brown hairs cloak the twigs between the bundles of needles, an identifying feature. Trunk bark is smooth and gray-brown. Cones are yellow-brown, upright, and about 5 inches long. They fall unopened to the ground, where birds and animals eat them and release the seeds. Use this somewhat formal tree in groves, as a windbreak, or as a specimen. From China, Japan, and Korea.

HOW TO GROW. Full sun to partial shade and almost any garden soil. Allow branches to remain all the way to the ground or prune for a more open effect. Usually pest-free. Zones 4a–7b; Zone 8b in the West.

CULTIVARS AND SIMILAR SPECIES. 'Glauca', P. 168, has blue-green needles and grows to 25 feet tall. 'Morris Blue' has excellent silver-blue needles and reaches 25 feet tall. 'Silveray' is identical to 'Morris Blue'. *P. cembra* (Swiss stone pine) looks similar but has shorter green needles and a dense cone shape when young, eventually becoming flat topped and spreading; grows to 35 feet tall; twigs have dense reddish hairs; cones are greenish violet, eventually turning purple-brown, and do not open; Zones 3b-7b. 'Pygmaea' forms a dense pyramid.

P. parviflora P. 169

p. par-veh-FLOR-ah. Japanese White Pine. This elegant, slow-growing pine creates a fine-textured, silvery blue effect. Dense and conical when young, it becomes more open and wide spreading as it matures, with a flat top and tiers of horizontal branches. It eventually reaches 35 to 50 feet tall and 20 to 35 feet wide. The slightly twisted, blue-green needles are stiff and short—only 2 to 2½ inches long—and very narrow, with white bands. They are in groups of five, forming clustered tufts at the tips of branches. Reddish brown, 2- to 4-inch-long, oval cones form even on young trees and decorate the branches for several years. Bark on older trunks is scaly and dark gray. This pine makes an excellent specimen in a border, small-scale garden, or seaside site. From Japan and Korea.

HOW TO GROW. Full sun and almost any well-drained, acid soil with moderate moisture. Tolerates salt and seashore conditions. Mulch to keep soil cool and moist. Remove lower limbs only if they die naturally. Wood is weak, and limbs are susceptible to storm damage. Usually pest-free. Zones 5b–9a.

CULTIVARS AND SIMILAR SPECIES. 'Glauca', P. 169, has silvery blue-green, more twisted needles and numerous cones; grows slowly to 30 feet tall; more commonly grown than the species. 'Glauca Brevifolia' has shorter, more tufted, blue-green needles. 'Glauca Nana' has blue-green needles and forms a narrower, shorter tree. 'Templehof' grows faster and is bluer than 'Glauca'. 'Venus' has shorter, bluer needles and a compact shape. *P. pumila* (Japanese stone pine) is similar but more shrublike and low spreading; grows only 10 to 15 feet tall.

P. resinosa   P. 170

p. rez-eh-NO-sah. Red Pine, Norway Pine. This very cold hardy, durable pine has a pyramidal or oval shape with heavy branches and grows to 50 or more feet tall and 25 feet wide. Though handsome, red pine is best used in cold, demanding sites where more beautiful pines perform poorly. The yellow-green needles are 6 inches long and arranged in pairs that form dense tufts along the branches. Needles are so brittle that they snap when bent, an identifying feature. Cones are light brown and 2 inches long. Older trunks have reddish brown bark that is broken into diamond-shaped plates, an attractive attribute that is revealed when lower limbs die naturally. Plant in groves or rows to use as a windbreak or screen in areas with demanding growing conditions. Makes a picturesque specimen to silhouette against the sky. From north-central and northeastern North America.

HOW TO GROW. Full sun and any well-drained, acid soil. Performs well in sandy or gravelly soil; very sensitive to poorly drained soil. Drought tolerant, but sensitive to air pollution. Remove competitive leaders if they form and lower limbs when they die. Usually pest-free, but quite susceptible to sawflies. Best suited to cold climates. Zones 2b–6b.

SIMILAR SPECIES. *P. ponderosa* (ponderosa pine, western yellow pine), **P. 169**, grows into a narrow or irregular, 60- to 100-foot-tall, 25- to 60-foot wide pyramid; deeply fissured, reddish brown bark; 5- to 10-inch-long needles in bundles of three; from western North America; tolerates drought and alkaline soil; Zones 3b–8a.

P. strobus   P. 170

p. STROH-bus. Eastern White Pine. Probably the most beautiful and widely grown pine, eastern white pine features graceful, horizontally spreading branches and a pyramidal shape, growing 50 to 80 feet tall and 20 to 40 feet wide. The long, narrow, light green or blue-green needles are 2 to 5 inches long and arranged in bundles of five, giving the tree a lovely texture. Older trunks feature deeply furrowed, gray-brown bark. The 6- to 8-

inch-long, brown cones are pendulous. Use this fast-growing pine as a fine-textured windbreak or specimen, or plant it in groves for a naturalistic effect. Can be pruned to develop a dense hedge. From eastern North America.

HOW TO GROW. Full to partial sun. Best in moist, well-drained, acid loam, but tolerates dry sites. Mulch soil to keep cool and moist. Does not tolerate poorly drained or heavy soil, road salt, air pollution, or seashore conditions. Limbs are susceptible to ice and snow damage. Prune to a single leader if several develop. Remove lower limbs that die naturally as the tree ages. To maintain as a tall hedge or screen, shear each spring when candles form. Cut back each limb only to a fork in the branch; pines do not resprout from leafless wood. White pine blister rust and white pine weevils can be serious. Becomes chlorotic in alkaline soil. Zones 3a–9a.

CULTIVARS. *P. s.* var. *glauca* has blue needles. 'Alba' has creamy white new growth that matures to blue-green. 'Fastigiata' is columnar when young and broadens with age, reaching 60 feet tall and 8 feet wide; excellent for screening. 'Contorta' is slow growing, with very twisted needles and contorted, ascending branches. 'Hillside Winter Gold' has green needles that turn a beautiful light yellow in winter. 'Pendula' forms a weeping specimen if staked and supported to the desired height. 'White Mountain' is a vigorous grower with beautiful powder blue needles. 'Torulosa' has twisted needles and a typical growth habit.

P. sylvestris
P. 171

p. sill-VES-tris. Scotch Pine, Scots Pine. This widely grown pine has an open structure with wide-spreading branches and an irregular, flat top; it becomes attractively craggy with age. Scotch pine grows quickly to 30 to 60 feet tall and 30 to 40 feet wide. Pairs of 2- to 3-inch-long needles are stiff, twisted, and tinted blue-green to gray-green, often turning yellowish green in winter. The flaky bark is an eye-catching orange-brown on the limbs and upper trunks and gray or reddish brown and fissured on older trunks. Cones are gray-brown and 3 inches long. Scotch pine works well as a specimen in a small garden or can be grouped for a naturalistic effect in a large landscape. From northern and central Europe.

HOW TO GROW. Full sun and any well-drained, acid to slightly alkaline soil. Tolerates infertile, dry sites and some road salt. Remove lower limbs if they die naturally; remove competitive leaders. Susceptible to storm damage. Often attacked and killed by pine wilt and tip blight in the East and Midwest. Zones 3a–8b.

CULTIVARS. 'Aurea' has bright yellow new growth that turns light green in summer and bright yellow in winter; very slow growing; useful as a shrub for many years. 'Auvergne' has the best green winter color. 'Arctic' is very cold hardy (Zone 2b); blue-green summer needles and bright yellow winter needles. 'East Anglia', **P. 171**, has a straight trunk and deep green needles even in winter. 'Fastigiata' has blue-green needles and forms a slow-growing, narrow column; grows to 25 feet tall and 5 feet wide. 'French Blue' has brighter blue needles and a compact shape. 'Spaan's Fastigiate' is a compact, vertical tree with blue-green needles; resists ice and snow damage. 'Waterii' is a favorite compact, rounded tree; grows 20 to 30 feet tall; blue-green needles and very orange bark.

P. taeda   P. 172

p. TEE-dah. Loblolly Pine. An important timber tree in the South, this native pine is pyramidal when young and becomes branched and rounded with age, maturing at 45 to 60 or more feet tall and half as wide. The dark yellow-green needles are 6 to 10 inches long and arranged in bundles of three. The narrow cones are 6 inches long and have sharp spines. Bark is gray and deeply furrowed and ridged. Though not as beautiful as many pines, this fast-growing, straight-trunked species adapts to adverse conditions and provides an effective screen in sites where other evergreens won't grow. Plant this and other native southern pines in a grove for a wooded effect and to shade azaleas and camellias, or plant in a staggered line for a quick screen. Established native stands of loblolly pine should not be cleared, because they provide shade and protection. From southeastern North America.

HOW TO GROW. Full sun to partial shade and moist, acid clay. Tolerates poor drainage and drought. Remove lower branches as they die naturally. Pine beetles and heart rot are sometimes serious. Zones 7b–9a.

CULTIVARS AND SIMILAR SPECIES. 'Nana' is a dwarf that grows slowly into a dense, rounded shape 15 feet tall. *P. palustris* (longleaf pine) is a southern native that reaches 80 feet tall; slender, 8- to 18-inch-long, bright green needles are in bundles of three and form fluffy tufts on short branches; grows in sandy soil; Zones 7b–9a. *P. elliotti* (slash pine), another southern native, reaches 80 feet tall; features pairs of 8- to 10-inch-long, yellow-green needles; tolerates poorly drained soil; Zones 8b–9a.

P. thunbergii (P. thunbergiana)   P. 172

p. thun-burr-gee-AY-nah. Japanese Black Pine. Open branched, with an irregular curving main trunk, this attractive small pine grows 35 to 60 feet tall and is a perfect choice for a seaside or high-desert garden, because it thrives in sandy soil and salt spray. Unfortunately, insect and disease problems may preclude planting the tree in some areas. The shiny, dark green needles are 2½ to 4½ inches long and arranged in bundles of two. The very prominent, silvery buds are an identifying feature. Trunk bark is dark gray to black and broken up into large plates. The 3-inch-long cones are shiny light brown. Use Japanese black pine as a specimen or windbreak or to stabilize dunes in areas where pests are not a problem. From Japan and Korea.

HOW TO GROW. Full sun. Best in fertile, moist soil, but tolerates sandy soil and drought. Tolerates heat and salt spray. Can be sheared and trained to emphasize its cloudlike branching in a Japanese-style garden. Pinewood nematodes (carried by long-horned beetles) and blue-stain fungus (carried by black turpentine beetles) attack and kill trees that are 20 or more years old in some regions, especially the East; check with local experts to see if pest problems preclude planting the tree in your area. Zone 6a–9a.

CULTIVARS AND SIMILAR SPECIES. 'Thunderhead', **P. 173**, features extra-large silver buds and is fast growing, with an upright shape. 'Majestic Beauty' tolerates smog. *P. leucodermis (P. heldreichii* var. *leucodermis)* (Bosnian pine) makes a good substitute for *P. thunbergii;* pairs of dark green, 3½-inch-long needles; smooth, gray-green bark and white-barked twigs; grows slowly into a 45-foot-tall, upright tree; tolerates dry or alkaline soil; resists *Diplodia* tip blight; Zones 5a–8a. *P. nigra* (Austrian pine) grows 60 to 100 feet tall; very dark green, long, sharp, stiff needles; furrowed, mottled bark; tolerates salt spray, sandy or clayey soil, and alkaline soil; in some areas, *Diplodia* tip blight devastates 15- to 20-year-old trees; resists oak root rot fungus; Zones 4a–8a. 'Arnold Sentinel' is columnar to 25 feet tall.

P. virginiana **P. 173**

p. ver-gin-ee-AY-nah. Virginia Pine, Scrub Pine, Jersey Pine. Pyramidal or flat topped and irregularly branching, Virginia pine grows 15 to 40 feet tall and 10 to 30 feet wide and is a durable pine where growing conditions challenge more attractive species. The stout green needles are somewhat twisted, 2 to 3 inches long, and arranged in pairs. In winter they may turn an unattractive yellowish green. The spiny cones are reddish brown, 2 inches long, and pendulous, with sharp spines. Bark is a colorful orange-brown. Use Virginia pine and similar species for a screen or specimen in a Xeriscape garden or in areas with infertile, dry soil. Virginia pine is also useful on reclamation sites. From eastern and central North America.

HOW TO GROW. Full sun. Best in clayey, acid to slightly alkaline loam, but performs well in poor, clayey or sandy soil. Tolerates drought and seashore conditions. May be sheared to increase density. Remove lower limbs if they die naturally. Canker, heart rot, and pine sawflies are sometimes troublesome. Zones 5b–9a.

CULTIVARS AND SIMILAR SPECIES. 'Watt's Gold', **P. 171**, is slow growing; light green needles in summer, turning bright gold in winter. *P. banksiana* (jack pine) is a fast-growing, cold-hardy, northern native with a pyramidal or shrubby, rugged shape that can grow to 50 feet tall; the paired, 1- to 2-inch-long needles are olive green and slightly twisted; makes a good coastal or poor-soil plant; Zones 2a–6a. *P. rigida* (pitch pine) is native to east-central North America; good for very poor, sandy sites; needles in bundles of three; susceptible to tip blight, tip moths, and pine needle scale; Zones 4b–7a. *P. edulis (P. cembroides* var. *edulis)* (pinyon pine) is a southwestern native that is bushy and stiff, growing 15 to 20 feet tall; 1- to 2-inch-long, dark green, paired needles; tolerates dry sites in the Midwest and West (in a Xeriscape or high-desert garden), but may be susceptible to insects in landscape situations; Zones 5a–7b; Zone 8b in the West.

P. wallichiana (P. griffithii)   P. 174

p. wall-lik-EE-ay-nah. Himalayan Pine, Bhutan Pine. Perhaps the most beautiful of all the pines, Himalayan pine is a soft-textured, broadly pyramidal tree that reaches 30 to 50 or more feet tall and wide, with branches all the way to the ground. The sharp-pointed needles are 6 to 8 inches long and arranged in soft, cascading groups of five. They are gray-green with white stripes, giving the tree a silvery sheen from a distance and creating an outstanding landscape effect. Light brown, pendulous cones are 6 to 10 inches long and 2 inches wide. Use this elegant tree as a specimen in a border or lawn. It's particularly beautiful with a dark background such as dark green or steel blue evergreens. From northern India and Pakistan.

HOW TO GROW. Full sun and moist, well-drained, fertile, acid, sandy loam. Does not tolerate drought, which may cause lower branches to die. Mulch to keep soil cool and moist. Shelter from wind. Do not shade lower branches, or they may die. Usually pest-free; resistant to white pine blister rust. Zones 5b–8b.

CULTIVARS. 'Zebrina' has unusual green needles with creamy yellow bands. 'Glauca' has very blue needles. 'Frosty' has very silvery needles. 'Morton' is cold hardy to Zone 4b.

❦ *Podocarpus*

poe-doe-CARP-us. Podocarp family, Podocarpaceae.

This genus of about 100 species hails from forested areas of the warm temperate and tropical zones of the Southern Hemisphere. The needle-like leaves are arranged spirally around the stems, and male and female catkins are borne on separate plants. Female plants develop showy, red or blue, berrylike, one-seeded cones. The several popular garden species are useful as specimens, screens, and hedges, because they take well to shearing.

P. macrophyllus   P. 175

p. mack-row-FYE-lus. Yew Pine, Yew Podocarpus. With a dense, upright or oval shape, yew pine matures at 20 to 30 feet tall and 10 to 15 feet wide and has many uses in the landscape, especially in the South, where it is quite common. The lance-shaped, leathery needles, which are arranged spirally around the stems, are waxy dark green with two white bands on their undersides and measure 3 to 8 inches long and ½ inch wide. They densely cloak the twiggy branches, giving the tree an intriguing, feathery texture. Trunk bark is reddish brown. The berrylike, pea-sized fruits ripen in fall to bright blue on thick red stalks. Use this dark green evergreen as a specimen in a border or foundation planting or as a privacy screen, or shear it for a formal hedge. Useful in seaside gardens. From China and Japan.

HOW TO GROW. Full sun to light shade. Best in moist, well-drained, fertile soil, but tolerates well-drained sandy loam or clay. Tolerates heat and salt spray, but not wet or alkaline soil. Stem tips may winterkill in sunny, windy sites in Zone 8a. Shear in spring and midsummer for a hedge. Usually pest-free. Zones 8a–9a.

CULTIVARS. *P. macrophyllus* var. *makii*, P. 175, is a 10-foot-tall dwarf form with 1½- to 2½-inch-long needles.

❦ *Pseudolarix*

soo-doh-LAR-ix. Pine family, Pinaceae.

Only one species belongs to this genus, an uncommon deciduous conifer that makes an unusual landscape specimen featuring beautiful, delicate foliage.

P. amabilis (P. kaempferi)

P. 176

p. ah-MAH-bil-lis. Golden Larch. Although it's a member of the pine family, this conifer drops its needles and stands leafless in winter. It grows slowly but after many years forms a 50-foot-tall, 40-foot-wide, open-branched pyramid with a straight central trunk and horizontally spreading branches. The very narrow, flattened needles are 1 to 2½ inches long. They are light green in spring, mature to soft green in summer, and finally turn a stunning yellow or russet-gold before dropping in autumn. They are arranged spirally around the young stems and in rosettes on the short spurs of older wood. The 3-inch-long, yellow-green cones ripen to reddish brown in autumn and are showy but soon shatter and drop off. Use golden larch as a specimen where it has plenty of room to grow. From China.

HOW TO GROW. Full to partial sun and moist, well-drained, acid to neutral, sandy loam. Intolerant of alkaline conditions. Shelter from wind. Allow branches to remain to the ground. Usually pest-free. Performs well in the South. Zones 6a–8a.

CULTIVARS. None.

❦ Pseudotsuga

soo-doh-SOO-gah. Pine family, Pinaceae.

This genus of six to eight firlike trees from North America and Asia is identified by its pendulous cones, which have conspicuous protruding bracts, and its pointed, many-scaled buds. These very important timber trees can grow to gigantic heights but are smaller in home landscapes. One species is a graceful landscape tree.

P. menziesii

P. 177

p. men-ZEE-zee-eye. Douglas Fir. In the wild, this is one of the tallest trees in North America, reaching 200 feet tall. In home landscapes, it usually grows into a spirelike, 50- to 80-foot-tall, 15- to 25-foot-wide pyramid. The branches are mostly horizontal—downswept at the bottom and upturned near the top of the single main trunk. The fine-textured, 1- to 1½-inch-long needles are arranged spirally in two ranks around the twigs. They are dark green in *P. menziesii* ssp. *menziesii,* which is from coastal areas, and blue-green or blue-gray in *P. menziesii* ssp. *glauca,* **P. 177**, which is from the Rocky Mountains. The mountain trees are more cold hardy than the coastal trees and are more commonly used in gardens. Douglas fir's young cones are a pretty rose-red and ripen to cinnamon brown, with forked bracts protruding from between the scales. Trunk bark is reddish and deeply fissured, becoming dark brown and corky on older trees. Use this attractive, fast-growing tree as a soft-textured specimen or screen, or plant in groups for a naturalistic effect. From western North America.

HOW TO GROW. Full sun and moist, well-drained, deep, acid to neutral soil. Blue types tolerate slightly alkaline soil. Sensitive to road salt. Protect from strong wind. Allow branches to remain to the ground. Branches may break if laden with snow or ice. Shear new growth annually for a hedge. May be troubled by canker, bark beetles, twig blight, budworms, gypsy moths, scale, tussock moths, and root weevils. Do not plant within 200 feet of Colorado spruce, as they are alternate hosts for cooly gall aphids. Rocky Mountain forms grow in Zones 3b–6b and cool areas of Zones 7 and 8; coastal forms grow in Zones 6a–8b.

CULTIVARS. 'Blue' has bright blue needles, like those of Colorado blue spruce. 'Fastigiata' is a narrow, columnar, green-needled form. 'Glauca' is a slow-growing, narrower form with blue-green needles. 'Glauca Pendula' has soft blue-green needles and a tall, narrow, weeping shape. 'Pendula' has weeping branches, a twisted leader, and green needles; wide spreading, growing to 11 feet tall.

❦ *Sciadopitys*

sy-uh-DOP-it-iss. Bald cypress family, Taxodiaceae.

The only species in this genus is a rare and unusual conifer that draws attention wherever it grows.

S. verticillata   P. 178

s. ver-tih-sih-LAH-tah. Japanese Umbrella Pine. Highly variable, depending on the seed source, this evergreen can grow into a narrow cone or a broad pyramid at least 25 to 30 feet tall and 15 to 20 feet wide, with symmetrical branches all the way to the ground. The flattened, thick needles are glossy dark green, 4 to 5 inches long, and ⅛ inch wide. They form dense whorls that spiral out from the branch tips, creating a billowy effect. Needles on some plants may turn bronze-green in winter. The 4-inch-long, egg-shaped, green cones ripen to dark reddish brown. The trunk is covered with shredding, reddish brown bark, which is not very noticeable because of the dense branches. Umbrella pine grows very slowly and is thus rare and costly. Use it as a focal point in a border or foundation planting, but allow room for it to mature into a noble specimen. From Japan.

HOW TO GROW. Full to partial sun; afternoon shade in the North and light shade in the South prevents desiccation. Best in fertile, moist, well-drained, acid soil. Protect from drying wind and full winter sun. Train to a single trunk if necessary. Allow low branches to remain to the ground. Usually pest-free and deer-proof. Zones 6a–8a.

CULTIVARS. 'Aurea' has golden needles. 'Wintergreen' retains an excellent dark blue-green color throughout the year.

❦ *Sequoia*

see-KWOY-ah. Bald cypress family. Taxodiaceae.

The only species in this genus is an evergreen native to coastal California and Oregon, where it thrives in the moist climate. Some of the largest trees growing in native stands are estimated to be 800 to 2,500 years old.

S. sempervirens P. 179

s. sem-per-VIE-rens. Redwood, Coast Redwood, California Redwood. The tallest tree in the world when grown in its native habitat, redwood reaches more than 300 feet tall in the wild, but it usually attains a height of only 60 to 80 feet under cultivation, especially outside its native area. It is densely branched when young but loses its lower branches with age, forming a slender pyramid with a tall, straight trunk. Trunk bark is an attractive reddish brown and ruggedly furrowed into broad ridges. The 1-inch-long needles are dark green to blue-green, have two white bands on the undersides, and are arranged opposite each other in two ranks, in dense flat sprays. The egg-shaped, reddish brown cones are about 1 inch long. Use this dramatic evergreen on a large property or in a park, allowing plenty of room for it to grow. From coastal California and Oregon.

HOW TO GROW. Full sun and rich, moist, acid soil. Remove suckers from the base. Performs best in the moist coastal conditions of the West but will grow in the East. Zones 7a–9a.

CULTIVARS. 'Adpressa' has very narrow shoots with smaller, bluer needles. 'Aptos Blue' has large green needles on horizontal branches. 'Kenwood' has blue needles. 'Los Altos' has shiny, green, coarse foliage on long, upwardly arching branches. 'Majestic Beauty' features blue-green foliage on dense, pendulous branchlets. 'Santa Cruz' has light green needles and slightly weeping branches.

⚜ *Sequoiadendron*

see-kwoy-uh-DEN-dron. Bald cypress family, Taxodiaceae.

Known as the world's largest tree because of its great mass and soaring height, the single member of this genus is a West Coast native that adapts readily to growing conditions in the East but will never grow as large outside its native habitat. Some of the largest and oldest giant sequoias are forest trees estimated to be 3,000 to 3,500 years old.

S. giganteum (Sequoia gigantea)   P. 179

s. jye-gan-TEE-um. Giant Sequoia, Big Tree, Giant Redwood, Sierra Redwood. A mammoth tree that can attain extreme old age in the wild, giant redwood grows much smaller in cultivation, usually forming a narrow pyramid and reaching only 60 to 100 feet tall, compared to the 250 to 300 feet it can reach in its native habitat. It naturally loses its lower branches, revealing a stout trunk covered with red-brown, fire-resistant, fibrous bark. The blue-green evergreen leaves are awl-shaped, ⅛- to ½-inch-long, pointed scales that press against the stems to create cordlike branches resembling *Juniperus* or *Cryptomeria*. The cones are egg shaped, reddish brown, and 1½ to 3 inches long. Use this unusual tree on a large property or in a park where it has room to mature; plant it in groves for a dramatic effect. From the western slopes of the Sierra Nevada.

HOW TO GROW. Full sun and fertile, moist, well-drained, acid to slightly alkaline, deep soil. Grows best with plentiful moisture, but tolerates occasional dryness. Remove lower branches as they die naturally. May be planted closely and sheared for a hedge. Usually pest-free, but needle blight and canker are rare problems. Grows best in the East or West. Zones 6b–9a.

CULTIVARS. 'Pendulum' has weeping branches. 'Glaucum' has pale blue-green needles. 'Hazel Smith' has deep blue-green needles and a uniform, pyramidal shape.

⚜ *Taxodium*

tax-OH-dee-um. Bald cypress family, Taxodiaceae.

This genus of deciduous and semievergreen conifers contains two species from the swampy areas of southern North America. Although they grow naturally in wet areas, they adapt readily to normal garden conditions, where they form stately trees even in climates colder than those in their natural range.

T. distichum

P. 180

t. DIS-tih-cum. Bald Cypress, Swamp Cypress. A deciduous conifer that grows to about 60 feet tall and 25 feet wide, bald cypress has a beautiful, symmetrical shape and delicate foliage, making it an eye-catching choice for a home landscape. The ½-inch-long, narrow, pointed needles are flattened and arranged in two-ranked sprays on delicate green twiglets that drop to the ground in autumn. Needles emerge bright green in spring, mature to gray-green, and turn golden rust-brown in fall before dropping. (Bald cypress can be distinguished from dawn redwood by the needle arrangement: bald cypress needles are arranged alternately, while dawn redwood's needles are opposite.) The trunk is very straight, buttressed at the base, and cloaked in pale brown, shredding bark. Naturally growing along streams or in other wet sites, bald cypress sends up odd, knobby growths called knees from its wide-spreading roots where soil is wet, but not in average or dry soil. Cones are round, dark brown, and about 1 inch around. Use this fast-growing tree as a specimen in a lawn or near water, or plant it in a grove in a wet or swampy site on a large property. From southern North America.

HOW TO GROW. Full to partial sun and deep, moist, acid, sandy loam or wet, swampy conditions. Adapts readily to average moisture and even to harsh midwestern sites, but will drop needles during a drought. Needs no pruning other than to remove any competing leaders. Usually problem-free, but may suffer from twig blight, wood rot, and spider mites. Becomes chlorotic in alkaline soil. Zones 4b–9a.

CULTIVARS. 'Shawnee Brave' has a tight pyramidal form with short branches and bronze-orange fall color. 'Monarch of Illinois' is much more wide spreading than the species. *T. distichum* var. *imbricarium (T. ascendens)* (pond cypress)', P. 181, is very similar, with light brown bark and small scalelike leaves that are held close to the upright twigs, creating a threadlike effect; Zones 6a–9a. 'Nutans' has weeping branchlets. 'Prairie Sentinel' has a threadlike leaf arrangement and very short, regularly spaced, horizontal branches that form a narrow column.

❦ Taxus

TAX-uss. Yew family, Taxaceae.

This genus contains seven or eight very similar species of evergreen trees and shrubs from North America, Europe, and Asia, including several very popular and common garden plants. In general, members of this genus have shredding, red-brown bark; two ranked or spirally arranged, somewhat fleshy needles; and fleshy, berrylike fruits on female plants. The needles and the seeds, though not the soft red flesh surrounding them, are poisonous. Unlike most conifers, which put out a single flush of growth in spring, yews grow continually from spring to fall, so they can be pruned at various times and will resprout from leafless wood if cut back severely in spring. Dwarf, shrubby cultivars are usually grown in home landscapes, but even they can grow much larger than expected. Unpruned and allowed to grow into their natural shapes, yews form elegant, dark-needled trees that stand out beautifully against a lighter background. They are a favorite food of deer.

T. baccata P. 181, 182

t. bah-KAY-tah. English Yew. When left to grow as it wishes, English yew forms a wide-spreading, multitrunked tree that matures at 45 feet tall and 20 feet wide. The flat, very dark green, waxy needles are about 2 inches long and somewhat curved or sickle shaped, with bluntly pointed ends. They are arranged spirally around upright shoots (which have green bark) but grow in two ranks on spreading shoots. Often pruned for use in foundation plantings and as hedges, English yew also makes an outstanding unpruned specimen for a lawn or shady border. The large, upright, narrow forms make excellent screens. From Europe.

HOW TO GROW. Full sun to full shade, although gold-leaved forms need good sun. Likes evenly moist, well-drained, fertile, acid to alkaline soil. May die in poorly drained sites. Does not tolerate drought. Strong winter wind and sun can desiccate foliage. May be pruned for a formal hedge. Remove lower limbs to reveal the showy trunks. Root weevils, mealybugs, and twig blight are occasional problems. Zones 6b–7b and cool areas of Zone 8a.

CULTIVARS. Many dwarf, shrublike forms are available. Only treelike forms are described here. 'Fastigiata' ('Stricta') (Irish yew) forms a dense column of upright branches; grows to 20 feet tall and 6 feet wide, with numerous red fruits. 'Fastigiata Aurea', P. 181, resembles Irish yew, with golden yellow new growth. 'Standishii', P. 182, is a compact, slow-growing, columnar form with eye-catching golden new growth.

T. cuspidata

t. cuss-peh-DAH-tay. Japanese Yew. Because it is so cold hardy, Japanese yew is the most common yew grown in North American landscapes. It can form a multitrunked, 25- to 40-foot-tall tree with upright or spreading branches, but dwarf types are grown more often than the species.

Needles are 1 inch long and pointed. They emerge bright green in spring, creating an eye-catching contrast against the very dark green older needles, which have yellowish green undersides. Needles are arranged in two irregular ranks on all the shoots, which have brown bark. This yew makes an excellent hedge or screen. Or you can use it as a specimen in a mixed border or shady garden. From Japan and Korea.

HOW TO GROW. See *T. baccata.* Zones 4b–7a.

CULTIVARS AND SIMILAR SPECIES. Many dwarf, shrublike forms are available. Only treelike forms are described here. 'Capitata', **P. 182**, is the name used for seed-grown treelike forms. *T.* × *media* (intermediate yew) is a hybrid of Japanese and English yew; it forms an upright or spreading shrub or tree that grows to 20 feet tall; two-ranked needles are borne on olive green shoots; Zones 5a–7b. 'Hicksii' forms a fast-growing, broad column that reaches 20 feet tall and 8 feet wide and has upright branches.

❦ *Thuja*

THEW-yah. Cypress family, Cupressaceae.

These evergreen trees and shrubs from North America and eastern Asia have small, rounded, brown cones and aromatic, scalelike or needlelike leaves borne on frondlike branches. Many cultivars are very popular landscape plants in cooler regions. They are ideal for screens and look better than most conifers when mass planted, because they have a softer, more informal outline.

T. occidentalis   P. 183

t. ox-seh-den-TAY-lis. Arborvitae, Eastern White Cedar, White Cedar. A columnar, 30- to 40-foot-tall, 15-foot-wide native evergreen, arborvitae is a common and very adaptable landscape plant with sprays of soft, aromatic foliage. Leaves are shiny, ½-inch-long scales that are tightly pressed to the twigs, which form flat, horizontal fans. The glossy green foliage cloaks the tree all the way to the ground. Unlike some species of *Thuja,* this one does not have white markings on the scales, an identifying feature. Foliage may remain green all winter or turn bronze, especially if exposed to full sun. In nature the tree usually forms a single trunk, but nursery-grown specimens are often multitrunked, which encourages splitting under ice or snow. Trunk bark is dark grayish brown and shredding. Cones are ½ inch long and ripen from yellow-green to light brownish yellow, with 8 to 10 woody scales. Use as a screen or a vertical accent in a border. From northeastern and north-central North America.

HOW TO GROW. Full sun to light shade; gold-leaved forms need sun. Best in fertile, moist, acid to alkaline, mulched soil, but tolerates wet soil and clay; tolerates dry soil as long it is cool and mulched. Adapts best to humid areas. Avoid storm damage by pruning young trees to a single leader or by tying multitrunked trees with an encircling support of twine for the winter. Trees are shallow rooted in wet soil and thus more likely to blow over in a storm. Does not resprout from old wood. Susceptible to deer. Bagworms are a problem in warmer areas. Zones 3a–7b.

CULTIVARS. Many dwarf, shrublike forms are available. Only treelike forms are described here. 'Affinity' forms a fast-growing, narrow, 30-foot-tall pyramid; yellow-green foliage; performs well in the Midwest. 'Emerald' ('Smaragd') forms a dense pyramid, growing to 15 feet tall and 3 to 4 feet wide; vertical sprays of bright green foliage; retains excellent color in winter. 'Elegantissima' forms a 12-foot-tall, 5-foot-wide tree with gold-tipped new growth that turns brownish in winter. 'Hills Dark Green' forms a narrow, 15-foot-tall pyramid with deep forest green foliage all year. 'Nigra' is slow growing but eventually forms a 20-foot-tall pyramid with dark green foliage all year. 'Pyramidalis' is a fast-growing, narrow, 25-foot-tall, 3-foot-wide cone best grown with a single leader. 'Sudworthii' is a 30-foot-tall tree with golden foliage that turns orange-yellow in winter. 'Sunkist' is a compact, broad, 15-foot-tall tree with orange-gold foliage. 'Techny' forms a slow-growing, 12- to 15-foot-tall, 4- to 6-foot-wide pyramid with excellent dark green foliage that lasts all year; resists snow damage. 'Wareana Lutescens' is a 30-foot-tall tree with creamy yellow foliage.

T. orientalis (Platycladus orientalis) P. 184

t. or-ee-en-TAY-lis. Oriental Arborvitae. This small, conical, stiffly symmetrical tree grows 20 to 25 feet tall and 10 to 15 feet wide in cultivation. It has graceful, ascending branches and vertical sprays of foliage—unlike arborvitae and western red cedar, which have horizontal sprays—giving it a very distinctive form. The scalelike needles are bright green or yellow-green without white markings. Some popular garden forms have only needlelike juvenile leaves or threadlike filamentous leaves. The 1-inch, woody cones have six woody scales and ripen from purplish blue to brown. Oriental arborvitae tolerates adverse growing conditions better than other species, and its attractive texture makes it an excellent specimen in a border. From China, Japan, and Korea.

HOW TO GROW. Full sun and moist, well-drained, fertile, mulched soil. Tolerates heat, humidity, and drought better than arborvitae. Foliage that is winter burned will usually sprout new growth. Does not respond well to shearing. Zones 6b–8b.

CULTIVARS. Many dwarf, shrublike forms are available. Only treelike forms are described here. 'Bakeri' has rich light green leaves and thrives in hot, dry sites. 'Blue Cone' is a 15-foot-tall, conical tree with dense blue-green foliage. 'Elegantissima' is a narrow, 20-foot-tall pyramid; bright gold–tipped vertical fans mature to greenish yellow in summer and bronze-green in winter.

T. plicata P. 185

t. ply-KAY-tah. Western Red Cedar, Giant Arborvitae. In cultivation, this beautiful, fast-growing, native evergreen forms a narrow, 50- to 60-foot-tall, 15- to 20-foot-wide pyramid with a dominant single trunk and horizontal branches all the way to the ground. In the wild, it can reach 120 feet tall. Western red cedar has an attractive, buttressed trunk with shredding, reddish brown bark. The horizontal, fanlike sprays of aromatic foliage consist of glossy, green, scalelike leaves with white markings on their undersides. Foliage is coarser and darker, and grows in narrower sprays, than that of arborvitae and may turn bronze in winter. Cones are ½ inch long, have 10 to 12 woody scales, and ripen from green to brown. This tree's tall, narrow shape makes it suitable as a screen or as a vertical accent in a border or near a building. From the Pacific Northwest.

HOW TO GROW. Full sun to partial or light shade and moist, fertile, acid to alkaline, mulched soil. Tolerates wet sites, but not drought. Prune when young to a single leader if needed. New growth sprouts from leafless old wood if cut back severely in spring. May be sheared for a hedge. Usually not bothered by deer. Bagworms may be a problem. Adapts best to the Northwest and East. Zones 4b–7b.

CULTIVARS. 'Atrovirens' is a fast-growing, tall pyramid with very shiny, dark green foliage in summer. 'Emerald Cone' forms a dense, 30- to 40-foot-tall column with bright green foliage year-round. 'Zebrina' looks yellow from a distance, but foliage is actually green with creamy yellow bands. 'Stoneham Gold' forms a broad cone; gold new growth stands out against dark green mature growth. 'Green Giant' is a hybrid with glossy, green, coarse summer foliage that turns yellow-green in winter; forms a 20-foot-tall, conical tree.

❧ *Thujopsis*

thew-YOP-sis. Cypress family, Cupressaceae.

This genus, which is closely related to *Thuja,* contains only one species.

T. dolabrata   P. 185

t. dole-ah-BRA-tah. Hiba Arborvitae. This uncommon tree has a conical shape and grows to 70 feet tall in its native habitat, although it is usually only 30 to 50 feet tall and 10 to 20 feet wide in cultivation. The scalelike leaves are bright glossy green with flashing silver-white undersides and are arranged in four ranks on the twigs, which form wide, flat, fan-shaped sprays. Leaves retain their vivid green color all year. Brownish gray bark cloaks the single trunk and peels off in strips. The ½-inch female cones are round and have silvery blue, leathery scales that ripen to brown. Each scale has a prominent spine in the center. This conifer is more striking than arborvitae *(Thuja occidentalis)* and deserves to be planted more often as a screen or specimen. From Japan.

HOW TO GROW. Full to partial sun and moist, humus-rich, acid or alkaline soil. Does not tolerate drought. Protect from winter wind. Usually pest-free. Grows best in the East or Northwest where the climate is cool and moist. Zones 6b–9a.

CULTIVARS. Many dwarf, shrublike forms are available. 'Variegata' is a tree form that has irregular creamy variegation.

❧ *Tsuga*

TSUE-gah. Pine family, Pinaceae.

This genus contains 14 species of trees from North America and Asia and has the smallest needles and cones of any member of the pine family. Needles are short, flat, and fine-textured. They have two white bands on their undersides and are arranged on slender, flexible twigs. Cones ripen in autumn and resemble miniature pine cones. All species do best in a cool, moist climate and look less formal than many other evergreens in a garden or home landscape. Unfortunately, a pest introduced from Asia in 1924 has been slowly migrating through the Mid-Atlantic States and New England, devastating cultivated and native Canada hemlocks. All American species are susceptible to this pest, called the woolly adelgid, but the Japanese species are probably immune. A parasitic mite that preys on this pest may offer biological control. Otherwise, a properly timed horticultural oil spray can be used to control and prevent the adelgid. It must be applied so as to drench the tree and coat the undersides of the needles in late winter and again in early summer, to coincide with the pest's life cycle. A professional arborist may be needed to treat large trees.

T. canadensis   P. 186

t. kan-ah-DEN-sis. Canada Hemlock, Eastern Hemlock. This elegant ever-green has wide-spreading, slightly pendulous, horizontal branches that cloak the central trunk from the top of its nodding leader all the way to the ground, creating a soft-textured, refined pyramid that can grow to 75 feet tall and 30 feet wide in a garden setting. The blunt-tipped needles are ⅔ inch long and shiny dark green or dark gray-green. They have two white stripes on their undersides and are arranged in two opposite rows along hairy, yellowish brown branchlets. Mature trees feature deeply fur-rowed, brown bark. The pretty cones are about ¾ inch around and re-semble miniature pine cones, ripening to brown in autumn. A beloved forest and landscape tree, Canada hemlock is perhaps the most fine-tex-tured evergreen commonly planted in gardens and also one of the few conifers that thrive in shade. Use it in a cool, lightly shaded location for a screen or hedge or in a naturalistic site or border. It does not work well in a lawn unless it is planted in a mulched bed. From northeastern North America.

HOW TO GROW. Full to partial sun; tolerates sun in a protected loca-tion where soil does not dry out. Needs moist, well-drained, acid, humus-rich soil. Sensitive to drought, heat, air pollution, and drying wind. Mulch to keep soil cool and moist. Protect from wind. Remove multiple leaders on new plants that are grown as trees. Allow limbs to remain to the ground. May be thinned or sheared as a hedge. Highly susceptible to woolly adelgids; suffers from mites if soil is dry. Zones 3a–8a.

CULTIVARS AND SIMILAR SPECIES. Many dwarf, shrublike forms are available. Only treelike forms are described here. 'Albospica' grows into a small, compact tree with bright white new growth; needs some af-ternoon shade. 'Summer Snow' has dark green needles that contrast beautifully with its bright white new growth; more attractive than 'Al-bospica'. 'Emerald Fountain' forms a narrow, rich green column with weeping branches. 'Emerald King' has rich green foliage all year. 'Golden Splendor' is a fast-growing form with golden needles. 'Pendula' is an up-right tree with weeping branches; can be variable. 'Sargentii', sometimes labeled as 'Pendula', is a slow-growing dwarf; needs staking to form a wide-spreading mound that eventually reaches 15 feet tall and 30 feet wide. 'Westonigra' is a fast-growing, compact tree with exceptionally dark green foliage. *T. caroliniana* (Carolina hemlock), **P. 186**, native to south-eastern North America, has a more open-branched, compact shape than Canada hemlock; grows to 50 feet tall; ¾-inch-long needles are arranged radially around reddish brown, hairy branchlets; tolerates more heat and is less susceptible (but not immune) to woolly adelgids; Zones 5b–7b and cool areas of Zone 8a. *T. heterophylla* (western hemlock) is native to the Pacific Northwest and grows best in sites with moist, cool summers; Zones 6a–8a.

T. sieboldii

t. see-BOL-dee-eye. Southern Japanese Hemlock. This broadly conical tree has a graceful, open shape and often multiple trunks. It grows to 50 feet tall and 25 feet wide. The shiny, dark green needles are about ¾ to 1 inch long and are broader than those of most other hemlocks. They have rounded, notched tips and are borne on waxy, yellowish brown branchlets. The attractive cones are about 1¼ inches long. This tree is not widely grown in North America, but it is being used more often as a replacement for Canada hemlock because of its resistance to pests and greater tolerance of adverse growing conditions. From Japan.

HOW TO GROW. Light to full shade and moist, well-drained, humus-rich, acid soil. Tolerates clayey soil, drought, and urban conditions better than other hemlocks. Good resistance to woolly adelgids. Zones 5a–8b.

SIMILAR SPECIES. *T. diverisifolia* (northern Japanese hemlock), **P. 187**, is a shrubby, fine-textured, 25- to 30-foot-tall tree; dark green, white-banded, ¼- to ½-inch-long needles are arranged radially on shoots, creating a shimmery appearance; Zones 5b–7b.

❧APPENDIX

TREES THAT TOLERATE ALKALINE SOIL

<small>DECIDUOUS</small>
Acer buergerianum (A. trifidum) (trident maple)
Acer campestre (hedge maple)
Acer griseum (paperbark maple)
Acer miyabei (miyabe maple)
Acer negundo (box elder, ash-leaved maple)
Acer platanoides (Norway maple)
Acer pseudoplatanus (sycamore maple)
Acer saccharinum (silver maple)
Acer tataricum ssp. *ginnala (A. ginnala)* (Amur maple)
Acer truncatum (Shantung maple, purpleblow maple)
Aesculus × carnea (red horse chestnut)
Aesculus flava (A. octandra) (yellow buckeye)
Aesculus glabra (Ohio buckeye)
Aesculus hippocastanum (horse chestnut)
Aesculus pavia (red buckeye)
Albizia julibrissin (silk tree, mimosa)
Alnus glutinosa (black alder, European alder)
Amelanchier spp. (shadblow, downy serviceberry, service tree, Juneberry)
Betula platyphylla var. *japonica* 'Whitespire Sr.' (whitespire birch)
Betula utilis ssp. *jacquemontii (B. jacquemontii)* (white-barked Himalayan birch)
Carpinus betulus (European hornbeam)
Carpinus caroliniana (American hornbeam, blue beech, musclewood)

Carya illinoinensis (pecan)
Carya ovata (shagbark hickory)
Castanea mollissima (Chinese chestnut)
Catalpa bignonioides (southern catalpa, Indian bean)
Catalpa speciosa (northern catalpa, western catalpa)
Celtis laevigata (sugar hackberry)
Celtis occidentalis (common hackberry)
Celtis sinensis (Japanese hackberry)
Cercidiphyllum japonicum (katsura tree)
Cercis canadensis (eastern redbud)
Cercis chinensis var. *texensis (C. reniformis)* (Texas redbud)
Chionanthus retusus (Chinese fringe tree)
Chionanthus virginicus (fringe tree, old man's beard)
Cladrastis kentukea (C. lutea) (yellowwood)
Cornus mas (cornelian cherry, cherry dogwood)
Corylus colurna (Turkish filbert, Turkish hazel)
Cotinus coggygria (smoke tree, smoke bush)
Cotinus obovatus (American smoke tree, smoke bush)
Diospyros virginiana (common persimmon)
Elaeagnus angustifolia (Russian olive, wild olive)
Eucommia ulmoides (hardy rubber tree)
Fagus sylvatica (European beech)
Fraxinus americana (white ash)
Fraxinus excelsior (European ash)
Fraxinus pennsylvanica (green ash, red ash)
Fraxinus velutina (velvet ash)
Ginkgo biloba (ginkgo, maidenhair tree)
Gymnocladus dioica (Kentucky coffee tree)
Koelreuteria paniculata (goldenrain tree)
Laburnum alpinum (Scotch laburnum)
Laburnum anagyroides (common laburnum)
Laburnum × watereri (golden chain tree, waterer laburnum)
Maackia amurensis (Amur maackia)
Magnolia acuminata (cucumber tree)
Malus spp. (crab apples)
Morus alba (white mulberry)
Ostrya virginiana (ironwood, hop hornbeam)
Phellodendron amurense (Amur cork tree)
Populus spp. (poplars, cottonwood)
Prunus 'Hally Jolivette' (Hally Jolivette cherry)

Prunus maackii (Amur chokecherry, goldbark cherry)
Pyrus calleryana (callery pear, flowering pear)
Quercus macrocarpa (bur oak, mossycup oak)
Quercus muehlenbergii (yellow chestnut oak)
Quercus robur (English oak)
Quercus shumardii (shumard oak)
Rhus glabra (smooth sumac)
Rhus javanica var. *chinensis* (Chinese sumac)
Rhus typhina (staghorn sumac)
Robinia pseudoacacia (black locust)
Sophora japonica (Styphnolobium japonicus) (Japanese pagoda tree,
   Chinese scholar tree)
Tilia americana (basswood, American linden)
Tilia cordata (littleleaf linden)
Tilia × *euchlora* (Crimean linden)
Tilia tomentosa (silver linden)
Ulmus alata 'Lace Parasol' ('Pendula')(winged elm)
Ulmus americana (American elm, white elm)
Ulmus davidiana var. *japonica* (David elm)
Ulmus parvifolia (lacebark elm, Chinese elm)
Ulmus pumila 'Cathedral' (Siberian elm, Chinese elm)

BROAD-LEAVED EVERGREENS
Prunus caroliniana (Carolina cherry laurel)
Quercus agrifolia (coast live oak)
Quercus chrysolepis (canyon live oak)
Quercus emoryi (Emory oak)
Quercus engelmanii (mesa oak)
Quercus fusiformis (upland live oak)
Quercus virginiana (live oak)

CONIFERS
Abies concolor (white fir)
Abies lasiocarpa (Rocky Mountain fir, alpine fir)
Abies nordmanniana (Nordmann fir)
Calocedrus decurrens (incense cedar)
Cedrus atlantica (C. libani ssp. *atlantica)* (Atlas cedar)
Cedrus deodara (deodar cedar)
Cedrus libani (cedar of Lebanon)
Chamaecyparis pisifera (sawara false cypress, retinospora)

× *Cupressocyparis leylandii* (Leyland cypress)
Cupressus arizonica var. *glabra* (Arizona cypress)
Cupressus sempervirens (Italian cypress)
Juniperus scopulorum (Rocky Mountain juniper, western red cedar)
Juniperus virginiana (eastern red cedar)
Larix decidua (European larch)
Podocarpus macrophyllus (yew pine, yew podocarpus)
Pseudotsuga menziesii (Douglas fir)
Thuja plicata (western red cedar, giant arborvitae)

TREES WITH ORNAMENTAL BARK

DECIDUOUS
Acer buergerianum (A. trifidum) (trident maple)
Acer cissifolium (ivy-leaved maple)
Acer davidii (David maple)
Acer griseum (paperbark maple)
Acer palmatum (Japanese maple)
Acer pensylvanicum (striped maple, moosewood)
Acer triflorum (three-flowered maple)
Acer truncatum (Shantung maple, purpleblow maple)
Betula spp. (birches)
Carpinus betulus (European hornbeam)
Carya ovata (shagbark hickory)
Chionanthus retusus (Chinese fringe tree)
Cornus kousa var. *chinensis* (Chinese dogwood)
Cornus mas (cornelian cherry, cherry dogwood)
Davidia involucrata (dove tree, handkerchief tree)
Fagus grandifolia (American beech)
Fagus sylvatica (European beech)
Franklinia alatamaha (Gordonia alatamaha) (franklinia, Franklin tree)
Halesia carolina (H. tetraptera) (Carolina silverbell)
Laburnum × *watereri* (golden chain tree, waterer laburnum)
Lagerstroemia indica (crape myrtle)
Maackia amurensis (Amur maackia)
Parrotia persica (Persian parrotia, Persian ironwood)
Platanus spp. (sycamores, plane trees)
Populus alba (white poplar)
Prunus maackii (Amur chokecherry, goldbark cherry)

Prunus sargentii (Sargent cherry)
Prunus serotina (black cherry, wild black cherry)
Prunus serrula (paperbark cherry, birchbark cherry)
Prunus serrulata Sato-zakura Group (Oriental cherry, Japanese flowering cherry)
Prunus subhirtella var. *pendula (P. pendula)* (higan cherry, weeping cherry)
Prunus × yedoensis (Yoshino cherry, Potomac cherry)
Stewartia monodelpha (tall stewartia)
Stewartia pseudocamellia (Japanese stewartia, Korean stewartia)
Syringa pekinensis (Peking lilac)
Syringa reticulata (S. amurensis var. *japonica)* (Japanese tree lilac)
Ulmus parvifolia (lacebark elm, Chinese elm)
Zelkova serrata (Japanese zelkova)

Conifers
Calocedrus decurrens (incense cedar)
Cryptomeria japonica (Japanese cedar, cryptomeria)
Metasequoia glyptostroboides (dawn redwood)
Pinus bungeana (lacebark pine)
Pinus densiflora 'Umbraculifera' (Japanese red pine, Tanyosho pine)
Pinus sylvestris (Scotch pine, Scots pine)
Sequoiadendron giganteum (Sequoia gigantea) (giant sequoia, big tree, giant redwood, Sierra redwood)
Taxodium distichum (bald cypress, swamp cypress)
Taxus baccata (English yew)

TREES THAT ATTRACT SONGBIRDS, HUMMINGBIRDS, AND OTHER WILDLIFE

Deciduous
Acer spp. (maples)
Aesculus spp. (buckeyes, horse chestnuts)
Amelanchier spp. (shadblow, downy serviceberry, service tree, Juneberry)
Aralia elata (Japanese angelica tree, devil's walking stick)
Aralia spinosa (devil's walking stick)
Betula spp. (birches)
Carpinus spp. (hornbeams)

Carya spp. (hickories)
Celtis laevigata (sugar hackberry)
Celtis occidentalis (common hackberry)
Chionanthus retusus (Chinese fringe tree)
Chionanthus virginicus (fringe tree, old man's beard)
Cornus spp. (dogwoods)
Corylus avellana (European hazelnut)
Corylus colurna (Turkish filbert, Turkish hazel)
Crataegus spp. (hawthorns)
Diospyros virginiana (common persimmon)
Fagus spp. (beeches)
Juglans (walnuts, butternuts)
Liquidambar styraciflua (sweet gum, gum tree)
Liriodendron tulipifera (tulip tree, yellow poplar)
Magnolia acuminata (cucumber tree)
Malus spp. (crab apples)
Morus alba (white mulberry)
Nyssa sylvatica (black gum, sour gum, pepperidge, tupelo)
Ostrya virginiana (ironwood, hop hornbeam)
Pistacia chinensis (Chinese pistache, Chinese pistachio)
Prunus cerasifera 'Atropurpurea' (purple-leaved plum, cherry plum)
Prunus maackii (Amur chokecherry, goldbark cherry)
Pyrus calleryana (callery pear, flowering pear)
Quercus spp. (oaks)
Rhus glabra (smooth sumac)
Rhus typhina (staghorn sumac)
Sorbus spp. (whitebeams, mountain ashes)
Ulmus americana (American elm, white elm)

BROAD-LEAVED EVERGREENS
Ilex aquifolium (English holly)
Ilex × *aquipernyi* 'San Jose' (San Jose holly)
Ilex opaca (American holly)
Ilex pedunculosa (long-stalk holly)
Magnolia grandiflora (southern magnolia, bull bay)
Magnolia virginiana var. *australis* (sweet bay magnolia)
Prunus caroliniana (Carolina cherry laurel)

CONIFERS
Abies spp. (firs)
Juniperus scopulorum (Rocky Mountain juniper, western red cedar)

Juniperus virginiana (eastern red cedar)
Picea spp. (spruces)
Pinus spp. (pines)
Thuja occidentalis (arborvitae, eastern white cedar, white cedar)

TREES THAT TOLERATE DROUGHT

DECIDUOUS
Acer buergerianum (A. trifidum) (trident maple)
Acer campestre (hedge maple)
Acer maximowiczianum (A. nikoense) (Nikko maple)
Acer negundo (box elder, ash-leaved maple)
Acer saccharinum (silver maple)
Acer truncatum (Shantung maple, purpleblow maple)
Aesculus glabra (Ohio buckeye)
Albizia julibrissin (silk tree, mimosa)
Aralia elata (Japanese angelica tree, devil's walking stick)
Aralia spinosa (devil's walking stick)
Carpinus betulus (European hornbeam)
Castanea mollissima (Chinese chestnut)
Castanea sativa (Spanish chestnut)
Catalpa bignonioides (southern catalpa, Indian bean)
Catalpa × rubescens 'Purpurea' (purple-leaved catalpa)
Catalpa speciosa (northern catalpa, western catalpa)
Celtis laevigata (sugar hackberry)
Celtis occidentalis (common hackberry)
Celtis sinensis (Japanese hackberry)
Cercis canadensis (eastern redbud)
Cercis canadensis var. *texensis (C. reniformis)* (Texas redbud)
Cercis chinensis (Chinese redbud)
Cercis occidentalis (western redbud)
Cornus racemosa (gray dogwood)
Cotinus coggygria (smoke tree, smoke bush)
Cotinus coggygria var. *purpureus* (purple smoke tree)
Cotinus obovatus (American smoke tree, smoke bush)
Crataegus crus-galli (cockspur hawthorn)
Crataegus crus-galli var. *inermis*
Crataegus laevigata (English hawthorn)
Crataegus × lavellei (Lavalle hawthorn)
Crataegus × mordenensis

Crataegus phaenopyrum (C. cordata) (Washington hawthorn)
Crataegus viridis (green hawthorn)
Elaeagnus angustifolia (Russian olive, wild olive)
Eucommia ulmoides (hardy rubber tree)
Fagus sylvatica (European beech)
Fraxinus pennsylvanica (green ash, red ash)
Fraxinus velutina (velvet ash)
Ginkgo biloba (ginkgo, maidenhair tree)
Gleditsia triacanthos var. *inermis* (thornless honey locust)
Gymnocladus dioica (Kentucky coffee tree)
Juglans cinerea (butternut)
Juglans nigra (black walnut)
Juglans regia (English walnut)
Koelreuteria bipinnata (Chinese goldenrain tree)
Koelreuteria paniculata (goldenrain tree)
Liquidambar styraciflua (sweet gum, gum tree)
Maackia amurensis (Amur maackia)
Maackia chinensis (Chinese maackia)
Morus alba (white mulberry)
Paulownia tomentosa (empress tree, princess tree)
Phellodendron amurense (Amur cork tree)
Platanus × acerifolia (London plane tree)
Platanus occidentalis (sycamore, American plane tree, buttonwood)
Platanus orientalis (Oriental plane tree)
Poncirus trifoliata (trifoliate orange, hardy orange)
Populus angustifolia (willowleaf poplar)
Prunus × blireana (blireana plum)
Prunus cerasifera 'Atropurpurea' (purple-leaved plum, cherry plum)
Pyrus betulaefolia (birch-leaf pear)
Pyrus calleryana (callery pear, flowering pear)
Pyrus salicifolia 'Pendula' (weeping willowleaf pear)
Pyrus ussuriensis (Ussuri pear)
Quercus acutissima (sawtooth oak)
Quercus macrocarpa (bur oak, mossycup oak)
Quercus palustris (pin oak)
Quercus phellos (willow oak)
Quercus robur (English oak)
Quercus rubra (Q. borealis) (northern red oak)
Quercus velutina (black oak)
Rhus glabra (smooth sumac)

Rhus javanica var. *chinensis* (Chinese sumac)
Rhus typhina (staghorn sumac)
Sophora japonica (Styphnolobium japonicus) (Japanese pagoda tree,
    Chinese scholar tree)
Tilia cordata (littleleaf linden)
Ulmus parvifolia (lacebark elm, Chinese elm)

BROAD-LEAVED EVERGREENS
Ilex opaca (American holly)
Laurus nobilis (sweet bay, bay laurel)

CONIFERS
Abies concolor (white fir)
Cedrus atlantica (C. libani ssp. *atlantica)* (Atlas cedar)
Cedrus deodara (deodar cedar)
Cedrus libani (cedar of Lebanon)
Cupressus arizonica var. *glabra* (Arizona cypress)
Juniperus chinensis (Chinese juniper)
Juniperus scopulorum (Rocky Mountain juniper, western red cedar)
Juniperus virginiana (eastern red cedar)
Picea pungens var. *glauca* (Colorado blue spruce)
Pinus aristata (bristlecone pine)
Pinus banksiana (jack pine)
Pinus flexilis (limber pine)
Pinus resinosa (red pine, Norway pine)
Pinus rigida (pitch pine)
Pinus strobus (eastern white pine)
Pinus sylvestris (Scotch pine, Scots pine)
Pinus thunbergii (P. thunbergiana) (Japanese black pine)
Pinus virginiana (Virginia pine, scrub pine, Jersey pine)
Taxodium distichum (bald cypress, swamp cypress)
Taxodium distichum var. *imbricarium (T. ascendens)* (pond cypress)

TREES WITH OUTSTANDING FALL COLOR

DECIDUOUS
Acer buergerianum (A. trifidum) (trident maple)
Acer campestre (hedge maple)
Acer cissifolium (ivy-leaved maple)

Acer × *freemanii* (Freeman maple)
Acer glabrum (Rocky Mountain maple)
Acer griseum (paperbark maple)
Acer japonicum (full-moon maple)
Acer palmatum (Japanese maple)
Acer pensylvanicum (striped maple, moosewood)
Acer platanoides (Norway maple)
Acer rubrum (red maple, swamp maple)
Acer saccharum (sugar maple, hard maple, rock maple)
Acer tataricum (Tatarian maple)
Acer tataricum ssp. *ginnala (A. ginnala)* (Amur maple)
Acer triflorum (three-flowered maple)
Acer truncatum (Shantung maple, purpleblow maple)
Aesculus glabra (Ohio buckeye)
Amelanchier arborea (shadblow, downy serviceberry, service tree,
    Juneberry)
Amelanchier × *grandiflora* (apple serviceberry)
Amelanchier laevis (Allegheny serviceberry)
Betula spp. (birches)
Carpinus betulus (European hornbeam)
Carpinus caroliniana (American hornbeam, blue beech, musclewood)
Carya spp. (hickories)
Cercidiphyllum japonicum (Katsura tree)
Cercis spp. (redbuds)
Chionanthus retusus (Chinese fringe tree)
Chionanthus virginicus (fringe tree, old man's beard)
Cladrastis kentukea (C. lutea) (yellowwood)
Cornus alternifolia (pagoda dogwood)
Cornus florida (flowering dogwood)
Cornus kousa (Kousa dogwood, Japanese dogwood, Korean dogwood,
    Chinese dogwood)
Cornus × *rutgersensis (C. florida* × *C. kousa)* (stellar dogwood, hybrid
    dogwood)
Cotinus spp. (smoke trees)
Franklinia alatamaha (Gordonia alatamaha) (franklinia, Franklin tree)
Fraxinus americana (white ash)
Fraxinus pennsylvanica (green ash, red ash)
Ginkgo biloba (ginkgo, maidenhair tree)
Gleditsia triacanthos var. *inermis* (thornless honey locust)
Gymnocladus dioica (Kentucky coffee tree)
Lagerstroemia indica (crape myrtle)

Lagerstroemia indica × *faureii* (hardy crape myrtle)
Liquidambar styraciflua (sweet gum, gum tree)
Liriodendron tulipifera (tulip tree, yellow poplar)
Magnolia acuminata (cucumber tree)
Magnolia stellata (M. tomentosa) (star magnolia)
Nyssa sylvatica (black gum, sour gum, pepperidge, tupelo)
Ostrya virginiana (ironwood, hop hornbeam)
Oxydendrum arboreum (sourwood, sorrel tree)
Parrotia persica (Persian parrotia, Persian ironwood)
Phellodendron amurense (Amur cork tree)
Pistacia chinensis (Chinese pistache, Chinese pistachio)
Prunus sargentii (Sargent cherry)
Prunus serotina (black cherry, wild black cherry)
Pyrus calleryana (callery pear, flowering pear)
Quercus acutissima (sawtooth oak)
Quercus alba (white oak)
Quercus bicolor (swamp white oak)
Quercus coccinea (scarlet oak)
Quercus falcata (southern red oak, Spanish oak)
Quercus imbricaria (shingle oak)
Quercus macrocarpa (bur oak, mossycup oak)
Quercus muehlenbergii (yellow chestnut oak)
Quercus palustris (pin oak)
Quercus rubra (Q. borealis) (northern red oak)
Quercus shumardii (shumard oak)
Quercus velutina (black oak)
Rhus spp. (sumacs)
Sorbus alnifolia (alder whitebeam, Korean mountain ash)
Sorbus aucuparia (European mountain ash)
Stewartia spp. (stewartias)
Styrax japonicum (Japanese snowbell)
Tilia americana (basswood, American linden)
Tilia cordata (littleleaf linden)
Ulmus alata 'Lace Parasol' ('Pendula') (winged elm)
Ulmus americana (American elm, white elm)
Zelkova serrata (Japanese zelkova)

CONIFERS
Larix spp. (larches)
Metasequoia glyptostroboides (dawn redwood)
Pseudolarix amabilis (P. kaempferi) (golden larch)

Taxodium distichum (bald cypress, swamp cypress)
Taxodium distichum var. *imbricarium (T. ascendens)* (pond cypress)

TREES WITH SHOWY FLOWERS

DECIDUOUS

LATE WINTER OR VERY EARLY SPRING

Acer rubrum (red maple, swamp maple)
Cornus mas (cornelian cherry, cherry dogwood)
Cornus officinalis (Japanese cornelian cherry)
Corylus avellana (European hazelnut)
Magnolia kobus (Kobus magnolia)
Magnolia stellata (M. tomentosa) (star magnolia)
Parrotia persica (Persian parrotia, Persian ironwood)
Prunus 'Hally Jolivette' (Hally Jolivette cherry)
Prunus mume (Japanese flowering apricot)
Prunus × 'Okame' (okame cherry)

SPRING

Acer × *freemanii* (Freeman maple)
Acer platanoides (Norway maple)
Acer tataricum ssp. *ginnala (A. ginnala)* (Amur maple)
Aesculus × *carnea* (red horse chestnut)
Aesculus flava (A. octandra) (yellow buckeye)
Aesculus glabra (Ohio buckeye)
Aesculus hippocastanum (horse chestnut)
Aesculus pavia (red buckeye)
Aesculus splendens (flame buckeye, Louisiana buckeye)
Amelanchier spp. (shadblow, downy serviceberry, service tree,
    Juneberry)
Cercis spp. (redbuds)
Chionanthus virginicus (fringe tree, old man's beard)
Cornus alternifolia (pagoda dogwood)
Cornus florida (flowering dogwood)
Cornus nuttallii (mountain dogwood)
Cornus × *rutgersensis (C. florida* × *C. kousa)* (stellar dogwood, hybrid
    dogwood)
Cotinus obovatus (American smoke tree, smoke bush)
Davidia involucrata (dove tree, handkerchief tree)
Halesia spp. (silverbells)
Laburnum spp. (golden chain trees)

Magnolia liliiflora (M. quinquepeta) (lily-flowered magnolia, Kosar hybrids)

Magnolia × *loebneri* (Loebner magnolia)

Magnolia × *soulangeana* (saucer magnolia)

Malus spp. (crab apples)

Poncirus trifoliata (trifoliate orange, hardy orange)

Prunus cerasifera 'Atropurpurea' (purple-leaved plum, cherry plum)

Prunus sargentii (Sargent cherry)

Prunus serotina (black cherry, wild black cherry)

Prunus serrulata Sato-zakura Group (Oriental cherry, Japanese flowering cherry)

Prunus subhirtella var. *pendula (P. pendula)* (higan cherry, weeping cherry)

Prunus × *yedoensis* (Yoshino cherry, Potomac cherry)

Pyrus calleryana (callery pear, flowering pear)

Pyrus ussuriensis (Ussuri pear)

Robinia × *ambigua* 'Idahoensis'

Robinia pseudoacacia (black locust)

Sorbus alnifolia (alder whitebeam, Korean mountain ash)

Sorbus americana (American mountain ash)

Sorbus aucuparia (European mountain ash)

Sorbus decora (showy mountain ash)

Sorbus rufoferrugenia 'Longwood Sunset'

Sorbus × *thuringiaca* 'Fastigiata' (oakleaf mountain ash)

Styrax americanus (American snowbell)

Styrax japonicum (Japanese snowbell)

Styrax obassia (fragrant snowbell)

EARLY SUMMER TO MIDSUMMER

Albizia julibrissin (silk tree, mimosa)

Aralia elata (Japanese angelica tree, devil's walking stick)

Aralia spinosa (devil's walking stick)

Catalpa bignonioides (southern catalpa, Indian bean)

Catalpa × *rubescens* 'Purpurea' (purple-leaved catalpa)

Catalpa speciosa (northern catalpa, western catalpa)

Chionanthus retusus (Chinese fringe tree)

Cladrastis kentukea (C. lutea) (yellowwood)

Cornus kousa (Kousa dogwood, Japanese dogwood, Korean dogwood, Chinese dogwood)

Cornus kousa var. *chinensis* (Chinese dogwood)

Cotinus coggygria (smoke tree, smoke bush)

Cotinus coggygria var. *purpureus* (purple smoke tree)

Crataegus spp. (hawthorns)
Koelreuteria bipinnata (Chinese goldenrain tree)
Koelreuteria paniculata (goldenrain tree)
Lagerstroemia indica (crape myrtle)
Lagerstroemia indica × *faureii* (hardy crape myrtle)
Maackia amurensis (Amur maackia)
Magnolia acuminata var. *subcordata* (yellow cucumber tree)
Oxydendrum arboreum (sourwood, sorrel tree)
Paulownia tomentosa (empress tree, princess tree)
Prunus subhirtella 'Autumnalis'
Rhus glabra (smooth sumac)
Rhus typhina (staghorn sumac)
Sophora japonica (Styphnolobium japonicus) (Japanese pagoda tree,
    Chinese scholar tree)
Stewartia monodelpha (tall stewartia)
Stewartia pseudocamellia (Japanese stewartia, Korean stewartia)
Stewartia pseudocamellia var. *koreana* and *S. koreana* (Korean stewartia)
Syringa pekinensis (Peking lilac)
Syringa reticulata (S. amurensis var. *japonica)* (Japanese tree lilac)
Syringa reticulata var. *mandushurica* (tree lilac)

LATE SUMMER TO FALL

Franklinia alatamaha (Gordonia alatamaha) (franklinia, Franklin tree)
Koelreuteria paniculata 'September Glory' (goldenrain tree)
Lagerstroemia indica × *faureii* (hardy crape myrtle)
Rhus javanica var. *chinensis* (Chinese sumac)
Stewartia ovata (mountain stewartia)

B R O A D - L E A V E D   E V E R G R E E N S

SPRING

Prunus caroliniana (Carolina cherry laurel)
Prunus laurocerasus (English laurel, cherry laurel)

EARLY SUMMER TO MIDSUMMER

Magnolia grandiflora (southern magnolia, bull bay)
Magnolia virginiana (sweet bay magnolia)
Magnolia virginiana var. *australis* (sweet bay magnolia)
Prunus lusitanica (Portuguese cherry laurel)

TREES THAT TOLERATE ROAD SALT AND SEA SALT

Deciduous

Acer campestre (hedge maple)
Acer cissifolium (ivy-leaved maple)
Acer griseum (paperbark maple)
Acer negundo (box elder, ash-leaved maple)
Acer platanoides (Norway maple)
Acer pseudoplatanus (sycamore maple)
Acer tataricum ssp. *ginnala (A. ginnala)* (Amur maple)
Acer triflorum (three-flowered maple)
Acer truncatum (Shantung maple, purpleblow maple)
Aesculus × carnea (red horse chestnut)
Aesculus hippocastanum (horse chestnut)
Albizia julibrissin (silk tree, mimosa)
Alnus glutinosa (black alder, European alder)
Amelanchier canadensis (shadblow, downy serviceberry, service tree,
      Juneberry)
Betula nigra (river birch)
Betula platyphylla var. *japonica* 'Whitespire Sr.' (whitespire birch)
Carya ovata (shagbark hickory)
Catalpa bignonioides (southern catalpa, Indian bean)
Catalpa × rubescens 'Purpurea' (purple-leaved catalpa)
Catalpa speciosa (northern catalpa, western catalpa)
Diospyros virginiana (common persimmon)
Elaeagnus angustifolia (Russian olive, wild olive)
Fraxinus americana (white ash)
Fraxinus excelsior (European ash)
Fraxinus pennsylvanica (green ash, red ash)
Fraxinus velutina (velvet ash)
Ginkgo biloba (ginkgo, maidenhair tree)
Gleditsia triacanthos var. *inermis* (thornless honey locust)
Gymnocladus dioica (Kentucky coffee tree)
Koelreuteria bipinnata (Chinese goldenrain tree)
Koelreuteria paniculata (goldenrain tree)
Lagerstroemia indica (crape myrtle)
Lagerstroemia indica × faureii (hardy crape myrtle)
Malus spp. (crab apples)
Morus alba (white mulberry)
Nyssa sylvatica (black gum, sour gum, pepperidge, tupelo)

Ostrya virginiana (ironwood, hop hornbeam)
Paulownia tomentosa (empress tree, princess tree)
Phellodendron amurense (Amur cork tree)
Platanus × *acerifolia* (London plane tree)
Platanus occidentalis (sycamore, American plane tree, buttonwood)
Platanus orientalis (Oriental plane tree)
Populus alba (white poplar)
Populus deltoides (cottonwood)
Populus fremontii (western poplar)
Prunus cerasifera 'Atropurpurea' (purple-leaved plum, cherry plum)
Prunus maackii (Amur chokecherry, goldbark cherry)
Prunus sargentii (Sargent cherry)
Prunus serrula (paperbark cherry, birchbark cherry)
Prunus serrulata Sato-zakura Group (Oriental cherry, Japanese
    flowering cherry)
Pyrus calleryana (callery pear, flowering pear)
Quercus acutissima (sawtooth oak)
Quercus alba (white oak)
Quercus bicolor (swamp white oak)
Quercus imbricaria (shingle oak)
Quercus muehlenbergii (yellow chestnut oak)
Quercus phellos (willow oak)
Quercus robur (English oak)
Quercus rubra (Q. borealis) (northern red oak)
Robinia pseudoacacia (black locust)
Salix alba var. *vitellina* (golden willow)
Salix matsudana (S. babylonica var. *pekinensis)* (Hankow willow, Peking
    willow)
Sophora japonica (Styphnolobium japonicus) (Japanese pagoda tree,
    Chinese scholar tree)
Styrax japonicum (Japanese snowbell)
Tilia tomentosa (silver linden)
Ulmus alata 'Lace Parasol' ('Pendula') (winged elm)
Ulmus americana (American elm, white elm)
Ulmus parvifolia (lacebark elm, Chinese elm)
Ulmus pumila 'Cathedral' (Siberian elm, Chinese elm)
Zelkova serrata (Japanese zelkova)

BROAD-LEAVED EVERGREENS

Ilex opaca (American holly)
Magnolia grandiflora (southern magnolia, bull bay)

Prunus caroliniana (Carolina cherry laurel)
Quercus virginiana (live oak)

CONIFERS

× *Cupressocyparis leylandii* (Leyland cypress)
Cupressus macrocarpa (Monterey cypress)
Cupressus sempervirens (Italian cypress)
Juniperus chinensis (Chinese juniper)
Juniperus scopulorum (Rocky Mountain juniper, western red cedar)
Juniperus virginiana (eastern red cedar)
Larix decidua (European larch)
Picea glauca (white spruce)
Picea pungens var. *glauca* (Colorado blue spruce)
Pinus elliotti (slash pine)
Pinus nigra (Austrian pine)
Pinus parviflora (Japanese white pine)
Pinus ponderosa (ponderosa pine, western yellow pine)
Pinus sylvestris (Scotch pine, Scots pine)
Pinus thunbergii (P. thunbergiana) (Japanese black pine)
Pinus virginiana (Virginia pine, scrub pine, Jersey pine)
Podocarpus macrophyllus (yew pine, yew podocarpus)
Taxodium distichum (bald cypress, swamp cypress)
Taxodium distichum var. *imbricarium (T. ascendens)* (pond cypress)

TREES FOR WINDBREAKS AND SCREENS

DECIDUOUS

Acer buergerianum (A. trifidum) (trident maple)
Acer campestre (hedge maple)
Acer tataricum ssp. *ginnala (A. ginnala)* (Amur maple)
Aesculus pavia (red buckeye)
Carpinus betulus (European hornbeam)
Carpinus caroliniana (American hornbeam, blue beech, musclewood)
Chionanthus retusus (Chinese fringe tree)
Crataegus crus-galli (cockspur hawthorn)
Elaeagnus angustifolia (Russian olive, wild olive)
Populus alba 'Pyramidalis' ('Boleana') (narrow white poplar)
Populus nigra 'Italica' (Lombardy poplar)
Quercus robur 'Skyrocket' ('Fastigiata') (narrow English oak)

B R O A D - L E A V E D   E V E R G R E E N S
Ilex aquifolium (English holly)
Ilex × *aquipernyi* 'San Jose' (San Jose holly)
Ilex opaca (American holly)
Ilex pedunculosa (long-stalk holly)
Laurus nobilis (sweet bay, bay laurel)
Prunus caroliniana (Carolina cherry laurel)
Prunus lusitanica (Portuguese cherry laurel)

C O N I F E R S
Abies spp. (firs)
Calocedrus decurrens (incense cedar)
Cephalotaxus harringtoniana (Japanese plum yew)
Chamaecyparis spp. (false cypresses)
Chamaecyparis spp. (false cypresses)
Cryptomeria japonica (Japanese cedar, cryptomeria)
× *Cupressocyparis leylandii* (Leyland cypress)
Cupressus sempervirens (Italian cypress)
Juniperus scopulorum (Rocky Mountain juniper, western red cedar)
Juniperus virginiana (eastern red cedar)
Pinus spp. (pines)
Podocarpus macrophyllus (yew pine, yew podocarpus)

TREES THAT TOLERATE FULL OR PARTIAL SHADE

D E C I D U O U S
Acer davidii (David maple)
Acer japonicum var. *aconitifolium* (fernleaf Japanese maple)
Acer palmatum (Japanese maple)
Acer palmatum var. *dissectum* (threadleaf maple, laceleaf maple)
Acer pensylvanicum (striped maple, moosewood)
Aesculus glabra (Ohio buckeye)
Aesculus pavia (red buckeye)
Amelanchier spp. (shadblow, downy serviceberry, service tree,
    Juneberry)
Aralia elata (Japanese angelica tree, devil's walking stick)
Aralia spinosa (devil's walking stick)
Asimina triloba (pawpaw)
Carpinus betulus (European hornbeam)
Carpinus caroliniana (American hornbeam, blue beech, musclewood)

Cercis canadensis (eastern redbud)
Chionanthus retusus (Chinese fringe tree)
Chionanthus virginicus (fringe tree, old man's beard)
Cornus florida (flowering dogwood)
Cornus kousa (Kousa dogwood, Japanese dogwood, Korean dogwood, Chinese dogwood)
Cornus kousa var. *chinensis* (Chinese dogwood)
Cornus mas (cornelian cherry, cherry dogwood)
Cornus officinalis (Japanese cornelian cherry)
Fagus grandifolia (American beech)
Halesia carolina (H. tetraptera) (Carolina silverbell)
Halesia diptera (two-winged silverbell)
Halesia monticola (mountain snowbell)
Ostrya virginiana (ironwood, hop hornbeam)
Oxydendrum arboreum (sourwood, sorrel tree)
Parrotia persica (Persian parrotia, Persian ironwood)
Stewartia monodelpha (tall stewartia)
Stewartia ovata (mountain stewartia)
Stewartia pseudocamellia (Japanese stewartia, Korean stewartia)
Stewartia pseudocamellia var. *koreana* and *S. koreana* (Korean stewartia)
Styrax japonicum (Japanese snowbell)
Styrax obassia (fragrant snowbell)

BROAD-LEAVED EVERGREENS
Ilex aquifolium (English holly)
Ilex× aquipernyi 'San Jose' (San Jose holly)
Magnolia virginiana (sweet bay magnolia)
Prunus caroliniana (Carolina cherry laurel)
Prunus laurocerasus (English laurel, cherry laurel)
Prunus lusitanica (Portuguese cherry laurel)

CONIFERS
Abies homolepis (Nikko fir)
Cephalotaxus harringtoniana (Japanese plum yew)
Chamaecyparis obtusa (Hinoki false cypress)
Cryptomeria japonica (Japanese cedar, cryptomeria)
× *Cupressocyparis leylandii* (Leyland cypress)
Podocarpus macrophyllus (yew pine, yew podocarpus)
Sciadopitys verticillata (Japanese umbrella pine)
Sequoia sempervirens (redwood, coast redwood, California redwood)
Taxus baccata (English yew)

Taxus cuspidata (Japanese yew)
Taxus × media 'Hicksii' (upright intermediate yew)
Tsuga canadensis (Canada hemlock, eastern hemlock)
Tsuga caroliniana (Carolina hemlock)
Tsuga diverisifolia (northern Japanese hemlock)
Tsuga heterophylla (western hemlock)
Tsuga sieboldii (southern Japanese hemlock)

TREES WITH COLORFUL FRUITS

DECIDUOUS
Acer circinatum (vine maple)
Acer palmatum (Japanese maple)
Acer tataricum (Tatarian maple)
Acer tataricum ssp. *ginnala (A. ginnala)* (Amur maple)
Amelanchier spp. (shadblow, downy serviceberry, service tree,
    Juneberry)
Chionanthus virginicus (fringe tree, old man's beard)
Cornus florida (flowering dogwood)
Cornus kousa (Kousa dogwood, Japanese dogwood, Korean dogwood,
    Chinese dogwood)
Cornus mas (cornelian cherry, cherry dogwood)
Cornus officinalis (Japanese cornelian cherry)
Crataegus spp. (hawthorns)
Elaeagnus angustifolia (Russian olive, wild olive)
Koelreuteria bipinnata (Chinese goldenrain tree)
Koelreuteria paniculata (goldenrain tree)
Magnolia acuminata (cucumber tree)
Nyssa sylvatica (black gum, sour gum, pepperidge, tupelo)
Oxydendrum arboreum (sourwood, sorrel tree)
Pistacia chinensis (Chinese pistache, Chinese pistachio)
Poncirus trifoliata (trifoliate orange, hardy orange)
Rhus glabra (smooth sumac)
Rhus javanica var. *chinensis* (Chinese sumac)
Rhus typhina (staghorn sumac)
Sophora japonica (Styphnolobium japonicus) (Japanese pagoda tree,
    Chinese scholar tree)
Sorbus alnifolia (alder whitebeam, Korean mountain ash)
Sorbus americana (American mountain ash)
Sorbus aucuparia (European mountain ash)

Sorbus decora (showy mountain ash)
Sorbus rufoferrugenia 'Longwood Sunset'
Sorbus × *thuringiaca* 'Fastigiata' (oakleaf mountain ash)

BROAD-LEAVED EVERGREENS
Ilex aquifolium (English holly)
Ilex × *aquipernyi* 'San Jose' (San Jose holly)
Ilex opaca (American holly)
Ilex pedunculosa (long-stalk holly)
Magnolia grandiflora (southern magnolia, bull bay)
Magnolia virginiana (sweet bay magnolia)
Magnolia virginiana var. *australis* (sweet bay magnolia)

CONIFERS
Juniperus virginiana (eastern red cedar)

STREET TREES

DECIDUOUS
SMALL
Acer buergerianum (A. trifidum) (trident maple)
Acer tataricum (Tatarian maple)
Acer tataricum ssp. *ginnala (A. ginnala)* (Amur maple)
Acer truncatum (Shantung maple, purpleblow maple)
Prunus serrulata (Japanese flowering cherry)
Syringa reticulata (S. amurensis var. *japonica)* (Japanese tree lilac)
MEDIUM
Acer campestre (hedge maple)
Acer maximowiczianum (A. nikoense) (Nikko maple)
Carpinus betulus (European hornbeam)
Crataegus viridis (green hawthorn)
Eucommia ulmoides (hardy rubber tree)
Fraxinus velutina (velvet ash)
Koelreuteria paniculata (goldenrain tree)
TALL
Acer × *freemanii* (Freeman maple)
Acer platanoides (Norway maple)
Acer pseudoplatanus (sycamore maple)
Acer rubrum (red maple, swamp maple)
Acer saccharum (sugar maple, hard maple, rock maple)

Betula nigra 'Heritage' (Heritage river birch)
Celtis occidentalis (common hackberry)
Fraxinus americana (white ash)
Fraxinus pennsylvanica (green ash, red ash)
Ginkgo biloba (ginkgo, maidenhair tree)
Gleditsia triacanthos var. *inermis* (thornless honey locust)
Liquidambar styraciflua (sweet gum, gum tree)
Maackia amurensis (Amur maackia)
Nyssa sylvatica (black gum, sour gum, pepperidge, tupelo)
Ostrya carpinifolia (European hornbeam)
Ostrya virginiana (ironwood, hop hornbeam)
Phellodendron amurense (Amur cork tree)
Platanus × acerifolia (London plane tree)
Prunus sargentii (Sargent cherry)
Pyrus calleryana (callery pear, flowering pear)
Quercus bicolor (swamp white oak)
Quercus coccinea (scarlet oak)
Quercus ellipsoidalis (northern pin oak)
Quercus imbricaria (shingle oak)
Quercus muehlenbergii (yellow chestnut oak)
Quercus nigra (water oak, possum oak)
Quercus nuttallii (Q. texana) (Nuttall's oak)
Quercus palustris (pin oak)
Quercus phellos (willow oak)
Quercus prinus (chestnut oak)
Quercus rubra (Q. borealis) (northern red oak)
Sophora japonica (Styphnolobium japonicus) (Japanese pagoda tree,
    Chinese scholar tree)
Tilia cordata (littleleaf linden)
Tilia × euchlora (Crimean linden)
Ulmus americana (American elm, white elm)
Ulmus parvifolia (lacebark elm, Chinese elm)
Zelkova serrata (Japanese zelkova)

URBAN SHADE TREES

DECIDUOUS
Acer buergerianum (A. trifidum) (trident maple)
Acer campestre (hedge maple)

Acer platanoides (Norway maple)
Acer rubrum (red maple, swamp maple)
Aesculus × carnea (red horse chestnut)
Betula nigra 'Heritage' (Heritage river birch)
Betula platyphylla var. *japonica* 'Whitespire' (Whitespire Asian birch)
Carpinus betulus (European hornbeam)
Catalpa bignonioides (southern catalpa, Indian bean)
Catalpa speciosa (northern catalpa, western catalpa)
Crataegus spp. (hawthorns)
Eucommia ulmoides (hardy rubber tree)
Fraxinus pennsylvanica (green ash, red ash)
Ginkgo biloba 'Princeton Sentry' (ginkgo, maidenhair tree)
Gleditsia triacanthos var. *inermis* (thornless honey locust)
Gymnocladus dioica (Kentucky coffee tree)
Koelreuteria paniculata (goldenrain tree)
Liquidambar styraciflua (sweet gum, gum tree)
Liriodendron tulipifera (tulip tree, yellow poplar)
Maackia amurensis (Amur maackia)
Paulownia tomentosa (empress tree, princess tree)
Phellodendron amurense 'Macho' (Amur cork tree)
Platanus × acerifolia 'Bloodgood' (London plane tree)
Pyrus calleryana (callery pear, flowering pear)
Pyrus ussuriensis (Ussuri pear)
Quercus acutissima (sawtooth oak)
Quercus bicolor (swamp white oak)
Quercus macrocarpa (bur oak, mossycup oak)
Quercus phellos (willow oak)
Quercus robur (English oak)
Quercus rubra (Q. borealis) (northern red oak)
Quercus shumardii (shumard oak)
Sophora japonica (Styphnolobium japonicus) (Japanese pagoda tree, Chinese scholar tree)
Sorbus alnifolia (alder whitebeam, Korean mountain ash)
Tilia cordata (littleleaf linden)
Tilia tomentosa (silver linden)
Ulmus parvifolia (lacebark elm, Chinese elm)
Zelkova serrata (Japanese zelkova)

BROAD-LEAVED EVERGREENS
Quercus virginiana (live oak)

<small>C O N I F E R S</small>
Calocedrus decurrens (incense cedar)
Juniperus virginiana (eastern red cedar)
Taxodium distichum (bald cypress, swamp cypress)

TREES THAT TOLERATE WET SOIL

<small>D E C I D U O U S</small>
Acer pensylvanicum (striped maple, moosewood)
Acer rubrum (red maple, swamp maple)
Acer saccharinum (silver maple)
Alnus glutinosa (black alder, European alder)
Alnus incana (gray alder)
Amelanchier arborea (shadblow, downy serviceberry, service tree, Juneberry)
Amelanchier × grandiflora (apple serviceberry)
Amelanchier laevis (Allegheny serviceberry)
Betula nigra (river birch)
Carya illinoinensis (pecan)
Catalpa bignonioides (southern catalpa, Indian bean)
Catalpa speciosa (northern catalpa, western catalpa)
Celtis occidentalis (common hackberry)
Fraxinus americana (white ash)
Liquidambar styraciflua (sweet gum, gum tree)
Liriodendron tulipifera (tulip tree, yellow poplar)
Magnolia acuminata (cucumber tree)
Magnolia acuminata var. *subcordata* (yellow cucumber tree)
Magnolia kobus (Kobus magnolia)
Magnolia liliiflora (M. quinquepeta) (lily-flowered magnolia, Kosar hybrids)
Magnolia × loebneri (Loebner magnolia)
Magnolia × soulangeana (saucer magnolia)
Magnolia stellata (M. tomentosa) (star magnolia)
Nyssa sylvatica (black gum, sour gum, pepperidge, tupelo)
Platanus × acerifolia (London plane tree)
Platanus occidentalis (sycamore, American plane tree, buttonwood)
Platanus orientalis (Oriental plane tree)
Populus × acuminata (lanceleaf poplar)
Populus alba (white poplar)

Populus angustifolia (willowleaf poplar)
Populus × *canadensis (P.* × *euramerica)*
Populus × *canescens* (hybrid poplar)
Populus deltoides (cottonwood)
Populus fremontii (western poplar)
Populus tremuloides (quaking aspen)
Quercus bicolor (swamp white oak)
Quercus ellipsoidalis (northern pin oak)
Quercus nigra (water oak, possum oak)
Quercus nuttallii (Q. texana) (Nuttall's oak)
Quercus palustris (pin oak)
Quercus phellos (willow oak)
Salix alba 'Tristis' *(S.* × *sepulcralis* 'Chrysocoma') (white willow, Niobe
    willow, golden weeping willow)
Salix alba var. *vitellina* (golden willow)
Salix babylonica (weeping willow)
Salix matsudana (S. babylonica var. *pekinensis)* (Hankow willow, Peking
    willow)
Ulmus americana (American elm, white elm)
Ulmus pumila 'Cathedral' (Siberian elm, Chinese elm)

B R O A D - L E A V E D   E V E R G R E E N S
Magnolia grandiflora (southern magnolia, bull bay)
Magnolia virginiana (sweet bay magnolia)
Quercus virginiana (live oak)

C O N I F E R S
Calocedrus decurrens (incense cedar)
Chamaecyparis thyoides (Atlantic white cedar, white cypress, swamp
    cedar)
Cryptomeria japonica (Japanese cedar, cryptomeria)
Larix larcinia (American larch, tamarack)
Metasequoia glyptostroboides (dawn redwood)
Taxodium distichum (bald cypress, swamp cypress)
Taxodium distichum var. *imbricarium (T. ascendens)* (pond cypress)
Thuja occidentalis (arborvitae, eastern white cedar, white cedar)
Thuja orientalis (Platycladus orientalis) (Oriental arborvitae)
Thuja plicata (western red cedar, giant arborvitae)
Thujopsis dolabrata (hiba arborvitae)

✿ Photo Credits

AGRICULTURAL RESEARCH SERVICE, USDA: 38–39

ALAN & LINDA DETRICK: 101 top, 161 top

MICHAEL DIRR: 90 top, 90 bottom, 105 bottom, 150 bottom, 151 top, 175 top, 175 bottom

DEREK FELL: 42 bottom, 45 top, 53 top, 57 top, 59 bottom, 60 top, 69 bottom, 71 top, 71 bottom, 72 top, 74 bottom, 76 top, 91 top, 99 bottom, 109 bottom, 111 bottom, 113 bottom, 119 top, 122 top, 124 top, 126 top, 137 top, 141 bottom, 142 top, 143 top, 156 top, 157 top, 158 top, 160 bottom, 185 top, 186 bottom

DENCY KANE: 138 bottom

CHARLES MANN: 75 bottom

JERRY PAVIA PHOTOGRAPHY, INC.: 70 top

SUSAN A. ROTH & CO.: ii–iii, vi–1, 2, 5, 7, 8, 9, 12, 15, 16, 19, 21, 23, 25, 30, 36, 40–41, 42 top, 43 top, 43 bottom, 44 top, 44 bottom, 45 bottom, 46 top, 46 bottom, 47 top, 47 bottom, 48 top, 48 bottom, 49 top, 49 bottom, 50 top, 50 bottom, 51 top, 51 bottom, 52 top, 52 bottom, 53 bottom, 54 top, 54 bottom, 55 top, 55 bottom, 56 top, 56 bottom, 57 bottom, 58 top, 58 bottom, 59 top, 60 bottom, 61 top, 61 bottom, 62 top, 62 bottom, 63 top, 63 bottom, 64 top, 64 bottom, 65 top, 65 bottom, 66 top, 66 bottom, 67 top, 67 bottom, 68 top, 68 bottom, 69 top, 70 bottom, 72 bottom, 73 top, 73 bottom, 74 top, 75 top, 76 bottom, 77 top, 77 bottom, 78 top, 78 bottom, 79 top, 79 bottom, 80 top, 80 bottom, 81 top, 81 bottom, 82 top, 82 bottom, 83 top, 83 bottom, 84 top, 84 bottom, 85 top, 85 bottom, 86 top, 86 bottom, 87 top, 87 bottom, 88 top, 88 bottom, 89 top, 89 bottom, 91 bottom, 92 top, 92 bottom, 93 top, 93 bottom, 94 top, 94 bottom, 95 top, 95 bottom, 96 top, 96 bottom, 97 top, 97 bottom, 98 top, 98 bottom, 99 top, 100 top, 100 bottom, 102 top, 102 bottom, 103 top, 103 bottom,

104 top, 104 bottom, 105 top, 106 top, 106 bottom, 107 top, 107 bottom, 108 top, 108 bottom, 109 top, 110 top, 110 bottom, 111 top, 112 top, 112 bottom, 113 top, 114 top, 114 bottom, 115 top, 115 bottom, 116 top, 116 bottom, 117 top, 117 bottom, 118 top, 118 bottom, 119 bottom, 120 top, 120 bottom, 121 top, 121 bottom, 122 bottom, 123 top, 123 bottom, 124 bottom, 125 top, 125 bottom, 126 bottom, 127 top, 127 bottom, 128 top, 128 bottom, 129 top, 129 bottom, 130 top, 130 bottom, 131 top, 131 bottom, 132 top, 132 bottom, 133 top, 133 bottom, 134 top, 134 bottom, 135 top, 135 bottom, 136 top, 136 bottom, 137 bottom, 138 top, 139 top, 139 bottom, 140 top, 142 bottom, 143 bottom, 144 top, 144 bottom, 145 top, 145 bottom, 146 top, 146 bottom, 147 top, 147 bottom, 148 top, 148 bottom, 149 top, 149 bottom, 150 top, 151 bottom, 152 top, 152 bottom, 153 top, 153 bottom, 154 top, 154 bottom, 155 top, 155 bottom, 156 bottom, 157 bottom, 158 bottom, 159 top, 159 bottom, 160 top, 161 bottom, 162 top, 162 bottom, 163 top, 163 bottom, 164 top, 164 bottom, 165 top, 165 bottom, 166 top, 166 bottom, 167 top, 167 bottom, 168 top, 168 bottom, 169 top, 169 bottom, 170 top, 170 bottom, 171 top, 171 bottom, 172 top, 172 bottom, 173 top, 173 bottom, 174 top, 174 bottom, 176 top, 176 bottom, 178 top, 178 bottom, 179 top, 179 bottom, 180 top, 180 bottom, 181 top, 181 bottom, 182 top, 182 bottom, 183 top, 183 bottom, 184 top, 184 bottom, 186 top, 187, 188–189

JOSEPH G. STRAUCH JR.: 101 bottom, 177 top, 185 bottom

MARK TURNER: 140 bottom, 141 top, 177 bottom

❧Index

Page numbers in italics refer to illustrations.

Abies, 312–16
 balsamea, 143, 313
 balsamea var. *phanerolepis,* 313
 concolor, 143, 314, 361, 367
 concolor 'Candicans', *144*
 firma, 144, 315
 fraseri, 313
 homolepis, 314–15, 377
 koreana, 145, 315
 lasiocarpa, 145, 315, 361
 nordmanniana, 146, 315, 361
 spp., 364, 376
Acer, 191–204
 buergerianum, 42, 192, 359, *362, 365,*
 367, 375, 379, 380
 campestre, 42, 192–93, 359, 365, 367,
 373, 375, 379, 380
 capillipes, 43, 196
 circinatum, 203, 378
 cissifolium, 196, *362,* 367, 373
 davidii, 196, *362, 376*
 × *freemanii,* 194–95, 368, 370, 379
 ginnala, 193–94, 359, 368, 370, 373, 375,
 378, 379
 glabrum, 192, 368
 griseum, 43, 193, 359, *362,* 368, 373
 japonicum, 202, 368
 japonicum var. *acontifolium, 44,* 203,
 376
 japonicum var. *acontifolium* 'Filicifolium', *44*
 japonicum var. *microphyllum,* 203–4

japonicum var. *microphyllum*
 'Aureum', *48,* 204
 maximowiczianum, 193, 365, 379
 miyabei, 193, 359
 mono, 198
 negundo, 18, 44, 195–96, 359, 365, 373
 nikoense, 193, 365, 379
 palmatum, 21, 45, 202–3, *362,* 368, *376,*
 378
 palmatum 'Aoyagi', 202–3
 palmatum 'Sango-Kaku', 202
 palmatum var. *dissectum,* 203, 376
 pensylvanicum, 196, *362,* 368, *376,* 382
 platanoides, 17, 18, 196–98, 359, 368,
 370, 373, 379, 380
 platanoides 'Crimson King', *45*
 pseudoplatanus, 46, 198, 359, 373, 379
 pseudoplatanus var. *erythrocarpum,*
 198
 pseudosieboldianum, 203
 rubrum, 46, 198–200, 368, 370, 379, 381,
 382
 rubrum var. *drummondii,* 199
 saccharinum, 17–18, 19, 200, 359, 365,
 382
 saccharum, 47, 201–2, 368, 379
 saccharum 'Bonfire', *47*
 saccharum ssp. *nigrum,* 201
 saccharum var. *grandidentum,* 201–2
 shirasawanum, 203–4
 shirasawanum 'Aureum', *48*
 spp., 363

Acer (cont.)
  tataricum, 48, 194, 368, 378, 379
  tataricum ssp. *ginnala*, 193–94, 359,
    368, 370, 373, 375, 378, 379
  tegmentosum 'White Tigress', 196
  trifidum, 42, 192, 359, 362, 365, 367, 375,
    379, 380
  triflorum, 193, 362, 368, 373
  truncatum, 198, 359, 362, 365, 368, 373,
    379
Aceraceae, 191–204
Adams golden chain, 95
Aesculus
  × *carnea*, 204–5, 359, 370, 373, 381
  × *carnea* 'Briotii', 49
  flava, 50, 205, 359, 370
  glabra, 50, 205, 359, 365, 368, 370, 376
  hippocastanum, 18, 206, 359, 370, 373
  hipposcastanum 'Baumanii', 51
  octandra, 50, 205, 359
  pavia, 51, 206, 359, 370, 375, 376
  pavia flavescens, 206
  splendens, 206, 370
  spp., 363
Ailanthus, 266
Alaska cedar, 321
Albizia julibrissin, 18, 52, 206–7, 359, 365,
    371, 373
alder
  black, 53, 359, 373, 382
  European, 53, 359, 373, 382
  gray, 208, 382
alder whitebeam, 125, 291–92, 369, 371,
    378, 381
alkaline soil, trees for, 5, 359–62
Allegheny serviceberry, 54, 208–9, 368,
    382
Alnus
  glutinosa, 53, 207–8, 359, 373, 382
  incana, 208, 382
alpine fir, 145, 315, 361
Amelanchier
  alnifolia, 209
  arborea, 209, 368, 382
  canadensis, 209, 373
  × *grandiflora*, 53, 209–10, 368, 382
  laevis, 54, 208–9, 368, 382
  spp., 359, 363, 370, 376, 378
American beech, 239, 362, 377
American chestnut, 218
American elm, 132, 298, 299–300, 361,
    364, 369, 374, 380, 383

American fringe tree, 70, 231–32
American holly, 137, 305–6, 364, 367, 374,
    376, 379
American hornbeam, 58–59, 216, 359,
    368, 375, 376
American larch, 161, 331–32, 383
American linden, 296–97, 361, 369
American mountain ash, 292, 371, 378
American plane tree, 269, 366, 374, 382
American smoke tree, 360, 365, 370
American snowbell, 294, 371
Amur chokecherry, 111, 273–74, 361, 362,
    364, 374
Amur cork tree, 104–5, 266–67, 360, 366,
    369, 374, 380, 381
Amur maackia, 90, 252, 360, 362, 366, 372,
    380, 381
Amur maple, 193–94, 359, 368, 370, 373,
    375, 378, 379
Anacardiaceae, 231–32, 286–87
Ann Kosar hybrid magnolia, 92
Annonaceae, 211
apple serviceberry, 53, 209–10, 368, 382
apricot, Japanese flowering, 275, 370
Aquifoliaceae, 303–6
Aralia
  elata, 210, 363, 365, 371, 376
  elata 'Variegata', 54
  spinosa, 210, 363, 365, 371, 376
Araliaceae, 210
arborvitae, 183–84, 353–54, 365, 383
  dwarf golden Oriental, 184
  giant, 185, 355, 362, 383
  hiba, 185, 356, 383
  Oriental, 354–55, 383
Arizona cypress, 157, 327, 362, 367, 376
ash
  blue, 241
  European, 241, 360, 373
  green, 80, 241, 360, 366, 368, 373, 380,
    381
  mountain (*See* mountain ash)
  red, 80, 241, 360, 366, 368, 373, 380, 381
  velvet, 241, 360, 366, 373, 379
  white, 79, 240–41, 360, 368, 373, 380, 382
ash-leaved maple, 18, 195–96, 359, 365, 373
Asimina triloba, 55, 211, 376
aspen, quaking, 110, 383
astilbes, 24
Atlantic white cedar, 323–24, 383
Atlas cedar, 317, 361, 367
Austrian pine, 344, 375

bald cypress, *180*, 351, 363, 367, 370, 375, 382, 383
bald cypress family
  Cryptomeria, 324–25
  Cunnighamia, 325
  Metasequoia, 332–33
  Sciadopitys, 348–49
  Sequoia, 349
  Sequoiadendron, 350
  Taxodium, 350–51
balled-and-burlapped (B&B), 10–13
ballerina Loebner magnolia, *92*
balsam fir, *143*, 313
basswood, 296–97, 361, 369
Baumanii horse chestnut, *51*
bay
  bull, *139*, 307–8, 364, 374, 379, 383
  sweet, 367, 376
bay laurel, *138*, 306–7, 367, 376
B&B, 10–13
bean family
  Laburnum, 247–48
beech
  American, 239, 362, 377
  attracting songbirds with, 364
  blue, *58–59*, 216, 359, 368, 375, 376
  copper, 239
  European, *77*, 238–39, 360, 362, 366
  fernleaf, 238
  purple, 239
  tricolor European, *78*
beech family, 217–19, 238–39, 280–86, 310–11
Betula, 211–15
  alba, 213–14
  albosinensis, 212–13
  alleghaniensis, 213
  ermanii, *55*, 215
  jacquemontii, *57*, 214–15, 359
  lenta, 213
  maximowicziana, 215
  nigra, *56*, 212–13, 373, 382
  nigra 'Heritage', 380, 381
  papyrifera, *56*, 213
  pendula, 213–14
  pendula 'Youngii', *57*
  platyphylla var. *japonica* 'Whitespire', 381
  platyphylla var. *japonica* 'Whitespire Sr.', 214, 359, 373
  populifolia, 213
  spp., 362, 363, 368

utilis, 215, 359
utilis ssp. *jacquemontii*, *57*, 214–15
Betulaceae
  Alnus, 207–8
  Betula, 211–15
  Carpinus, 215–16
  Corylus, 230
  Ostrya, 263–64
Bhutan pine, *174*, 345
bigleaf magnolia, 253
Bignoniaceae, 219–20
bignonia family, 219–20
big tree, *179–80*, 350, 363
birch
  attracting songbirds with, 363
  canoe, *56*, 213
  cherry, 213
  Chinese paper, 212–13
  Erman, *55*
  erman, 215
  European, 213–14
  for fall color, 368
  gray, 213
  Heritage river, 380, 381
  monarch, 215
  and ornamental bark, 362
  paper, *56*, 213
  red-barked Himalayan, 215
  river, *56*, *212*–13, 373, 382
  sweet, 213
  weeping European, *57*
  white-barked Himalayan, 359
  white-barked Himilayan, *57*, 214–15
  whitespire, 359, 373
  Whitespire Asian, 381
  Whitespire Senior Asian, 214
  yellow, 213
birchbark cherry, 363, 374
birch family
  Alnus, 207–8
  Betula, 211–15
  Carpinus, 215–16
  Corylus, 230
  Ostrya, 263–64
birch-leaf pear, 280, 366
Bishop's hat, 24
bitternut hickory, 217
black alder, *53*, 207–8, 359, 373, 382
black cherry, *112*, 274, 363, 369, 371
black gum, *100*, 262–63, 364, 369, 373, 378, 380, 382
Black Hills spruce, *36*, 334–35

black locust, *123*, 287–88, 361, 371, 374
black maple, 201
black oak, 282, 366, 369
black walnut, *5*, 18, *84*, 246, 364, 366
blireana plum, 273, 366
blue ash, 241
blue Atlas cedar, *147–48*, 317
blue beech, *58*–59, 216, 359, 368, 375, 376
blue heaven Rocky Mountain juniper,
    158
blue Korean pine, *168*
blue Lawson false cypress, *151*
blue limber pine, *167*
'Bonfire' sugar maple, *47*
Bosnian pine, 344
box elder, 18, *44*, 195–96, 359, 365, 373
Bradford pear, 277–78
branch collar, 3
briotii red horse chestnut, *49*
bristlecone pine, *165–66*, 337, 367
broad-leaved evergreens, 4
    with colorful fruits, 379
    in gallery of trees, 136–42
    pruning of, 28–34
    with showy flowers, 370–72
    that attract songbirds, 364
    that tolerate alkaline soil, 361
    that tolerate drought, 367
    that tolerate salt, 374–75
    that tolerate shade, 377
    that tolerate wet soil, 383
    for urban shade, 381
    for windbreaks and screens, 376
buckeye
    attracting songbirds with, 363
    flame, 206, 370
    Louisiana, 206, 370
    Ohio, *50*, 205, 359, 365, 368, 370, 376
    red, *51*, 206, 359, 370, 375, 376
    yellow, *50*, 205, 359, 370
bull bay, *139*, 307–8, 364, 374, 379, 383
bur oak, 284, 361, 366, 369, 381
butternut, 246, 364, 366
buttonwood, 269, 366, 374, 382

California redwood, *179*, 349, 377
callery pear, *115*, 278–79, 361, 366, 369, 371,
    374, 380, 381
Calocedrus decurrens, *146–47*, 316, 361,
    363, 376, 382, 383
camperdown elm, 301
Canada fir, 313
Canada hemlock, *186*, 357–58, 378

canary American holly, *137*
candicans white fir, *144*
canoe birch, *56*, 213
canopy trees, 3, 4
canyon live oak, 310, 361
capitata Japanese yew, *182–83*
care of trees, 22–28
Carolina cherry laurel, 309, 361, 364, 372,
    375, 376, 377
Carolina hemlock, *186*, 358, 378
Carolina silverbell, *83–84*, 245, 362, 377
Carpinus
    betulus, 215–16, 264, 359, 362, 365, 368,
        375, 376, 379, 381
    betulus 'Fastigiata', *58*
    caroliniana, *58*–59, 216, 263, 359, 368,
        375, 376
    japonicus, 216
    spp., 363
Carya, 216–17
    cordiformis, 217
    illinoinensis, 217, 360, 382
    laciniosa, 217
    ovata, *59*, 217, 360, 362, 373
    spp., 364, 368
cashew family, 231–32, 267–68, 286–87
Castanea, 217–19
    dentata, 218
    mollissima, *60*, 218–19, 360, 365
    sativa, 219, 365
Catalpa
    bignonioides, *61*, 220, 360, 365, 371, 373,
        381, 382
    × *rubescens* 'Purpurea', 220, 365, 371,
        373
    speciosa, 219–20, 360, 365, 371, 373, 381,
        382
cedar
    Alaska, 321
    Atlantic white, 323–24, 383
    Atlas, 317, 361, 367
    blue Atlas, *147–48*, 317
    cypress, 319
    deodar, *148*, *149*, 318, 361, 367
    eastern red, *159*, 329–30, 362, 365, 367,
        375, 376, 379, 382
    eastern white, *183–84*, 353–54, 365, 383
    incense, *146–47*, 316, 361, 363, 376, 382,
        383
    Japanese, *155*, 324–25, 363, 376, 377, 383
    of Lebanon, *149*, *150*, 318–19, 361, 367
    lobbii Japanese, *155*
    Port Orford, 320–21

swamp, 323–24, 383
western red, 158, 185, 328–29, 355, 362, 364, 367, 375, 376, 383
white, 183–84, 353–54, 365, 383
Cedrus
  atlantica, 317, 361, 367
  atlantica 'Glauca', 147–48
  brevifolia, 319
  deodara, 148, 318, 361, 367
  deodara 'Aurea', 149
  libani, 149, 318–19, 361, 367
  libani 'Pendula', 150
  libani ssp. *atlantica,* 317, 361, 367
  libani ssp. *brevifolia,* 319
Celtis
  laevigata, 221, 360, 364, 365
  occidentalis, 62, 220–21, 360, 364, 365, 380, 382
  sinensis, 221, 360, 365
Cephalotaxaceae, 319–20
Cephalotaxus
  fortunei, 320
  harringtonia, 150–51, 319–20, 376, 377
Cercidiphyllaceae, 221–22
Cercidiphyllum
  japonicum, 62, 221–22, 360, 368
  japonicum var. *magnificum* 'Pendulum', 222
Cercis
  canadensis, 63, 222–23, 360, 365, 377
  canadensis 'Forest Pansy', 63
  canadensis var. *alba,* 222
  canadensis var. *texensis,* 222, 365
  chinensis, 223, 365
  chinensis var. *texensis,* 360
  occidentalis, 223, 365
  reniformis, 222, 360, 365
  spp., 368, 370
Chamaecyparis
  lawsoniana, 320–21
  lawsoniana 'Glauca', 151
  lawsoniana 'Lanei', 152
  nootkatensis, 321
  nootkatensis 'Lutea', 152
  nootkatensis 'Pendula', 153
  obtusa, 321–22, 377
  obtusa 'Crispii', 153
  obtusa 'Gracilis Aurea', 154
  pisifera, 154, 322–23, 361
  spp., 376
  thyoides, 323–24, 383
cherry
  birchbark, 363, 374

black, 112, 274, 363, 369, 371
cornelian, 68, 228–29, 360, 362, 370, 377, 378
goldbark, 111, 273–74, 361, 362, 364, 374
Hally Jolivette, 360, 370
higan, 9, 114, 276–77, 363, 371
Japanese cornelian, 229, 370, 377
Japanese flowering, 114, 363, 371, 374, 379
Kwanzan, 2
okame, 112–13, 274–75, 370
Oriental, 363, 371, 374
paperbark, 363, 374
Potomac, 115, 277, 363, 371
Sargent, 113, 363, 369, 371, 374, 380
Shirofugen Oriental, 114
weeping, 114, 276–77, 363, 371
wild black, 112, 274, 363, 369, 371
Yoshino, 115, 277, 363, 371
cherry birch, 213
cherry dogwood, 68, 228–29, 360, 362, 370, 377, 378
cherry laurel, 140–41, 310, 372, 377
cherry plum, 110, 273, 364, 366, 371, 374
chestnut
  American, 218
  Chinese, 60, 218–19, 360, 365
  horse (*See* horse chestnut)
  Spanish, 219, 365
chestnut oak, 283, 380
China fir, 156, 325
Chinese chestnut, 60, 218–19, 360, 365
Chinese dogwood, 227–28, 228, 362, 368, 371, 377, 378
Chinese elm, 18, 133–34, 134, 301–2, 302, 361, 363, 367, 374, 380, 381, 383
Chinese fringe tree, 64, 223, 360, 362, 364, 368, 371, 375, 377
Chinese goldenrain tree, 247, 366, 372, 373, 378
Chinese juniper, 330, 367, 375
Chinese maackia, 366
Chinese paper birch, 212–13
Chinese pistache, 105, 267–68, 364, 369, 378
Chinese pistachio, 105, 267–68, 364, 369, 378
Chinese redbud, 223, 365
Chinese scholar tree, 290–91, 361, 367, 372, 374, 378, 380, 381
Chinese sumac, 287, 361, 367, 372, 378
Chinese tulip tree, 251

Chionanthus
  retusus, *64*, 223, 360, 362, 364, 368, 371,
    375, 377
  virginicus, *64*–65, 223–24, 360, 364,
    368, 370, 377, 378
Chionodoxa, 254
chokecherry, Amur, *111*, 361, 362, 364, 374
choosing trees, 2, 10–11, 16–22
Cladrastis
  kentukea, *65*, 224–25, 360, 368, 371
  lutea, *65*, 224–25, 360, 368, 371
coast live oak, *141*, 311, 361
coast redwood, *179*, 349, 377
cockspur hawthorn, 232–33, 365, 375
coffee tree, Kentucky, *82*–83, 244, 373, 381
Colorado blue spruce, *165*, 336, 367, 375
common hackberry, *62*, 220–21, 360, 364,
  365, 380, 382
common laburnum, 248, 360
common persimmon, *74*–75, 235–36, 360,
  364, 373
conifers
  about, 4–6
  with colorful fruits, 379
  in encyclopedia of trees, 312–58
  in gallery of trees, *143*–87
  with ornamental bark, 363
  with outstanding fall color, 369–70
  pruning, 34–36
  that attract songbirds, 364–65
  that tolerate alkaline soil, 361–62
  that tolerate drought, 367
  that tolerate salt, 375
  that tolerate shade, 377–78
  that tolerate wet soil, 383
  for urban shade, 382
  for windbreaks and screens, 376
container-grown, 11–13
copper beech, 239
coral-bark maple, 202
corkscrew willow, *124*, 290
cork tree, Amur, *104*–5, 360, 366, 369, 374,
  380, 381
Cornaceae, 225–30
cornelian cherry, *68*, 228–29, 360, 362,
  370, 377, 378
Cornus
  alternifolia, 225–26, 368, 370
  alternifolia 'Argentea', *66*
  controversa, 226
  florida, *66*–67, 226–27, 368, 370, 377,
    378

  florida × *C. kousa*, *69*, 229–30, 368, 370
  kousa, 227–28, 368, 371, 377, 378
  kousa 'Summer Stars', *67*
  kousa var. *chinensis*, 228, 362, 371, 377
  mas, *68*, 228–29, 360, 362, 370, 377, 378
  nuttallii, 227, 370
  officinalis, 229, 370, 377, 378
  racemosa, 226, 365
  × *rutgersensis*, 229–30, 368, 370
  × *rutgersensis* 'Aurora', *69*
  spp., 364
Corylus
  avellana, 230, 364, 370
  colurna, *69*, 230, 360, 364
Cotinus
  coggygria, *70*, 231, 360, 365, 371
  coggygria var. *purpureus*, 231–32, 365,
    371
  obovatus, *70*, 231–32, 360, 365, 370
  spp., 368
cottonwood, 18, *108*–9, 271–72, 360, 374,
  383
crab apple
  for alkaline soil, 360
  attracting songbirds with, 364
  Japanese flowering, 258–59
  for road and sea salt, 373
  rosybloom, 257
  for showy flowers, 371
  Siberian, 257–58
cranston Norway spruce, *162*
crape myrtle, *87*, 248–49, 362, 368, 372, 373
  hardy, 369
  Natchez hybrid, *87*
Crataegus
  cordata, *72*, 233–34, 366
  crus-galli, 232–33, 365, 375
  crus-galli var. *inermis*, 233, 365
  laevigata, *71*, 233
  × *lavellei*, 233, 365
  × *mordenensis*, 233, 365
  phaenopyrum, *72*, 233–34, 366
  spp., 364, 372, 378, 381
  viridis, 234, 366, 379
  viridis 'Winter King', *72*–73
Crimean linden, 297–98, 361, 380
Crimson King Norway maple, *45*
crispii Hinoki false cypress, *153*
crown thinning, 32–34
Cryptomeria
  japonica, *155*, 324–25, 363, 376, 377, 383
  japonica 'Lobbii', *155*

cucumber tree, *91*, 253, 360, 364, 369, 378, 382
  yellow, 372
Cunninghamia
  lanceolata, 156, 325
  lanceolata 'Glauca', *156*
Cupressaceae
  Calocedrus, 316
  Chamaecyparis, 320–24
  × *Cupressocyparis,* 326
  Cupressus, 327–28
  Juniperus, 328–30
  Thuja, 353–55
  Thujopsis, 356
× *Cupressocyparis leylandii, 157,* 326, 362, 375, 376. 377
Cupressus
  arizonica var. *glabra, 157,* 327, 362, 367, 376
  macrocarpa, 158, 327–28, 375
  sempervirens, 327, 362, 375, 376
custard apple family, 211
cut-leaved staghorn sumac, *122,* 287
cypress
  Arizona, *157,* 327, 362, 367, 376
  bald, *180,* 351, 363, 367, 370, 375, 382, 383
  Italian, 327, 362, 375, 376
  Leyland, *157,* 326, 362, 375, 376, 377
  Monterey, *158,* 327–28, 375
  pond, 351, 367, 370, 375, 383
  prairie sentinel pond, *181*
  swamp, *180,* 351, 363, 367, 370, 375, 382, 383
  white, 323–24, 383
cypress cedar, 319
cypress family
  Calocedrus, 316
  Chamaecyparis, 320–24
  × *Cupressocyparis,* 326, 376
  Cupressus, 327–28
  Juniperus, 328–30
  Thuja, 353–55
  Thujopsis, 356

damage, avoiding, 26–28
David elm, 361
Davidia
  involucrata, 73–74, 235, 362, 370
  involucrata var. *vilmoriniana,* 235
David maple, *196,* 362, 376
dawn redwood, *161–62,* 332–33, 363, 369, 383

dead nettle, 24
deciduous trees
  with colorful fruits, 378–79
  in encyclopedia, 191–303
  in gallery, 42–135
  leaves of, 3
  with ornamental bark, 362–63
  with outstanding fall color, 367–69
  with showy flowers, 370–72
  for streets, 379–80
  that attract songbirds, 363–64
  that tolerate alkaline soil, 359–61
  that tolerate drought, 365–67
  that tolerate salt, 373–74
  that tolerate shade, 376–77
  that tolerate wet soil, 382–83
  for urban shade, 380–81
  for windbreaks and screens, 375
definitions, 1–3
deodar cedar, *148, 149,* 318, 361, 367
devil's walking stick, *54,* 210, 363, 365, 371, 376
Diospyros
  kaki, 236
  virginiana, 74–75, 235–36, 360, 364, 373
diseases, 36–37
dogwood
  attracting songbirds with, 364
  cherry, *68,* 228–29, 360, 362, 370, 377, 378
  Chinese, 228, 362, 368, 371, 377, 378
  family, 225–30
  flowering, *66–67,* 226–27, 368, 370, 377, 378
  giant, 226
  gray, 226, 365
  hybrid, *69,* 229–30, 368, 370
  Japanese, 368, 371, 377, 378
  Korean, 368, 371, 377, 378
  Kousa, 368, 371, 377, 378
  mountain, 370
  pagoda, 225–26, 368, 370
  stellar, *69,* 229–30, 368, 370
  summer stars Kousa, *67*
  variegated pagoda, *66*
Douglas fir, *177,* 347–48, 362
dove tree, *73–74,* 235, 362, 370
downy serviceberry, 209, 359, 363, 368, 370, 373, 376, 378, 382
dragon's-eye pine, *167,* 339
drop crotching, 32–34
drought, trees that tolerate, 365–67

dwarf Alberta spruce, *163*, 334
dwarf golden Oriental arborvitae, *184*
dwarf yew pine, *175*
dwarf yew podocarpus, *175*

eastern hemlock, *186*, 357–58, 378
eastern redbud, *63*, 222–23, 360, 365, 377
eastern red cedar, *159*, 329–30, 362, 365, 367, 375, 376, 379, 382
eastern white cedar, *183–84*, 353–54, 365, 383
eastern white pine, *170*, *171*, 341–42, 367
Ebenaceae, 235–36
ebony family, 235–36
Elaeagnaceae, 236–37
Elaeagnus angustifolia, 18, *75–76*, 236–37, 360, 366, 373, 375, 378
elder, box, 18, *44*, 195–96, 359, 365, 373
elm
    American, *132*, 298, 299–300, 361, 364, 369, 374, 380, 383
    Chinese, 18, *133–34*, *134*, 301–2, 361, 363, 367, 374, 380, 381, 383
    David, 361
    lacebark, *133–34*, 301–2, 361, 363, 367, 374, 380, 381
    Siberian, 18, *134*, 361, 374, 383
    white, 299–300, 361, 364, 369, 374, 380, 383
    winged, 361, 374
elm family, 220–21, 298–302, 303
Emory oak, 310, 361
empress tree, *103–4*, 265–66, 366, 372, 374, 381
English hawthorn, *71*, 233, 365
English holly, *136*, 304–5, 364, 376, 377, 379
English laurel, 310, 372, 377
English oak, *120–21*, 285–86, 361, 366, 374, 381
English walnut, 246, 366
English yew, 352, 363, 377
Epimedium, 24
Ericaceae, 264
erman birch, *55*, 215
Eucommiaceae, 237–38
Eucommia ulmoides, *76–77*, 237–38, 360, 366, 379, 381
European alder, *53*, 207–8, 359, 373, 382
European ash, 241, 360, 373
European beech, *77*, 238–39, 360, 362, 366
European birch, 213–14
European hazelnut, 230, 364, 370

European hornbeam, 215–16, 264, 359, 362, 365, 368, 375, 376, 379, 380, 381
European larch, *160*, 330–31, 362, 375
European mountain ash, *126*, 292–93, 369, 371, 378
evergreens, broad-leaved
    in encyclopedia of trees, 303–12
    in gallery of trees, 136–42
    leaves of, 3

Fabaceae
    Albizia, 206–7
    Cercis, 222–23
    Cladrastis, 224–25
    Gleditsia, 243–44
    Gymnocladus, 244
    Laburnum, 247–48
    Maackia, 252
    Robinia, 287–88
    Sophora, 290–91
Fagaceae, 217–19, 238–39, 280–86, 310–11
Fagus
    grandifolia, 239, 362, 377
    spp., 364
    sylvatica, *77*, 238–39, 360, 362, 366
    sylvatica purpurea, 238
    sylvatica purpurea 'Apslenifolia', 238
    sylvatica purpurea 'Riversii', 239
    sylvatica 'Roseo-marginata', *78*
    sylvatica 'Tricolor', *78*
fall color, trees with outstanding, 367–70
false cypress, 320–24
    blue Lawson, *151*
    crispii Hinoki, *153*
    golden Hinoki, *154*
    golden nootka, *152*
    Hinoki, 321–22, 377
    Lane Lawson, *152*
    Lawson, 320–21
    Nootka, 321
    sawara, *154*, 361
    weeping nootka, *153*
    for windbreaks and screens, 376
fastigate European hornbeam, *58*
fernleaf beech, 238
fernleaf Japanese maple, 203
ferns, 24
fertilization, 24–26
figwort family, 265–66
filbert, Turkish, *69*, 230, 360, 364
fir
    alpine, *145*, 361
    attracting songbirds with, 364

balsam, *143*, 313
Canada, 313
candicans white, *144*
China, *156*, 325
Douglas, *177*, 347–48, 362
Fraser balsam, 313
Korean, *145*
momi, *144*
Nikko, 314–15, 377
Nordmann, *146*, 361
Rocky Mountain, *145*, 361
Rocky Mountain Douglas, *177*
white, *143*, 314, 361, 367
for windbreaks and screens, 376
flame buckeye, 206, 370
flowering dogwood, *66–67*, 226–27, 368,
370, 377, 378
flowering pear, *115*, 278–79, 361, 366, 369,
371, 374, 380, 381
fragrant snowbell, *127*, *128*, 295, 371,
377
Franklinia alatamaha, 78–79, 239, 362,
368, 372
Franklin tree, *78–79*, 239, 362, 368, 372
Fraser balsam fir, 313
Fraxinus
americana, 79, 240–41, 360, 368, 373,
380, 382
excelsior, 241, 360, 373
pennsylvanica, 80, 241, 360, 366, 368,
373, 380, 381
quadrangulata, 241
veluntina, 241, 366, 373, 379
Freeman maple, 194–95, 368, 370, 379
fringe tree, *64–65*, *70*, 223–24, 231–32,
360, 364, 368, 370, 377, 378
Chinese, *64*, 362, 375, 377
fruits, trees with colorful, 378–79
full-moon maple, 203, 368

giant arborvitae, *185*, 355, 362, 383
giant dogwood, 226
giant redwood, *179–80*, 350, 363
giant sequoia, *179–80*, 350, 363
Ginkgoaceae, 242
Ginkgo biloba, 80–81, 242, 360, 366, 368,
373, 380
Ginkgo biloba 'Princeton Sentry', 381
Gleditsia triacanthos var. *inermis*, 81,
243–44, 366, 368, 373, 380, 381
Gleditsia triacanthos var. *inermis* 'Sunburst', 82

goldbark cherry, *111*, 273–74, 361, 362, 364,
374
golden chain
Adams, 95
redbud, 99
sargent, 98, 259–60
strawberry parfait, 97
tea, 95, 259
Zumi, 99
golden chain tree, *86*, 248, 360, 362, 371
golden English yew, *181*
golden full-moon maple, *48*, 204
golden Hinoki false cypress, *154*
golden black locust, *123*
golden larch, *176*, 347, 369
golden Nootka false cypress, *152*
goldenrain tree, *85*, 247, 360, 366, 372,
373, 378, 379, 381
golden weeping willow, *124*, 289, 383
golden willow, 289, 374, 383
gold-tipped Oriental spruce, *164*
Gordonia alatamaha, 78, 239, 362, 368,
372
gray alder, 208, 382
gray birch, 213
gray dogwood, 226, 365
green ash, *80*, 241, 360, 366, 368, 373, 380,
381
green-bark maple, 202–3
green hawthorn, 234, 366, 379
green vase Japanese zelkova, *135*
ground covers, 23–24
gum
black, *100*, 364, 369, 373, 378, 380,
382
sour, *100*, 364, 369, 373, 378, 380, 382
sweet, 364, 366, 369, 380, 381, 382
tree, *88*, 250–51, 364, 366, 369, 380, 381,
382
Gymnocladus dioica, 82–83, 244, 360, 366,
368, 373, 381

hackberry
common, *62*, 220–21, 360, 364, 365,
380, 382
Japanese, 221, 360, 365
sugar, 221, 360, 364, 365
Halesia
carolina, 83–84, 245, 362, 377
diptera, 245, 377
monticola, 245, 377
spp., 371

Halesia (cont.)
   tetraptera, *83–84*, 245, 362, 377
Hally Jolivette cherry, 360, 370
Hamamelidaceae, 250–51, 264–65
handkerchief tree, 73–74, 235, 362, 370
Hankow willow, 289–90, *374*, 383
hardiness zone map, 38–39
hard maple, *47*, 201–2, 368, 379
hardy crape myrtle, 369, 372, 373
hardy orange, *107*, 269, 366, 371, 378
hardy rubber tree, 76–77, 237–38, 360,
   366, 379, 381
hardy windmill palm, *142*, 312
hawthorn
   attracting songbirds with, 364
   cockspur, 232–33, 365, 375
   with colorful fruits, 378
   English, *71*, 233, 365
   green, 234, 366, 379
   Lavalle, 233, 365
   for showy flowers, 372
   for urban shade, 381
   Washington, *72*, 233–34, 366
   winter king green, *72–73*
hazel, Turkish, *69*, 230, 360, 364
hazelnut, European, 230, 364, 370
heath family, 264
hedge maple, *42*, 192–93, 359, 365, 367,
   373, 375, 379, 380
hemlock
   Canada, *186*, 357–58, 378
   Carolina, *186*, 358, 378
   eastern, *186*, 357–58, 378
   northern Japanese, *187*, 358, 378
   southern Japanese, 358, 378
   western, 358, 378
Heritage river birch, 380, 381
hiba arborvitae, *185*, 356, 383
hickory
   attracting songbirds with, 364
   bitternut, 217
   for fall color, 368
   family, 216–17
   shagbark, *59*, 217, 360, 362, 373
   shellbark, 217
higan cherry, *9*, *114*, 276–77, 363, 371
Himalayan pine, *174*, 345
Hinoki false cypress, 321–22, 377
Hippocastanaceae, 204–6
holly, 303–6
   American, *137*, 305–6, 364, 367, 374,
   376, 379

canary American, *137*
   English, *136*, 304–5, 364, 376, 377, 379
   long-stalk, *138*, 306, 364, 376, 379
   San Jose, 364, 376, 377, 379
honey locust
   sunburst thornless, *82*
   thornless, *81*, 243–44, 366, 368, 373,
   380, 381
hop hornbeam, *101*, 263–64, 360, 364,
   369, 374, 377, 380
hornbeam
   American, 58–59, 216, 359, 368, 375, 376
   attracting songbirds with, 363
   European, 215–16, 264, 359, 362, 365,
   368, 375, 376, 379, 380, 381
   fastigate European, *58*
   hop, *101*, 263–64, 360, 364, 369, 374,
   377, 380
   Japanese, 216
horse chestnut, 18, 206, 359, 363, 370, 373
   Baumanii, *51*
   briotii red, *49*
   family, 204–6
   red, 204–5, 359, 370, 373, 381
hostas, 24
hybrid dogwood, *69*, 229–30, 368, 370

Ilex, 303–6
   × *altaclarensis*, 304
   × *altaclarensis* 'San Jose', 376
   aquifolium, *136*, 304–5, 364, 376, 377,
   379
   × *aquipernyi*, 305
   × *aquipernyi* 'San Jose', 364, 377, 379
   opaca, *137*, 305–6, 364, 367, 374, 376, 379
   opaca 'Canary', *137*
   pedunculosa, *138*, 306, 364, 376, 379
   pernyi, 305
incense cedar, *146–47*, 316, 361, 363, 376,
   382, 383
Indian bean, *61*, 220, 360, 365, 371, 373,
   381, 382
injury, avoiding, 26
insects, 36–37
intermediate yew, 353
Irish yew, 352
ironwood, *101*, 263–64, 360, 364, 369, 374,
   377, 380
   Persian, *103*, 265, 362, 369, 370, 377
Italian cypress, 327, 362, 375, 376
ivy-leaved maple, 196, 362, 367, 373

jack pine, 345, 367

Japanese angelica tree, *54*, 210, 363, 365, 371, 376

Japanese black pine, *172*, 343–44, 367, 375

Japanese cedar, *155*, 324–25, 363, 377, 383

Japanese cornelian cherry, 229, 370, 377

Japanese dogwood, 227–28, 368, 371, 377, 378

Japanese flowering apricot, 275, 370

Japanese flowering cherry, *114*, 275–76, 363, 371, 374, 379

Japanese flowering crab apple, 258–59

Japanese hackberry, 221, 360, 365

Japanese hornbeam, 216

Japanese larch, *160*, 331

Japanese maple, *21*, *45*, 202–3, 362, 368, 376, 378

Japanese pagoda tree, *125*, 290–91, 361, 367, 372, 374, 378, 380, 381

Japanese plum yew, *150*–51, 319–20, 376, 377

Japanese red pine, 338–39, 363

Japanese snowbell, *128*, 294, 369, 371, 374, 377

Japanese stewartia, *126*–27, 293–94, 363, 372, 377

Japanese stone pine, 341

Japanese tree lilac, *129*, 295–96, 363, 372, 379

Japanese umbrella pine, *178*, 348–49, 377

Japanese white pine, *169*, 340–41, 375

Japanese yew, 352–53, 378

Japanese zelkova, 303, 363, 369, 374, 380, 381

Jersey pine, 344–45, 367, 375

Juglandaceae, 216–17, 245–46

Juglans, 245–46, 364
  cinerea, 246, 366
  nigra, *5*, *18*, *84*, 246, 366
  regia, 246, 366

Juneberry, 209, 359, 363, 368, 370, 373, 376, 378, 382

juniper
  blue heaven Rocky Mountain, *158*
  Chinese, 330, 367, 375
  Rocky Mountain, 328–29, 362, 364, 367, 375, 376
  Wichita blue Rocky Mountain, *159*

Juniperus
  chinensis, 330, 367, 375
  horizontalis, 257
  scopularum, 256–57, 328–29, 362, 364, 367, 375, 376
  scopularum 'Blue Heaven', *158*
  scopularum 'Wichita Blue', *159*
  virginiana, *159*, 257, 329–30, 362, 365, 367, 375, 376, 379, 382

katsura tree, *62*, 221–22, 360, 368

Kentucky coffee tree, *82*–83, 244, 360, 366, 368, 373, 381

Kobus magnolia, 256, 370, 382

Koelreuteria, 246–47
  bipinnata, 247, 366, 372, 373, 378
  paniculata, *85*, 247, 360, 366, 372, 373, 378, 379, 381
  paniculata 'September Glory', 372

Korean dogwood, 227–28, 368, 371, 377, 378

Korean fir, *145*, 315

Korean maple, 203

Korean mountain ash, *125*, 291–92, 369, 371, 378, 381

Korean pine, 339–40

Korean stewartia, *126*–27, 293–94, 363, 372, 377

Kosar hybrid magnolia, *91*, 382

Kousa dogwood, 227–28, 368, 371, 377, 378

Kwanzan cherry, 2

laburnum
  common, 248, 360
  Scotch, 248, 360
  waterer, 248, 360, 362

Laburnum, 247–48
  alpinum, 248, 360
  anagyroides, 248, 360
  spp., 371
  × *watereri*, *86*, 248, 360, 362
  × *watereri* 'Vossii', *86*

lacebark elm, *133*–34, 301–2, 361, 363, 367, 374, 380, 381

lacebark pine, *166*, 338, 363

laceleaf maple, 203, 376

Lagerstroemia
  fauriei, 249
  indica, *87*, 248–49, 362, 368, 372, 373
  indica × *faureii*, 369, 372, 373

Lagerstroemia indica × *faureii* 'Natchez', *87*

Lamium, 24

lanceleaf poplar, 271–72, 382

Lane Lawson false cypress, *152*

larch
American, *161*, 331–32, 383
European, *160*, 331, 362, 375
for fall color, 369
golden, *176*, 347, 369
Japanese, *160*
western, 332
Larix
decidua, 160, 330–31, 362, 375
kaempferi, 160, 331
larcinia, 161, 331–32, 383
occidentalis, 332
spp., 369
lateral buds, 3
lateral roots, 3
Lauraceae, 306–7
laurel
bay, *138*, 306–7, 367, 376
Carolina cherry, 309, 361, 364, 372, 375, 376, 377
cherry, *140–41*, 310, 372, 377
English, 310, 372, 377
Portuguese cherry, 309–10, 372, 376, 377
Laurus nobilis, 138, 306–7, 367, 376
Lavalle hawthorn, 233, 365
Lawson false cypress, 320–21
leaves, 3
Leyland cypress, *157*, 326, 362, 375, 377
Libocedrus decurrens, 146–47
lilac
Japanese tree, *129*, 363, 372, 379
Peking, *129*, 296, 363, 372
tree, 372
lily-flowered magnolia, 254, 371, 382
limber pine, 339, 367
linden
American, 296–97, 361, 369
Crimean, 297–98, 361, 380
littleleaf, *131*, 297–98, 361, 367, 369, 380, 381
redmond American, *130*
silver, *132*, 298, 361, 374, 381
Liquidambar styraciflua, 88, 250–51, 364, 366, 369, 380, 381, 382
Liriodendron
chinense, 251
tulipifera, 89, 251–52, 364, 369, 381, 382
littleleaf linden, *131*, 297–98, 361, 367, 369, 380, 381
live oak, *142*, 311, 361, 375, 381, 383
lobbii Japanese cedar, *155*

loblolly pine, *172*, 343
locust, black, *123*, 287–88, 361, 371, 374
Loebner magnolia, 254, 371, 382
Lombardy poplar, *109*, 272, 375
London plane tree, *106*, 268–69, 366, 374, 380, 381, 382
longleaf pine, 343
long-stalk holly, *138*, 306, 364, 376, 379
loosestrife family, 248–50
Louisiana buckeye, 206, 370
Lythraceae, 248–50

Maackia
amurensis, 90, 252, 360, 362, 366, 372, 380, 381
chinensis, 252, 366
magnolia
Ann Kosar hybrid, 92
ballerina Loebner, 92
bigleaf, 253
family, 251–52, 252–56, 307–8
Kobus, 256, 370, 382
Kosar hybrid, *91*, 371, 382
lily-flowered, 254, 371, 382
Loebner, 254, 382
pink star, *94*
saucer, *23*, *93*, 255, 371, 382
southern, *139*, 364, 374, 379, 383
star, *94*, 255–56, 369, 370, 382
sweet bay, *140*, 308, 364, 372, 377, 379, 383
Magnolia, 252–56
acuminata, 91, 253, 360, 364, 369, 378, 382
acuminata var. *subcordata*, 253, 372, 382
as broad-leaved evergreen, 307–8
denudata, 253
grandiflora, 139, 307–8, 364, 374, 379, 383
grandiflora 'Edith Bogue', *139*
kobus, 256, 370, 382
× *liliflora, 91*
× *liliflora* 'Ann', 92
liliiflora, 254, 371, 382
× *loebneri*, 254, 371, 382
× *loebneri* 'Ballerina', 92
macrophylla, 253
quinquepeta, 254, 371, 382
× *soulangeana, 23*, *93*, 255, 371, 382
stellata, 255–56, 369, 370, 382
stellata 'Rosea', *94*

tomentosa, *94*, 255–56, 369, 370, 382
virginiana, *140*, 308, 372, 377, 379, 383
virginiana var. *australis*, 308, 364, 372, 379
Magnoliaceae, 251–52, 252–56, 307–8
maidenhair tree, *80–81*, 242, 360, 366, 368, 373, 380, 381
maintenance, 32
Malus, 256–61
  'Adams', *95*
  baccata, 257–58
  floribunda, 258–59
  × *floribunda*
    'Red Jewel', *96*
    'Sugar Tyme', *96*
  hupehensis, *95*, 259
  × *hupehensis* 'Strawberry Parfait', *97*
  sargentii, *98*, 259–60
  spp., 360, 364, 371, 373
  zumi, 260
  × *zumi* 'Calocarpa', *99*, 260–61
map, hardiness zone, 28–29
maple
  Amur, 193–94, 359, 368, 370, 373, *375*, 378, 379
  ash-leaved, 18, *44*, 195–96, 359, 365, 373
  attracting songbirds with, 363
  black, 201–2
  'Bonfire' sugar, *47*
  coral-bark, 202
  Crimson King Norway, *45*
  David, 196, 362, 376
  family, 191–204
  fernleaf Japanese, *44*, 203, *376*
  Freeman, 368, 370, 379
  full-moon, 203, 368
  golden full-moon, *48*, 204
  green-bark, 202–3
  hard, *47*, 201–2, 368, 379
  hedge, *42*, 192–93, 359, 365, 367, 373, 375, 379, 380
  ivy-leaved, 196, 362, 367, 373
  Japanese, *21*, *45*, 202–3, 362, 368, 376, 378
  Korean, 203
  laceleaf, 203, 376
  miyabe, 193, 359
  Nikko, 193, 365, 379
  Norway, 17, 18, 196–98, 359, 368, 370, 373, 379, 380
  paperbark, *43*, 193, 359, 362, 368, 373
  purpleblow, 359, 362, 365, 368, 373, 379

red, *46*, 368, 370, 379, 381, 382
rock, *47*, 201–2, 368, 379
Rocky Mountain, 192, 368
Shantung, 359, 362, 365, 368, 373, 379
Shirasawa, 203–4
silver, 17–18, *18*, 200, 359, 365, 382
small, 192–94
snakebark, *43*, 196
striped, 196, 362, 368, 376, 382
sugar, *19*, *47*, 201–2, 368, 379
swamp, *46*, 368, 370, 379, 381, 382
sycamore, *46*, 359, 373, 379
tall shade-tree, 194–202
Tatarian, *48*, 194, 368, 378, 379
threadleaf, 203, 376
three-flowered, 193, 362, 368, 373
trident, *42*, 192, 359, 362, 365, 367, 375, 379, 380
vine, 203, 378
mesa oak, 311, 361
Metasequoia glyptostroboides, 161–62, 332–33, 363, 369, 383
mimosa, 18, *52*, 206–7, 359, 365, 371, 373
miyabe maple, 193, 359
momi fir, *144*, 315
monarch birch, 215
Monterey cypress, *158*, 327–28, 375
moosewood, 196, 362, 368, 376, 382
Moraceae, 261–62
Morus alba, 18, *99*, 261–62, 360, 364, 366, 373
mossycup oak, 284, 361, 366, 369, 381
mountain ash
  American, 292, 371, 378
  attracting songbirds with, 364
  European, *126*, 292–93, 369, 371, 378
  Korean, *125*, 291–92, 369, 371, 378, 381
  oakleaf, 293, 371, 379
  showy, 292–93, 371, 379
mountain dogwood, 227, 370
mountain snowbell, 245, 377
mountain stewartia, 294, 372, 377
mulberry white, 18, *99*, 261–62, 360, 364, 366, 373
mulches, *23*, 23–24
musclewood, *58–59*, 216, 359, 368, 375, 376
myrtle, 24. *See also* crape myrtle

narrow English oak, 375
narrow white poplar, 375
Natchez hybrid crape myrtle, *87*
Nikko fir, 314–15, 377

Nikko maple, 193, 365, 379
Niobe willow, *124*, 289, 383
Nootka false cypress, 321
Nordmann fir, *146*, 315, 361
northern catalpa, 219–20, 360, 365, 371, 373, 381, 382
northern Japanese hemlock, *187*, 358, 378
northern pin oak, 281, 380, 383
northern red oak, *121*, 281, 282, 366, 369, 374, 380, 381
Norway maple, 17, *18*, 18, 196–98, 359, 368, 370, 373, 379, 380
Norway pine, *170*, 341, 367
Norway spruce, 333–34
Nuttall's oak, 281, 380, 383
Nyssaceae, 262–63
Nyssa sylvatica, 100, 262–63, 364, 369, 373, 378, 380, 382

oak
    attracting songbirds with, 364
    black, 280–82, 282, 366, 369
    bur, 284, 361, 366, 369, 381
    canyon live, 310, 361
    chestnut, 283, 380
    coast live, *141*, 311, 361
    Emory, 310, 361
    English, *120–21*, 285–86, 361, 366, 374, 381
    live, *142*, 311, 361, 375, 381, 383
    mesa, 311, 361
    mossycup, 284, 361, 366, 369, 381
    narrow English, 375
    northern pin, 281, 380, 383
    northern red, *121*, 281, 282, 366, 369, 374, 380, 381
    Nuttall's, 281, 380, 383
    pin, 25, *119*, 281–82, 366, 369, 380, 383
    possum, 284–85, 380, 383
    red, 280–82
    sawtooth, *116*, 282–83, 366, 369, 374, 381
    scarlet, *117–18*, 280–81, 369, 380
    shingle, *118*, 285, 369, 374, 380
    shumard, 282, 361, 369, 381
    southern red, 282, 369
    Spanish, 282, 369
    swamp chestnut, 283
    swamp white, 283–84, 369, 374, 380, 381, 383
    upland live, 311, 361
    water, 284–85, 380, 383
    white, *117*, 282–86, 284, 369, 374

willow, *119–20*, 285, 366, 374, 380, 381, 383
    yellow chestnut, 283, 361, 369, 374, 380
oakleaf mountain ash, 293, 371, 379
Ohio buckeye, *50*, 205, 359, 365, 368, 370, 376
okame cherry, *112–13*, 274–75, 370
old man's beard, *64–65*, 223–24, 360, 364, 368, 370, 377, 378
Oleaceae, 223–24, 240–41, 295–96
oleaster family, 236–37
olive
    Russian, 18, *75–76*, 236–37, 360, 366, 373, 375, 378
    wild, 18, *75–76*, 236–37, 360, 366, 373, 375, 378
olive family, 223–24, 240–41, 295–96
orange, *107*, 269
Oriental arborvitae, 354–55, 383
Oriental cherry, 275–76, 363, 371, 374
Oriental persimmon, 236
Oriental plane tree, 269, 366, 374, 382
Oriental spruce, *164*, 335–36
ornamental bark, trees with, 362–63
ornamentals, flowering, 4, *8*
Ostrya
    carpinifolia, 264, 380
    virginiana, *101*, 263–64, 360, 364, 369, 374, 377, 380
Oxydendrum arboreum, *102*, 264, 369, 372, 377, 378

pachysandra, 24
pagoda dogwood, 225–26, 368, 370
painted maple, 198
palm, hardy windmill, *142*, 312
Palmae, 311–12
palm family, 311–12
paperbark cherry, 363, 374
paperbark maple, *43*, 193, 359, 362, 368, 373
paper birch, *56*, 213
Parrotia persica, *103*, 264–65, 265, 362, 369, 370, 377
Paulownia tomentosa, *103*–4, 265–66, 366, 372, 374, 381
pawpaw, *55*, 211, 376
pea family
    Albizia, 206–7
    Cercis, 222–23
    Cladrastis, 224–25
    Gleditsia, 243–44

Gymnocladus, 244
Maackia, 252
Robinia, 287–88
Sophora, 290–91
pear
    birch-leaf, 280, 366
    Bradford, 277–78
    callery, 115, 278–79, 361, 364, 366, 369,
        371, 374, 380, 381
    flowering, 115, 278–79, 361, 364, 366,
        369, 371, 374, 380, 381
    Ussuri, 279, 366, 371, 381
    weeping willowleaf, 116, 279, 366
pecan, 217, 360, 382
Peking lilac, 129, 296, 363, 372
Peking willow, 289–90, 374, 383
pepperidge, 100, 262–63, 364, 369, 373,
    378, 380, 382
Persian ironwood, 103, 265, 362, 369, 370,
    377
Persian parrotia, 103, 265, 362, 369, 370,
    377
persimmon, 74–75, 235–36, 360, 364, 373
Phellodendron amurense, 104–5, 266–67,
    360, 366, 369, 374, 380
Phellodendron amurense 'Macho', 381
Phellodendron amurense var. *sachali-*
    nense, 267
Picea
    abies, 333–34
    abies 'Cranstonii', 162
    aristata, 165–66
    glauca, 334–35, 375
    glauca var. *albertina* 'Conica', 163, 334
    glauca var. *densata,* 36, 334–35
    omorika, 163, 335
    orientalis, 164, 335–36
    orientalis 'Aureo-spicata', 164
    pungens var. *glauca,* 165, 336, 367, 375
    spp., 365
Pinaceae
    Abies, 312–16
    Cedrus, 317–19
    Larix, 330–32
    Picea, 333–36
    Pinus, 337–45
    Pseudolarix, 346–47
    Pseudotsuga, 347–48
    Tsuga, 356–58
pine
    attracting songbirds with, 365
    Austrian, 344, 375

Bhutan, 174, 345
blue Korean, 168
blue limber, 167
Bosnian, 344
bristlecone, 165–66, 337, 367
dragon's-eye, 167, 339
dwarf yew, 175
eastern white, 170, 171, 341–42, 367
Himalayan, 174, 345
jack, 345, 367
Japanese black, 172, 343–44, 367, 375
Japanese red, 338–39, 363
Japanese stone, 341
Japanese umbrella, 178, 348–49, 377
Japanese white, 169, 340–41, 375
Jersey, 344–45, 367, 375
Korean, 339–40
lacebark, 166, 338, 363
limber, 339, 367
loblolly, 172, 343
longleaf, 343
Norway, 170, 341, 367
pinyon, 345
pitch, 345, 367
ponderosa, 169, 341, 375
red, 170, 341, 367
Scotch, 171, 342–43, 363, 367, 375
Scots, 171, 342–43, 363, 367, 375
scrub, 344–45, 367, 375
slash, 343, 375
Swiss stone, 340
Tanyosho, 338–39, 363
thunderhead Japanese black, 173
Virginia, 173, 344–45, 367, 375
Watt's gold Virginia, 174
western yellow, 169, 341, 375
yew, 346, 362, 375, 376, 377
pine family
    Abies, 312–16
    Cedrus, 317–19
    Larix, 330–32
    Picea, 333–36
    Pinus, 337–45
    Pseudolarix, 346–47
    Pseudotsuga, 347–48
    Tsuga, 356–58
pink star magnolia, 94
pin oak, 25, 119, 281–82, 366, 369, 380, 383
Pinus
    aristata, 337, 367
    banksiana, 345, 367
    bungeana, 166, 338, 363

Pinus (cont.)
  cembra, 340
  cembroides var. edulis, 345
  densiflora, 338–39
  densiflora 'Oculus-draconis', 167
  densiflora 'Umbraculifera', 363
  edulis, 345
  elliotti, 343, 375
  flexilis, 339, 367
  flexilis 'Glauca', 167
  griffithii, 174, 345
  heldreichii var. leucodermis, 344
  koraiensis, 339–40
  koraiensis 'Glauca', 168
  leucodermis, 344
  nigra, 344, 375
  palustris, 343
  parviflora, 340–41, 375
  parviflora 'Glauca', 169
  ponderosa, 169, 341, 375
  pumila, 341
  resinosa, 170, 341, 367
  rigida, 345, 367
  spp., 365, 376
  strobus, 170, 341–42, 367
  strobus var. glauca, 171
  sylvestris, 342–43, 363, 367, 375
  sylvestris 'Fastigiata', 171
  taeda, 172, 343
  thunbergiana, 172, 173, 343–44, 367, 375
  thunbergii, 172, 343–44, 367, 375
  thunbergii 'Thunderhead', 173
  virginiana, 173, 344–45, 367, 375
  virginiana 'Watt's Gold', 174
  wallichiana, 174, 345
pinyon pine, 345
pistache, Chinese, 105, 364, 369, 378
pistachio, Chinese, 105, 364, 369, 378
Pistacia chinensis, 105, 267–68, 364, 369, 378
pitch pine, 345, 367
plane tree
  American, 269, 366, 374, 382
  London, 106, 268–69, 366, 374, 380, 381, 382
  Oriental, 269, 366, 374, 382
  for ornamental bark, 362
planting, 10, 11–14, 12
Platanaceae, 268–69
Platanus
  × acerifolia, 106, 268–69, 366, 374, 380, 382

  × acerifolia 'Bloodgood', 381
  × hispanica, 106
  occidentalis, 269, 366, 374, 382
  orientalis, 269, 366, 374, 382
  spp., 362
Platycladus
  orientalis, 354–55, 383
  orientalis 'Aurea Nana', 184
plum
  blireana, 273
  cherry, 110, 273, 364, 366, 371, 374
  purple-leaved, 8, 110, 273, 364, 366, 371, 374
plum yew family, 319–20
Podocarpaceae, 346
Podocarpus macrophyllus, 346, 362, 375, 376, 377
Podocarpus macrophyllus 'Mackii', 175
Poncirus trifoliata, 107, 269, 366, 371, 378
pond cypress, 351, 367, 370, 375, 383
ponderosa pine, 169, 341, 375
poplar, 19
  and alkaline soil, 360
  lanceleaf, 271–72, 382
  Lombardy, 109, 272, 375
  narrow white, 375
  western, 272, 374, 383
  white, 108, 270–71, 362, 374, 382
  willowleaf, 270–71, 366, 383
  yellow, 89, 251–52, 364, 369, 381, 382
Populus
  × acuminata, 271, 382
  alba, 108, 270–71, 362, 374, 382
  alba 'Boleana', 375
  alba 'Pyramidalis', 272, 375
  alba 'Raket', 272
  angustifolia, 270–71, 366, 383
  × canadensis, 271–72, 383
  × canescens, 383
  × canescens 'Tower', 271, 272
  deltoides, 108–9, 271–72, 374, 383
  deltoides 'Prairie Sky', 272
  × euramerica, 271–72, 383
  fremontii, 272, 374, 383
  nigra 'Italica', 109, 272, 375
  tremula, 271
  tremuloides, 110, 271, 383
Port Orford cedar, 320–21
Portuguese cherry laurel, 309–10, 372, 376, 377
possum oak, 284–85, 380, 383
Potomac cherry, 115, 277, 363, 371

prairie sentinel pond cypress, *181*
princess tree, *103–4*, 265–66, 366, 372, 374,
   381
pruning, 28–36, *30*
Prunus, 272–77
  × *blireana*, 273, 366
  as broad-leaved evergreens, 309–10
  campanulata, 274
  caroliniana, 309, 361, 364, 372, 375, 376,
    377
  cerasifera 'Atropurpurea', 273, 364, 366,
    371, 374
  cerasifera 'Thundercloud', *110*
  'Hally Jolivette', 360, 370
  incisa, 274
  × 'Kwanzan', *2*
  laurocerasus, 310, 372, 377
  lusitanica, 140–41, 309–10, 372, 376, 377
  maackii, *111*, 273–74, 361, 362, 364, 374
  mume, 275, 370
  × 'Okame', *112–13*, 274–75, 370
  pendula, *114*, 276–77, 363, 371
  sargentii, *113*, 275, 363, 369, 371, 374, 380
  serotina, *112*, 274, 363, 369, 371
  serrula, 274, 363, 374
  serrulata, 379
  serrulata Sato-zakura Group, 275–76,
    363, 371, 374
  serrulata 'Shirofugen', *114*
  subhirtella 'Autumnalis', 277, 372
  subhirtella var. *pendula*, *9*, *114*, 276–77,
    363, 371
  × 'Thundercloud', *8*
  × *yedoensis*, *115*, 277, 363, 371
Pseudolarix, 346–47
  amabilis, *176*, 347, 369
  kaempferi, *176*, 347, 369
Pseudotsuga
  menziesii, 347–48, 362
  menziesii ssp. *glauca*, *177*, 347
  menziesii ssp. *menziesii*, *177*, 347
purple beech, 239
purpleblow maple, 198, 359, 362, 365, 368,
   373, 379
purple-leaved catalpa, 365, 371, 373
purple-leaved plum, *8*, *110*, 273, 364, 366,
   371, 374
purple smoke tree, 365, 370
Pyrus
  betulaefolia, 280, 366
  calleryana, *115*, 278–79, 361, 364, 366,
    369, 371, 374, 380, 381

  calleryana 'Bradford', 277–78
  salicifolia 'Pendula', *116*, 279–80, 366
  ussuriensis, 279, 366, 371, 381

quaking aspen, *110*, 271, 383
Quercus
  acutissima, *116*, 282–83, 366, 369, 374,
    381
  agrifolia, *141*, 311, 361
  alba, *117*, 284, 369, 374
  bicolor, 283–84, 369, 374, 380, 381, 383
  borealis, *121*, 282, 366, 369, 374, 380, 381
  as broad-leaved evergreens, 310–11
  chrysolepsis, 310, 361
  coccinea, *117–18*, 280–81, 369, 380
  ellipsoidalis, 281, 380, 383
  emoryi, 310, 361
  engelmanii, 311, 361
  falcata, 282, 369
  fusiformis, 311, 361
  imbricaria, *118*, 285, 369, 374, 380
  macrocarpa, 284, 361, 366, 369, 381
  michauxii, 283
  muehlenbergii, 283, 361, 369, 374, 380
  nigra, 284–85, 380, 383
  nuttallii, 281, 380, 383
  palustris, *25*, *119*, 281–82, 366, 369, 380,
    383
  phellos, *119–20*, 285, 366, 374, 380, 381,
    383
  prinus, 283, 380
  robur, *120–21*, 285–86, 361, 366, 374, 381
  robur 'Fastigiata', 375
  robur 'Skyrocket', 375
  rubra, *121*, 281, 282, 366, 369, 374, 380,
    381
  shumardii, 282, 361, 369, 381
  spp., 364
  texana, 281, 380, 383
  velutina, 282, 366, 369
  virginiana, *142*, 311, 361, 375, 381, 383
  × *warei* 'Regal Prince', 286

red ash, *80*, 241, 360, 366, 368, 373, 380,
   381
red-barked Himalayan birch, 215
red buckeye, *51*, 206, 359, 370, 375, 376
redbud
  Chinese, 223, 365
  eastern, *63*, 222–23, 360, 365, 377
  for fall color, 368
  Forest Pansy, *63*

redbud *(cont.)*
for showy flowers, 370
Texas, 360, 365
western, 223, 365
redbud golden chain, *99*, 260–61
red horse chestnut, 204–5, 359, 370, 373, 381
red maple, *46*, 198–200, 368, 370, 379, 381, 382
redmond American linden, *130*
red pine, *170*, 341, 367
redwood
California, *179*, 349
coast, *179*, 349
dawn, *161–62*, 363, 369, 383
giant, *179–80*, 350, 363
and shade, 377
Sierra, *179–80*, 350, 363
retinospora, *154*, 322–23, 361
Rhus
glabra, 122, 287, 361, 364, 366, 372, 378
javanica var. *chinensis,* 287, 361, 367, 372, 378
spp., 369
typhina, 286–87, 361, 364, 367, 372, 378
typhina 'Laciniata', *122*, 287
river birch, *56*, 212–13, 373, 382
Robinia
× *ambigua* 'Idahoensis', 288, 371
pseudoacacia, 123, 287–88, 361, 371, 374
pseudoacacia 'Frisia', *123*
rock maple, *47*, 201–2, 368, 379
Rocky Mountain Douglas fir, *177*
Rocky Mountain fir, *145*, 315, 361
Rocky Mountain juniper, 328–29, 362, 364, 367, 375, 376
Rocky Mountain maple, 192, 368
roots, 3
Rosaceae
Amelanchier, 208–10
Crataegus, 232–34
Malus, 256–61
Prunus, 272–77, 309–10
Pyrus, 277–80
Sorbus, 291–93
rose family
Amelanchier, 208–10
Crataegus, 232–34
Malus, 256–61
Prunus, 272–77, 309–10
Pyrus, 277–80
Sorbus, 291–93

rosybloom crab apple, 257
rue family, 266–67, 269
Russian olive, 18, *75–76*, 236–37, 360, 366, 373, 375, 378
Rutaceae, 266–67, 269

Salicaceae, 270–72, 288–90
Salix, 288–90
alba, 289
alba 'Tristis', *124*, 289, 383
alba var. *vitellina,* 289, 374, 383
babylonica, 289, 383
babylonica var. *pekinensis,* 289–90, 374, 383
matsudana, 289–90, 374, 383
matsudana 'Torulosa', *124*
× *sepulcralis* 'Chrysocoma', 289, 383
specularis 'Chrysocoma', *124*
spp., 18
salt, trees that tolerate, 373–75
San Jose holly, 364, 376, 377, 379
Sapindaceae, 246–47
Sargent cherry, *113*, 275, 363, 369, 371, 374, 380
Sargent golden chain, *98*, 259–60
saskatoon, 209
saucer magnolia, *23*, *93*, 255, 371, 382
sawara false cypress, *154*, 322–23, 361
sawtooth oak, *116*, 282–83, 366, 369, 374, 381
scarlet oak, *117–18*, 280–81, 369, 380
Sciadopitys verticillata, 178, 348–49, 377
Scilla siberica, 254
Scotch laburnum, 248, 360
Scotch pine, *171*, 342–43, 363, 367, 375
Scots pine, *171*, 342–43, 363, 367, 375
screen, 6
Scrophulariaceae, 265–66
scrub pine, 344–45, 367, 375
Sequoia
gigantea, *179–80*, 350, 363
sempervirens, *179*, 349, 377
Sequoiadendron giganteum, *179–80*, 350, 363
Serbian spruce, *163*, 335
serviceberry
Allegheny, *54*, 208–9, 368, 382
apple, *53*, 209–10, 368, 382
downy, 209, 359, 363, 368, 370, 373, 376, 378, 382
service tree, 209, 359, 363, 368, 370, 373, 376, 378, 382

shadblow, 209, 359, 363, 368, 370, 373, 376, 378, 382
shade, trees that tolerate, 4, 5, 376–78
shagbark hickory, 59, 217, 360, 362, 373
Shantung maple, 198, 359, 362, 365, 368, 373, 379
shapes, 9–10
shellbark hickory, 217
shingle oak, 118, 285, 369, 374, 380
Shirasawa maple, 203–4
Shirofugen Oriental cherry, 114
showy flowers, trees with, 370–72
showy mountain ash, 292–93, 371, 379
shumard oak, 282, 361, 369, 381
Siberian crab apple, 257–58
Siberian elm, 18, 134, 302, 361, 374, 383
Sierra redwood, 179, 350, 363
silk tree, 18, 52, 206–7, 359, 365, 371, 373
silverbell, Carolina, 83–84, 245, 362, 371, 377
silverbell, two-winged, 377
silver linden, 132, 298, 361, 374, 381
silver maple, 17–18, 18, 200, 359, 365, 382
slash pine, 343, 375
smoke bush, 70, 231–32, 360, 365, 371
smoke tree, 360, 365, 368, 371
smooth-leaf elm, 300–301
smooth sumac, 122, 287, 361, 364, 366, 372, 378
snakebark maple, 43, 196
snowbell
    American, 294, 371
    fragrant, 127, 128, 295, 371, 377
    Japanese, 128, 294, 369, 371, 374, 377
    mountain, 245, 377
soapberry family, 246–47
songbirds, trees that attract, 363–65
Sophora japonica, 125, 290–91, 361, 367, 372, 374, 378, 380, 381
Sorbus
    alnifolia, 125, 291–92, 369, 371, 378, 381
    americana, 292, 371, 378
    aucuparia, 126, 292–93, 369, 371, 378
    decora, 292–93, 371, 379
    × hybrida, 293
    rufoferrugenia 'Longwood Sunset', 293, 371, 379
    spp., 364
    × thuringiaca 'Fastigiata', 293, 371, 379
sorrel tree, 102, 264, 369, 372, 377, 378
sour gum, 100, 262–63, 364, 369, 373, 378, 380, 382

sourwood, 102, 264, 369, 372, 377, 378
southern catalpa, 61, 220, 360, 365, 371, 373, 381, 382
southern Japanese hemlock, 358, 378
southern magnolia, 139, 307–8, 364, 374, 379, 383
southern red oak, 282, 369
Spanish chestnut, 219, 365
Spanish oak, 282, 369
spruce
    attracting songbirds with, 365
    Black Hills, 36, 334–35
    Colorado blue, 165, 336, 367, 375
    cranston Norway, 162
    dwarf Alberta, 163, 334
    gold-tipped Oriental, 164
    Norway, 333–34
    Oriental, 164, 335–36
    Serbian, 163, 335
    white, 334–35, 375
staghorn sumac, 286–87, 361, 364, 367, 372, 378
staking and wrapping, 14–16, 15, 16
standishii English yew, 182
star magnolia, 255–56, 369, 370, 382
stellar dogwood, 69, 229–30, 368, 370
Stewartia
    koreana, 293, 372, 377
    monodelpha, 294, 363, 372, 377
    ovata, 294, 372, 377
    pseudocamellia, 126–27, 293–94, 363, 372, 377
    pseudocamellia koreana, 293
    pseudocamellia var. koreana, 372, 377
    spp., 369
strawberry parfait golden chain, 97
streets, trees for, 21, 379–80
striped maple, 196, 362, 368, 376, 382
Styphnolobium japonicus, 361, 367, 372, 374, 378, 380, 381
Styracaceae, 245, 294–95
Styrax
    americanus, 127, 294, 371
    family, 245, 294–95
    japonicum, 128, 294, 369, 371, 374, 377
    obassia, 128, 295, 371, 377
sugar hackberry, 221, 360, 364, 365
sugar maple, 19, 47, 201–2, 368, 379
sumac
    Chinese, 287, 361, 367, 372, 378
    cutleaf staghorn, 122, 287
    for fall color, 369

sumac *(cont.)*
  smooth, *122*, 287, 361, 364, 366, 372, 378
  staghorn, 286–87, 361, 364, 367, 372, 378
summer stars Kousa dogwood, *67*
sun, blocking, 6–7, *7*
sunburst thornless honey locust, *82*
swamp cedar, 323–24, 383
swamp chestnut oak, 283
swamp cypress, *180*, 351, 363, 367, 370, 375, 382, 383
swamp maple, *46*, 198–200, 368, 370, 379, 381, 382
swamp white oak, 283–84, 369, 374, 380, 381, 383
sweet bay, 367, 376
sweet bay magnolia, *140*, 308, 364, 372, 377, 379, 383
sweet birch, 213
sweet gum, *88*, 250–51, 364, 366, 369, 380, 381, 382
Swiss stone pine, 340
sycamore, 268–69, 362, 366, 374, 382
sycamore maple, *46*, 198, 359, 373, 379
Syringa
  Amurensis var. *japonica*, *129*, 295–96
  amurensis var. *japonica*, 363, 372, 379
  pekinensis, *129*, 296, 363, 372
  reticulata, *129*, 295–96, 363, 372, 379
  reticulata var. *mandushurica*, 296, 372

tall stewartia, 294, 363, 372, 377
tamarack, *161*, 331–32, 383
Tanyosho pine, 338–39, 363
Tatarian maple, *48*, 194, 368, 378, 379
Taxaceae, 351–53
Taxodiaceae
  Cryptomeria, 324–25
  Cunnighamia, 325
  Metasequoia, 332–33
  Sciadopitys, 348–49
  Sequoia, 349
  Sequoiadendron, 350
  Taxodium, 350–51
Taxodium, 350–51
  ascendens, 351, 367, 370, 375, 383
  ascendens 'Prairie Sentinel', *181*
  distichum, *180*, 351, 363, 367, 370, 375, 382, 383
  distichum var. *imbricarium*, 351, 367, 370, 375, 383
  distichum var. *imbricarium* 'Prairie Sentinel', *181*

Taxus, 351–53
  baccata, 352, 363, 377
  baccata 'Fastigiata Aurea', *181*
  baccata 'Standishii', *182*
  cuspidata, 352–53, 378
  cuspidata 'Capitata', *182–83*
  × *media*, 353
  × *media* 'Hicksii', 378
tea family, 239, 293–94
tea golden chain, *95*, 259
Texas redbud, 360, 365
Theaceae, 239, 293–94
thornless honey locust, *81*, 243–44, 366, 368, 373, 380, 381
threadleaf maple, 203, 376
three-flowered maple, 193, 362, 368, 373
Thuja
  occidentalis, *183–84*, 353–54, 365, 383
  orientalis, 354–55, 383
  orientalis 'Aurea Nana', *184*
  plicata, *185*, 355, 362, 383
Thujopsis dolbrata, *185*, 356, 383
thunderhead Japanese black pine, *173*
Tilia
  americana, 296–97, 361, 369
  americana 'Redmond', *130*
  cordata, *131*, 297–98, 361, 367, 369, 380, 381
  × *euchlora*, 297–98, 361, 380
  tomentosa, *132*, 298, 361, 374, 381
Tiliaceae, 296–98
topping, 34
Trachycarpus fortunei, *142*, 311–12
training, 29–32
tree lilac, 372
tree of heaven, 266
trees, shade, 380–82
tricolor European beech, *78*
trident maple, *42*, 192, 359, 362, 365, 367, 375, 379, 380
trifoliate orange, *107*, 269, 366, 371, 378
trunk, 1–3
Tsuga, 356–58
  canadensis, *186*, 357–58, 378
  caroliniana, *186*, 358, 378
  diversifolia, *187*, 358, 378
  heterophylla, 358, 378
  sieboldii, 358, 378
tulip tree, *89*, 251–52, 364, 369, 381, 382
tupelo, *100*, 262–63, 364, 369, 373, 378, 380, 382
Turkish filbert, *69*, 230, 360, 364

Turkish hazel, *69*, 230, 360, 364
twigs, 3
types, 4
    with bad reputations, 17–19
    for streets, 20–22, 379–80
    for urban setting, 19–20

Ulmaceae, 220–21, 298–302, *303*
Ulmus
    alata 'Lace Parasol', 301, 361, 369, 374
    alata 'Pendula', 301, 361, 369, 374
    americana, *132*, 298, 299–300, 361, 364,
        369, 374, 380, 383
    carpinifolia, 300–301
    davidiana, 300
    davidiana var. *japonica*, 361
    davidiana var. *japonica* 'Discovery', 300
    glabra 'Camperdownii', *133*, 301
    japonica, 302
    minor, 300–301
    parvifolia, *133–34*, 301–2, 361, 363, 367,
        374, 380, 381
    pumila, 18, *134*, 302, 361
    pumila 'Cathedral', 374, 383
    × *wilsoniana* 'Accolade', 300
    wilsoniana 'Prospector', 300
umbrella catalpa, 220
understory trees, 4
upland live oak, 311, 361
upright intermediate yew, 378
Ussuri pear, 279, 366, 371, 381

variegated pagoda dogwood, *66*
velvet ash, 241, 360, 366, *373*, 379
village green Japanese zelkova, *135*
vinca, 24
vine maple, 203, 378
Virginia pine, *173*, 344–45, 367, *375*
visual effects, creating, 7–9

walnut, 245–46, 364
    black, *5*, *18*, *84*, 246, 366
    English, 246, 366
Washington hawthorn, *72*, 233–34, 366
waterer laburnum, *86*, 248, 360, 362
watering, 22–23
water oak, 284–85, 380, 383
Watt's gold Virginia pine, *174*
weeping cherry, *114*, 276–77, 363, 371
weeping European birch, *57*
weeping Nootka false cypress, *153*

weeping willow, 289, 383
weeping willowleaf pear, *116*, 279–80, 366
western catalpa, 219–20, 360, 365, 371,
    373, 381, 382
western hemlock, 358, 378
western larch, 332
western poplar, 272, 374, 383
western redbud, 223, 365
western red cedar, *158*, *159*, *185*, 328–29,
    355, 362, 364, 367, 375, 376, 383
western yellow pine, *169*, 341, *375*
wet soil, trees that tolerate, 382–83
white ash, *79*, 240–41, 360, 368, *373*, 380,
    382
white-barked Himalayan birch, *57*,
    214–15, 359
whitebeam, alder, *125*, 291–92, 364, 369,
    371, 378, 381
white cedar, *183–84*, 353–54, 365, 383
white cypress, 323–24, 383
white elm, 299–300, 361, 364, 369, 374,
    380, 383
white fir, *143*, 314, 361, 367
white mulberry, 18, *99*, 261–62, 360, 364,
    366, 373
white oak, *117*, 284, 369, 374
white poplar, *108*, 270–71, 362, 374, 382
Whitespire Asian birch, 381
whitespire birch, 359, 373
Whitespire Senior Asian birch, 214
white spruce, 334–35, 375
white willow, 289, 383
Wichita blue Rocky Mountain juniper,
    159
wild black cherry, *112*, 274, 363, 369, 371
wild olive, 18, *75–76*, 236–37, 360, 366,
    373, 375, 378
willow, 19
    corkscrew, *124*, 290
    golden, 289, 374, 383
    golden weeping, *124*, 289, 383
    Hankow, 289–90, 374, 383
    Niobe, 383
    niobe, *124*, 289
    Peking, 289–90, 374, 383
    weeping, 289, 383
    white, 289, 383
willow family, 270–72, 288–90
willowleaf poplar, 270–71, 366, 383
willow oak, *119–20*, 285, 366, 374, 380, 381,
    383
wind, blocking, 7

windbreaks and screens, trees for, 6,
  375–76
winged elm, 361, 374
winter king green hawthorn, 72–73
witch hazel family, 250–51, 264–65

yellow birch, 213
yellow buckeye, 50, 205, 359, 370
yellow chestnut oak, 283, 361, 369, 374,
  380
yellow cucumber tree, 253, 372, 382
yellow poplar, 89, 251–52, 364, 369, 381,
  382
yellowwood, 65, 224–25, 360, 368, 371
yew
  capitata Japanese, 182–83
  English, 352, 363, 377
  golden English, 181

intermediate, 353
Irish, 352
Japanese, 352–53, 377
Japanese plum, 150–51, 319–20, 376,
  378
standishii English, 182
upright intermediate, 378
yew family, 351–53
yew pine, 346, 362, 375, 376, 377
yew podocarpus, 345, 362, 375, 376, 377
Yoshino cherry, 115, 277, 363, 371

Zelkova
  serrata, 303, 363, 369, 374, 380, 381
  serrata 'Green Vase', 135
  serrata 'Village Green', 135
zumi crab apple, 260–61
zumi golden chain, 99